General George H. Thomas

ALSO BY ROBERT P. BROADWATER
AND FROM MCFARLAND

*Did Lincoln and the Republican Party
Create the Civil War? An Argument* (2008)

*American Generals of the Revolutionary War:
A Biographical Dictionary* (2007)

*Civil War Medal of Honor Recipients:
A Complete Illustrated Record* (2007)

*Chickamauga, Andersonville, Fort Sumter and
Guard Duty at Home: Four Civil War Diaries
by Pennsylvania Soldiers* (2006)

*The Battle of Olustee, 1864:
The Final Union Attempt to Seize Florida* (2006)

*The Battle of Perryville, 1862:
Culmination of the Failed Kentucky Campaign* (2005)

General George H. Thomas

*A Biography of the Union's
"Rock of Chickamauga"*

Robert P. Broadwater

McFarland & Company, Inc., Publishers
Jefferson, North Carolina, and London

LIBRARY OF CONGRESS CATALOGUING-IN-PUBLICATION DATA

Broadwater, Robert P., 1958–
General George H. Thomas : a biography of the Union's
"Rock of Chickamauga" / Robert P. Broadwater.
p.   cm.
Includes bibliographical references and index.

ISBN 978-0-7864-3856-3
softcover : 50# alkaline paper ∞

1. Thomas, George Henry, 1816–1870.   2. Thomas, George Henry,
1816–1870 — Military leadership.   3. Generals — United States — Biography.
4. United States. Army — Biography.   5. United States — History — Civil War,
1861–1865 — Campaigns.   6. Unionists (United States Civil War) —
Virginia — Biography.   I. Title.
E467.1.T4B76   2009   973.7'83092 — dc22 [B]   2008055207

British Library cataloguing data are available

©2009 Robert P. Broadwater. All rights reserved

*No part of this book may be reproduced or transmitted in any form
or by any means, electronic or mechanical, including photocopying
or recording, or by any information storage and retrieval system,
without permission in writing from the publisher.*

On the cover: General George H. Thomas portrait, Library of Congress;
Civil War era map ©2009 Clipart.com

Manufactured in the United States of America

*McFarland & Company, Inc., Publishers
Box 611, Jefferson, North Carolina 28640
www.mcfarlandpub.com*

To my granddaughter Sophia —
a joy in every way

Table of Contents

Introduction   1

ONE. Early Life and Military Training   5
TWO. A Martial Career Begun   12
THREE. First Glory in Mexico   18
FOUR. Service Throughout the South   32
FIVE. The Outbreak of Civil War   46
SIX. To the West and Mill Springs   58
SEVEN. Early Battles in the West   71
EIGHT. Savior at Stones River   87
NINE. The Tullahoma Campaign   103
TEN. The Rock of Chickamauga   115
ELEVEN. Chattanooga and Missionary Ridge   139
TWELVE. With Sherman Through Georgia   158
THIRTEEN. From Kennesaw to the Gate City   175
FOURTEEN. Back to Tennessee   190
FIFTEEN. The Sledge of Nashville and the End of the War   205
SIXTEEN. The Final Years   222

Conclusion   233
Appendix I. General Officers Serving Under Thomas   237
Appendix II. Units Serving Under Thomas   238
Appendix III. George H. Thomas Chronology   241
Chapter Notes   243
Bibliography   251
Index   259

Introduction

George Henry Thomas won praise, distinction, and promotion in three wars. He was among the top field commanders on either side in the Civil War. At Chickamauga, he displayed his tenacious abilities of defense, saving the Union army from destruction, and earning the sobriquet of "The Rock of Chickamauga." At Nashville, he exhibited to the fullest his capacities for offensive action, scoring what many military historians feel to be one of the most complete victories of all time, second only to Napoleon's triumph at Austerlitz, earning him the title of "The Sledge of Nashville." He began the war in the east, winning two minor affairs against the Confederate leader who would later be known as "Stonewall" Jackson, before being transferred to Kentucky, following the battle of First Manassas. Thomas won the first major victory of the war in the west at Mill Springs, was instrumental in staving off disaster at Stones River, delivered a crushing blow to Confederate forces at Missionary Ridge, and provided the power behind General William T. Sherman's drive through Georgia to capture the city of Atlanta. He was one of the most solid and dependable commanders to serve on either side during the war, and his accomplishments have earned his inclusion, along with Lee, Jackson, Grant, and Sherman, as one of the foremost military minds to come out of that terrible conflict. While most military historians rate Thomas among the top four Union generals of the war — behind Grant, Sherman, and Sheridan — there are some who rank him even higher, ahead of Sheridan, Sherman, and, for a few historians, even Grant. It would stand to reason, therefore, that General Thomas would be one of the most written-about figures of the Civil War, and one of the best known participants of that great national tragedy. Such is not the case, however, as Thomas has been relegated to the status of a footnote of the era, and his hope that history would do him justice has been sorely disappointed.

The reasons for Thomas's relative obscurity and lack of fame are varied. To begin with, he was a Southerner, born and raised in Virginia. When the nation split and entered into the destruction of civil war, he chose to remain true to the national government and the old flag, earning him the enmity and disdain of his fellow Virginians, and of Southerners as a whole. To those of the South, he had betrayed his own people, and was a traitor to his native land. This being the case, Thomas lacked the support of family, friends, and constituents enjoyed by all of the other leading figures in the war. There were to be no hometown supporters, no local members of Congress pushing for his recognition or advancement, no hometown newspapers extolling his virtues and accomplishments. All of the people who could have aided his career or ensured his proper place in history had sided with the Confederacy, and he was thus deprived of support and publicity enjoyed by every other prominent member of the military on both sides.

But what of the North? Surely, those who adhered to the preservation of the Union would embrace one who, for reasons of conscience, had given up everything to defend the old flag and make war against his own people. Such was not to be the case. Despite the fact that Thomas had sacrificed everything in response to his own convictions of right and wrong, he was viewed with suspicion within the government and the military, by virtue of his Southern birth. With the nation splitting apart along geographic lines of north and south, the civil and military leaders of the Federal government found it difficult to conceive that Thomas, a Southerner, could truly be a champion of national unity. Winfield Scott, the aged hero of the Mexican War and the commanding general of all Union forces, was a fellow Virginian. The nation praised his allegiance to the Federal government, and he enjoyed the unqualified confidence and support of his superiors. Thomas was to be afforded no such approbation. While Winfield Scott had been a figure of public renown for almost two decades and was a name known to almost every child of school age, Thomas was relatively unknown at the outbreak of the war, a major serving in the 2nd United States Cavalry, familiar only to those within the tight-knit circle of the military. Though he was already in his second decade of service to the nation, and had won distinction and promotion in the Seminole and Mexican Wars, he was a relative stranger to the national stage, so, unlike Scott, no one was quite sure what to expect of him. His Southern birth, previous affiliations with the institution of slavery, and membership in the fraternity of West Point graduates all played against him at the time he offered his sword to President Lincoln in 1861, and would continue to influence his career throughout the war.

Thomas would also be the target of ambition and political intrigue from brother officers who sought to advance their own stations or enhance their own reputations. He would fall victim to the bonds of loyalty that existed between Grant and Sherman, as each of these officers pushed him aside while extolling the virtues and achievements of the other. William T. Sherman's brother, John Sherman, occupied a seat in Congress, from which he could supervise the public relations spin of his brother and his brother's closest friends. Following the lifting of the Confederate siege of Chattanooga, a campaign that saw Sherman's troops falter while Thomas's excelled, Sherman was nonetheless placed in com-

George Henry Thomas as he appeared in the early stages of the Civil War. He had become a hero in the Seminole and Mexican Wars, but the Civil War would showcase his talents and make him a household name (United States Army Military History Institute).

mand of the combined Union armies of the west. During the course of the Atlanta Campaign, Sherman was given the credit, while Thomas performed the assignments that ensured the success of the enterprise. Without a highly placed advocate in the government, Thomas was forced to endure alone the many slights and slanders from his superiors, intended to keep him in a subordinate position. Even his greatest victory of the war, at Nashville, was soiled by the issuance of information that Grant had ordered his removal as commander of the army, prior to his utter destruction of the Confederate Army of Tennessee, due to his alleged hesitation in making the attack. This despite the fact that Thomas was forced to create an army with which to face the Confederate threat from the scraps and remnants left him by Sherman, who had taken the best of the available manpower with him on his March to the Sea.

The last reason for the relative obscurity of George H. Thomas is that he destroyed most of his personal records and documents prior to his death in 1870. Researchers have been left to piece together the essence of the man without the benefit of the insight that could have been garnered by examination of his private writings and correspondence. To be sure, this is a handicap to the Civil War historian, and makes Thomas a difficult man to come to grips with, in terms of character, beliefs, and motivation, but there is sufficient material available, without his private files, to enable the diligent researcher to construct a picture of the mind and soul of the man. Through official records and the writings of intimates and contemporaries, the image of Thomas the man emerges clear and distinct, and his character and personality can be witnessed and examined.

As noted, most serious students of the war rank Thomas among the top four commanders on the Union side, behind Grant, Sherman, and Sheridan. This placement is curious when one examines and compares the overall performance of the members of this quartet.

Grant, to be sure, was in command of the Union armies at the conclusion of the war and thereby was widely acclaimed as the master and architect of the Northern victory. A closer look at his campaigns in 1864 and 1865 reveals that he was defeated in almost every battle in which he engaged with Robert E. Lee's Army of Northern Virginia. The Wilderness, Spotsylvania, and Cold Harbor were all blood-baths resulting in Union defeats. In fact, Grant lost more men to the casualty lists during his summer campaign of 1864 than Lee had in his entire army at its inception. Having an advantage of more than two-to-one in manpower, with the ability to replace his battlefield losses, Grant conducted a war of attrition that the North could not possibly lose: not exactly a measure of tactical or strategic expertise.

When one looks at Sherman's record on the battlefield, his defeat at Chickasaw Bayou is followed by a lackluster performance at Chattanooga. His Atlanta Campaign on the surface appears to be a master stroke of strategy and maneuver. When one considers that the Union Signal Corps had broken the Confederate code, and knew exactly what the Southerners were doing as they were doing it, a little of the luster fades away. When the Confederates changed their code and Sherman no longer had inside information, the result was the bloody Union defeat at Kennesaw Mountain, and a refusal, on Sherman's part, to ever after mount a frontal assault. In his most celebrated campaign of the war, he marched to the sea against almost non-existent opposition, John Bell Hood and his Confederate army having entered Tennessee to face the pick-up force Thomas would array against him. In his final great battle of the war, Sherman came close to receiving a check by Joe Johnston's army at Bentonville, even though the Confederate force was only about one-third the size of the Federals.

Sheridan's record of independent command is harder to evaluate, and is basically limited to the Valley Campaign of 1864. His greatest victory, at Cedar Creek, was a stroke of luck for the Union commander. His army had been defeated while he himself was at Winchester, and for all intents and purposes, the issue had already been decided. Sheridan was given the opportunity to redeem his loss only because the hungry Confederates stopped to forage supplies in the Union camp, becoming disorganized in the process, and presenting the Federals with a chance to regroup and counterattack. Confederate hunger dictated the outcome of the day, not Union tactics or strategy.

By comparison, Thomas won at Bunker Hill, Falling Waters, and Mill Springs. His actions were responsible for saving the Union army at Stones River and Chickamauga, and his army broke the back of the Confederates at Missionary Ridge. His army provided the muscle for Sherman's drive for Atlanta, before he was detached to deal with and eventually destroy Hood in Tennessee. Throughout the war, beginning with his actions at Bunker Hill and Falling Waters and ending at Nashville, Thomas compiled a record of victory unequalled by any other Union commander in the war. He never failed to hold his ground or gain his objective, a record second to none for the commanders on either side.

History is an inexact science, and many variables often influence who gets the headlines and who does not. In the case of George Henry Thomas, the variables were all stacked against him, resulting in an injustice being done to one of the most dependable and competent military leaders this nation has ever produced. Fame and recognition were not to be the reward of his efforts during his lifetime, or in the decades that followed his death. Historians would largely plod along a path blazed during the war, and would continue to focus emphasis and research on other leading actors of the great national drama, relegating Thomas to a supporting role, at best. It is the purpose of this work to, in some small way, right this wrong, and to preserve for posterity the memory and achievements of General George Henry Thomas. It is the hope of the writer that this offering to the archives of the period may spark further interest in this great American, serving to enhance the reputation of one who has heretofore not received the approbation due to a life so noble and worthy of celebration.

In 1870, James A. Garfield, an officer who had served with Thomas in the Western Theater, and a man who would become president of the United States, addressed a gathering of the Society of the Army of the Cumberland, paying tribute to the man who had been its leader through so many hard-fought campaigns.

> Who shall collect and unite into one worthy picture, the bold outlines, the innumerable lights and shadows which make up the life and character of our past leader? Who shall condense into a single hour the record of a life which forms so large a chapter of the nation's history, and whose fame fills and overfills a hemisphere? No line can be omitted ... which you, his soldiers, will not detect and deplore. I know that each of you here present, sees him in memory at this moment, as we often saw in life; erect and strong like a tower of solid masonry; his broad, square shoulders and massive head; his abundant hair and full beard of light brown, sprinkled with silver; his broad forehead, full face, and features that would appear colossal, but for their perfect harmony of proportion; his clear complexion, with just enough color to assure you of robust health and a well regulated life; his face lighted up by an eye which was cold gray to his enemies, but deep blue to his friends; not a man of iron, but of live oak; his attitude, form and features all assure you of inflexible firmness, of inexpugnable strength; while his welcoming smile set every feature aglow with a kindness that won your manliest affection.[1]

Chapter One

Early Life and Military Training

George Henry Thomas was born at his family home, Thomaston, near Newsom's Depot, Southampton County, Virginia, five miles north of the North Carolina border, on July 31, 1816. His father, John C. Thomas, was of Welsh descent, and his mother, Elizabeth Rochelle, was descended of French Huguenot ancestors who had fled France during the reign of Louis XIV to escape religious persecution from the Catholic majority there. The couple were married on February 9, 1808, in Southampton County, by the Episcopal minister, Joseph Curley. George Henry Thomas was to be the fourth of nine children born to the couple before John's untimely death from a farming accident on April 20, 1829, which left Elizabeth Thomas to raise her large family alone.[1] At the tender age of thirteen, young George was thrust into a position of assisting in the responsibility, along with his two elder brothers, John William and Benjamin, for his mother and siblings, a situation not unlike that experienced by two other famous Virginians who went on to forge records of dignified service to their country: George Washington and Robert E. Lee.[2]

Though he was not born into the same social status as either Washington or Lee, Thomas's family had managed to become notable and respectable throughout Southampton County. While John Thomas could by no means have been considered to be among the planter class, he had managed to acquire several hundred acres for his estate at Thomaston, and while no elaborate manor house graced the grounds, visitors were greeted by a warm and comfortable structure befitting a family that had worked hard to attain its position in the upper middle class. The family home symbolized the rise of the Thomas family in class and stature. Prior to George's birth, it was a small structure, having only two rooms on the first floor, with one room above. George was born on the first floor of the modest home, but as the boy grew, so did the residence that was to become known as Thomaston.[3]

As a boy, young George was doubtless influenced by the examples of civic responsibility set forth in the personal conduct of his father. John Thomas involved himself in numerous activities for the public good, including service as overseer of elections, guardian in settling estates, and commissioner of highways.[4] John was not the sort to aspire to position by means of affiliation with any prominent group. He believed that people should be judged and rated according to their own achievements and character, and through his civic-minded service and industrious management of his own affairs, he had succeeded, by the time of his death, in becoming a respected and venerated member of the community. The examples of service and accomplishment he had witnessed in his father became deeply engrained in the character of young George, and when he was called upon to assist in the role of "man of the house," he endeavored to emulate those qualities he had come to admire and respect in his father.

Precious little else is known of George Thomas's boyhood or early life. Just prior to his death, he made known his intention to chronicle the events of his youth, but that goal was never attained.[5] It is known that young George had few playmates, and spent a great deal of time with a couple of slave children on the family farm. Accounts would seem to indicate that this time was not spent in boyhood merriment, however, but was instead focused on education. Virginia state law forbade the education of slaves, specifically instruction in reading and writing. Young George defied this law by tutoring the slave children, passing along to them the teachings he had learned at school and church. Indeed, he had endeavored to teach the fifteen slaves owned by the family to read the Bible, along with a free Negro named Artise who lived with the family.[6] The humane and indulgent treatment of the Thomases toward their slaves undoubtedly saved their lives when the greatest drama ever to play itself out in Southampton County took place in 1831: Nat Turner's Raid.

Nat Turner was a slave who had taught himself to read the Bible, becoming a religious fanatic who claimed to be able to read the signs of God in the heavens. He reportedly received a divine command to free his fellow slaves by leading an insurrection against their masters. On the night of August 21, 1831, he gathered together 60 followers in a patch of woods near the home of his master. The group ate a midnight meal, washed down with apple brandy mixed with gunpowder, and then set out on its mission of death and destruction. The first stop was at the home of Nat's masters, Mr. and Mrs. Joseph Travis. The Travises and their children were all murdered before the now-drunken mob set forth to visit like vengeance on the rest of Southampton County. Armed with a variety of weapons, from knives and clubs to swords and guns, Turner's band fanned out over a twenty-seven mile swath of the county, spreading death and destruction to all in their path.

Being a rural society, the white population of Southampton County proved to be an easy target for the insurgents. Homes were often isolated from their neighbors by considerable distance, making any effort to stop the marauders a difficult undertaking. Families that did not receive warning of the approach of Turner's band were left to fend for themselves against overwhelming odds. Many of those who did not receive advance notice were still asleep in their beds when they fell into the hands of the insurgents. The Thomas family did receive advance notice, though the warning came only moments before Turner and his band descended upon Thomaston. Elizabeth Thomas, along with her daughters, fled in a buggy toward Jerusalem, Virginia, but, fearing that they would be overtaken, abandoned the buggy to make their way to town through the intervening woods.

A family slave by the name of Sam, who was the overseer of the farm, kept a cool head when the marauders swarmed over the Thomas home. He instructed his son, Leonard, to escape at the first opportunity, and to make his way back to where his mother was hidden. Leonard was to tell his mother to retrieve the keys to the house, which Sam had hidden in the cider press, and to look after the property until the family could return. The Thomas slaves declined to join with Turner's band. Instead, they fled to the woods and hid until they could make their way to Jerusalem to rejoin their mistress. Once there, they were locked up in the local jail for their own protection, to safeguard them from angry whites who might mistake them for members of Turner's band.

The raiders were turned back on the outskirts of Jerusalem by a dozen whites armed with muskets, but the rampage continued for another day before help could arrive from neighboring counties. After two days of terror, most of Turner's men were killed or captured. Turner himself escaped, only to be captured six weeks later. He was subsequently tried and hanged for crimes against the state. During the raid, fifty-seven whites, many of them women and children, were killed by Turner and his followers.[7] Turner's Raid brought fear to the hearts of whites throughout the South, and altered the way in which blacks were viewed by many white Southerners.

As to the activities of George during the time of the insurrection, accounts are sketchy and somewhat contradictory. General William T. Sherman related a story told to him by Thomas while both men were serving as cadets at West Point. Thomas had told his young comrade that President Andrew Jackson had signed his appointment to the Academy as a reward for his services during the Turner Raid, when he had ridden from house to house sounding the alarm to the residents. Historians have never found any information to corroborate this statement, however, and, as the reader will later discover, it does not coincide with the record of events that landed Thomas at West Point. Contemporaries never knew Thomas to lie or stretch the truth, but there is no evidence to support the claim.[8] Even so, the story did not come directly from Thomas. It was told by Sherman and recorded in the papers of the Army of the Cumberland proceedings about a decade after the end of the war.

From contemporaries, it has been learned that George was a quiet and thoughtful boy. He has been described as an individual "of few words and of an excellent spirit." He liked to work with his hands, and had an aptitude for things of a mechanical nature. Possessed of an inquisitive mind, he had an affinity for building and creating, as evidenced by the saddle and several pieces of house furniture created by his youthful efforts.[9] It was told that Thomas would frequently visit the shops of the saddle-maker and the cabinet-maker, spending many hours observing the craftsmen at their trade. By observation alone he was able to learn and master the trades to the point of being able to make the articles himself without supervision.[10] As to his formal education, Thomas was instructed in his primary studies at Southampton Academy, where his keen mind and intellectual aptitude were praised by his teachers. His courage, judgment, and independent thinking also won the accolades of his schoolmates, making him a favorite among his peers.

Upon his graduation from Southampton Academy at the age of eighteen, Thomas undertook legal studies in the office of James Rochelle, his uncle on his mother's side, even though he showed no special interest in becoming a lawyer. Rochelle served as county clerk of Southampton County. As the ranking administrative officer of the county, he was responsible for all county court proceedings, collected and disbursed taxes, and enforced the laws and statutes of the county and state. Thomas applied himself to his study of the law with the same enthusiasm and vigor as he had always evidenced in regard to education. When James Rochelle died on August 17, 1835, Thomas was subsequently appointed deputy clerk of the county.[11]

In the spring of 1836, John Young Mason, the United States congressman serving the district in which Thomas lived, visited the clerk's office to announce that he had an appointment to the Military Academy at West Point. Mason was searching for a special individual upon whom he could bestow the appointment, as no one from his congressional district had ever been successful in completing the course of studies and graduating from the academy. Mason had heard good things about the deputy county clerk living in Jerusalem, and felt that young Thomas might be just the candidate who could become the first West Point officer from the region. A meeting with Thomas convinced Mason that he had indeed found his man, and upon his return to Washington, he wrote a letter to Lewis Cass, Secretary of War: "Sir: I have the honor to recommend George Thomas of Southampton County, for admission into the Academy at West Point as a cadet. He is Seventeen or Eighteen years of age, of fine size, and of excellent talents with a good preparatory education."[12] Actually, Thomas was nineteen, and just about to turn twenty. As such, he was a couple of years older than the normal cadet in the plebe class.

Even so, Thomas still needed the consent of his mother in order to attend the academy. That was forthcoming within a month of Mason's nomination. "This is to certify that I give my consent for George H. Thomas to sign any articles by which he will bind himself to serve five years as a cadet in the United States Military Academy at West Point, unless sooner discharged. Given under my hand this 26th day of March, 1836. Elizabeth Thomas-Guardian."[13] Cass accepted the appointment from Mason and forwarded it to President Andrew Jackson for approval. Everything progressed in rapid succession, and Thomas was in Washington in April to pay Congressman Mason a visit and offer his thanks. Mason reminded Thomas of the poor performance of his previous nominations to West Point, and his expectations for Thomas's future success. As a final admonition, he stated, "If you should fail to graduate, I never want to see your face again."[14]

On June 1, 1836, the name of George Henry Thomas was entered on the rolls of the Military Academy at West Point as a plebe in the class of 1840. Thomas was embarking on the initial phase of a journey into military service that would last for the remainder of his life. Thomas was assigned to the Old South Barracks, and among his room mates were William Tecumseh Sherman and Stewart Van Vliet, both of whom would later see service in the Civil War. Van Vliet was the elder statesman of the group, at almost twenty-one years of age. According to Van Vliet:

> Sherman, George H. Thomas and I arrived at West Point on the same day, and all three were assigned to the same room on the south side of the old south barracks. A warm friendship commenced in that room, which continued, without a single break, during our lives. We were all three sturdy fellows, which prevented our being annoyed by older cadets. They commenced to haze us, as was the fashion of those days, but Thomas put a stop to it. One evening a cadet came into our room and commenced to give us orders. He had said but a few words when Old Tom, as we always called him, stepped up to him and said, "Leave this room immediately, or I will throw you through the window." It is needless to say that the cadet lost no time in getting out of the room. There were no more attempts to haze us. When we graduated we consulted as to the regiments we should apply for. The Florida [Seminole] war was then going on, and we all concluded that we would apply for some regiment then in Florida, for we all wanted to see some actual fighting, and if we did not go to Florida we should never see any; so we all joined the Third Artillery. History shows how near we came to the facts in our reasoning.
>
> Fifty-three years — over half a century — have passed since we separated at West Point, and, of course, one forgets many things in that time."[15]

Erasmus D. Keyes, a West Pointer and future general in the Union army, left an interesting perspective on life at the academy. Keyes felt that the cadets were in "the only society of human beings that I have known in which the standing of an individual is dependant wholly on his own merits as far as they can be ascertained without influence. The son of the poorest and most obscure man, being admitted as a cadet, has an equal chance to gain the honors of his class with the son of the most powerful and richest man in the country. All must submit to the same discipline, wear the same clothes, eat at the same table, come and go upon the same conditions. Birth, avarice, fashion and connections are without effect to determine promotion or punishment." Keyes felt the academy to be a "model republic in all things saving respect to constituted authority and obedience to orders, without which an army is impossible."[16] Descended of modest but industrious lineage, the talented and disciplined young Thomas would thrive in such an environment.

The first order of business for the new plebes was initial examinations to determine which among them would be allowed to stay, and which would be sent home. Physical and academic testing culled the appointees, leaving only those thought to be sound enough in mind and body to endure the rigors of the four years of instruction to come. One cadet who had successfully passed the initial examinations wrote with compassion regarding those who had been sent home. "It is not thought a disgrace to be dismissed from here, for the studies and discipline are very hard, and a man who succeeds should be thought uncommonly talented, and one found deficient should not be blamed, for I verily believe that not one half of those appointed can possibly graduate."[17]

George Thomas and the rest of the plebes who passed the initial testing now settled in to begin their education as officers of men. Life at West Point was a confusing combination of pageantry mixed with Spartan existence. To be sure, one could be awe-struck by the grandeur of the handsome, brass-buttoned uniforms, the stately and commanding demeanor of the officers, and the quality of the education they were to receive. At the same time, the simple manner in which they lived and trained served to humble any thoughts of personal ambition or superiority.

Mealtime exemplified the Spartan portion of a plebe's experience at West Point. The typical breakfast consisted of bread, butter, and desiccated potatoes, cooked with whatever meat was left over from the previous evening's meal, and coffee. A typical dinner saw a beef roast with boiled potatoes. Supper was more of a snack, with only bread, butter, and tea serving as the usual fare.[18] The sparse offerings at mealtime led Sherman to amass a staggering 109 demerits for misconduct in his first year. A large number of those disciplinary points were given due to nighttime forays that Sherman would make in search of food to augment their diet. Sherman gained the reputation of being the best hash maker at the academy, and though there is no record of Thomas's participation in the food-gathering excursions, the stout appearance he maintained throughout his cadet years suggests that he benefited from them.[19]

Samuel G. French, a cadet at West Point during Thomas's time there, and a future general in the Union army, left a description of life at the academy:

> We have five in our room, which you know is about 10 by 12. At 5 a.m. which is ½ an hour after the morning gun, the drums are beat by the barracks, & the cry grows — "fall in there," when we all have to be in the ranks or be reported. The roll is then called, we go to our rooms & have 15 minutes to roll up our blankets, put them up, wash, clean the room, etc., when everything must be in order. We have no mattresses & only 2 blankets to lay on the floor and cover ourselves with, & when we all five spread ourselves out we just cover the floor — (In camp we have no more). We then remain in our rooms until the drums beat for breakfast, again if missing we are reported. We then march to the mess hall, & if one speaks, raises his hand, looks to the right or left (which is the case on all parade) we are reported for everything. I have been so fortunate as to escape as yet. When we arrive at the tables, the command is given "take seats," & then such a scrambling you never saw.... We have to eat fast as we can, & before we get enough, the command is given "Squad rise." ... We have to drill twice a day, & a good many faint away. It is terrible, but I like the whole of it, after we have marched from tea, we stay in our room till ½ hour past 9 when we can go to bed if we choose, & at taps at 10 every light must be out & after that the inspector happens in all times of night.[20]

The course of studies for the first-year cadets included French, algebra, trigonometry, application of trigonometry to geometry, ministration of planes and solids, and school of the soldier. At the end of the initial year, Thomas finished close to the upper third of his class, with a standing of twenty-sixth in a class of seventy-six. The second-year courses were French, rhetoric, geography, history, and artillery. Thomas rose to a standing of fifteenth in a class of fifty-eight during his sophomore year, and exhibited a particular ability for artillery practice. Third-year subjects included drawing, natural philosophy and chemistry, school of the battalion, another artillery course, and duties of the sergeant. Thomas's standing slipped a slight bit in his junior year, and found him finishing seventeenth in a class of forty-six. The final year at the academy focused on engineering, science of war, mineralogy and geology, moral philosophy, political science, rhetoric, and a final installment of artillery. Thomas was able to improve his class standing in the final year, based largely upon his good marks in artillery, in which he stood seventh in the entire class. Overall, he graduated twelfth out of the forty-two members who remained. He had acquired a grand total of 87 demerits during his four years, or approximately 22 per year, as compared to the staggering total of 380 which Sherman amassed. His class position rated him the highest of any of the four cadets who would go on to attain fame in the Civil War, namely Grant, Sherman, Sheridan, and himself. During his time at the academy, he had advanced through the ranks to cadet lieutenant, while Sherman attained the rank of sergeant, only to find himself busted back down to private as punishment for infractions.[21] By contrast, Thomas's deportment, his low level of demerits, and his sterling character were the source of the first of many nick-names to be associated with him: his fellow cadets called him George Washington. It must have been a Virginia trait, as a number of years before, the same comparison had been made of Robert E. Lee, who became known at the academy as the Marble Model for his exemplary record.

His high grades in artillery, along with a desire to see action in actual combat, led Thomas to apply for appointment to that branch of the service in hopes of seeing action in Florida in the war that was being waged against the Seminoles. The graduates received their diplomas in June of 1840, and were then assigned to their first posts as new lieutenants in the army. Thomas received an appointment as second lieutenant in the 3rd United States Artillery, and was ordered to report to the commanding officer at Fort Columbus, Governor's Island, New York.[22]

Before reporting for duty, however, all graduates were granted a leave of absence to return home and visit their families. This leave provided the new lieutenants with a perfect opportunity to be the toast of their towns in their handsome new uniforms, and George Thomas was no exception. He returned to Southampton County with his first military laurels to display to his friends and family, and to Congressman Mason: a diploma from West Point. One is left to wonder what Congressman Mason, a Virginian and Southerner, would have thought if he had known that his first successful appointment to the academy would be to a man who would go on to seek everlasting glory fighting against his home region. But that was all in the future. For the present, Thomas and his neighbors celebrated his most recent accomplishments.

Most of the cadets who attended West Point during the time Thomas was there would have to make difficult decisions when the Civil War came, and many would attain fame and distinction for their service in that struggle. Thomas became intimate with a large number of future generals on both sides through his acquaintances at the Point. The list of future greats Thomas counted as friends or acquaintances included: Don Carlos Buell, Class of 1841; William S. Rosecrans, Class of 1842; Ulysses S. Grant, Class of 1843; Braxton Bragg, Class of 1837; Daniel H. Hill, Class of 1842; William J. Hardee, Class of 1838; James Longstreet,

Class of 1842; in addition to his classmates, Sherman and Van Vliet. Thomas would serve under Grant, Buell, and Rosecrans in the Civil War, and he would fight against Bragg, Hardee, and Longstreet. But for now, they were all still on the same side, facing a common enemy, the Seminoles.

Following Thomas's leave at home, he reported to Fort Columbus to receive his orders, along with the rest of the army replacements gathered at that post. The wild and untamed wilderness of Florida was to be the site of his first active service.

Chapter Two

A Martial Career Begun

In October of 1840, Thomas was ordered to report to that portion of the 3rd Artillery then serving in the Florida Everglades. He would make his journey aboard the *Zenobia* to Savannah, Georgia, where more recruits for the 3rd Artillery were met. In all, two companies of new men for the regiment were bound for Florida. Thomas and his company sailed aboard the *Forester*, landing at Fort Lauderdale. Other companies were spread out along the coast from St. Augustine to Key Biscayne.

Thomas was to be surrounded by classmates and comrades from West Point during his time in Florida. Braxton Bragg was stationed at St. Augustine. Both Sherman and Van Vliet were attached to Company A, stationed at Fort Pierce. Thomas, along with the rest of Company D, was assigned to the post at Fort Lauderdale.[1] What Thomas discovered when he got off the boat at Fort Lauderdale was little more than a cluster of cane-built huts, and a few Indian wigwams, all located about 200 feet from the ocean. The post was quite filthy, and all of the lodgings were overrun with cockroaches. The bunks were thoroughly infested with fleas, and mosquitoes swarmed everywhere to round out the three-pronged insect attack on the soldiers, which lasted day and night. Looking inland from the beach, one was struck by the dense, jungle-like tropical undergrowth, out of which could occasionally be heard the cries of the panther and the bellows of the alligator. At night, the troops could see campfires of the enemy on the western horizon. All in all, Fort Lauderdale was an imposing and difficult post, and would try the bodies and spirits of the men stationed there.[2]

The United States army had been involved in active operations against the Seminole Indians in the region since 1835 in this, the second war against the tribe. The first expedition against the Seminole had taken place from 1817 to 1818, when Andrew Jackson led a campaign that successfully subdued the tribe. Now, the new generation of Seminoles were again fighting against white intrusion upon their land, and were proving to be a fearsome and elusive enemy to the United States military. The Seminole were not the only enemies the soldiers would face while campaigning in Florida. Disease, alligators, water moccasins, mosquitoes, and a host of other natural dangers challenged the troops as they lived and struggled in the 4,000-square-mile watery wasteland that was the Everglades.

In a letter to Charles P. Kingsbury, graduating second in the Class of 1840, Thomas wrote of his early experience with army life on this wilderness outpost.

> Dear Kingsbury: Owing to the quantity of business on my hands at this time, I have not been able to answer yours of the 23d May before.
> What do you ordnance officers do for quartermasters and commissaries? Do you do the duty yourselves, or have you staff officers at your arsenals to perform those duties?
> My duties at this post are so many that my whole time is taken up. I have to do the duty of

commissary, quartermaster, ordnance officer, and adjutant; and if I find time to eat my meals, I think myself most infernal fortunate.

So the Democrat was not dismissed after all, you have, however, got him away from Watervliet, which must be some consolation at least. Old Van has become much pleased with line duty that I hardly think he could be bribed to accept an appointment in a staff corps. I saw him yesterday; he came down in the boat with Major Childs, who has gone to Fort Dallas, below this place, with sixty men from his post and sixty from here, for the purpose of making an expedition into the Everglades to oust Sam Jones from his cornfields. I think it highly probable that they may do something if they will go to work properly, for the Indians are there, I know, as we have frequently seen their fires at night, and they do not expect to see any of our men there at this season of the year; therefore, if the major will only manage the affair well, he may he may add fresh laurels to those he has already won. I have been left behind to take care of this infernal place in consequence of being commissary, etc.

This will be the only opportunity I shall have of distinguishing myself, and not to be able to avail myself of it is too bad. They say at St. Augustine that the Third will be ordered to Old Point this fall, but there have been so many sayings of the kind this summer that I begin to have no faith in them.

Colonel Worth has been on a grand scout, but did not succeed in discovering any fields or Indians. Major Childs thinks that some regiment of infantry will come to these lower posts this fall, and we will be concentrated at Fort Pierce preparatory to a grand expedition to the Okechobee, where they think the whole Indian force has retired as the last point of safety.

I am glad you exposed the doings of those people of the Academic Board; they deserved something worse than exposition of the Engineer Department.

I have not heard from Gardiner or Martin yet; what they are doing I can not learn. Herbert has written only once since my arrival in Florida; he had just then returned from furlough. From his accounts, I should say that he has been enjoying himself in fine style.

I have just heard that poor Job Lancaster has been killed by lightening. I have heard no news lately that has distressed me more, for he was one of the very best of men. Wardwell is also dead; he had the fever which has been prevailing in the western part of the territory. You must write again soon. Yours truly, George H. Thomas.[3]

In this letter to a comrade and classmate Thomas strays from his usual stoic adherence to duty and his strict obedience to orders. The friendship he shared with Kingsbury obviously allowed him the rare opportunity to lower his guard and do something he rarely ever did: complain. Thomas was less than pleased with his situation in Florida, but he maintained a professional and uncomplaining veneer with his superiors at Fort Lauderdale. To Kingsbury, he complained of his numerous duties, rued his lack of personal time, and chafed at the possibility of being left behind when the opportunity for glory in the field was at hand. In talking about Van Vliet, one could surmise that he is making a comparison between himself and his old friend, and that his estimation of line duty is somewhat diminished from Van Vliet's. Then again, Van Vliet would see action against the Seminole. In fact, he would be one of the very few to not only come to close quarters with the elusive foe, but to kill one of the enemy in action.

A 19th-century biographer of William T. Sherman relates the story of the capture of one of the Seminole chiefs in the summer of 1841. According to the story, the Seminole chief Coacoochee, or Wild Cat, had been induced to come to Fort Pierce to discuss laying down his arms and surrendering to United States authorities. The chief and a dozen of his warriors met with Major Childs, Sherman, and other officers, and told them that he was tired of war and only desired to be transported with his people to the Indian Territory, where they could live in peace. He informed Childs that he would need one month's rations for his people while they prepared to leave their homes and make the journey to the Oklahoma Territory. Childs readily agreed to this provision, at which point Coacoochee proceeded to get infamously drunk. When the chief sobered up, he took his rations and disappeared into the Everglades, but when one month had passed there were no Indian families at the fort, and all that had transpired were the frequent requests from Coacoochee for whiskey and additional rations. The chief was not preparing his people to surrender; he was merely subsisting them at the expense of the United States government. Coacoochee and some of his warriors were once more induced to come to the fort for a council, and in the course of the proceedings they all became drunk. Sherman and some of his men slapped irons on all of the drunken Seminoles, and they were promptly transferred to the Indian Territory. At the time of the capture, the biographer states that "Among Sherman's associates were Lieutenants Ransom, Ord, George H. Thomas, Field, and Van Vliet."[4] It is to be noted that mention of this incident appears no where in any of the biographical works devoted to the life of George H. Thomas, as most historians do not credit the story. Regrettably, the biographer did not cite a source for the information, leaving the matter open to question. It is hard to believe, however, that Thomas, with all of his pressing duties at Fort Lauderdale, would have made a trip to Fort Pierce to see Sherman and be present at the council when the Seminole chief was captured.

Thomas would spend a year in Florida performing the commissary, quartermaster, and ordnance duties that used up all his available time and prevented him from experiencing the active service he longed for. To him, it was a year of almost intolerable drudgery, devoid of honor or glory, but the assignments were making him proficient in necessary components of supervising an army in the field, and, as with all things undertaken by him, Thomas excelled at his tasks.

Finally, in November of 1841, Captain Richard A. Wade, the commander at Fort Lauderdale, was ordered to mount an expedition into the interior for the purpose of subduing the inhabitants of several Seminole villages. Thomas was named second in command for the expedition, and put in charge of sixty men. Captain Wade left a complete description of the expedition in his official report:

Sir,—In pursuance to the instructions contained in your communication of the 24th September, I set out on the morning of the 5th inst., accompanied by Lieutenant Thomas, Third Artillery, Assistant Surgeon Emerson and sixty non-commissioned officers and privates, embarked in twelve canoes and provisioned for fifteen days. We proceeded by the inland passage to the northward, coming out at the bay in the Hillsborough Inlet, and in such manner that our canoes were concealed from the view of an Indian whom I there discovered fishing on the northern point of the inlet. I made the requisite dispositions immediately to land, and succeeded in surprising him. By operating on his hopes and fears, I induced him to lead us to his Indian village, fifteen miles distant in a westerly direction. This we reached on the morning of the 6th; surprised and captured twenty Indians, men, women, and children; took six rifles, destroyed fourteen canoes and much provisions of the usual variety. Of those who attempted to escape eight were killed by our troops. We returned to our boats the same forenoon with our prisoners, and proceeded up a small stream towards the Orange Grove haul-over, where we encamped for the night. On the morning of the 7th, after proceeding three miles farther north, the stream became too shallow for canoe navigation, and we made here a camp, leaving the prisoners, boats, and a sufficient guard in charge of Dr. Emerson. Under the guidance of an old Indian found among our prisoners, who is called Chia-chee, I took up the line of march through nearly a mile of deep bog and saw-grass, then through the pine barren and some hummocks to a cypress swamp a distance of some thirty miles northward. Here (on the 8th inst.) we were conducted to another village, which we also surrounded, and surprised and captured twenty-seven Indians, took six rifles and one shot-gun, and destroyed a large quantity of provisions and four canoes. The next morning (November 9) we set out on our return to the boats, on a more easterly route than the former, which led us to the shores of Lake Worth, where we found and destroyed a canoe, a field of pumpkins, and an old hut. In the afternoon of this day one man came in and surrendered himself, thus making the whole number of our Indian prisoners forty-nine. At 11 A.M. of the 10th we arrived at our boats and proceeded to the little Hillsborough bar by evening, and in the afternoon of the next day (November 11) we returned to Fort Lauderdale without any loss on our part, after an absence of six days. Having seen much in the old man Chia-chee to inspire my confidence in his integrity, I permitted him to go out from our camp (on the 10th November) to bring in other Indians, which he promised to do in three or four days. This promise he subsequently redeemed, having on the 14th inst. brought in six (four men and two boys) at Fort Lauderdale.

My warmest thanks are due to Dr. Emerson and Lieutenant Thomas for their valuable and efficient aid in carrying out my orders, and of the conduct of the troops likewise, without any exception, I can speak only in terms of the highest praise.

I have the honor to be, very respectfully, Your obedient servant, R.D.A. Wade, Captain Third Artillery, Commanding Expedition.[5]

There had not been much fighting and little glory to be gained in the hunting down of the small, isolated pockets of resistance that Wade's force encountered in the course of the expedition, but Thomas had at last seen action, and had performed his duties in a manner deserving of praise in his commander's official report of the campaign. Thomas doubtless relished the opportunity to escape from the rigors and tedium of his post duties, and the expedition had to seem a great adventure to him, regardless of the lack of any appreciable combat. He had led his first field command, a mere sixty men, to be sure, but he had once more proven himself equal to the task and able to accept more responsibility.

When Wade's report was received by Colonel William J. Worth, commander of the 3rd Artillery, he forwarded it to the War Department with the following endorsement: "I have the satisfaction to forward the following report of the successful operations of Captain Wade, Third Artillery, acting under the orders of his immediate commander, Major Childs. This very creditable affair will operate the most favorable influence upon the closing scenes of this protracted contest, and I but do equal justice to the distinguished merit and conduct of captain Wade, and the expectations of the service, in respectfully asking that the special notice of the Department of War may be extended to him and his gallant assistant, Second Lieutenant G.H. Thomas, of the same regiment. Respectfully, etc., W.J. Worth, Colonel Commanding."[6] The War Department concurred with Worth's request in bestowing the brevet rank of first lieutenant on Thomas, retroactive to November 8, 1841, "for gallantry and good conduct in the war against the Florida Indians."[7] Finally, Thomas had had the opportunity to prove his mettle in the field, and the resultant promotion had been the reward for his actions.

Captain Wade also received a reward, of sorts, for his participation in the expedition, in the form of a transfer away from the bleak post at Fort Lauderdale. His replacement was Captain Erasmus D. Keyes. Keyes and Thomas soon struck up a mutual admiration, and spent a great deal of time together, though Keyes was many years Thomas's senior. Keyes described his new friend as being about twenty-six years of age, six feet tall, with a symmetrical form, inclined to plumpness, with a blond complexion and large, deep blue eyes. He stated that "The shape and carriage of his head and facial expression corresponded with my idea of a patrician of ancient Rome."[8] Keyes saw the potential of greatness in Thomas. He also saw that the new brevet first lieutenant was encumbered with too many duties to perform at the post, so he assigned another officer to act as post quartermaster, maintaining Thomas in his other assignments.

Aside from the friendly relations Keyes and Thomas were cultivating, life at the post remained a droll and tiresome assignment. Keyes, who had previously been stationed in Washington, D.C., recalled how life in Florida lacked the amenities he had become accustomed to at the nation's capital when he described his first experience at the officer's mess.

> I went into another thatched hut, and sat down on a block of wood at a table composed of two unpainted planks which rested upon stakes driven into the sand. A complement of tin plates, pewter spoons, rusty knives, and two-pronged forks, constituted the table setting. The breakfast was brought in, and it consisted in muddy coffee without milk, brown sugar, hard bread, tough buckwheat cakes, and semi-fluid rancid butter, held in a cracked teacup.
>
> My first dinner at Fort Lauderdale differed from my first breakfast by substitution of bean soup and salt pork for buckwheat cakes and commissary whiskey for muddy coffee which recalled the sumptuous fare in Washington."[9]

Though post life at Fort Lauderdale offered few delicacies or epicurean delights, there was never a shortage of food for the men, due largely to the efforts of Thomas. The ocean and rivers near the post literally swarmed with fish and green turtles, both of which were liberally used to supplement the soldiers' diet. In fact, Thomas's commissary served up so many turtle steaks that the men looked forward to a normal ration of salt pork. Being a good shot, he would also make periodic hunting trips into the jungle-like interior, in search of deer and turkey with which to augment the dining fare of the post. The menu was sometimes monotonous and unappetizing, but no one at Fort Lauderdale ever went hungry for want of provisions.[10]

Keyes would not have to long endure or ponder the privations of a frontier post. Expeditions such as the one mounted by Captain Wade had forced the Seminoles to retreat deep into the interior of the Everglades. Although the war was not ended, and the Seminole did not surrender, their removal to the interior made all of the coastal posts of the army secure, and lessened the need for military presence in the region. Accordingly, Company D received orders in December of 1841 to transfer to Fort Brooke at Tampa Bay. After a brief stay on the west side of the state, the company was ordered to relocate itself once more, to New Orleans, to refit and reorganize in February of 1842. Despite the fact that there were still Seminole Indians deep in the Everglades who had not surrendered to the United States Army, the War Department considered the war in Florida to be over.

Thomas and Keyes continued to

Erasmus D. Keyes, one of George Thomas's earliest friends in the military. Their paths would cross several times in the 1840s through the 1860s (United States Army Military History Institute).

serve together at New Orleans Barracks from February to June of 1842, at which point Thomas was ordered to Fort Moultrie in Charleston, South Carolina. While stationed at New Orleans, Thomas took the opportunity to visit Chalmette Battlefield, where Andrew Jackson had saved New Orleans by defeating a British army twice the size of his own, inflicting 2,036 casualties, while sustaining only 71 himself. He drank in the lay of the ground, the manner in which Jackson had used his defensive position to batter the waves of attacking British, and the effect of superior marksmanship. More than two decades later, he would employ the same sort of barricades and the same unerring marksmanship to shatter the waves of Confederate soldiers General James Longstreet threw against him on Horseshoe Ridge at Chickamauga.[11]

Thomas performed garrison duty at Fort Moultrie until December of 1843, when he was ordered to Fort McHenry in Baltimore, Maryland. In October of 1844, he was detached from his garrison post and assigned to recruiting duty at Charleston, South Carolina. He would arrive in Charleston with a new promotion in hand, and the War Department had upgraded his brevet to an official commission as first lieutenant in the 3rd Artillery on April 30, 1844. The promotion was in recognition of his service during the Seminole War, even though it came nearly two and one-half years after Wade and Thomas had completed their successful expedition into the Everglades. Recruitment service continued until March of 1845, when Thomas was reassigned to garrison duty with his company at Fort Moultrie.

The ominous clouds of a new war were clearly visible on the horizon, however, and on June 26, 1845, Company D was ordered to transfer to Texas, in anticipation of hostilities with Mexico.[12] Back in Florida, Thomas had worried that he would not have the opportunity to distinguish himself in combat. His only foray into the field had not only dispelled that fear, it had resulted in commendation and promotion from his superiors. Now, there was a possibility that he could once more see field service and enhance his career. It is important for the reader to understand that the United States Army was essentially a small organization in the decades prior to the Civil War. Chances for promotion were few and often long in coming. It was not uncommon for a junior officer to remain in grade for ten years or more. Only through proving oneself on the field of battle could an officer even hope to attain rapid promotion. Thomas had elevated himself from second lieutenant to first lieutenant in the space of four years, and now he would have the chance to advance himself even further.

Certainly, he had already secured the attention of many of his superiors, and so long as his performance mirrored the opinions already held about him, that advancement would be relatively assured. Captain Keyes spoke for many officers who had come into contact with the young first lieutenant when he left his own assessment of the man. Keyes described Thomas as being of even temperament, stated that he was never violently demonstrative, and was calm when entering or leaving a battle. He said that Thomas was seldom early for an appointment, but he never knew him to be late, impatient, or in a hurry. In his movements, he was deliberate. Though supremely self-possessed, he was not arrogant, and he issued and followed orders with serenity. His deportment was dignified when with friends, reserved when with strangers and casual acquaintances. He was sociable, and possessed of a subtle sense of humor that could be seen through his use of illustrations and smiles. Keyes felt him to be a most accomplished and capable officer, with a scientific mind, who was inclined toward good reading and other worthy pursuits. He felt that Thomas excelled his peers when it came to judgment, impartiality, and integrity.[13] For such a man as Keyes described, surely the sky was the limit, and all that was needed was a chance to prove himself.

Chapter Three

First Glory in Mexico

Ever since Texas had won its independence from Mexico in 1836, there had been a wave of support in the United States to welcome the new republic into the Union with the status of statehood. Texas had already been recognized as an independent nation by many of the powers of the world, including the United States, and a large portion of the population residing there had come from the states. But the sticking point boiled down to a controversy between the Whigs and the Democrats over the extension of slavery in the new territories and states of the west. For nine years, the debate raged in the halls of Congress, while Texas went about the business of running its own affairs as an independent nation. One of the most pressing issues facing the republic was a border dispute with Mexico regarding the southern and western boundary of Texas. Texans claimed that the boundary was the Rio Grande to its source, thence due north to 42 degrees north latitude. General Santa Anna and the Mexican authorities contested this, claiming that the Nueces River and not the Rio Grande was the true boundary of Texas. Tensions had been mounting between the two sides for a considerable period by the time the United States got around to granting Texas statehood in December of 1845. One of the conditions for statehood was the understanding that the United States would be responsible for settling the dispute with Mexico over the boundaries.

The United States government did not wait until Texas's admission to the Union had been officially ratified to make its official presence known to the Mexican authorities. During the summer of 1845, several regiments of regular troops received their orders to proceed to Texas and await further instructions. One June 26, 1845, George Thomas received orders to take Company E, 3rd U.S. Artillery to Texas, and to report to General Zachary Taylor, who had already set up a headquarters in the state. Thomas and his command arrived in New Orleans on July 19, and departed that city on July 24, arriving at Corpus Christi, Texas, in August. Along with the 3rd and 4th Infantry Regiments, Company E set up a garrison position at Corpus Christi. These were the first American troops to enter the Republic of Texas, and their presence was intended to act as a deterrent to Santa Anna and the Mexican government should any acts of aggression be planned before Texas statehood could be ratified.[1]

Once Texas officially became a state, President James K. Polk ordered General Taylor to move his troops to the east bank of the Rio Grande, to exhibit to the Mexican government that the United States intended to uphold the Texan claim that the river was the boundary. As far as Santa Anna and the Mexican government were concerned, Texas and United States authority ended at the Nueces, meaning that the Americans were 100 miles beyond their border, and occupying territory sovereign to Mexico. From the point of view of the Mexican authorities, a state of war therefore already existed between their country and the United States.

On August 23, 1843, while the annexation of Texas was still very much in doubt and being passionately debated in the halls of Congress, the Mexican ambassador to the United States had warned that the admittance of Texas into the Union would be viewed as an act of war against Mexico, and would be dealt with accordingly. The American State Department took the stance that Texas was an independent nation, recognized by several members of the world community, and was free to do as she wished. Mexico contested this claim on the grounds that Mexico did not recognize Texas's independence, and therefore it was still subject to Mexican rule. When Secretary of State John C. Calhoun suggested that the United States would be willing to negotiate all differences between the two countries, including compensation for damages and negotiation over the boundary dispute, the Mexican ambassador seemed in agreement. He was overruled by the Mexican Cabinet, however, when it reviewed the substance of Calhoun's proposal. Any attempt to annex Texas would result in a state of war between the two other nations. Nevertheless, the annexation of Texas was brought before Congress, where it was defeated in the Senate.

This turn of affairs left Texas in a most precarious position. The republic had declined alliances offered by both England and France in favor of statehood in the United States. Now it stood alone, denied of the annexation it sought, and having strained relations with the European powers it had snubbed. To make matters worse, General Santa Anna had requested that the government raise the funds and manpower to mount a second invasion of Texas, to return it to Mexican rule. With 30,000 troops, he promised to regain the northern territory and end the dispute once and for all. Secretary Calhoun attempted to defuse the impending crisis by stating to the Mexican authorities that the United States was responsible for the present difficulties, not Texas. He further stated that while the annexation of Texas had been stalled in the Senate, the issue was still pending, and would be brought before that body for another vote in the future. Calhoun advised that because of American interests, the nation would not allow the situation in Texas to be settled by threats and hostile action, a not-so-subtle warning that any use of force by Santa Anna would be responded to in kind.[2]

During the summer of 1845, in a joint resolution, Congress finally voted for the annexation of Texas. The Mexican government promptly broke off diplomatic relations with the United States, and when Texas officially accepted the offer of statehood in July of 1845, both sides prepared for war. George H. Thomas, Company E, and the rest of the troops who had been sent to Corpus Christi formed an American presence that the government hoped would dissuade the Mexicans from launching a pre-emptive strike before the annexation of Texas could be completed. At the time of their arrival in the republic, Texas was not yet part of the United States, even if the wheels of government were traveling in that direction.

Diplomacy might yet have been sufficient to settle the differences between the two nations following the annexation of Texas. Both sides prepared for war, but open hostilities were not yet a certainty. It was not until after President Polk ordered General Taylor to occupy the east bank of the Rio Grande that the situation reached a point of no return. Both sides braced for the conflict that was sure to follow, and on May 12, 1846, the United States Congress passed a declaration of war against the nation of Mexico. President Polk signed the document the following day.[3]

Thomas would find himself under a new immediate superior in Texas, as Captain Braxton Bragg was assigned to command of Company E. Erasmus Keyes described Bragg as being "ambitious and of saturnine disposition and morbid temperament." Of fiery temper, he had nearly fought a duel when a citizen of Charleston jokingly referred to his native North Carolina as "a strip of land lying between two states." Violence was only averted through the intercession of Sherman and John Reynolds, who managed to delay and subsequently eliminate the proposed meeting on the field of honor.[4] Bragg could be prideful, petty, and vindictive. His ambition for promotion and distinction dictated his actions, and caused him to sometimes be dictatorial and harsh with subordinates. A man on a mission, with much to prove, he would stand in stark contrast to the unassuming and even-tempered Thomas, who would be serving as his executive officer.

By all accounts, the pair worked well together, however. Thomas, always one to subordinate himself to proper authority, was an able and efficient second-in-command to Bragg. For Bragg's part, he found in Thomas a junior officer whose competence and ability were without question, and whose loyal performance of his duties posed no threat to the position or authority of his commander. It can be assumed from the cordial relations that existed between the two men that Bragg never felt the need to let loose with any tyrannical tirades toward Thomas, and that he instead treated him in a cordial and respectful manner. Thomas's interaction with his commander would certainly bear out this assumption, as his later life showed he was not one to silently bear the sting of what he felt to be unjust or intolerable treatment.

On March 26, 1846, Company E, 3rd U.S. Artillery, along with Company I, 1st U.S. Artillery, and the 7th United States Infantry, under the command of Major Jacob Brown, were ordered to occupy a Fort Texas (named Fort Taylor by the troops) on the Rio Grande opposite Matamoras, Mexico. In the meantime, General Taylor located the remainder of his force at Port Isabel, where a base of supply was established. For six days, from May 3 to 8, the fort was subjected to almost constant bombardment from the Mexicans. Although the shelling did little material damage to the fort and inflicted few casualties upon its defenders, Major Brown was killed, and the fort was subsequently named in his honor.[5]

The American troops responded to the Mexican bombardment with vigor, even though their fire did as little damage to the enemy as that which they were enduring. Captain E.S. Hawkins, who had assumed command of the works following the death of Major Brown, found Lieutenant Thomas calmly sitting on a keg of powder during the shelling and asked him what he thought of the proceedings. Thomas responded "Service excellent, but I am thinking you will need the ammunition you are throwing away."[6] Even then, he had started to exhibit the tendencies toward conservation of resources that came to define him as a field commander.

On May 9, the Mexicans ceased their attack on Fort Brown and withdrew to form a junction with General Ampudia and his forces at Resaca de la Palma. General Ampudia had that same day been forced to retire from Palo Alto, a position lying between Fort Brown and Port Isabel, when General Taylor's forces, advancing to the relief of Fort Brown, engaged the Mexicans in a heavy skirmish. The fighting was minor and indecisive, excepting for the fact that Ampudia quit the field and retired to Resaca de la Palma. On May 9, General Taylor attacked the Mexicans at Resaca de la Palma, driving Ampudia's men from the field. As the Mexican soldiers, pressed by Taylor's victorious troops, sought safety by crossing the Rio Grande and re-entering Mexico, they were forced to pass under the guns of Fort Brown. Thomas and his comrades helped turn their retreat into a rout by pouring a merciless hail of shot and shell into their fleeing ranks. The damage to the Mexican army was not as extensive as it might have been, however, for the prophecy of Thomas had come to pass: the guns of the fort were running short on ammunition.[7]

From May 3 to 9, the defenders of Fort Brown had sustained casualties of 13 wounded and 2 killed. Major Brown had been among the latter. Two of the wounded had come from Company E, 3rd Artillery. Captain Hawkins left a written history of the defense of the fort in his official report to General Taylor:

Head Quarters, Fort Taylor, Texas, May 10, 1846
Sir — I have the honor to report that on the morning of the 6th instant, during the third day of the bombardment of this fort its gallant commander, Major Brown, received a severe wound, which caused his death at 2 o'clock on the 9th instant. I immediately assumed command, and have the honor to report the result of the bombardment since 7 o'clock A.M., on the 4th, at which time Capt. [Samuel H.] Walker left with a report of the result up to that time.

At 9 o'clock P.M. on the 4th, firing of musketry was heard in our rear, about three or four hundred yards distant, and apparently extended a mile up the river; the firing was very irregular. This continued until half-past 11 o'clock P.M. The garrison was under arms, batteries and defenses all manned, and continued so during the night. On the 5th instant, at 5 o'clock A.M., the fire was recommenced from the enemy's batteries, which was immediately returned from the eighteen-pounder battery [Capt. Allen Lowd's] and six-pounder howitzer, placed in embrasure on the southeast bastion. The firing was kept up one hour, receiving during that time about fifty round shot and shells from the enemy. The batteries on both sides ceased firing at the same time. Our expenditure of ammunition was thirty rounds of both caliber.

At 8 o'clock A.M., Valdez, a Mexican, came in and reported that a party of dragoons had been driven back from the prairie to the point, and also a party to the fort; that he had seen thirty deserters from Arista's army, who stated that the Mexicans were without subsistence-stores, that they were tired, and left for their homes; that it was stated in the Mexican camp that Arista had received an express from Mexico informing him that another revolution had broken out in Mexico, and that he could receive no support from the government. At 9 o'clock A.M. it was reported that a reconnaissance of officers escorted by mounted men of the enemy, was going on in rear within eight hundred yards of the fort; and that other parties, mounted and infantry, were at some distance, extending from the bend of the lagoon to the river. Lieut. [Charles] Hanson, Seventh Infantry, asked permission to take the dragoons and go and look at them. This was granted, and in an hour he returned, reporting that the enemy was establishing a battery at the cross roads; his appearance among them created great alarm, and they were soon concentrated at a distance under cover of their work. Every man at work to-day strengthening the defenses. Several parties of cavalry and infantry seen to-day occupying our old encampment. At 11 o'clock P.M. musketry was heard in our rear, from bend of lagoon to the river. The troops all at their places in the bastions during the night.

Wednesday, May 6 — At 5 o'clock A.M., the cannonade commenced from the lower fort and mortar battery. Many round shot and shells thrown until 6 o'clock, when there was a cessation of firing. During the last hour, the shot and shells were well directed, bursting in all directions in the interior of the fort, tearing our tents to pieces, and injuring several horses. At half past 6 o'clock the signal eighteen-pounders were fired, at which the enemy opened their batteries in our front and rear, and the cannonade continued from two mortars and a howitzer in front, and a mortar established at or near the cross roads in rear, until 10 o'clock A.M. when our gallant commander [Major Brown] received a mortal wound from a falling shell.

Large mounted parties and infantry were seen at this time in rear. At 7 o'clock one mortar was playing upon us from town, and two from the rear. At 10 o'clock a small party of infantry crept up in ravine, and fired musketry; but, being out of range, the fire was not returned. At half past 10 o'clock A.M., several parties of infantry and mounted men were seen surrounding us in rear. Several rounds of canister were fired from Lieut. Bragg's battery, which soon dispersed them. Several were afterwards heard to have been killed. Immediately afterwards, and until half past 12 o'clock P.M., we received a continual shower of shells from the enemy's batteries. At 2 o'clock five shells were thrown. At half past 4 o'clock P.M. a white flag was shown at the old building in the rear, and a parley sounded by the enemy. Two officers advanced and were met by two officers of my command....

The night was passed very quietly, but constant vigilance was exercised in the command; every man kept at his post, as an attack was confidently expected in the morning.

Thursday, May 7 — At half past 5 o'clock A.M., the enemy's batteries opened with shells, and continued for about an hour and a half, and then ceased. At half past 7 A.M., several rounds of canister and grape were fired into the enemy's picket guards, at the houses in rear, and at the old guardhouse of the Second brigade, which caused them to abandon their positions. This was replied to by a discharge of some ten or twelve shells. At 9 o'clock A.M., we received a shower of some four or five shells, and then stopped. About this time the enemy commenced firing iron shells, having previously thrown composition shells, and it was discovered that one of the mortars had been removed from our rear, and returned to the city [of Matamoras]. At a quarter past 10 A.M., we received three shells; at 11 A.M., eight shells; at 12 P.M., six shells, by which four of Lieut. Bragg's horses were killed, and the wheel of one of his caissons disabled. At half past 12 the batteries were opened with round shot and shells, and continued for an hour and a half. By this time our bombproofs were so far advanced, that our troops were relatively protected. At 2 o'clock small parties of commenced [firing] on us with random musketry, on the bank of the river, and from the ravine. At half past 2 P.M., a regular bombardment with shot and shells, from a howitzer and the mortars, was kept up with little intermission until sunset. At 5 o'clock during this bombardment, a shell struck in a tent, almost entirely destroying the instruments of the Seventh infantry band, to the value of three hundred dollars. The accuracy of their firing now evidently increased, as at least one-half of the shells thrown fell in the fort. A sentinel [Private Moody] to-day lost his arm by a round shot from the enemy. As soon as it was dark enough, a party headed by our indefatigable engineer, Capt. [Joseph K.F.] Mansfield, was sent out to level the traverse thrown up by Gen. [William J.] Worth, and cutting down the chaparral, which served as a cover to the sharp shooters of the enemy. At 12 o'clock at night, a random fire of musketry commenced around us, followed by two bugles; this continued for about one hour, and from 3 A.M., was continued until near daylight.

Friday, May 8 — At a quarter past 5 o'clock A.M., the enemy's batteries again opened with shells from the lower fort, from the sand-bag battery, and from our rear. The fire this morning was kept up until 8 o'clock A.M., without cessation. A party was sent out this morning, and burnt the old houses on the traverse, on the river bank. This drew from them [the Mexicans] several round shot and shells; from 12 to half past 2 P.M., a heavy bombardment of shells was kept up, at least fifty thrown at us during that time. At half past 3 they again opened their shells upon us, accompanied by round shot. At this time the enemy had established a mortar on the ridge of the chaparral across the river, and immediately west of us. Mortars were now playing upon us from the north, south, and west, four in number. The firing of round shot was kept up for two hours and that of shells until half past 7 P.M. About half past 2 P.M., a heavy cannonading was heard, supposed to be a little north and east of us, it apparently approached until half past 4, when it became very distinct, it lasted until nearly 7 P.M. [This was from the Battle of Palo Alto.] This we supposed to be an action between our forces and the enemy.

A little before sunset, a Mexican came running in with a white flag, from the direction of the Second brigade guard-house, claiming protection. He stated that our forces had come in contact with those of the enemy, had driven them back; that he was a prisoner in charge of the picket guards fired on by our batteries; that while they were burying the dead, and carrying off the wounded, he effected his escape. During the cannonade this afternoon, a small column of infantry from above, and one of cavalry from below, were seen advancing, supposed to be reinforcements to the enemy. The excitement in our command during this distant cannonading was intense. During the day we received from one hundred and fifty to two hundred shells, and from seventy-five to one hundred round shot, and not a man disabled. During the previous night the halliards of the flag on the outside had become unrigged, and as the firing had become too intense to re-establish them, a temporary staff was erected on the inside, and the national flag of the Seventh Infantry raised as a substitute. We passed a very quiet night — the men on the alert at their guns.

Saturday, May 9 — An officer of the Seventh succeeded in lowering the topmast of the flagstaff, and rigging the halliards, but found he could not raise it again without great labor and exposure; he therefore lashed it in position, and raised the national flag, after having stood a succession of round shot, canister, and shells from the enemy's batteries for fifteen or twenty minutes. At 10 o'clock, a sergeant and ten men fired the houses on the road which had been successively occupied by our men and the enemy's pickets. It brought a heavy discharge of shells, canister and round shot from the enemy's batteries. Shells, with slight intervals, continued until half past 2 o'clock P.M., the mortar on our west silent, and one firing from a position between us and the fort, at the upper ferry; it was much further off, fired accurately.

Two P.M., Major Brown died, and in a short time we heard the re-engagement between the armies [the Battle of Resaca de la Palma]. Quarter to six, quite a number of Mexican cavalry and a few infantry were seen in retreat. At this time we received a heavy fire of round shot and shells. From the time the battle commenced, and continued to increase, an eighteen-pounder and six-pounder were fired in the direction of the upper ferry, when, finding it difficult to distinguish between friend and foe, the firing was discontinued. I cannot close this report, and pass in silence the gallant and laborious of the soldiers and men of this command, to fulfill the high trust reposed in them by the commanding general. Under the most disadvantageous circumstances, labor was performed by the men with the greatest alacrity, and always in good cheer. The indefatigable engineer, Capt. Mansfield, is entitled to the highest praise. I have the honor to report a list of the killed and wounded during the seven days' bombardment of Fort Taylor, Texas.

I am, sir, respectfully, your obedient servant ... E.S. Hawkins, Capt. Seventh Infantry, commanding post.[8]

Following the engagement between Taylor's forces and the Mexicans at Resaca de la Palma, the American army was forced to allow the Mexican army to seek refuge in Mexico unimpeded by an active pursuit. This was due to the fact that Taylor was running short of supplies and was compelled to send back to Port Isabel to obtain them before he could re-engage the enemy. George Thomas took note of this situation and mentally logged that the necessity of being "prepared for eventualities, come what may, was an outstanding characteristic throughout his career."[9]

General Taylor's relief of Fort Brown prompted the Mexican army to withdraw from Matamoras, and the town was promptly occupied by the American forces. On June 6, General Taylor made plans for the capture of Reynosa by organizing a flying column made up of four companies of the 1st U.S. Infantry, two twelve-pounders under the command of Lieutenant Thomas, and a company of Texas Rangers. The occupation of Reynosa was viewed to be an easy assignment, as the alcalde of that town had contacted General Taylor to seek his protection from the roving partisan troops of General Antonio Canales and the marauding Comanches of the area. With this open invitation to take possession of the town, Taylor prepared to move his flying column forward.[10]

In early September, Taylor's army was ready to undertake a movement against the fortified city of Monterrey. By this time, Thomas had been returned from detached duty, and was once more serving under Bragg with the rest of Company E. It took two weeks for the American column to come within sight of Monterrey, a distance of about 100 miles. The march was a pleasant one for the troops, all in all, as they plodded through a land abundant with provisions. Fields of vegetables ready for harvest and heavily laden fruit trees greeted their every step. Lieutenant Samuel French, serving with Thomas in Company E, stated "We had oranges, lemons, limes, pomegranates, bananas, and grapes."[11] Though there was a force of 1,000 Mexican dragoons constantly hovering around the column, the enemy horsemen made no attempt to engage or harass the Americans.

As they neared Monterrey, the troops got their first glimpses of the Sierra Madre Mountains. They were so high and extensive that many of the men speculated as to whether they were indeed mountains or were merely clouds. What they beheld was an adobe and stone fortified city, containing from 8,000 to 10,000 soldiers, commanded by General Pedro de

Ampudia. Taylor would be assuming the role of the aggressor, even though he had only about 6,000 men in his army, and thus commanded the inferior force. The breakdown of Taylor's army was as follows: 3,080 were regulars, and 3,150 were volunteers. Approximately 1,350 of the total were mounted men. The artillery consisted of four field batteries, a pair of twenty-four-pounder howitzers, and one 10-inch mortar. There was no real siege artillery with which to invest the fortifications of the city.[12]

Monterrey boasted five strong forts to defy the advance of the American army. Of these, the strongest and most formidable were the Citadel (known as Black Fort by the Americans), the Cathedral, and the Bishop's Palace. The Citadel guarded the northern approach to the city, while the Bishop's Palace served as the main western defense. Taylor and his advance guard approached to within artillery range of the Citadel to reconnoiter the defenses, drawing the fire of several guns from within the fortification. Despite the barrage of shot and shell, they remained targets on the plain in front of the city for half an hour while their commander noted the various approaches and defenses of Monterey. Taylor then withdrew to the woods of San Domingo, to a position called Walnut Springs, about three miles from the city, to await the arrival of the remainder of his army. Here, under the shade of live oaks, and amid an abundant supply of good water, he established his base camp for operations against the Mexican army.[13]

On September 20, Taylor opened the engagement when he ordered his artillery to open fire on the walls of the Citadel. General Worth had been sent with his division on a flanking maneuver to cut the supply line of the Mexican army. Major Mansfield, in charge of a party of engineers, had discovered that the road leading southwest from the city to Saltillo could be taken and held by the Americans, thus depriving Ampudia of receiving any supplies or reinforcements. General Taylor had ordered Worth to seize the objective, covered by the diversionary bombardment of the artillery against the Citadel. Once the road was taken, Worth was to move against the city's defenses from that side, if practicable. Though Worth's men were able to secure possession of the road, their movements had been observed by the Mexicans, and an advance against the Bishop's Palace was deemed inadvisable under the current conditions. Taylor ordered General David E. Twiggs's division to make a demonstration, on Worth's behalf, against the Citadel, which was continued until dark, but the situation to the west of town still made it imprudent for an assault against the Bishop's Palace to be made. Worth bedded his men down for the night beyond the range of the enemy's artillery as he awaited further developments.[14]

That night, Taylor had the two twenty-four-pounder howitzers and the 10-inch mortar brought up and placed in position to bear upon the walls of the Citadel. On the morning of September 21, Taylor opened fire on the fortification with all his available guns. In the meantime, Worth had begun his advance against the Bishop's Palace, with the Texas Volunteers in the lead. On approaching the fortification, the Texans were attacked by a force of Mexican cavalry, which they soon put to flight with well-aimed volleys from their muskets. "The enemy retired in disorder, leaving on the ground 100 killed and wounded, among the former, Juan N. Najera, colonel of the permanent regiment of lancers. The enemy retired upon the Saltillo Road, and was closely pursued until possession of the gorge was secured, where all debouches from Monterrey unite; whereby the force just defeated, were excluded from entering the city."[15]

While Worth progressed against the Bishop's Palace, Taylor's men were making substantial headway in assaulting the Citadel and the northern approach to the city. The Americans had breached the outer defenses and were fighting a bitter contest in the very streets of the city. Bragg's Battery was summoned forward to cover the advance, and he galloped his men too far forward, where they became trapped in a narrow alley, bordered on either side by stone walls. In the cramped and confined quarters, only Thomas's gun could be brought to bear. Enemy snipers, firing from the roof tops of the surrounding houses, were taking a terrible toll on the men and horses of the battery. "A few of his artillerymen and more than a dozen horses were down in the same spot, making the ground about the guns slippery with their gasped foam and blood." The battery was ordered to retreat, but Thomas calmly took the time to reload his cannon and fire a parting shot at the enemy. The gun had to raised and wheeled around by hand in order to extricate it from the narrow street, but once that was accomplished, it was found that there were no remaining horses to draw it. Thomas stood patiently by his gun, amid the constant buzzing of sniper bullets, until fresh horses could be located and brought to the spot, refusing to allow his piece to fall into the hands of the enemy. While he and his men waited, they removed the harness from the fallen animals so that it could not be recovered and used by the Mexicans.[16]

The guns of the Citadel now concentrated on the men of the First Ohio Volunteers, as a troop of enemy lancers, led by a woman dressed in a captain's uniform, emerged from the fort and charged the wavering Americans. The Ohio troops were ordered to take a prone position, and as they were lying there, aiming their muskets, they could feel the ground shaking beneath the hooves of the Mexican cavalry mounts. Panic began to take hold in the ranks of the defenders, and the Ohioans were on the verge of fleeing when aid came from an unexpected quarter. The discharge of artillery announced the arrival of Bragg's refitted battery, as the men of Company E poured round after round of canister and grape into the advancing horsemen. Bragg, Thomas, and French stood to their guns in front of the stampeding lancers, delivering a merciless barrage that caused the Mexicans first to falter, and then to fall back in confusion to the protection of their own works.[17]

On September 22, Thomas and the rest of Company E were pulled out of the line to refit the guns. Worth was making progress against the Bishop's Palace and the twenty-four-pounder guns were being brought to bear against the Cathedral, in the heart of the city. After prolonged fighting, Worth succeeded in capturing the Bishop's Palace. Most of the Mexican defenders had fallen back into the city itself, and the Cathedral was being prepared for a last stand against the Americans.

As the sun rose on September 23, General Taylor prepared to make the final thrust against Monterrey as he pushed his men forward to wrest control of the city away from the defenders in house-to-house fighting. Lieutenant French described not only some of the action that transpired, but also gave an account of the character and disposition of General Taylor that exemplifies why he became so popular with his men. Amidst the fury of the battle,

> General Taylor and staff came down the street on foot, and very imprudently he passed the cross street, escaping the many shots fired at him. There he was, almost alone. He tried to enter the store on the corner. The door being locked, he and the Mexican within had a con fab, but not understanding what was said, he called to Colonel Kinney, the interpreter.... The Colonel said "damn," and went over at double-quick and made the owner open the door. The store was empty. Here General Quitman joined him with some troops and a gun in charge of Lieutenant G.H. Thomas. Quitman directed me to take my howitzer to the next cross street but to save my men and horses. I suggested that Thomas should put his gun in position first and let me pass through the smoke. Comprehending the matter at once, he said: "No, you remain here and let Thomas pass over when you fire [under cover of the smoke]." Thomas moved to the next street and turned his gun into it. That street was barricaded also and defended by a piece of artillery.

The infantrymen and riflemen now made good progress in gaining possession of the houses and driving the enemy toward the plaza.[18]

Thomas and French kept their guns both moving and firing, as they blasted away barricades and silenced enemy cannon. The supporting infantry cleared the neighboring houses of Mexican snipers, as the defenders fell steadily back. General Worth was exerting similar pressure from the direction of the Bishop's Palace as Ampudia's men were all being herded toward the Cathedral and the central plaza of the city, where the Mexican commander was at length induced to accept terms of surrender. Thomas and French were ordered to retire to camp with their guns, at which time French, who had been slightly wounded in the affair, was dispatched to the hospital, leaving Thomas in charge of both guns. Bragg received a brevet promotion to major for his services at Monterrey, and Thomas was rewarded with a brevet to the rank of captain. He also attained a new nick-name among his contemporaries for his battlefield prowess: Old Reliable.[19]

Thomas did not possess the esteem of all of his superior officers, however. Following the battle, he had entered into a controversy with Brigadier General David Twiggs over a team of mules. Twiggs had requested Thomas to give him a battery team of mules for his personal convenience at headquarters. Thomas denied the request, which enraged Twiggs, but the decision of the artillerist was upheld by higher authority, leaving a bitter rift between Twiggs and Thomas that would later surface when the vindictive general sought vengence.[20]

General Taylor did not receive the congratulations of his superiors. Instead, he got himself into trouble with President Polk and many of the Whig politicians in Washington over the surrender terms given to General Ampudia. The Mexicans were permitted to retain their side arms and a six gun battery of artillery, and to march out of Monterrey with their army intact. Taylor defended his actions on the basis that it would have cost too many American lives to have stormed the Mexicans in their remaining strongholds, and that he did not have the resources to handle such a large number of prisoners. Regardless of whether President Polk approved of the surrender terms or not, Taylor was viewed as a hero across the nation following his victory. Taylor's officers sensed the rift arising with Washington, and they rallied solidly around their commander.

Following their victory, the men of Taylor's army received a welcome rest period. There was plenty of leisure time to do sightseeing, hunting, gambling, and just relaxing in the warm and restful climate. An industrious entrepreneur even showed up with an American circus shortly after the capture of the city, providing the troops with an outlet for both their surplus time and money. But the time spent at Monterrey was not all frivolity. Fully one-third of the army came down with chills and fever, which many believed to be a reaction to their recent exertions, combined with a too-liberal consumption of the local fruits.[21]

President Polk demonstrated his displeasure with Taylor's surrender terms by naming General Winfield Scott to be the supreme commander of American forces in Mexico and ordering that a portion of Taylor's force be transferred to Scott for his proposed campaign against Mexico City. In fact, Taylor was effectively eliminated from the war, as far as the administration was concerned. He was conspicuously bypassed when orders were given to his subordinate, General Robert Patterson, to advance with his men to discover a route to Tampico, where he would form a junction with Scott. Taylor had been ordered to remain where he was, but he instead led the column headed toward Tampico, after directing General Worth to remove his division to Saltillo. General John A. Quitman was chosen to lead the advance to Tampico, which got underway early in November, and he asked for artillery support, specifically requesting Thomas, Reynolds, and French, of Bragg's Battery, with Thomas in command.[22]

The first objective of the expedition was the capital of the state of Tamaulipas: Victoria, located in the Sierra Madres. By Christmas, the column had advanced east to Villa Gran, a few days' march from Victoria, where the troops prepared to celebrate the holiday as best they could. Lieutenant French went hunting, hoping to bag a turkey for a Christmas feast, but returned from his search empty-handed. Thomas and Reynolds stayed closer to camp, but were on a search of their own. The pair secured all of the necessary ingredients to make eggnog, and the only thing lacking was liquor. In a rare example of high jinks, Thomas, French, and Reynolds kidnapped the regimental surgeon, demanding a bottle of medicinal rum or brandy for his ransom. The doctor's ransom was speedily delivered, and he helped the trio toast the day with the traditional drink.[23]

Four days later, on December 29, Quitman's advance column entered Victoria and officially took possession of the city. Taylor arrived on January 4, 1847, with Twiggs's Division, followed a couple of days later by Patterson. After a few days of rest, Taylor ordered Twiggs and Paterson to proceed to Tampico on January 12. He remained behind, hoping that orders would come allowing him to also make a junction with Scott. But Taylor was to be excluded from the coming campaign against the Mexican capital. He was even stripped of Worth's Division, which was ordered to march from Saltillo to Tampico. All of these moves left Taylor with a force of about 800 regulars and 5,000 volunteers, mostly new recruits who had not seen action. Bragg's Battery was to be among the small force of regulars remaining with their fallen leader. As Taylor faced his small army around and retraced his steps, back to Monterrey, all must have thought that their chances to attain further dis-

Winfield Scott, hero of the Mexican War and future general-in-chief of the United States Army. Thomas would become suspicious of politicians because of governmental intrigue on behalf of Scott that impaired the effectiveness of General Zachary Taylor (United States Army Military History Institute).

tinction were over.²⁴ Fate would prove them wrong. For Thomas, a sincere distrust of political interference in military matters was planted. The seed would grow and develop for the rest of his life.

A courier sent from General Scott, bearing orders detailing the disbursement of Taylor's troops, was captured and murdered by the Mexicans, and his dispatch fell into the hands of General Santa Anna. In possession of the American plans, and advised of the weakened condition of Taylor's army, Santa Anna decided to eliminate Taylor before taking the field against Scott. Once Taylor had retraced his route, he determined to reinforce the garrison at Saltillo. Lieutenant Thomas led a detachment twenty miles south of that place, to Agua Nueva, where he was soon after joined by Taylor and the main body. In all, Taylor's army contained just over 4,600 men. It was soon discovered that Santa Anna was advancing on the American position, with a force more than four times the size of Taylor's army. Upon receipt of this news, Taylor withdrew his men a short distance to La Angosture, meaning the Narrows, just south of Buena Vista, where the ground was felt to be more easily defended.

La Angosture provided Taylor with a natural defensive stronghold. Bordered to the east and west by ridges of the Sierra Madre, it would serve to funnel the Mexican troops into the battle, instead of allowing them to maneuver against the American flanks. Gorges on the left flank, and deep gullies on the right, only served to add to the strength of the position, which was a total of only two miles wide. Santa Anna would be sorely restricted in the use of his artillery and cavalry, and would have to depend largely on his infantry to dislodge Taylor's army from this natural bastion.

On the morning of February 22, 1847, Santa Anna's army was in position and ready to make its assault. Observing the signs of the withdrawal from Agua Nueva, he supposed that the Americans were in full flight, and prepared to bag the whole lot of them. Necessity prodded the Mexican commander forward, for his supplies were running desperately low, and a quick victory over the Americans was needed before the situation became acute.

Taylor's men greeted the day to the strains of "Hail Columbia," played by the regimental bands. The watchword, "Honor of Washington," was passed through the ranks, and wild cheering accompanied the first sightings of the dust cloud that indicated the approach of Santa Anna's army.²⁵

The American line of battle had eight guns of the 4th United States Artillery under Captain John M. Washington astride the road to Agua Nueva. On the right of the artillery, toward the mountains, were two companies of the 1st Illinois Volunteer Infantry, behind breastworks. To the left of Washington were the remainder of the 1st Illinois, the 2nd Illinois Volunteer Infantry, and a company of Texas Volunteers. The 2nd Kentucky Volunteer Infantry occupied a ridge to the left and rear of the main line, and the extreme left, at the base of the mountains, was held by a regiment each of Kentucky and Arkansas Cavalry. Taylor massed his reserve on the ridges immediately behind the front line, consisting of the 2nd and 3rd Indiana Volunteer Infantry, the Mississippi Rifles, the 1st and 2nd U.S. Dragoons, and the 3rd U.S. Artillery batteries of Bragg and Thomas W. Sherman. This dispersement of forces meant that the reserve line and the front line were approximately equal in strength. General Wool was in tactical command of the front line.²⁶ Thomas would be serving in his regular capacity, as a 1st lieutenant of artillery, in charge of a gun in the battery commanded by Thomas Sherman. This was a recent development. When Bragg had been promoted to captain and assumed command of another battery, Thomas was placed in temporary charge of Battery E, effective November 21, 1846. He had continued in this capacity until February 14, 1847, at which time Captain Sherman was assigned to command of the battery, and became Thomas's immediate superior.[27]

As Santa Anna scanned the American battle line, the strength of the position was at once made evident to him, and he decided to await the arrival of all of his troops before making an assault against it. In the meantime, he dispatched his chief medical officer, Dr. Vanderlinden, to take a message to Taylor, informing him that he was surrounded by a vastly superior force, and requesting his surrender to avoid the useless slaughter of his men. Taylor was given one hour in which to make a response, but his reply to Santa Anna was given immediately upon receipt of the message: "Sir: In reply to your note of this date summoning me to surrender my forces at discretion, I beg leave to say that I decline acceding to your request. With high respect, I am, sir, your obedient servant, Z. Taylor, Major-General United States Army."[28]

Santa Anna tested the American line by sending General Ampudia against the left, at the base of the mountains. At the same time, another Mexican force was sent against the right, while still another was directed to march even further to the right, in the obvious hope of turning this flank. The first column sorely pressed the left, outflanking that portion of the line, but it was unable to turn the flank. The latter column ran into the Bragg's Battery and the 2nd Kentucky. A spirited fire-fight erupted in front of all of the Mexican forces, but a general engagement was not brought on by either side, and night was permitted to fall with the combatants occupying the aforementioned positions.

At dawn on February 23, fighting resumed on the American left. General Wool was in command, as Taylor had gone to Saltillo the previous night with a detachment of troops. An attempt to get at the Americans by moving a Mexican column into a ravine separating the combatants was met with devastating fire from a 12-pound howitzer commanded by Lieutenant O'Brien. A 12-pound howitzer, commanded by French, and a 6-pounder, commanded by Thomas, were to the left of the 2nd Illinois Volunteer Infantry. All guns were supporting the infantry. Santa Anna directed General Blanco's division to advance against Washington's artillery, supported by cavalry and a 12-pounder. General Manuel Lombardini's and General F. Pacheco's divisions were then to advance to the right of Blanco, connecting with Ampudia's division, already on the American left flank, and assist in turning that flank and sweeping the Americans from the field. Blanco's division was met by withering fire from Washington's Battery that tore gaping holes in the Mexican line and forced the survivors to flee for cover. General Pacheco's division was blunted by the 2nd Indiana, along with O'Brien's gun, and for about half an hour the fighting raged ferociously on this part of the field. General Joseph Lane ordered his 3rd Indiana forward in support of the 2nd Indiana, in an effort to sweep Pacheco from the front. O'Brien moved his gun forward along with Lane, and effectively peppered the Mexican force with grape and canister. At this time, for unknown reasons, the commander of the 2nd Indiana suddenly ordered his regiment to retreat. The withdrawal soon turned into a rout, with four companies of the Arkansas troops getting caught up in the panic. Mexican cavalry added to the confusion as it pursued the escaping Americans. The disintegration of this portion of the line left O'Brien heavily pressed and without infantry support, compelling him to withdraw, leaving a four-pounder behind.[29]

Lombardini's division had been delayed getting into position, but it arrived at the American line just as the stampede of the 2nd Indiana was taking place. Lombardini was wounded, and command of the division passed to F. Perez, who changed front and pressed against the retiring Americans. This left the 2nd Illinois, a troop of dragoons, and the guns of French and Thomas, on the left and right of the 2nd Illinois, as the only troops still holding the line. French and Thomas poured a terrible fire into the ranks of the oncoming Mexicans, but they could not halt their advance. Perez's men overlapped the left flank and rear of the 2nd Illinois, threatening to drive them from the field. The guns of Sherman and Reynolds were ordered forward, and they unlimbered to deliver a terrific and continuous fire into the faces of the advancing Mexicans. The 2nd Kentucky moved in support of Sherman's gun, and was soon joined by the remainder of Bragg's Battery, with all of the American forces converging on the enemy at the base of the mountains to the left.

General Taylor had returned from Saltillo by this time, and was greeted by General Wool, who exclaimed: "General, we are whipped!" Taylor showed that he was by no means ready to concede defeat when he snapped back at Wool, "That is for me to determine." Wool left Taylor at once to resume command of the front line, where he was effective in rallying the faltering troops on the shattered left flank. The Mexicans brought up a battery of sixteen-pounder guns and placed it at the spot recently vacated by O'Brien, in an effort to drive back the infantry and artillery still holding the line where French and Thomas were fighting. The big Mexican guns punished the line, but were in turn brought under the fire of Bragg's and Sherman's cannon, which so effectively decimated the supporting infantry that the Mexicans were forced to retire. O'Brien brought his guns forward again, and the combined artillery, along with the musketry of the 2nd Illinois and 2nd Kentucky, stopped the Mexican advance.[30]

A force of some 1,500 Mexican cavalry surged forward in an attempt to cut the Saltillo road, behind the American lines. With the American line of retreat in sight, the Mexican horsemen inexplicably slowed down, then stopped, right in range of the muskets of the Mississippi Rifles, the 2nd and 3rd Indiana, and Sherman's 12-pounder howitzer. The Americans opened fire with volleys that tore the Mexican troopers to pieces, and forced them to make a hasty retreat from the area.

What followed was one of the most confusing episodes of the battle. Several white flags were seen advancing from the Mexican line, as a few of Santa Anna's officers took it upon themselves to offer terms of surrender to Taylor's army. The Americans, by and large, stopped firing, out of respect for the flags of truce, but the volume of fire from the Mexican line continued unabated. Mexican troops that had been caught against the base of the mountain took advantage of the truce to withdraw from their exposed position and reform. Santa Anna then called forward all of his reserves, throwing them against the American line in an all-out effort to break through. The 2nd Kentucky and 1st Illinois took heavy casualties from fire on their right flank, and the men ran from the position to take refuge in the nearest gorge. When the advancing Mexicans reached the rim of the gorge, a terrible slaughter of the cowering Americans took place. O'Brien and Thomas were firing canister into the Mexican ranks as quickly as their guns could be served, in an unsuccessful effort to protect their trapped infantry comrades. The ground was strewn with the enemy dead and wounded, but the gun crews of O'Brien and Thomas were also sustaining heavy casualties. Each discharge of O'Brien's guns drove them backward on the field, but they were not giving ground as rapidly as the advancing Mexicans were gaining it. Finally, with most of his men and horses down, faced with impending capture, O'Brien fired one last charge into the very faces of the enemy and hobbled away, leaving his guns.

That left Thomas to engage the victorious enemy alone. He worked his gun in a deliberate and defiant manner, despite the fact that it was about to be overrun by the charging Mexicans. Just when all seemed about to be lost, Bragg and Sherman arrived with their guns to add to Thomas's firepower. The Mississippi Rifles and the 2nd Indiana also came forward to provide infantry support for the guns. Thomas would later state, "I saved my section of Bragg's Battery at Buena Vista by being a little slow."

The fighting now became both general and desperate. "The cannonade on both sides was incessant, the roar of musketry loud and continuous; it was impossible, above the general clamor and din, to distinguish the report of any single gun.... The whole air vibrated with the rushing current of balls."[31] Taylor rode forward to order Bragg to load his guns with double canister, admonishing the artillerist to "give 'em hell," and each discharge of the guns tore gaping holes in the enemy line, which wavered, then hesitated, and finally broke in retreat in the face of the iron and leaden hailstorm it was facing.[32] American units surged forward to kill and capture isolated pockets of Mexican resistance still trapped on the battlefield, but for all intents and purposes the battle was over.

Mexican casualties, in killed and wounded, amounted to approximately 1,800 men, or just under 10 percent of Santa Anna's available force. While the Americans suffered only about a third that total, or 673 casualties, that number represented around fifteen percent of the men in Taylor's army. The army commanders were very congratulatory toward the artillerists for their part in sustaining the American line and bringing about the victory. Captain Sherman acknowledged Thomas by stating that he had "more than sustained the reputation he has long enjoyed in his regiment as an accurate and scientific artillerist." Taylor said that he felt the artillery had always been in exactly the right place at exactly the right time, and General Wool voiced the opinion that the army could not have held its position for one hour without the efforts of the artillery. Thomas, for his part, was extremely self-deprecating as far as his part in the battle was concerned. He merely wrote: "The Battle of Buena Vista was fought 22 Feb. '47 and I was under fire from 6 o.c A.M. until 4 P.M."[33]

While the war with Mexico had yet to see its final conclusion, the victory at Buena Vista ended the fighting in the northern portion of the country. Taylor's army would now be granted an extended period to rest and refit.

Chapter Four

Service Throughout the South

Following the victory at Buena Vista, General Taylor assigned a burial detail, and granted the remainder of the army three day's rest. The victory at Buena Vista was lauded as being one of the most impressive feats in military history. Zachary Taylor had defeated a superior enemy force approximately four times the size of his own. General Taylor became the hero of the hour, and was toasted all across the nation. The victory would serve as a springboard which would eventually land Taylor in the White House.

Many of Taylor's officers were also in line for accolades and promotion. Braxton Bragg had won the special notice of his superiors, and was the recipient of high praise. The commanding general wrote, "Without infantry to support him and at the imminent risk of losing his guns [Bragg] came rapidly into action, the Mexican lines being but a few yards from the muzzles of his pieces. The first discharge of canister caused the enemy to hesitate; the second and third drove him back in disorder and saved the day." The brevet rank of lieutenant colonel was bestowed upon Bragg, making him, along with Robert E. Lee, the most highly promoted of the regular officers in the American army. George Thomas was also among those who had been put on the fast-track of promotion as a result of his war service. In recognition for his gallant service at Buena Vista, he received his third brevet of the war, to the rank of major.[1] As such, he had leapt over many of his peers, who would later attain distinction in the Civil War. As already noted, Robert E. Lee was promoted to the rank of lieutenant colonel, as was Braxton Bragg. George Thomas, Samuel French, Thomas Sherman, and John Reynolds all received brevet commissions as majors. George B. McClellan and George G. Meade were given brevets as captains, while Thomas J. Jackson and Ulysses S. Grant were still 1st lieutenants at the close of the war.

On July 19, 1847, a large number of citizens of Southampton County gathered at Jerusalem Court House to honor their native son. The reserved and unassuming Thomas was treated to numerous public resolutions proclaiming his courage, skill, and exemplary military deportment. It can be assumed that Thomas would have spent an uneasy day as the focus of everyone's attention, even though the attainment of martial distinction had been his goal, if he had not still been stationed with Taylor's army. The high point of the tribute was the authorization to order a beautifully custom-made officer's sword as a token of the esteem with which the citizens of Southampton County held Thomas. Horstman & Sons of Philadelphia was commissioned to produce the sword. "The pattern of the saber is that used by the United States Dragoons. The blade is of the truest and prettiest steel, finished in a manner that would defy superiority of workmanship. The scabbard is of solid silver, standard value, beautifully enriched with engraved scroll work encircling military trophies, with the words: Florida, Ft.

Brown, Monterey, Buena Vista, and an engraved vignette of the Battle of Monterey [sic]. The hilt is of basket form, most elaborately chased. The grip is of solid silver, also enriched and engraved with scrolls. The pommel is of gold, grasping an amethyst, and the rings and hands in bass-relief, and upon its grip is engraved an elephant." Coming as it did from his friends, neighbors, and fellow Southampton County residents, it would be one of his most prized possessions. In a letter dated March 31, 1848, Thomas acknowledged receipt of the sword, and thanked the residents of Southampton County for the honor paid to him:

> Your letter of 8th February transmitting the Resolutions of the citizens of Southampton County at a meeting in their court house on the 19th July, 1847, was received by the last mail. In accepting the Sword presented me by my fellow country-men, and in acknowledging the very high compliment paid me in these resolutions, I beg you will present to the committee, and through my old friends of Southampton my sincere and heart-felt thanks — Aware that the little service I have been able to render my country, although performed with cheerfulness, and to the utmost of my ability, does not in the least entitle me to this very high compliment from my old friends and fellow citizens. I shall always regard it as the result of kindness of heart, and friendliness of feeling on their part, which renders the obligation doubly grateful, and as such will ever be a proud collection to the last hour of my life. "Next to the consciousness of having done his duty the sympathy of friends is the highest reward of a soldier." In conclusion, I beg you will accept my hearty acknowledgement for the very flattering and friendly manner in which you have communicated, to me, these resolutions, and with every wish for long continued health and happiness to yourself and family, I remain your friend and obedient servant, George H. Thomas.[2]

For Thomas and his brother officers still in the regular army at the conclusion of the Mexican War, it must have seemed as if the most significant part of their military careers had already come to pass, as the nation embraced the realities of a peacetime army. Following the end of the war, all of the volunteer regiments had been mustered out of the service, as well as a few of the regular ones that had been raised to fill the needs of the war. The prospects for advancing one's career in the small standing army of a nation at peace were indeed limited, and to many it seemed as if there was no future in continued military service. Many of Thomas's comrades and brother officers resigned their commissions in the years following the conclusion of the Mexican War to seek fame and fortune in the private sector. Thomas, it would seem, was never faced with the trying dilemma of what to do with the rest of his life. For him, the

Robert E. Lee. Thomas would serve under Lee in the 2nd United States Cavalry in Texas, where the two became close friends (United States Army Military History Institute).

choice was easy. He was an officer in the United States Army, and had taken an oath to serve. Regardless of whether or not the chances for advancement had all but disappeared, Thomas would remain in the service. A possible reason for that was the fact that he had already attained great distinction and promotion, rising from second lieutenant to brevet major, in the short span of only seven years following his graduation from West Point. His advancement must surely have already surpassed any expectations he had entertained upon assuming active duty, and therefore the need to attain fame and recognition may not have been as acute with him as it was with some of his brother officers.

It was about this time in his life that a contemporary wrote the following description of Thomas:

> He was cast in a strong and large mold, and had many of the personal traits of Washington, whom, in his intellectual and moral character, he greatly resembled. He was just six feet high and well proportioned, without too much flesh; he was very erect. He had a walk that was at once military and easy; it was that of a man who marched straight to his purpose. Bright blue eyes, later in life somewhat sunken, changeable expression from mildness to strong purpose; a heavy overhanging brow, with a horizontal furrow at the base. His nose was well shaped and proportioned; he had firm-set lips falling a little at the extremities; a strong chin; light-brown waving hair and full but short bread. His head gave altogether the suggestion of a self-reliant man; dignified and courteous, asking little from others, but ready to impart much. When men first knew him they respected and feared him; on longer acquaintances, especially such as exists between a commander and his soldiers, they trusted and loved him. They learned to associate his appearance with sure victory and constant care for their comfort and safety.[3]

Thomas would remain with the army in Mexico until August 20, 1847, at which time Company E was ordered back to Texas to assume garrison duties at Brazos de Santiago, near the mouth of the Brazos River. In addition to his other duties, Thomas once more was detailed as commissary officer of the post, a position he held till February 1, 1849, when he was granted a six-month leave. This was only the second such leave he had taken since his graduation from West Point in 1840, and would be only his second opportunity to visit home and hearth in the nearly thirteen years that had passed since he had left Southampton County to attend West Point. Following this extended furlough, Thomas rejoined his company, then stationed at Fort Adams in Rhode Island, on August 1, 1849. Five days later, he severed the ties to Company E that had lasted almost a decade when he was assigned to Company B of the same regiment. The Seminole had renewed hostilities, and Company B was being shipped to Florida to keep the peace. Obviously, Thomas's prior service in the state was a main factor in his being transferred to the company before its departure. The company was ordered to Florida on September 12, 1849, and shortly after its arrival Thomas was charged with making an expedition against the enemy.[4]

Thomas had narrowly and unknowingly missed having a singular honor bestowed upon him that would have drastically altered his military assignment. There was a vacancy in the artillery department at West Point for the scholastic year of 1849, requiring the appointment of a suitable officer to act as instructor. The position was offered to Braxton Bragg, who was at that time on leave in Mobile, visiting family. Bragg declined the honor, but took it upon himself to seek the appointment on behalf of Thomas. He wrote a letter to John Young Mason, Secretary of the Navy under President Polk, in an effort to influence the appointment. This was the same John Young Mason who had appointed Thomas to West Point when he had been a congressman serving the district Southampton County was part of. Bragg wrote, "The vacancy, I think, would suit your young friend Brevet Major George H. Thomas 3rd Artillery and it is one for which he is eminently qualified. Without knowing his views, I presume on requesting your influence in his behalf.... No officer of the army has been so long in the field without relief, and to my personal knowledge no one had rendered more arduous, faithful and brilliant service.... He is certainly entitled to some consideration from his government." Mason must have been gratified to have played a part in beginning the career of one who was now so highly esteemed by his military peers, and Thomas's name was forwarded for consideration. However, the vacancy was filled by First Lieutenant William H. Shrover, also of the 3rd Artillery, whose permanent rank in the army was two years senior to that of Thomas.[5]

While in Florida, Thomas would once more resume association with one of the officers he had served under in Mexico, namely General David Twiggs. Twiggs had not forgotten the perceived slight Thomas had issued him back at Monterrey when he had refused to give him a battery team of mules, and his vindictive nature would not allow him to let the matter pass. While no specific incidents between the two officers took place in Florida, Thomas was definitely serving under a hostile commander who held a grudge. After a fourteen month tour of duty in Florida, Thomas was ordered once more to Texas, but upon arrival at New Orleans en route to Texas, he received orders directing him to report instead to Fort Independence in Boston Harbor. Thomas performed an act of seafaring heroism that some historians believe took place during his voyage to Fort Independence.

The vessel on which Thomas was sailing ran into a savage storm off the coast of Cape Hatteras that threatened to capsize the ship. To add to the seriousness of the situation, the ship's captain was intoxicated beyond the point of being able to perform his duties, though he continued to issue commands. The first officer outlined the danger of the situation to Thomas, explaining further that he could not assume command of the ship without violating the code of maritime law and exposing himself to a charge of mutiny. Thomas at once settled upon a course of action. He instructed the captain to confine himself to his stateroom, while he assume the responsibility for the ship. Then, with the able assistance of the first officer, the vessel was brought through the storm without incident, and with no loss of life. This incident gives example of Thomas's constant willingness to take charge in difficult situations, and insight to his confidence in his own abilities and judgement.[6]

Duty at Fort Independence differed dramatically from that in sunny Florida. To be sure, there were no alligators or water moccasins to deal with, and there was no enemy to fight except the cold, damp, dreary existence of garrison duty in an antiquated island fort that had been built several decades before. Fort Independence was not without its lore and legend, though, and a favorite of these would become the basis for a well-known piece of published fiction.

In 1817, a young Virginia lieutenant by the name of Robert F. Massie was involved in a game of cards when his captain accused him of cheating. The code of honor, so prevalent in the military, was brought to bear, and the charge prompted Massie to challenge his accuser to a duel. On Christmas Day, 1817, the two men met to settle the matter, and Massie was shot to death. Owing to his popularity with his comrades and brother officers, hard feelings were held for the captain who had both accused him and been responsible for his demise. After taking up a collection to buy a marble marker for his grave, Massie's comrades concocted a plan to even the score with the captain. They invited the officer to join them in a drinking binge, during which time the captain became completely intoxicated. While he was in this drunken state, they led him to a windowless underground casemate, where he was gagged, shackled, and chained to the floor. They then commenced to wall up the opening with brick and mortar, condemning the officer to an isolated and lingering death. Legend or fact, the story has been told since shortly after Massie's death, and continues so to this day. What is known is that in the early part of the 1900s a work crew opened a casemate that had been sealed off to discover a skeleton clad in an officer's uniform from the period of the War of 1812. Edgar Allan Poe, while serving as a private in the army, was stationed at Fort Independence in the late 1820s, and story of Massie and the captain was certainly related to him. In later years, he would assimilate it when he wrote "The Cask of Amontillado," in which one of the characters was similarly imprisoned.[7]

Thomas served at Fort Independence until March of 1852. Lieutenant Shrover passed away early in 1852, once more creating a vacancy for an artillery instructor at West Point. Thomas was again nominated for the opening, this time by Captain William S. Rosecrans, the supervising engineer officer at Fort Adams, who had come to know and appreciate the qualities of the officer when he was stationed there. This time the nomination met with approval, and Thomas was ordered to the Point to start training cadets to become officers in the United States Army. Upon reaching the academy, Thomas placed his few belongings in his quarters and then went to the post library, where he checked out some French military text books to review in preparation for assuming his new position.[8]

Among his new duties, Thomas was to instruct the cadets in artillery and cavalry tactics. Generally, instructors at West Point held the grade of captain or above, but an exception had been made in Thomas's case, for though he held the brevets of captain and major, he was still a 1st lieutenant as far as his permanent rank was concerned. Thomas would serve at the academy under a superintendent who was from his native state of Virginia. Robert E. Lee had been assigned to the top spot at the academy on September 1, 1852, and when Thomas arrived there it was to be the first meeting between the already famous sons of the Old Dominion. In many ways the two men were very similar. In fact, one of the only differences between them was their social status, Lee coming from one of the finest families in the state, while Thomas was the product of more humble birth. Erasmus D. Keyes, who was also an instructor at the academy at that time, later stated that of the hundreds of Southern men he had come to know intimately, Lee and Thomas were the fairest he had ever come in contact with, as far as their judgment of Northern men was concerned. Their Southern birth, combined with their gracious and amiable conduct toward Northern men, made Lee and Thomas favorites with both cadets and fellow instructors alike.[9]

Lee's son, Robert E. Lee, Jr., remembered those days at the academy, and the esteem with which his father was held.

As Superintendent of the Military Academy at West Point my father had to entertain a good deal, and I remember well how handsome and grand he looked in uniform, how genial and bright, how considerate of everybody's comfort of mind and body. He was always a great favorite with the ladies, especially the young ones. His fine presence, his gentle, courteous manners and kindly smile put them at once at ease with him.

Among the cadets at this time were my eldest brother, Custis, who graduated first in his class in 1854, and my father's nephew, Fitz Lee, a third classman, besides other relatives and friends. Saturday being a half-holiday for the cadets, it was the custom for all social events in which they were to take part to be placed on that afternoon or evening. Nearly every Saturday a number of these young men were invited to our house to tea, or supper, for it was a good substantial meal. The misery of some of these lads, owing to embarrassment, possibly from awe of the Superintendent, was pitiable and evident even to me, a boy of ten or eleven years old. But as soon as my father got command, as it were, of the situation, one could see how quickly most of them were put at their ease. He would address himself to the task of making them feel comfortable and at home, and his genial manner and pleasant ways at once succeeded.[10]

Listed among the faculty and staff of the academy were several officers who would rise to distinction within the next decade, including Robert S. Garnett, Seth Williams, Robert W. Weir, and Fitz John Porter.[11] Among the cadets who attended the academy while Thomas was an instructor was a veritable who's who of Civil War leaders and commanders: Kenner Garrard, David S. Stanley, Alexander McD. McCook, George Crook, James McPherson, Phil Sheridan, John Schofield, Oliver O. Howard, John Bell Hood, George Washington Custis Lee, James Deshler, and James Ewell Brown Stuart.[12] Lee would help to mold these individuals into the officers they would become a decade later.

David Stanley left his impression of the academy while he was a cadet there, during Thomas's tenure as an instructor: "I have tramped by horse and foot and in railroad cars over much of the finest scenery in these United States and some of the other four corners of the globe and never have I looked at more lovely scenery than that at West Point. Either in summer when its mountains, hills and plains are covered with brightest green or in crisp winter when these mountains, snow clad, glisten, like diamonds, West Point is always lovely." But all was not splendor, nor was every memory so pleasant. "Furlough soon ended and we were back at West Point and in gray again. The morning after we reported I was awakened by the sharp crack of the morning cannon and I never, in all my war experience, heard such a startling report. Sleeping as I was, on the ground, it fairly lifted me up, and as they say a drowning man reviews his life in an instant, so in the moment of that rude awakening, I saw two years of hard study, of drills, of toils, as a sudden vision before me, but reveille and a basin of cold water soon dispelled this gloomy vision."[13]

Oliver O. Howard, another of Thomas's cadets, would later describe him with unfettered fondness. He recalled how the cadets regarded their artillery instructor with admiration and respect. Some of this was due to his commanding presence, and some to the tone of his voice when he spoke, which brought all eyes to him and demanded the undivided attention of all those within earshot. But the main reason his students were drawn to him was the fact that he was a man who had already proven himself on the field of battle. Thomas's three brevets for heroic service loomed large among cadets who one day hoped to prove their own mettle in conflict, and added weight to anything and everything he had to say. In short, he was deemed a hero by the cadets at West Point. He was the sort of man they wished to emulate, and had already lived the sort of life they dreamed of. Howard described him as a man of valor, but he also made reference to his easy and kind manner, and the habit he had of giving good grades for indifferent recitations in class, which endeared him to the cadet corps, and would cause many to exclaim, "God bless Major Thomas!"[14]

George H. Thomas was in his mid–30s at the time of his appointment to West Point. As such, his body was changing, and he was beginning to take on the rotund appearance for which he was known during the Civil War. Gone were the days when he tipped the scales at a solid and muscular 175 pounds. The instructor the cadets would come to know could already be considered stout, and over the next decade or so his weight would continue to rise, until he weighed more than 240 pounds. Thomas's appearance combined with his naturally steady and methodical approach to teaching to bring him yet another nick-name from the cadets. While teaching cavalry tactics, Thomas would conduct the boys through the various evolutions in something of a slow-motion drill. He would put them through their paces, over and over again, until the commands and responses became second nature. At times, some of the cadets would feel themselves sufficiently advanced to attempt the evolutions at a fast trot, or gallop, which would always bring about the cry of "Slow trot! Slow trot!" from their instructor. That, along with the fact that the cadets always kidded about the strain Thomas's horse suffered under his increasing size, produced one of the names that would stay with him through the Civil War and beyond: Old Slow Trot.

The appointment as an instructor at the academy was to be only one of several changes in Thomas's life. One of his cadets, Lyman M. Kellogg, was to indirectly play a great role in shaping Thomas's personal life. Kellogg's aunt, Mrs. Abigail Paine Kellogg, was a widow from Troy, New York, who made numerous trips to West Point to see her nephew during the spring and summer of 1853. She was usually accompanied on her visits by her two unmarried daughters, Frances and Julia. It had become common place for a lady with unmarried daughters to take them to West Point in search of a proper suitor, and such was probably the intention of Mrs. Kellogg. George Thomas made the acquaintance of Frances during one of her visits to the academy, and was apparently smitten with her from the start. The post library shows that the books he withdrew changed during this period, from military texts to novels and tales of romance. Since he was direct and to the point in all things, a prolonged courtship would be out of the question where George Thomas was involved, and after only a few months of getting to know one another, he proposed to Frances, and she accepted. Frances was five years younger than Thomas, and was said to be an exact match for him. His fellow officers described her as a "noble" woman who was "good natured and congenial," and her tall, stately, and attractive appearance complemented his splendidly. She was said to have excellent manners and to be a gifted conversationalist.

The couple were married on November 17, 1853, at the home of Frances's uncle, Daniel Southwick, in Troy, New York. The groom was dressed in full dress uniform, complemented by the presentation sword given to him by the citizens of Southampton County. It was the only time in his life that Thomas would wear the treasured memento. Following the wedding, the happy couple spent part of Thomas's extended leave from the army seeing the sights in New York City. Thomas did not return to his duties at the academy until the middle of January, 1854, to discover that he had been promoted during his absence. In November of 1853, the War Department had granted his long overdue advancement to the grade of captain in the regular army, the rank which West Point instructors were supposed to hold. The commission was dated in December of that same year.[15]

Upon their return to the academy, the happy couple settled into the regular routine of married life. The surroundings at West Point provided almost a fairy-tale setting for the couple, but alas, their time of wedded bliss together was to be all too short. Six months after he had reported back to duty at the academy Thomas received orders assigning him to one of the most desolate posts occupied by the United States Army: Fort Yuma, in the Arizona Territory. Erasmus D. Keyes was given the instructor's position he was vacating at the academy, and on May 1, Thomas bade farewell to General Lee, saw to the details of the relocation of his wife back to her home in Troy, and began the journey to Arizona. He had been placed in command of Company A, 3rd U.S. Artillery, and would be responsible for four companies of artillery that had also been ordered to the territory.

The man responsible for his new assignment was none other than General David Twiggs. It can be assumed that Twiggs still smarted over the perceived slight Thomas had done him at Monterrey, as this was one of the most undesirable postings in the country, not at all the sort of assignment that would normally be given to an officer who had already distinguished himself and won the plaudits of his superiors. The story was told of a soldier, stationed at Fort Yuma, who had died and gone to Hell. The soldier returned to Fort Yuma to get blankets with which to warm himself, as Hell was not nearly as hot as Fort Yuma. Though bound for possibly the most hated post in the army, the victim of petty, vindictive ego, Thomas was too much the soldier to utter a word of protest or complaint.[16]

It would take a month for Thomas to make the first leg of the journey. He would travel by ship down the east coast, through the Isthmus of Panama, thence westward to San Francisco, where he arrived with the men in his charge on June 1, 1854. Many of the soldiers had become ill during the trip, and Thomas was aggravated to discover that there were insufficient hospital facilities at San Francisco to care for them. He spent two weeks in the city looking to the comfort of his sick men, while he awaited the arrival of the artillery baggage that was lagging behind the troops. Finally, he embarked his men on a coastal steamer that took them to San Diego. From there he began the last leg of the trek to Fort Yuma, an overland march of some 200 miles through the desert and the scorching Imperial Valley. They would be marching through this formidable country in July, the worst month of the year to do so, when temperatures soared as high as 130 degrees, making it necessary to march the column only at night, and to seek what cover and shade they could during the heat of the day.[17]

When the column finally reached Fort Yuma, Thomas wrote a letter to Major Townsend at the War Department, that came as close to complaining as the captain had ever been known to do: "The excessive heat and scarcity of water on the Desert caused the most intensive suffering, and it was only by the utmost precaution that I have succeeded in reaching the post with the command in an exhausted condition. For the six days we were on the Desert the Thermometer ranged from 115 degrees to 130 degrees in the sun, rendering it necessary to make our march at night and lay by during the day. This naturally broke in upon the rest of the men and animals, and if I had not finally determined to make a depot of all the heavier stores.... I doubt if I should have succeeded in getting half the command there." He went on to recommend that "troops should never be marched across the Desert during the summer."[18]

Thomas occupied his spare time at Fort Yuma trying to learn the various languages of the Indian tribes that lived in the area, particularly Yuma, which he learned to speak and attempted to reduce to writing. He even compiled a 70 word dictionary of the local language. He also collected samples of the plants and minerals in the area, and sent a specimen of an unusual variety of bat to the Smithsonian Institution for further research.[19] His official duties largely revolved around providing military protection for parties of immigrants passing near the fort, and in mounting punitive expeditions against Indians who had committed depredations against settlers and prospectors.

Thomas became especially interested in the case of the Oatman sisters, Mary Ann and Olive. They had been captured by Yavapai Indians, a tribe in the Apache Nation, in the fall of 1852, after the wagon their parents had been traveling in on the Gila Trail became separated from its train. Their parents, Mr. and Mrs. Royce Oatman, and four other siblings were murdered, while one brother had managed to escape from the Indians. Mary Ann was seven years old, and Olive was fifteen, at the time of their capture. After about a year, the Yavapai traded the girls to the Mohave tribe. The Mohave were an extremely warlike society, but they relied heavily on farming for their existence. Mary Ann Oatman perished from starvation due to tribal famine shortly after their captivity with the Mohave began, but Olive was reported to be still alive and in need of rescue. George H. Thomas took a personal interest in finding and releasing the girl. He gathered information and sifted through the rumors and gossip in order to ascertain Olive's whereabouts, while he sought mediation to secure her freedom. The investigation he began would end in successful fruition almost a year after he was no longer stationed at Fort Yuma, when the United States government paid a ransom to the Mohave to secure Olive's release in 1856.[20]

Thankfully, Thomas's banishment to Fort Yuma was to be of relatively short duration. Secretary of War Jefferson Davis had use of his talents for a more important assignment, and on May 12, 1855, he was promoted to the rank of major in the regular army and ordered to report to Jefferson Barracks, Missouri. The orders would take almost two months to reach Fort Yuma, however, and Thomas did not officially quit the post until July 21 of that year. Braxton Bragg once more figured importantly in Thomas's receiving both the promotion and the assignment. Bragg had been offered the position, but, having just tendered his resignation from the army, was forced to decline. He named Thomas as the most qualified officer to be his replacement, and Davis and the War Department concurred, elevating him to the rank of major, even though he was junior to many other captains in the service.

The assignment Thomas was heading for was one of the most coveted and esteemed in the entire army. Congress had enacted legislation on March 3, 1855, establishing the 1st and 2nd United States Cavalry Regiments. Jefferson Davis endeavored to staff the officer corps of the two new regiments with the best the army had to offer, especially in the 2nd Regiment, where he clustered together a veritable who's who of army leadership. To be named to service with either of the two regiments was a distinct honor, but to serve with Davis's pet 2nd Cavalry was the ultimate stamp of approval from the War Department.[21]

Historians have added their voices to Davis's contemporaries in accusing the Secretary of War of having a personal agenda in selecting the officers he chose to command the 2nd U.S. Cavalry. Seventeen of the twenty-five officers were Southern men. It has been alleged that Davis foresaw the coming sectional difficulties and sought to create a regiment that would be loyal to the South in the event of war. The veracity of these allegations can neither be proved nor disproved, and continue to be argued by historians and buffs alike. What is certain is that more than half of the Southern-born officers in the 2nd Cavalry would go on to lead independent commands in Civil War campaigns. Colonel Albert Sidney Johnston, reputed to be the finest soldier in the nation, was named commander of the regiment. Lieutenant Colonel Robert E. Lee, who was esteemed by Davis only slightly less than Johnston, was second in command. William J. Hardee served as the senior major, while George H. Thomas acted as the junior major. Earl Van Dorn and E. Kirby Smith were captains, while John Bell Hood served as lieutenant.[22] Never in the history of the United States military had so many talented and proven officers been brought together into one command. The regiment was the pride of the War Department, and a source of hero-worship for every school boy in the land.

The 1st U.S. Cavalry was not without its stars, even if the greatest concentration of talent existed in the 2nd regiment of horse. Edwin V. Sumner was colonel of the 1st, with Joseph E. Johnston serving as lieutenant colonel and second in command. Among the subordinate officers was James E.B. Stuart, a second lieutenant. Stuart told of how desperately officers wished to receive assignments with one of the two regiments, and how sharp the competition was for the postings. All knew that assignment to one of these two elite regiments could do nothing but enhance their future careers. "Expectation is on tiptoe to see the correct list," he wrote at the time the War Department issued its listing of officers selected to receive the desired duty. Luckily for Stuart, his name appeared upon the list.[23]

Thomas reported to Jefferson Barracks in September of 1855. The first order of business was the recruitment of men to serve in the regiment, followed by the training of the new recruits, as well as their officers, and the appropriation of good horse-flesh with which to mount the troopers. Albert Sidney Johnston selected Thomas to oversee all training, for officers and men alike. His expertise in this duty can be judged by the fine record of the regiment before the war, and the record achieved by its officers following the commencement of the sectional strife. On October 17, 1855, little more than a month after the regiment had been brought together, the 2nd U.S. Cavalry received orders to proceed to Fort Belknap, Texas. It had been a colossal effort to gather the men and horses needed to fill out the regiment, and to do it in such a short space of time. Ten days more were required to get everything in readiness for the march to Texas, which was begun on October 27.[24]

The 2nd Cavalry was intended to be the showpiece of the entire army, and its appearance on the march certainly lived up to that expectation. At first sight, one was immediately struck by the mounts. Each company was issued horses that were color coded specifically to that company. The practice not only provided a grand martial spectacle, it also made it possible to know at a glance what company a particular trooper belonged to, and on the battlefield, it would help a trooper find his company if he became separated. Thomas's squadron was made up of Company A, mounted all on gray horses, and Company F, mounted solely on bay horses. The troopers' uniforms were designed to impress. A dark blue jacket and pants of pale azure were accented by yellow braid, brass shoulder scales, and a silk sash. A large black Stetson completed the attire, with the brim pulled up on the right and attached to the crown by means of an eagle symbol. Ostrich plumes completed the beau sabre appearance of the hat. It was nothing but the best for the 2nd Cavalry, and that included its weaponry. The troopers were all issued the latest Colt revolvers, rifled carbines, and Model 1840

James E.B. Stuart was a subordinate officer in the 2nd United States Cavalry. Thomas would face his cavalry in Virginia during the Manassas campaign (United States Army Military History Institute).

cavalry swords. Even the saddles were special, complete with polished wooden stirrups and brass appointments. One can readily understand why officers like J.E.B. Stuart were so anxious to seek appointment in one of the two elite new regiments.[25]

The squadrons of the regiment were disbursed among a chain of forts extending through central Texas to regimental headquarters at San Antonio, and continued onward to Brownsville. All posts were charged with operating against the Comanche Indians, who were then marauding over the Texas plains. Thomas was assigned to command at Fort Mason. Robert E. Lee would be his nearest neighbor, at Camp Cooper, some 170 miles away, so it is easy to see that a post commander, by necessity, commanded in a semi-autonomous fashion. The posts contrasted greatly with the martial splendor of the troopers who were stationed there. When Lee arrived at Camp Cooper, he found a barren stretch of plains, with no buildings constructed upon it. The troopers were forced to live in tents under the merciless sun that regularly drove temperatures to over 100 degrees. The ground was infested with snakes, most of them of poisonous varieties, as well as tarantulas, which seemed to be everywhere. Lee had brought seven chickens with him in order to ensure a regular supply of eggs. It was necessary to build a coop that was elevated off the ground to try to protect the fowl from the serpents that crawled upon it. All in all, the region was a dry, dusty, sun-baked piece of barren frontier, infested with creeping and crawling nightmares to humanity. Indeed, everything in this country would stick you, sting you, or bite you.[26]

But neither Lee nor Thomas would spend a great deal of time at his respective post during their initial service in Texas. Both were assigned to court-martial duty, requiring them to travel the state to hear the various cases against soldiers that were being tried. Thomas and Lee had ample opportunity to renew the friendship they had initiated at West Point over the course of the trials they sat together on. The two men were so similar in their deportment, ideas, and judgment that they became fast friends, and Lee would later pay tribute to his admiration of Thomas when he allowed him almost independent command of his squadron.

Thomas was still doing court-martial duty, at Fort Washita in December of 1856, when he finally received permission to rejoin his regiment. He was also given a short leave, and permission to rejoin his regiment by way of New York City, so that he could spend a short visit with Frances. He was also authorized to recruit musicians for the regiment while he was in the city. The couple had spent precious little time together since their marriage, and plans were made for Frances to join him in Texas, which she did in March of 1857. Thomas's mother died on January 26, 1857, as a result of a farming accident. There is no evidence that Thomas was able to attend her funeral, and reticent as he was about family matters, he left no information concerning her death. As Elizabeth Thomas left no will, the family farm was legally divided between her living children.[27]

Mrs. Thomas's arrival at Fort Mason witnessed an increase in the social exchanges between Thomas and Lee, as the two men frequently spent off-duty time together, and partook in several small dinner parties that helped to enliven the barren and dismal atmosphere of their surroundings. However, Lee was somewhat bothered by a problem he faced arising from this social circle. Mrs. Thomas and her servant, who helped her cook, always spread the table with a delicious assortment of food, and the preparation of each was exquisite. Lee, who also had a servant who acted as his cook, wrote despairingly to Mrs. Lee, still in Virginia suffering from poor health, that he was embarrassed by the difference between the Thomas table and the fare he in turn offered Mrs. Thomas when it was his turn to entertain. Though the food at his dinners was plentiful, his cook was not as adept at preparing it as was Mrs. Thomas or her servant, and he feared his dinners were not up to the standard they should be. "The Major can fare as I do," he confided to his wife, "but I fear that she will fare badly as my man Kremer is both awkward and unskilled."[28]

In July of 1857, Thomas once more came into conflict with General David Twiggs, the department commander in Texas, when he was assigned to another court-martial case. It seems that an officer had had been accused by some settlers of stealing a drunken man's purse. Thomas examined all the information, culled the testimony for malice, and then rendered his decision that the officer be exonerated of the accusation. General Twiggs, in an effort to curry local political favor, overturned Thomas's decision and pronounced the officer guilty. Thomas at once reported the incident to Secretary of War John B. Floyd, and the War Department not only upheld Thomas's ruling, it gave Twiggs a light reprimand and instructed him not to interfere in the affairs of the court-martial. For the second time, Twiggs had received a reproof from his superiors at the hands of Thomas, and the animosity he felt for the Virginian was intensified. He sought vengeance in whatever manner he could find.

In October of 1857 Lee was granted leave to go home owing to the death of his father-in-law, leaving Thomas in temporary command of the regiment. Twiggs took this opportunity to issue orders that Thomas's squadron be attached to the squadron of Earl Van Dorn, recently promoted to major, and that the combined force was to make a scouting expedition in the Wachita Mountains. This left Thomas virtually without a command, as was the intention of the insult when it was committed. Once more, Thomas apprised the War Department of the situation at hand, and he went so far as to request a formal inquiry of Twiggs's actions. Secretary Floyd sided with Thomas, and instructed him to personally assume command of the expedition, but he did not feel that a court of inquiry was necessary to deal with Twiggs. A letter from the War Department was sufficient to produce the desired effect. Twiggs was reminded that the 2nd Cavalry was a special breed, and officers of that regiment were a class above. Therefore, they were not to be trifled with by mere department commanders, regardless of their rank.[29]

Lee did not return to Texas until February of 1859, at which time he wrote to Thomas requesting him to come and take over command at Camp Cooper, where tensions were rising between white settlers and Comanche on the nearby reservation. Early that spring, a band of renegade Comanche stirred the pot when they stole some horses and hid out on the reservation. Thomas knew that there were but a few guilty parties, and that the vast majority of the Indians on the reservation had broken no laws, but the white settlers did not see it that way. They banded together to punish all the Indians and made an attack on the reservation under cover of night. The result of the hostilities were nine dead, leading Thomas to direct Van Dorn to send him two additional companies to help keep the peace.

Thomas held to his conviction that the settlers were wrong in their punishment of all of the Indians, as only a few renegades were responsible for the acts of theft, but angry letters from the local population prompted the Commissioner of Indian Affairs to take further action. He ordered the reservation to be closed and its residents moved to the Indian Territory. Thomas was assigned to supervise the relocation of the Comanche even though he had fought against it with the officials at Washington. The move was begun on July 30, and Thomas, always solicitous of the needs of women and children, set a slow pace so as not to wear them out. As such, he did not return to Camp Cooper until August 21, at which time he addressed all marauding Indians in his area of operations by declaring that any Kiowa or Comanche that were found off the reservation would be automatically treated as if they were hostile. He added weight to his words by mobilizing a five-company expedition that went on a fifty-three-day sweep of the plains to round up every stray Indian they could find.[30]

In late February of 1860, Thomas reported to Lee that a white man had been murdered by marauding Kiowa near Camp Cooper. This renegade band was also responsible for stealing a number of horses from the Indian Agency. Lee, who was engaged in dealing with Mexican bandits in his region, gave Thomas full authority to deal with the Kiowa as he saw fit. Thomas spent a few months getting organized for a campaign against the Indians, and waiting for the summer grass on the plains to become sufficient to forage his horses. He was meticulous in his attention to detail, down to personally making sure that all weapons were cleaned and all horses were newly shod.

By July, all was in readiness, and Thomas, along with twenty-six officers and men and three Indian scouts, rode south out of Camp Cooper, in search of the foe. He had made arrangements for his column to be reinforced along its line of march. Lieutenant Fitzhugh Lee and his thirty men joined Thomas at the Colorado River, where the troopers turned west, en route to Kiowa Creek. There Captain Richard W. Johnson's squad was added, bringing Thomas's total command to approximately 100 men. Thomas then divided his force to sweep a seven-county area in search of renegade Kiowa. The campaign lasted for a month, with no sightings of the Indians by any of the troopers. Supplies began to run low, prompting Thomas to send Johnson and Lee back to their posts and continue on with only his own detachment. The major gave a thorough description of the latter portion of the campaign in his official report:[31]

> I have the honor to submit for the information of the department commander, the following report of the operations of the expedition under my command, to the head waters of the Concho and Colorado rivers, during the months of July and August.... On the morning of the 25th inst. about fourteen miles east of the mountain pass, one of the Indian guides (Dloss) discovered a fresh horse trail crossing the road. As soon as the packs could be arranged and our wagons dispatched with the remains of our baggage to the post, with the teams (two sick — the hospital steward and a private of the band — too sick to ride) I followed the trail with all the remainder of the department and three guides, in a west northwest direction for about forty miles that day, traveling as long as we could see the trail after nightfall. On the 26th, about 7 A.M., the Delaware guide (Dloss) discovered the Indians, eleven in number, at camp. He and their spy discovered each other about the same time, and giving the signal agreed upon, the party moved at once in a gallop for a mile and a half before coming in sight of their camp, which was located on the opposite side of a deep ravine, (running North, and I presume, into the Clear Fork), impassable except at a few points. Here we lost considerable time searching for a crossing, and only succeeded finally, in getting over by dismounting and leading our animals. In the meantime the Indians being already mounted and having their animals collected together, had increased their distance from us by at least half a mile. As soon as the crossing was effected and the men remounted, we pursued them at full speed for about three miles and a half further, pushing them so closely that they abandoned their loose animals, and continued their flight, effecting their escape solely from the fact that our animals had been completely exhausted by the fatiguing pace at which the pursuit had been kept up. As we were gradually over-hauling them, one fellow, more persevering than the rest, suddenly dismounted and prepared to fight, and our men, in their eagerness to dispatch him, hurried upon him so quickly that several of his arrows took effect, wounding myself in the chin and chest, also Private William Murphy of Company D, in the left shoulder, and Privates John Tile and Casper Siddle, of the band, each in the leg, before he fell, by twenty or more shots.... By this time the main body of the Indians, who were mounted on their best animals, were at least two miles from us, retiring at a rapid pace, and it being impossible to overtake them, on account of the exhausted condition of our animals, the pursuit was discontinued.[32]

Thomas had not been hit by two arrows. The shaft that had struck him on the chin had glanced off, embedding itself in his chest. After the wounded were cared for and the dead Indian was buried, the detachment rounded up the horses that had been abandoned by the Indians in their flight and prepared to return to Camp Cooper. The horsemen spoke of the courage of the Kiowa brave who had fought against them single-handedly, and his action became the topic of normal conversation around the campfires once they had returned to their post. Captain Johnson voiced his opinion that a wounded Indian was more dangerous than four unhurt ones. He went on to state that such was not the case with white soldiers, saying that when a white man was wounded he not only became useless for further fighting, but four men were required to carry him to the rear for medical aid.[33]

The campaign against the Kiowa was to be Thomas's last action in Texas. On November 12, 1860, he was granted a six-month leave to go home and visit his wife, who had departed from Texas about a year before. The presidential election dominated the attention of most of the citizens of the east, and Abraham Lincoln's election would put in motion a series of events that would lead Thomas to the most important decision of his military career. But when Thomas took his leave from Camp Cooper he was not embarking on a momentous journey; he was going to visit Frances, from whom he had long been absent.

Chapter Five

The Outbreak of Civil War

When Thomas came north, he brought with him his body servant and cook, his two slaves. Despite the fact that it had many times been inconvenient for him to retain these servants, he had declined to sell them, fearing that they would not be properly cared for by their new owners. The cook spent the next five years either with Thomas or at Thomaston, and following the end of the war, she remained with the family as a paid employee.

The fact that Thomas owned slaves and wore the uniform of an officer in the United States Army might be considered by most to have been the crux of the choice he would soon have to make. That would be an incorrect assumption, however. Many officers from the North or from the border states owned slaves. In fact, during the course of the war, many more Northern officers were slave holders than were Southern officers. The source of controversy with Thomas would not arise because of slavery, but instead from the fact that he was a Virginian. In the sectional crisis that was looming, most Americans aligned themselves with their friends and neighbors in supporting their home state, and back in Southampton County, it was assumed that their favorite son would follow course and tender his sword to the Old Dominion. For Thomas, however, the decision was not as simple as where he was born. His mind demanded a more thorough examination of the issues, and his honor would permit him to do no less than to pursue and uphold what his mind told him was right.

The national election had been held on November 6, 1860, and Lincoln had been successful in garnering the needed number of electoral votes to capture the White House. Sectional differences were now at a head, and Thomas would be arriving in the east just in time to take a hand in them.

It is necessary to provide the reader with some insight into the political atmosphere that existed in the nation at the time Thomas was making his way from Texas. The Republican Party was still a newcomer to the national scene in 1860, having been founded only six years before. Though Republicans had made inroads into the government in the Midwest and northeast, it was still far from being a national powerhouse, or a serious threat to Democratic domination of the affairs of the central government. The Democratic candidates for their party's nomination for president were so self-assured of their final victory in the fall election that they took it upon themselves to argue personal platforms and ideology instead of uniting to defeat the Republicans. What followed was a split in the Democratic Party, and the eventual nomination of three different candidates to oppose Lincoln: Stephen Douglas, John C. Breckinridge, and John Bell. The Democratic vote was split so badly that Lincoln was able to win the election even though he had received only about 39 percent of the popular vote. One can come to more clearly realize the rift between the sections when you examine the fact that Lincoln did not receive one vote in nine of the Southern states. In fact, he carried only 9 of 996 counties in the South and received but 26,395 votes, or 2 percent, of the more than 1.3 million cast. These numbers become even more glaring when one considers that 17,028 of the Southern votes he received came from the state of Missouri, leaving but 9,368 from all the remainder of the states south of the Mason-Dixon line, and of the border states where slavery existed. Even in Kentucky, where he was touted as a native son, Lincoln received but 1,364 votes of the 146,216 cast, or less than 1 percent.[1]

With that in mind, the reaction of the South to Lincoln's election can be more easily understood. The average Southerner had voted against Lincoln and the Republicans, regardless of which of the other three candidates their ballot went to. In their minds, they were about to come under the rule of a man who only 2 percent of the people in their section of the country had voted for, and this was, to them, an intolerable situation. States'-rights fire-eaters in the cotton states had been warning since before the election was held that if the Republicans won they would sever their ties with the Union and secede, and now that that eventuality had come to pass, they took steps to make good their threat. On December 15, 1860, South Carolina left the Union, followed by Mississippi on January 9, 1861, and Florida the following day.

One by one, the Southern states gathered together to oppose what they viewed to be a central government that no longer represented their interests. Passions raged on all sides as the nation moved ever closer to open hostilities and a fratricidal civil war that would rip the country asunder. These were the current events of the time when George H. Thomas was making his way for the east and a long-overdue reunion with his wife.

Thomas began his journey by stagecoach, heading for New Orleans, where he caught a steamer that brought him up the Mississippi River to Memphis, Tennessee. From there, he boarded a train for Chattanooga, where it was necessary to change cars for the next portion of the trip. When the train he was riding on stopped at Lynchburg, Virginia, to take on water, Thomas determined to step off of the car to stretch his legs. It was night time, and in the poor light he thought that there was a road bed outside of the car, but his first step proved his assumption to be incorrect, sending him on a tumble down a steep embankment, and severely injuring his spine in the process. He was able to get himself back into the car with great difficulty, and endured great pain during the trip to Norfolk, where he disembarked and gave up all hope of trying to reach New York City. Instead, he sought lodging in the city and sent word to Frances of his accident, along with a request that she join him there. On December 15, he had recovered sufficiently to attempt the thirty mile trip to Thomaston, where he recuperated for another three weeks. In early January, though still in great pain, he determined to resume his journey north, leaving his military baggage, along with his cook, in the care of his sister.

The trip to New York City was interrupted by a stop-over in Washington, where Thomas made a personal report to General-in-Chief Winfield Scott, concerning the military situation in Texas. In particular, he warned the fellow Virginian that it was his belief that General Twiggs was conspiring with local secessionists to perform some acts of treachery against the federal government. Though there had been a long-standing difficulty between the two men, Thomas was making his report solely on the basis of facts. For him, personal feelings could not be allowed to bias one's perception of a situation. General Scott and the War Department would have done well to heed his warning, for on February 18, 1861, General Twiggs acted exactly as Thomas thought he would when he surrendered federal troops, property, and equipment to a secessionist body of Texas Rangers at San Antonio.[2]

The defection of Twiggs proved to be a particularly bitter pill for General Scott to swallow. Twiggs's loyalty to the national government had been questioned in the past, but he had always enjoyed the uncompromising support of the General-in-Chief, who had many times defended his "discretion, firmness, and patriotism."[3] Twiggs was to be only the first of scores of defections from the old army that would disappoint and sadden the aging hero of the War of 1812 and the Mexican War. The secession of each Southern state took with it a complement of active army officers, as well as numbers of men from the private sector who had previously obtained military training at West Point. The people of the South anxiously awaited Scott's own defection, as it was hoped his Virginia lineage would induce him to cast his lot with his own kind. But Scott had his own ideas of where his duty lay. When he was approached by a delegation of Virginia friends intent on ascertaining his intentions, Scott was insulted by the idea that he would cast his lot with rebellion: "I have served my country under the flag of the Union, for more than fifty years, and so long as God permits me to live, I will defend that flag with my sword, even if my own native State assails it."[4] Few Southerners shared Scott's devotion to the old flag. One by one the ranks of the Union army were reduced as men of talent and ability like Joseph E. Johnston, Albert Sidney Johnston, Braxton Bragg, John Bell Hood, and even Robert E. Lee joined their fortunes with the new Confederacy. With defections rampant in the army, it was assumed in Virginia that Thomas would answer his state's call, should it become necessary.

Thomas's back was still tormenting him when he finally reached New York City, to the extent that he despaired of his ability to continue in the active service of the military, and felt that his days as a cavalry officer were over. He was, by now, in his third month of recuperation, and though the blinding pain that he had first experienced was past, it could be brought back again through movement or exertion. Fearing himself to be in a semi-invalid condition that would prevent him from continuing in the army, and having a wife to provide for, he began casting about in search of another form of livelihood he felt he could perform.

By coincidence, the Virginia Military Institute was at that time publicly advertising to fill the vacant seat for a commandant of cadets. Thomas felt that he was qualified for such a position, based on his long service in the army, as well as his academic work at West Point. The Virginia Military Institute was a prestigious academy, considered by most to be second only to West Point as a training ground for those seeking a commission in the army, and as such, it would provide worthy and dignified employment for a man who had made the profession of arms his livelihood. Thomas made inquiry to Superintendent Francis H. Smith about the availability of the position: "I would be under obligation if you would inform me what salary and allowances pertain to the situation, as from present appearances I fear that it will soon be necessary for me to be looking up some means of support."[5]

Much controversy has surrounded this inquiry on the part of Thomas, and detractors maintain that it is proof positive that Thomas entertained the idea of resigning his commission and casting his lot with the Confederacy. Dabney Maury, in a paper written for the Southern Historical Society, declared that his inquiry to Superintendent Smith was evidence of his intentions to join with his state. He details how Thomas's name was discussed by members of the secession convention as being a suitable man to be named general of the Virginia State Forces, should the state secede. He eludes to the fact that these discussions were taking place even before Robert E. Lee or Joseph E. Johnston had resigned as a sort of testimony to show that Thomas had performed some sort of treachery against his native state by entering into a covenant that he then refuted. Possibly the most revealing statement made by Maury was: "Thomas was a tower of strength in the Federal army. He alone of all the Virginians who remained in that army was the one we could not well spare."[6] In this statement can be found the reason for the false assertions made against Thomas's character and purpose. He was, as Maury freely states, the officer that Virginia could least afford to lose, and the recriminations against him were derived out of resentment that he did not offer his sword to the state, and not from any facts in the matter.

When Thomas inquired about the vacancy at V.M.I., Virginia had not yet made any move to secede from the Union. That action was still some three months away. In mid–January, state officials were still trying to mediate a peaceful solution between the federal government and their disaffected Southern brethren. But the most substantial refutation to Maury's claim is the fact that Smith's written endorsement of Thomas's inquiry insinuated that Thomas could not be trusted to assume the position, presumably because his loyalties were not clear. Instead, he recommended to Governor Letcher that Thomas be assigned as chief ordnance officer for the state militia, a position that was promptly declined. If, as Maury asserts, Thomas intended to cast his lot with the Confederacy, and was the toast of the state's secessionists, why then was he viewed with suspicion by Francis Smith? It can be further asked that if he desired to resign from the service of the United States, as alleged, would not the position of chief artillery officer for the state of Virginia be a substantial incentive to do so? The fact of the matter is that Thomas's actions were much maligned, both North and South, and that his inquiry to V.M.I. came solely from a desire to seek honorable employment should he not be able to continue in the service of the United States. A great deal has been made over this innocent action because it served the agenda of those who were making the accusations, and nothing more. Evidence that Thomas experienced turmoil over his course of action in regard to his allegiance is available, but not in the instance of his application to V.M.I.

Later, when responding to Governor Letcher's offer of command of the state's ordnance, he gives a glimpse of the struggle between service to the state and the oath he took to the federal government. In a letter dated March 12, he wrote: "I have the honor to state, after expressing my most sincere thanks for your very kind offer, that it is not my wish to leave the service of the United States as long as it is honorable for me to remain in it, and therefore as long as my native State remains in the Union it is my purpose to remain in the army, unless required to perform duties alike repulsive to honor and humanity."[7] Many have considered this rejection of Letcher's offer to have been Thomas's way of keeping the door open, just in case he should determine to resign his commission. His words certainly give rise to such a possibility, and it must be assumed that he was wrestling with his own conscience and sense of duty at the time.

A very short time after the death of Thomas in 1870, Fitzhugh Lee, who had served with him in the 2nd Cavalry, had a letter published in a Richmond newspaper claiming that he had personal knowledge of Thomas's intention to join the Confederate army. He stated "that just before the war Thomas' feelings were strongly Southern; that in 1861 he expressed his intention to resign; and about the same time, sent a letter to Governor Letcher, offering his services to Virginia."[8]

General James Garfield refuted Lee's assertions, demanding to see proof of the alleged letter, which Lee could never produce. "To this statement I invite the most searching scrutiny," Garfield advised.

> That prior to the war the sentiments of Thomas were generally in accord with those which prevailed in Virginia, and that he strongly reprobated many of the opinions and much of the conduct of Northern politicians, were facts well known to his friends and always frankly avowed by himself.

That in the winter of 1860–61, he contemplated the resignation of his commission, we have no proof except the declaration of Fitzhugh Lee. But it would not be in the least surprising or inconsistent, if, at that time, it seemed to him more than probable that disunion would be accomplished, and the army dissolved by political action and without war. Should that happen, he must perforce abandon his profession and seek some other employment. If it should appear that at that time he made inquiries looking toward a prospective employment as professor in some college, the fact would only indicate his fear that the politicians would so ruin both his country and its army, that the commission of a soldier would be no longer an object of honorable desire.

When Fitzhugh Lee's letter was published, he was challenged on all sides to produce the letter which he alleged Thomas had written, tendering his services to the rebellion. His utter failure to produce any such letter, or any proof that such a letter was ever written, is a complete refutation of the charge.[9]

While Garfield's defense of Thomas is admirable, his allusion to his lofty reasons for applying to V.M.I. are as fictitious as was Lee's letter to Governor Letcher. Garfield's idealistic explanation goes far beyond the simple truth of the matter, that Thomas's spinal injury caused him serious concern over his future prospects.

As the secession crisis intensified, and more and more Southern states took their leave of the Union, Thomas began to feel some relief from his injured back. Though he would never fully recover, the pain had subsided to the point that he dispelled his previous notions about having to resign due to disability. On April 10, he received a message from the War Department canceling the remainder of his leave and ordering him back to active duty. The 2nd Cavalry had been one of the units surrendered to Texas authorities by General Twiggs, and remnants of the regiment had begun to arrive in New York City in early April. Thomas was directed to take command of these companies and march them to Carlisle Barracks, Pennsylvania, to be reorganized and refitted.

While he was en route, Confederate forces fired on Fort Sumter, South Carolina, prompting President Lincoln to make a call for 75,000 volunteers to put down the rebellion. Each state still in the Union was given a quota of men to supply for Federal service. The governor of Virginia balked at the prospect of raising troops that were to be used to invade sister Southern states, and a secession conference speedily took the Old Dominion out of the Union. Thomas, hearing news of these events, sought out a local magistrate upon his arrival at Carlisle, for the purpose of publicly renewing his oath of allegiance to the United States. On April 20, Robert E. Lee left the Federal service to fight with Virginia. Five days later, Thomas was promoted to the rank of lieutenant colonel to fill the spot made vacant by Lee's departure. On May 3, he was promoted to the rank of colonel and given command of the 2nd Cavalry, due to the fact that Albert Sidney Johnston's resignation had just been received.[10]

Many contemporaries and historians have pointed to the fact that Thomas's wife was Northern-born as a sustaining reason why he stayed with the Union. His old friend and comrade Erasmus D. Keyes expressed his conviction that Frances exerted influence over him to remain true to the old flag, but this statement is clearly denounced by Mrs. Thomas in a letter written to a friend after the war: "General Keyes' private opinion that I was the cause of General Thomas remaining in the service is decidedly a mistake. I do not think they met from the time General Thomas went to Kentucky to join that army until they met in San Francisco years after. There was never a word passed between General Thomas and myself, or any one of the family, upon the subject of his remaining loyal to the United States Government. We felt that whatever his course, it would be from a conscientious sense of duty; that no one could persuade him to do what he felt was not right."[11]

Thomas believed in adherence to the Constitution and in the continuance of the Union, and as such had been in favor of John Bell in the presidential election. He was opposed to extremists on either side, and refused to allow himself to be aligned with them. One New Yorker who had the opportunity to obtain his views said, "General Thomas was strong and bitter in his denunciation against all parties North and South that seemed to him responsible for the condition of affairs, but while he reprobated, sometimes very strongly, certain men and parties North, in that respect going as far as any of those who afterward joined the rebels, he never, in my hearing, agreed with them respecting the necessity of going with their States, but denounced the idea and denied the necessity of dividing the country or destroying the Government."[12]

Thomas knew that he would be branded as a traitor no matter which side he chose. If he sided with the South, he would be accused of violating his oath to the United States Army, and if he remained in that army he would be charged with abandoning his own people and his native state. For Thomas, the question was not nearly so personal, however. In fact, it was not much of a decision at all. While he must have labored over the decision, it had, in reality, already been made before he had pondered over it for the first minute, even if he did not realize it himself. Thomas believed in the compact of the Constitution, and strongly opposed the destruction of the Union. Even if he felt that parties in the North had contributed heavily toward breaking up that Union, he could not go against his own convictions and fight against the flag he had taken an oath to defend. His Unionist principles allowed that his honor could only be served by continued loyalty to that flag, just as Robert E. Lee's principles dictated that his honor could only be served by defending his native state. Thomas believed in allegiance to nation more than he did in allegiance to his state, and that being the case, he was not willing to suffer what he felt to be a stain on his honor or reputation by forsaking the uniform he wore, or the country it represented.

General Robert Patterson expressed his complete confidence in Thomas and his loyalty to the Union: "General Thomas contemplated with horror the prospect of a war between the people of his own State and the Union; but he never for a moment hesitated, never wavered, never swerved, from his allegiance to the nation that had educated him and whose servant he was. From the beginning I would have pledged my hopes here and hereafter on the loyalty of Thomas.... He was the most unselfish man I ever knew; a perfectly honest man, who feared God and obeyed his commandments."[13]

On April 27, 1861, the Department of Pennsylvania was created, with General Patterson as its commander. On April 29, Thomas was assigned to command of the 1st Brigade in this department, consisting of his own 2nd Cavalry and three regiments of three-month Pennsylvania Militia. Thomas trained and outfitted his brigade in preparation for the offensive operations he knew would come, probably in his home state. After five weeks in Carlisle, the brigade was directed to move to Chambersburg, where Thomas renewed acquaintances with Fitz John Porter and Abner Doubleday, both officers he had known in the past.

Alexander K. McClure, the influential Pennsylvania publisher of an abolitionist newspaper, extended the courtesy of his dinner table to a number of the officers then stationed at Chambersburg, including Thomas and Doubleday. After the meal, several officers began discussing the probability that the war would be over after just one battle, and most agreed that the conflict would be a short one. According to McClure, "Thomas, with that modesty which always characterized him, was silent. Doubleday had met the Southerners in battle at Sumter and he knew how desperately earnest they were, and Thomas was a son of Virginia who knew that the Southern people were as heroic as any in the North.... Doubleday surprised his fellow officers by declaring it would be one of the most desperate and bloody wars of modern history ... and that they [the Rebels] meant to make it a fight to the death. He was the first to leave after dinner, and when he was gone several leading officers ridiculed his ideas of a long and terrible war, and I well remember the remark of one of them that Doubleday was a Spiritualist and a little gone in the head."[14]

On June 12, Thomas received orders to march his brigade to Williamsport, Maryland, where it was to be held in readiness for a possible crossing into Virginia. On July 2, the 1st Brigade was ordered across the Potomac to engage the enemy. Some 12,000 of the men in Patterson's army were to be discharged at the end of their three months' service on July 24, and if any good was to come from their enlistments, they must be put into action immediately. Major General Irvin McDowell, with a force of about 30,000 men, was finally bowing to pressure from the government and making a campaign against the Confederate capital at Richmond. Arrayed against him were some 20,000 Confederates, under the command of Major General P.G.T. Beauregard, in the vicinity of Centreville, Virginia. Major General Joseph E. Johnston commanded a second Confederate army, some 9,000 strong, in the vicinity of Winchester, and Patterson and his army had been given the assignment of holding Johnston's forces in place and not allowing them to reinforce Beauregard in front of McDowell.

Thomas's brigade followed Patterson's advance across the Potomac and into Virginia at 4:00 A.M. on the morning of July 2. After a march of some four miles, at Falling Waters, they encountered an enemy force of between 2,500 and 3,000 men, commanded by Brigadier General Thomas J. Jackson and Colonel J.E.B. Stuart. Colonel John J. Abercrombie, commanding the lead brigade, deployed his men at once, and Thomas brought his brigade into line on Abercrombie's right. Jackson was under orders from General Johnston not to bring on a general engagement, but he held his line until the Federal force moved forward and a lively fire ensued. The Confederates then retreated, and were pursued by the victorious Federals until darkness ended the contest. The victory at Falling Waters was Thomas's first action in the Civil War. It was also one of the first engagements in the east between the contending armies.

There is a lack of reliable information concerning the numbers engaged, or the casualties sustained by the forces on either side. Jackson's force was assailed by two full brigades of Union troops, meaning that the Confederates must have been greatly outnumbered. That much can be assumed even without reliable statistical information. Estimates of Federal losses were eight killed and fifteen wounded, while Confederate casualties were listed at thirteen killed and approximately fifty wounded.

J.E.B. Stuart was personally responsible for what would be the majority of all the losses suffered by the Federals on that day. Following Jackson's withdrawal, Stuart's cavalry remained behind to keep an eye on Patterson's army. Stuart was riding alone, in advance of his men, through a patch of woods when he came upon a body of Federal troops on the opposite side of a rail fence. Stuart continued boldly forward, and when he reached the fence he directed several of the enemy troops to tear down a section of it. The soldiers, believing Stuart to be one of their own officers, readily complied. Stuart then leveled his revolver at the group and demanded that they throw down their arms and surrender before he opened fire. The ruse worked until the Federals caught sight of the Confederate troopers riding to join their leader. Several Union soldiers then attempted to resist capture, resulting in three of their number being shot dead. By the time the affair was concluded, Stuart had captured forty-six members of Company I, 15th Pennsylvania Volunteer Infantry, including their lieutenant and surgeon.[15]

Falling Waters was not much of a battle, but the North hailed it as a triumph. Now there could be no doubt from any quarter where Thomas's loyalties lay. He had crossed into the Old Dominion and engaged Virginia troops on the field of battle. He was part of an army dedicated to bringing his home state back into the Union, "to help whip her back again," as he put it.[16] Thomas's conduct on the battlefield was commended by his superiors, as well as by the men under his command. Samuel J. Randall, a soldier in his ranks who would later rise to become Speaker of the United States House of Representatives, was so impressed with his commander that he later wrote a letter to Thomas A. Scott, Assistant Secretary of War:

General Thomas J. "Stonewall" Jackson suffered one of his few defeats in Thomas's first engagement of the war at Falling Waters, Virginia (United States Army Military History Institute).

> I notice that the Government is now considering the appointment of proper persons to be brigadier-generals. In the name of God, let them be men fully competent to discharge the duties to which they may be assigned. Inefficiency is the evil of the hour. This opinion is based upon our observation of nearly three months. Most of the time, in fact nearly all of the time, we have been under the command of Colonel George H. Thomas, now commanding one of the brigades here. He is thoroughly competent to be a brigadier-general, has the confidence of every man in his command for the reason that they recognize and appreciate capacity — which to them in every hour of the day is so essential to their safety. Now let me as a friend of this administration, in so far as the war is concerned and the preservation of the Union is involved, urge upon General Cameron to select Colonel Thomas as one of the proposed brigadiers. I am, as perhaps you know, a private in the First City Cavalry of Philadelphia, and I never saw Colonel Thomas until I saw him on parade, and our intercourse has only been such as exists between a colonel and one of his soldiers; hence, you see my recommendation comes from pure motives, and entirely free from social or political considerations. I speak for and write in behalf of the brave men who, in this hour of our country's peril, are coming forward and endangering their own lives, and perhaps leaving those most dear to them without support. I write warmly, because I think I know the necessity of the case. You will do the country a service by giving my letter a serious consideration.[17]

Jackson's force retreated to Martinsburg on July 3, while the Union advance, led by Thomas, skirmished with the retreating foe. On the Fourth of July, the Confederates abandoned Martinsburg, and Patterson's army celebrated the holiday with a martial display in their newly captured prize. The next move of the army was discussed at mess that evening, with

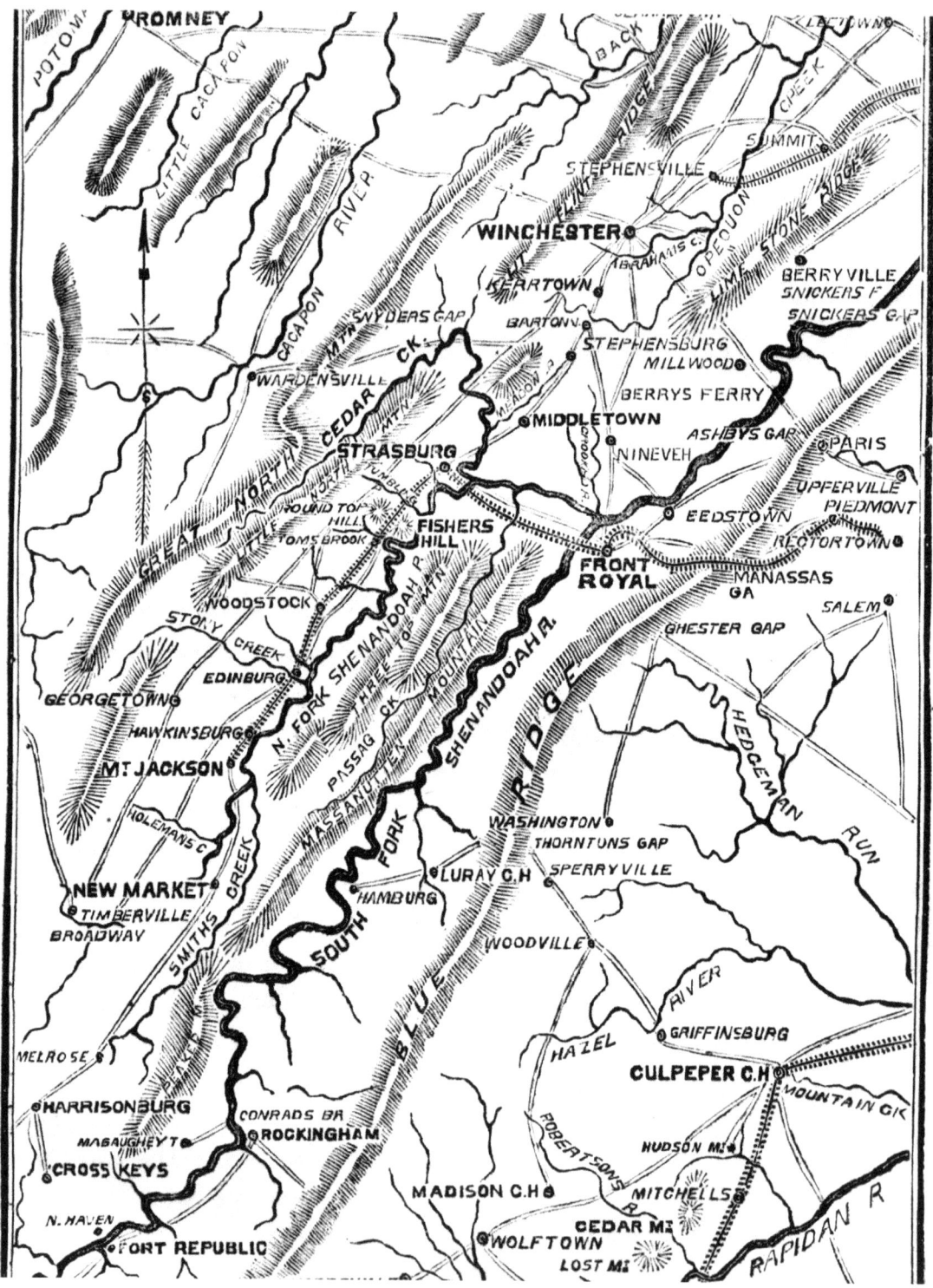

Map of the Shenandoah region of Virginia in 1861, showing the area of Falling Waters and Bunker Hill. From *History of the Civil War in the United States*, by Samuel M. Schmucker. Published by Jones Brothers & Co., Philadelphia, Pa., 1865.

Thomas supporting an immediate drive on Winchester. Fitz John Porter was against such an operation because of his lack of confidence in the volunteer regiments that made up the larger portion of the army. Thomas countered that the Confederate army was also made up of volunteers, and that both sides were equal in this regard. Patterson agreed with Thomas, and the following morning an advance on Winchester was begun. By the end of the day, however, Patterson changed his mind and called off the advance after seeing some of his troops who had no shoes.

The situation remained static for several days. Patterson was hesitant to bring on a general engagement since he had not been specifically ordered to do so. Instead, his instructions directed him to occupy Johnston's forces, and the general took those orders literally. He finally settled on a plan to flank Johnson out of Winchester, without attacking his position there, and his columns were accordingly set in motion. On July 15, Thomas approached to within nine miles of the Confederate camp, where he ran into an enemy force of some 600 men at Bunker Hill. Thomas easily brushed aside this Confederate force, compelling them to retire upon their main defensive position at Winchester. The road was now open for further operations against that city, but Patterson reconsidered his options and called off the advance. Instead, he ordered the army to back-track to Charleston, some twenty-two miles away from the enemy.

In part, Patterson had arrived at this decision because of news that McDowell had already made contact with Beauregard's army at Fairfax Court House. He believed that he had already achieved his mission in holding Johnston's forces in check, as he felt they could not possibly reinforce Beauregard before the deciding battle between him and McDowell took place. Also, he was highly concerned over the reliability of his volunteer troops. Their three month enlistments were to expire shortly and most of the men in the ranks vowed that they would not serve one day longer than they had signed up for. A telegram from General Scott warned, "Do not let the enemy amuse and delay you with a small force in front while he reinforces the [Manassas] Junction with his main body." But Patterson remained indecisive. He wired back to Scott asking if the commander desired him to attack the Southerners in his front. The reply showed agitation on the part of his superior: "I have certainly been expecting you to beat the enemy ... [or] at least had occupied him by threats and demonstrations." In Patterson's mind, that was precisely what he was doing.[18]

On July 18, one of Thomas's scouts observed dust clouds on the horizon and immediately discerned their meaning. He reported to Thomas, who, once advised, rushed to Patterson's headquarters without stopping to button his coat or put on his hat. Johnston's army was on the move, probably headed for a junction with Beauregard with several thousand reinforcements. Thomas pushed for an attack on the column but Patterson balked. He felt that enough time had elapsed for McDowell to defeat Beauregard, making Johnston's march useless, and thus allowed the Confederates to leave his front unmolested. Johnston was permitted to entrain his men at Piedmont, and they arrived at Manassas in time to stem the retreat of Beauregard's army and turn defeat into a crushing victory for Southern arms. Scott was outraged over Patterson's failure to keep Johnston in the vicinity of Winchester, and Patterson was duly relieved of command of the Department of Pennsylvania.

Though Thomas had urged his superior several times to take action other than that which Patterson settled upon, he steadfastly supported the decisions of his commander. In a letter to Patterson, written in the third year of the war, he fully endorses his chief's actions, an act of loyalty he would exhibit throughout the Civil War:

In the council of war at Martinsburg, I in substance advised an advance towards Winchester, at least as far as Bunker Hill, and if your information, after the army reached Bunker Hill, led you to believe that Johnston still occupied Winchester in force, then to shift our troops over to Charleston, as that would place our communications with our depot of supplies in safety, and still threaten and hold Johnston at Winchester, which I understand was all that you were expected to do. I should have advised a direct advance on Winchester, but for the character of the troops composing your army. They were all, with the exception of a couple squadrons of the Second U.S. Cavalry and two batteries of regular artillery, three-month's men, and their terms of service would expire in a few days. Judging of them as of other Volunteer troops, had I been the commander, I should not have been willing to risk them in a heavy battle, coming off within a few days of the expiration of their service.

I have always believed, and have frequently so expressed myself, that your management of the three-months campaign was able and judicious, and was in the best interest of the service, considering the means at your disposal, and the nature of the troops under your command.[19]

In this letter, Thomas exhibits tendencies he held throughout his life. He defers to Patterson and his judgment to the point of stating that he had concurred with all of the general's decisions, even though he had several times urged for more active measures to be taken. His statement regarding the volunteer troops may seem odd, considering that he was the one who had been stressing that the Confederate soldiers were just as green and inexperienced as the Federals, and that should be no reason to hesitate to attack. What the reader finds in Thomas's letter to Patterson is a man who refuses to do damage to the reputation or career of a brother officer who, in his opinion, had done the best he could. This, despite the fact that he had personally disagreed with decisions made by that officer, even though time had proven Thomas's decisions as the proper course of action. He was too much the gentleman and professional soldier to advance himself by detracting from the good name of a superior. Throughout the war, he would remain the loyal and humble servant of all those who were placed over him, the consummate lieutenant and team player.

Following the disaster at Manassas, the Federal army took time to refit and reorganize for another drive on Richmond. New regiments, three-year regiments, were raised to replace the men who had been mustered out of the service, and these men were to have a new commander as well. Major General George B. McClellan had replaced McDowell as commander of the main Federal army in the east. McClellan had been considered one of the bright young stars of the old army before resigning to seek fame and fortune in the private sector. Upon his return to active duty, he was assigned to a command in western Virginia, where he won the greatest Union victory of the war to date, at Philippi. This triumph catapulted him to national fame, and paved the way for his rapid advancement to commander of the Federal army around Washington. An able organizer and drillmaster, the Army of the Potomac was created under his watchful eye, and while his leadership of that army is a topic of controversial discussion, all that it later accomplished was a result of his efforts and instruction.

Back in the Valley of the Shenandoah, little had transpired since the battle at Manassas. On August 3, 1861, Congress passed a bill that consolidated the dragoons, mounted infantry, and cavalry into one branch of the service. As a result of this reorganization, the 2nd U.S Cavalry was redesignated as the 5th U.S. Cavalry. Two weeks later, on August 26, Thomas was relieved of command of the 5th Cavalry and the 1st Brigade, and ordered to report to Brigadier General Robert Anderson at Louisville, Kentucky. Anderson had been the Union commander at Fort Sumter, and enjoyed hero status throughout the land for his defense of that post in the opening engagement of the war. He had been promoted to the rank of major general and assigned command of the Federal troops in his native state of Kentucky, in hopes of his being able to assist in keeping that border state in the Union.

Anderson accepted the assignment under the condition that he could choose the four brigadier generals who would serve under him. Thus far, he had already selected William T. Sherman, Don Carlos Buell, and Ormsby M. Mitchell. Anderson desired Simon B. Buckner, a fellow Kentuckian, for his fourth brigadier, but his nephew, Lieutenant Thomas M. Anderson, informed him that Buckner intended to cast his lot with the Confederates. The younger Anderson had served under Thomas in the 2nd and 5th Cavalry, and urged his uncle that this was the man who should be appointed to the remaining vacancy. Thomas was known to General Anderson, as he had been one of his cadets when Anderson served as an instructor at West Point. He had also derived a favorable opinion of him from his service with General Patterson, who was a friend of Anderson's.

According to Sherman, Anderson was won over to the side of Thomas, but he had a difficult time convincing President Lincoln to confirm the appointment. In his memoirs, Sherman contends that Lincoln was hesitant to approve the appointment because of Thomas's Southern lineage, and the fact that so many Southern officers had proven themselves disloyal. He states that both he and Anderson vouched for Thomas's devotion to the Union, and that only after considerable conversation on their part did Lincoln relent and favor the appointment with his blessing. There is no corroborating evidence that this conversation ever took place, however, and though Sherman contends that he was Thomas's best friend with the administration at this time, his subsequent actions tend to cast doubt on that assertion.[20]

It is known that a small number of congressman opposed the appointment of Thomas as a brigadier, namely Andrew Johnson and Horace Maynard, both of Tennessee, and Carey Trimble of Ohio. These men favored Buckner for the position, believing that he would then deliver the Kentucky Home Guard Militia over to Federal service, thus ensuring that the state would stay in the Union. Lieutenant Anderson addressed this group in a meeting at a hotel, informing them categorically that Buckner intended to resign his commission and fight for the South. He told them of how Buckner had offered him a commission in the Home Guard, which was known to be a Rebel organization. He advocated strongly on behalf of Thomas, and was joined by Sherman, who also happened to be at the meeting. This is perhaps the incident Sherman refers to in his memoirs, and it is possible that he mistakenly believed that Lincoln had been in attendance.[21]

Thomas's commission as a brigadier general of volunteers was officially dated August 17, 1861, ranking him fifty-fifth on the list of brigadiers on active duty, in terms of seniority. Pursuant to complying with his orders to report to Kentucky, Thomas marched his brigade to Hyattsville, Maryland, where he turned it over to the new department commander, General Nathaniel P. Banks. Following this, he was allowed a brief leave in order to see his wife, who happened to be in New Haven, Connecticut, at the time. Six days were spent in the round trip to Connecticut, and the abbreviated visit with Frances, and the new general was once more ready to assume his duties in the Bluegrass State. He reported to General Anderson on September 6, upon his arrival at Louisville, and was assigned to command at Camp Dick Robinson, reaching that post on September 15.[22]

Chapter Six

To the West and Mill Springs

Camp Dick Robinson, established on July 2, 1861, was located between Danville and Lexington. It was considered to be the most important post in the department, so Anderson showed great confidence in Thomas by appointing him as the officer responsible for turning its raw recruits into soldiers.

General William Nelson had been selected by President Lincoln to recruit volunteers from Kentucky and east Tennessee. Nelson, a Kentuckian, had been an officer in the U.S. Navy prior to accepting Lincoln's appointment. As such, he became the only naval officer in the service to attain the rank of general in the army during the course of the war. An imposing figure, he stood six feet four inches tall and weighed about 300 pounds. His influence among the citizens of Kentucky and east Tennessee who remained loyal to the Union was almost as impressive as his size. By the time Thomas arrived in Kentucky, Nelson had been successful in raising four regiments of soldiers from Kentucky and two from east Tennessee, or approximately 6,000 men.

These men had been raised to counter the influence of the Kentucky State Guard, the state militia under the command of Simon B. Buckner, which was known to be in sympathy with the new Confederacy. Though the government of the state maintained a policy of neutrality, refusing to choose sides in the conflict, it was feared in Washington that preparations were afoot to take Kentucky out of the Union, and Nelson's force was intended to prevent such an occurrence by providing loyal men a rallying point from which such a move could be resisted. If hostilities erupted within the state, it would also provide the Union with a ready fighting force. To Thomas would fall the responsibility of training these men to handle their part of the war if it came to Kentucky.

By the time Thomas reached Camp Dick Robinson on September 15, Kentucky's neutrality was already becoming a failed dream. On September 5, Brigadier General Leonidas Polk moved his Confederate forces across state lines to occupy Hickman and Chalk Bluffs, Kentucky. Brigadier General Ulysses S. Grant responded by moving his Union forces into Paducah, Kentucky, supported by two Union gunboats. Brigadier General Felix K. Zollicoffer supported Polk's move a few days later when he occupied Cumberland Gap and moved a portion of his command across the line into Kentucky. Any illusions or pretensions of neutrality were now out of the question. The state troops within the borders of Kentucky were now compelled to choose sides and they aligned themselves exactly as had been anticipated, with Buckner and his State Guard adopting the Confederate flag as their banner.[1]

The Southerners were aware of Thomas's appointment and made plans to capture him before he had the opportunity to assume command. Confederate sympathizers intended to abduct him while he was en route from Louisville, but the plans somehow went awry, and the opportunity was missed. They would shortly rue this failure, as Thomas would exert almost immediate influence over affairs in Kentucky that helped to change the balance of power in the state.

General Buckner had planned to capture the Frankfort Arsenal at Lexington. To accomplish this, he publicly announced that the State Guard was to assemble at that place on September 20 for the purpose of drills, and invited all men in Kentucky who favored states' rights and peace to join them there. By means of this subterfuge, he hoped to secure the much needed arms contained in the arsenal before the Federals could divine his true purpose, and without having to fight a battle. When Thomas was made aware of the public proclamation he anticipated Buckner's true intentions, immediately deciding that this was to be no peaceful training maneuver. He at once ordered Colonel Thomas E. Bramlette to march to Lexington with his 3rd Kentucky Infantry, to take possession of the fairgrounds and deny its use by the Rebels. Bramlette's move was conducted with such alacrity and secrecy that it took Buckner by surprise and forced him to cancel his own plans of operation. By sound judgment and quick action Thomas had succeeded in securing the arsenal and had probably thwarted the best opportunity the Confederate sympathizers had of taking the state out of the Union by force of arms.[2] It was a bloodless victory, one only slightly noticed by his superiors in Washington. Thomas's actions at Lexington, however, would prove to be one of the most significant accomplishments of the early war in the west, and would provide the Union with the opportunity to gain the advantage in the region.

Major General Oliver O. Howard, in a paper read before the New York Military Order of the Loyal Legion of the United States in 1904, described the situation in Kentucky which Thomas inherited. Thomas "assumed command of that hatcher of armies, that source of regiments and brigades, discipline, frill, instruction, and supply, 'Camp Dick Robinson.'"

It is not difficult to imagine all the chaos of that large wild camp — the ever-changing commanders of the department, or district, and the ambition of those great men, who, unused to war, had come from civil

General Robert Anderson. The hero of Fort Sumter and native Kentuckian who became Thomas's first department commander in the west, Anderson would give way to William T. Sherman shortly after Thomas's arrival in Kentucky (United States Army Military History Institute).

pursuits to assert their prerogatives. Above and below Thomas' volunteer rank there was commotion and perpetual unrest. Steady, strong, firm, deliberate, he soon brought order out of confusion. He declined to be subordinated to juniors in the command given him, [and he] managed to keep his camp till he had gotten in a fair state of readiness one field division."[3]

In October of 1861, General Robert Anderson applied for leave from the army due to illness. The leave was granted on October 8, and General Sherman subsequently replaced him in command of the forces in Kentucky and east Tennessee. In a message to the troops, Anderson conveyed his hope that Sherman "may be the means of delivering this department from the marauding bands, who, under the guise of relieving and benefiting Kentucky, are doing all the injury they can to those who will not join them in their accursed warfare."[4] In the meantime, Thomas had responded to the threat posed from Zollicoffer's army by creating an advanced camp at Rockcastle Hills, some 30 miles southeast of Camp Dick Robinson. This position was named Camp Wildcat, and was garrisoned by four regiments of infantry, a battalion of artillery, and a detachment of cavalry, all under the command of Brigadier General Albin F. Schoepf. When Sherman made an inspection tour of the department he heartily approved of Thomas's dispositions to blunt the further advance of the Confederates.[5]

For his part, Sherman was largely paralyzed by the new responsibilities that had recently been placed upon his shoulders. General Polk threatened the state from the west, while General Zollicoffer exerted pressure from the east. General Albert Sidney Johnston, the newly appointed Confederate commander in the Western Theater, was collecting to himself an army at Nashville, Tennessee, with which he designed to invade central Kentucky and settle once and for all the question of who would control the state. When Johnston moved his army to Bowling Green, Kentucky, Sherman went on the defensive, both militarily and emotionally. He began telegraphing Washington to warn of what he perceived to be the desperate situation in Kentucky, and voiced his opinion that 60,000 men would be needed to hold the state. He preached of a long and bloody war that would rival anything in the history of Europe, and his volatile temperament was stretched to the point that local reporters started to portray him as being unstable, or even mentally deranged. Many historians believe that Sherman did indeed suffer a nervous breakdown while commanding in Kentucky.[6]

On October 21, General Zollicoffer

General Simon B. Buckner. Leader of the Kentucky Home Guard during the state's neutrality, he would later rally thousands of Kentuckians to fight for the Confederacy (United States Army Military History Institute).

made an attempt to push back the advance forces of Thomas when he directed his division to attack Camp Wildcat. A grueling march of some eighty miles had been made on the Wilderness Road, a well named thoroughfare passing through the rocky and barren regions of east Tennessee and Kentucky. The march exhausted his men and stretched the army's supply line to its limit. Zollicoffer's footsore Confederates were thrown at Schoepf's camp, but found it too formidable a position to capture. The fortified camp was protected by natural barriers of deep gorges, steep bluffs, and fallen timber that kept Zollicoffer from being able to maximize his superiority of numbers on the broken and rugged ground, and the attack resulted in a repulse that forced the Confederates to withdraw back to their base at Cumberland Gap.[7] The affair at Camp Wildcat resulted in only minor casualties on both sides. According to Union reports only about thirty of the enemy had been killed in the attack, out of a force of more than 4,000. Regardless of the casualty rates, Zollicoffer's offensive movement had been blunted, and Thomas once more proved the solid reliability of his command decisions.

But Thomas's judgment and action did not receive validation or recognition from his superiors. Instead, events had transpired that relegated him to a subordinate role in the department and snubbed both his past and recent accomplishments. Thomas had been in contact with the War Department to forward his plans for a campaign against Cumberland Gap, with the goal of liberating east Tennessee from Confederate occupation. His superiors in Washington heartily approved, and the plan had the full endorsement of Andrew Johnson, the Unionist governor of Tennessee. But Thomas was to receive no credit for planning or organizing the campaign. That honor was to go to Brigadier General Ormsby M. Mitchell. It is unclear whence Mitchell's support derived, but on October 10, he notified Thomas that Secretary of War Simon Cameron had placed him in command at Camp Dick Robinson: "General: Under orders from the Secretary of War of this date, I am directed to repair to Camp Dick Robinson, and there prepare the troops for onward movement, the object being to take possession of Cumberland Ford and Cumberland Gap, and ultimately seize the East Tennessee and Virginia Railroad." Thomas was to act as second in command for the expedition, under the direction of Mitchell. Though Mitchell's commission to brigadier general was senior to Thomas's by a few days, the intended slight was obvious to all, especially to the conscientious and honorable Thomas.

General William T. Sherman. Sherman served briefly as Thomas's department commander before becoming overwhelmed by the responsibilities of command and suffering what many historians believe was a nervous breakdown. Sherman would become Thomas's immediate superior again during the Atlanta campaign, in the last year of the war (United States Army Military History Institute).

The reasons for such a change in command are unclear, even at this time when historians have had ample opportunity to review all the records. Thomas's detractors have long stated that this was nothing more or less than an example of the lack of faith the administration held in him due to his Southern birth and questions regarding his loyalty to the cause. While this is a plausible argument, this writer finds it hard to believe that such would be the case since Thomas had already been assigned to such an important post as commander at Camp Dick Robinson. If there had been any serious questions concerning his loyalty, the administration would never have entrusted him with a position so crucial in maintaining the all-important state of Kentucky in the Union. Instead, it is probable that the change in command resulted from the political arena and from Ohio politicians who were promoting the career of their own native son.[8]

Regardless of the root cause, the relegation of Thomas to a subordinate position was more than that officer's honor could bear. On October 11 he sent Mitchell acknowledgment of the orders: "General: Your communication of the 10th instant was received today at the hands of Governor Johnson of Tennessee. I have been doing all in my power to prepare the troops for a move on Cumberland Ford and to seize the Tennessee and Virginia Railroad, and shall continue to do all I can to assist you until your arrival here; but justice to myself requires that I ask to be relieved from duty with these troops, since the Secretary has thought it necessary to supersede me in the command, without, as I conceive, any just cause for so doing." That same day, he followed up with a letter to his immediate commander, Sherman, stating: "General: I received an official communication to-day from Brigadier-General O.M. Mitchell, informing me that he had been ordered by the Secretary of War to repair to this Camp and prepare the troops for a forward movement, first to Cumberland Ford, and eventually to seize upon the Tennessee and Virginia Railroad. As I have been doing all in my power to effect this very thing, to have the execution of it taken from me when nearly prepared to take the field, is extremely mortifying. I have therefore respectfully to ask to be relieved from duty with the troops on the arrival of General Mitchell."[9]

Sherman replied that he was so tied up with administrative duties at the present that he would not be able to come to Camp Dick Robinson and meet with Thomas personally, but he instructed that officer to continue forward with his plans and preparations. He assured Thomas, "I will, if possible, give you the opportunity of completing what you have begun." Sherman would later claim that he interceded on Thomas's behalf, which resulted in the rescission of the orders to Mitchell, so that Thomas retained command. However, there is no record to be found of Sherman's communicating with his superiors on this matter. The only evidence that would tend to support his claim was his response to Thomas himself.

Governor Johnson also claimed in later years to have been Thomas's benefactor in retaining him in command at this critical time, and to have been a steadfast supporter of the general. The record shows that Johnson had not been a particularly warm supporter of Thomas at the time of the Mitchell incident. He was convinced to lend his support only after canvassing Tennessee troops under the general's command and finding them to be in unified opposition to the impeding removal of Thomas. The most likely cause of the change in orders for Mitchell was the reputation and popularity Thomas enjoyed with his troops and with the public. It is probable that the War Department reconsidered its action based on the political considerations that had dictated the move in the first place, and determined that appeasement of a few Ohio politicians was not worth alienation of Tennessee and Kentucky politicians.

Whatever the causes, Thomas had survived this unjustified attempt to remove him from an important command. In doing so, he had given further proof that the accusations of his detractors were unfounded. An officer with questionable loyalty or devotion to the cause would surely have taken this slight as a reason to resign his commission. Thomas, on the other hand, understandably requested to be relieved from an embarrassing situation, but never entertained the possibility of leaving the service of his country.

Following the repulse of Zollicoffer's army at Camp Wildcat, Thomas joined Schoepf and pushed his forces forward thirty miles to London, where a defensive position was established at a fork in the road. Two additional regiments of Tennessee troops were added to Schoepf's force, while Thomas went back to Camp Dick Robinson. On October 26, he advanced with the rest of his army to establish an advanced post at Crab Orchard. Zollicoffer was on the defensive, and Thomas was determined to seize the moment. Sensing that the time was right for the proposed offensive that would liberate east Tennessee and secure the Tennessee and Virginia Railroad, he sent a message to Sherman asking for reinforcements. "With four more good regiments we could seize the railroad yet," he said. "With my headquarters at Somerset, I can easily seize the most favorable time for invading East Tennessee which ought to be done this winter."[10]

But Thomas was permitted to proceed no further toward the Tennessee border. Sherman was becoming alarmed by rumors that Albert Sidney Johnston's army, at Bowling Green, was poised to make a thrust toward Louisville, Lexington, and even Cincinnati. Estimating Johnston's army to be three times its actual size, Sherman began alerting Washington that he was soon to be assailed by overwhelming enemy forces and requested immediate reinforcements be sent to the state to avert disaster. By Sherman's count, it would take 60,000 additional Union troops to ensure Kentucky's safety, and that number would be sufficient only in a defensive posture. Of course, the government did not have such a reserve force available, even if Sherman had been correct in his assumptions, and the request for such large scale reinforcements was denied. The department command was becoming too heavy a weight for Sherman to cope with, and the lack of the reinforcements he thought he needed was pushing him to his breaking point. He acknowledged his overwhelmed condition in a letter to Thomas dated November 6: "It would be better if some more sanguine mind were here, for I am forced to order according to my convictions."

On November 11, Sherman succumbed to his fears of impending attack by Johnston and ordered Thomas to withdraw from his advanced positions, with a view to consolidating the forces of the department. Thomas obeyed, but tried to convince Sherman that the move was unnecessary: "I am sure the enemy is not moving between us. All my information is that they are moving south." Sherman remained unmoved, and the order remained intact. Though he was merely obeying orders in withdrawing from Crab Orchard and London, Thomas came under severe criticism in the press, where his loyalty was once more questioned and he was accused of intentionally allowing Zollicoffer's army to evade defeat and capture. Horace Maynard, the congressman from Tennessee who had previously objected to Thomas's appointment as brigadier general, made a personal attack on the general and hinted that his actions were to be investigated.[11]

This would be one of the last orders Sherman would give as department commander. Authorities at Washington came to the conclusion that he was not the right man for the job and took measures to replace him. The final decision to remove Sherman rested largely on a personal interview between Sherman, Secretary Cameron, and Adjutant-General Lorenzo Thomas that took place in late October. Though Thomas should have been the leading candidate for the administration, owing to his solid leadership and firm commitment to the campaign to liberate east Tennessee, a pet project of Lincoln and the administration, he was to be passed over for political reasons. Major General George B. McClellan, who had been appointed General-in-Chief of the army on November 1, opted instead to assign his friend Don Carlos Buell to the command. McClellan's reasoning was that Buell was a native Kentuckian, making him more acceptable to the people of the state. His commission to brigadier general was also senior to Thomas's by about three months.[12]

On November 15, General Buell officially replaced Sherman as commander of the department. Sherman retired to St. Louis, Missouri, where he reported to Major General Henry Halleck for assignment.[13] Buell's appointment was not to be the only change that took place that day. The Department of the Cumberland had been expanded to include Ohio, Indiana, and Michigan, and effective November 15 its primary fighting force would be known as the Army of the Ohio.

Buell was a West Point graduate in the class of 1841, and was well known to Thomas, who had graduated a year earlier. The two men had shared similar prewar experiences, both having served in the Seminole and Mexican Wars, Buell with the 3rd U.S. Infantry. Like Thomas, Buell had received multiple brevets for gallant conduct in Mexico, and had been advanced to the rank of brevet major by the conclusion of that conflict. Buell was subsequently transferred to the adjutant general's office, and served for thirteen years in that capacity. The outbreak of the war found him stationed in San Francisco, serving as adjutant general for the Department of the Pacific, with the rank of lieutenant colonel. He was commissioned a brigadier general of volunteers on May 17, 1861, and ordered east. September of 1861 found him employed in assisting General McClellan to train and organize the Army of the Potomac. It was through this association with the General-in-Chief that Buell won the confidence that catapulted him to command of the department.[14]

Buell's first order of business after taking command was to organize his army into brigades and divisions. The 1st Division, consisting of four brigades, was assigned to Thomas. The 2nd Division, also four brigades strong, was given to Brigadier General Alexander McDowell McCook. The remaining divisions all contained three brigades, with the 4th being assigned to Brigadier General William Nelson, the 5th to Brigadier General Thomas L. Crittenden, and the 6th to Brigadier General Thomas J. Wood. Buell assigned a battery of artillery to each brigade. Cavalry regiments were also dispersed throughout the various brigades, with no specific cavalry organization being formed for army useage.[15]

Buell had been appointed to command with instructions to make a vigorous campaign against Cumberland Gap and east Tennessee. Instead, he ordered Thomas to make a retrograde movement on November 17, leaving one brigade behind at London under the command of Lieutenant Samuel P. Carter, U.S. Navy. On November 20, Thomas received instructions to move his men to Lebanon.[16] General Zollicoffer watched with interest as Thomas's army was withdrawn from his sector, and decided that the time was right to make an advance upon Somerset. When Thomas learned of the movement of the Confederates he ordered Shoepf, then at Lebanon, to march at once to Somerset, supported by a regiment of cavalry from Columbia. His subsequent orders to reinforce Shoepf were countermanded by Buell, who felt that Shoepf's force was sufficient to deal with the threat from Zollicoffer. Buell also clipped Thomas's wings by instructing him that he did not have the discretionary authority to issue such orders and that from this point forward orders were not to be issued without Buell's personal approval.[17]

By December 29, Buell was forced to admit that Thomas's initial reaction to Zollicoffer's move had been the correct one. The Confederates had occupied a fortified position at Beach Grove, near Somerset, on the north bank of the Cumberland River, which was posing a threat to Union positions in that sector. Thomas was ordered to advance the remainder of his division forward for the purpose of making an attack on Zollicoffer's stronghold. It was precisely the action that Thomas proposed to make when he had sent Schoepf's brigade forward, but now Zollicoffer had been given time to dig in and prepare a defensive position.[18]

Thomas marched his troops out of Lebanon on January 1, 1862. Cold January rains made the roads a muddy quagmire that was almost impassable. Troops slogged along in ankle-deep mud, and artillery carriages sank in to their hubs and had to be man-handled forward. The march was slowed to a snail's pace, and for an eight day period no more than five miles a day could be achieved. Finally, on January 17, the army arrived at a point ten miles north of the Confederate fortifications and ten miles west of Somerset, variously known by the locals as Logan's Cross Roads, Fishing Creek, and Mill Springs. Thomas established a camp at this site as he prepared for a junction with Schoepf's brigade, and waited for his rear guard to catch up with the main body before resuming offensive operations against the enemy. Picketts were thrown out to guard against surprise from the Confederates, and word was sent to Shoepf to send three of his regiments to Mill Springs at once. While he waited for the concentration of his forces, Thomas directed Colonel James B. Steedman, with his 14th Ohio Infantry, to capture or disperse an enemy supply train that was supposed to be foraging close to Steedman's camp.[19]

General Thomas Crittenden. During the Mill Springs campaign, he would fight against his brother, George Crittenden, who commanded the Confederate forces on that field (United States Army Military History Institute).

While Thomas's army was en route to Mill Springs a change had been made in the command of the Confederate forces in his front. Major General George B. Crittenden, brother of Thomas L. Crittenden, commander of Buell's 5th Division, was assigned to overall command of the Confederate forces in the vicinity of Somerset. Zollicoffer had ignored the wishes of Albert Sidney Johnston by advancing his command into Kentucky. With appropriate bravado, he announced: "People of Southeastern Kentucky. The brigade I have the honor to command is here for no other purpose but war upon those Northern hordes who with arms in their hands are attempting the subjugation of a sister Southern State."[20] By the time Crittenden arrived on the scene he found that the dice had already been cast: Zollicoffer's fortifications had been constructed with the Cumberland River at their back, and the Confederates now were faced with a Union army to their front. Crittenden was placed in an unenviable position, not of his own making, and with few reasonable choices.[21]

A few days prior to the arrival of Thomas's advance guard General Crittenden had held a council of war with his regimental and brigade commanders to canvass their opinions as to what the army should do next. The Cumberland River was in flood stage because of the same heavy rains Thomas's men had slogged through in their advance, and the Confederates did not possess the necessary means to convey the army across the river in the face of an enemy attack. All present agreed that the camp could not be held against a serious assault by the force Thomas would be able to bring against them once he had merged his army with Schoepf's force. The only viable solution was to attack Thomas before he could meet for a junction with Schoepf, and while his own main body was not yet consolidated. Only by striking before Thomas was fully prepared could Crittenden hope to salvage victory from the tenuous situation he had inherited from Zollicoffer. His regimental and brigade commanders agreed with this decision, and orders were issued to put the campaign in motion. The appointed time for the advance was set for midnight on January 18.[22]

Crittenden's army marched out to meet Thomas with eight regiments of infantry, two of cavalry, and a few pieces of artillery, or some 6,250 men in all. The regiments were considerably below full strength, mostly due to sickness in the ranks. George P. Faw, a member of the 29th Tennessee Infantry, gave insight just how severe the problem of absent men in the army was in a letter to his brother. "Our Regiment is much reduced by sickness," he wrote. "We have about 5 hundred men in camp and 300 at home."[23] Even so, Crittenden's force would have a numerical superiority to Thomas's, owing to the fact that Shoepf's brigade was caught on the wrong side of Fishing Creek, and some of the rear regiments in the march were still plodding along in the muddy mire trying to reach the Union position. In all, Thomas would have only about 4,000 troops on hand with which to resist the Confederates when Crittenden decided to make the advance, but more were trudging in every hour. By the time the Confederates would be able to launch an attack the Federal force would number some 4,400 men.

The Confederates slogged their way forward some eleven miles to Thomas's position, through a heavy rain and the resulting mud. General Crittenden fortified himself against the cold through the use of spirits, and he did such a commendable job of it that he ended up being intoxicated and unfit for command. Zollicoffer would have to lead the army in its campaign after all. George C. Porter, a member of the 20th Tennessee Infantry, left an account of the march stating that the "night was dark and the road softened by the rainfall rendered the march slow and difficult. The batteries, distributed at different parts of the line, were constantly miring and lengthened the column several miles. As the movement was intended to be a surprise, the plan adopted by the commanding general was for the regiments to assail the enemy as soon as he was reached."[24] Crittenden had planned for a pre-dawn assault, but the column was so slowed by the weather that they did not arrive at Thomas's position until about daylight, at 6:30 A.M. At that hour, the 1st Kentucky Cavalry, which had been posted in advance of the camp, sighted the Confederates and sounded the alarm. Musket fire erupted from both sides as the Union pickets gave ground and retired upon the main body. As George Porter phrased it: "The enemy was neither divided, as supposed, nor surprised, as expected. General Zollicoffer, whose brigade was in the front, formed his line of battle, placing the Fifteenth Mississippi and the Twentieth Tennessee on the right of the road.... These were the only forces ready for the advance. An Indiana regiment was already in line and awaited the attack."[25]

The Indiana regiment Porter spoke of was the 10th Indiana Infantry, under the command of Colonel Mahlon D. Manson. Along with the soldiers in the 10th Indiana was an elderly civilian by the name of Edwin B. Wood. Wood had tried to enlist in the regiment the previous August, but had been denied admittance because of his advanced age. Nevertheless, he had accompanied the unit into the field, had been given a uniform and a musket, and had done the service of a soldier for five months without pay. Now, he was fighting on the front line as a true citizen-soldier. He would survive a close call when a Confederate buck shot pierced his jacket but failed to penetrate his breast.[26]

Thomas had formed his line of battle behind some trees and brush with the Hoosiers on the right and Colonel Speed S. Fry's 4th Kentucky Infantry on the left, supported by guns of the 1st Ohio Light Artillery. Firing became general along the line as the opposing forces came together. William H. Honnell, chaplain of the 1st Kentucky Cavalry, said, "The darkness of the morning was increased by the heavy rain and dense smoke of the battle, so that it became difficult to distinguish the battle line." Unknown to Porter and the rest of the 20th Tennessee, lost from view through the smoke and haze, the 16th Alabama Infantry was also on the field, far to the right, attempting to skirt the left flank of the 4th Kentucky. They were stopped in their tracks by fire from the 1st Ohio Light Artillery.[27]

Thomas, dressed for the first time in his new brigadier general's uniform, was calmly addressing his men and putting the regiments into line. Honnell stated that Thomas and "Capt. Joseph Breckinridge sat on their horses twenty steps only to the rear, with limbs, cut from trees overhead, falling upon them." When Thomas was informed that the regiments in front were beginning to run low on ammunition, he ordered "Tell them to hold the line, that McCook is coming up on their right."[28] Colonel Daniel L. McCook was leading his 3rd Brigade of the 9th Ohio Infantry and 2nd Minnesota Infantry into line, to assume a position on the front line while the 10th Indiana and 4th Kentucky replenished their cartridge boxes. One soldier in the 2nd Minnesota told how "we started through a thick piece of woods and came up to the enemy just as the 19th [10th] Indiana was retreating [withdrawing to draw ammunition]. The enemy was advancing with fixed bayonets, but the Minnesota boys came up to them with an Indian yell and such a volley as there was poured upon them for about 40 minutes, was never before heard. When the enemy gave way for us, we were so close to each other that some of our boys pulled their guns out of their hands. There was nothing but a fence between us. Fortunate for our side, they shot too high."[29]

Colonel Fry's regiment received the needed ammunition and quickly returned to the front. Along the way, they were greeted by a mounted officer dressed in a light-colored raincoat and accompanied by an aide. The officer rode straight toward Colonel Fry and his men, and when he got within hailing distance, he cautioned Fry against firing on his own men. The officer was General Zollicoffer, and he had mistaken the 4th Kentucky to be one of his own regiments. Fry was in undress uniform, and by the time Zollicoffer had ridden to within touching distance of him the mistake became clear. Fry responded, "I do not intend to fire upon our men," at which time Zollicoffer turned his horse and began riding back toward his own lines. Though he made no comment, Zollicoffer had obviously seen the uniforms of the men in front of him and realized his mistake. The Federals were still uncertain of the true identity of the officers in front of them until Zollicoffer's aide, Lieutenant Fogg, drew his pistol and fired in the direction of Colonel Fry, killing his horse. Fry returned the fire with his pistol, and was immediately joined by the muskets of his surrounding men. Zollicoffer and Fogg both fell from their horses, shot dead by the fearful volley.[30] Most contemporary reports credited Fry as having been the one to deliver the fatal bullet to Zollicoffer's heart, but Chaplain Honnell, who examined the body, casts doubts on that commonly held belief. "As there were three wounds on his body, and only one of them of immediately deadly effect, and that by a large ball," it was doubtful that Fry's pistol shot was actually the one that killed the general.[31]

The Confederates continued to press the attack, despite the fact that their field commander had been shot down, but the effort seemed doomed to failure. About half of the six Tennessee regiments in the command had been armed with antiquated flintlock muskets. When fired at a range of only 200 yards, the balls fell woefully short of their targets. The rain further complicated the situation, making it difficult or impossible for the flints to fire charges and discharge the muskets. Some members of the 20th Tennessee vainly attempted to fire their weapons half a dozen times before smashing them against trees and fence posts in utter frustration.[32] Lieutenant Baille Peyton, of Gallatin, Tennessee, stood alone in front of the Union line, defiantly challenging the Yankees to fight him. He resolutely declined all offers to surrender himself and was shot dead where he stood.[33]

Thomas directed a flank movement against the Confederate right, and Sergeant J.N. Haggard, of the 1st Tennessee Infantry (Union), said "we was ordered to flank the Rebels on their right which we did. They shot their cannons at us but did not hurt us. We intered [sic] the field in time of the fight and raised a yell, and you ought to see those tories throw down their guns and run." Another Union soldier witnessed "Our artillery and rifles did the work. We threw shell and grape and canister so fast that they could not stand it."[34] Without overall leadership, and handicapped in their ability to fight, the Confederates lost the impetus of their attack and some of the men began to fall back. The firing was hot on both sides. Colonel Fry had a ball pass so near to his left temple that it brushed his hair, and another round pierced his clothing without hitting his body. A captured Confederate told him, "So many of us pointed our guns directly at you, I congratulate you that you are still alive, but you must be mighty hard to shoot." Another Confederate from Tennessee took advantage of the confusion to change sides and joined Fry's men. He picked up the musket of a fallen Federal and fought the rest of the battle against the men he had so recently served with, taking particular pleasure in shooting the officer who had forced him to join the Southern army.[35]

A number of Confederates took shelter behind some log huts and outhouses to their rear and attempted to rally and make a stand. By this point, the fighting had been going on for about an hour. Thomas had no intention of allowing the enemy to reform, and he immediately ordered his battle line forward in a bayonet charge. Colonel McCook, though having his horse shot out from under him and sustaining a flesh wound in the leg himself, led his 3rd Brigade (9th Ohio and 2nd Minnesota) forward "with fixed bayonet and loaded guns. They charged up the hill against the Mississippi Tigers (15th Mississippi Infantry) who were behind a fence. They shoved their bayonets through the fence when the devils up and used their legs. Then the old Dutchman [McCook, who was not German, though most of the members of his 9th Ohio were] gave the order, fire, and the rebels fell like grass before the wind and the victory was ours."[36]

The advance of Thomas's line broke the back of all Confederate resistance. The fire of the 9th Ohio Battery only added to the weight of the assault being launched by the Federals. Private Joseph Durfee said "We fired our shells in earnest. One of them struck a stub, and, bursting, killed 10 and wounded 8. I saw and counted them. Finally, the cry 'They flee,' was heard and we followed in the rear of the infantry."[37] Indeed, the Southern lines were breaking, and a panic was beginning to seize upon the Confederate troops, many of whom were throwing down their inferior flintlocks and fleeing the field. Trooper Robert Deaderick of the 4th Tennessee Cavalry Battalion (Confederate) related: "The infantry broke ranks. I do not know what regiment made the break. We were ordered to fall back some distance and try to stop the infantry, who were leaving, but in this we failed. Retreat was then ordered. We were to cover the retreat, and this we did by allowing the infantry to go in front of the retreat."[38]

Thomas allowed his men to stop for a brief respite while they refilled their depleted cartridge boxes, and then took up the pursuit. It was now about 8:00 A.M., and the battle had been raging for approximately one and one half hours. When the Federals were once more thrown forward, only scattered musketry fire came from Confederate stragglers and their rear guard. Rebel prisoners, mostly men who had been wounded and could not keep up with the retreat, were brought into the fold, as the Union troops tried to overtake the fleeing foe. But the Federals were experiencing difficulties of their own during the chase. The rain had spoiled the rations the men were carrying in their haversacks, and they had been issued nothing further to eat. Already tired from the fighting and now from the pursuit, they were also battling the effects of the hunger pangs that gnawed at their stomachs with each forward step. But on they marched, for ten miles, until they came upon the fortified Confederate camp at Beach Grove, on the Cumberland River.

Thomas ordered forward his artillery and began to shell the position. A steamer was seen crossing the river, and it drew the immediate attention of the gunners. Unknown to the Federals, it was filled with Confederate officers who were trying to gain the relative safety of the opposite shore. Thomas examined the strength of the enemy position and determined that it was too strong to risk making a frontal assault against. Darkness was allowed to fall with the Confederates molested only by the Federal big guns. It was during this time that Thomas was accused of making the only mistake of the war thus far, when he neglected to send forward a surrender demand to the Confederates huddled in the camp. When Colonel Fry asked him that evening why he neglected to do so, Thomas replied, "Hang it all, Fry, I never once thought of it."[39] Later that night, Thomas reconsidered and felt that the retreating Confederates "did our cause more good by their terror spread over Middle and East Tennessee, than all who had been taken in and held as prisoners of war."[40]

The Confederates used the cover of darkness to extricate the remainder of their army to the Tennessee shore by using several flatboats Crittenden had commandeered. Only the men themselves could be saved. Artillery, horses, camp equipment, all were to be left behind for the victorious Federals. Trooper Deaderick said:

> I was told by one of the officers to have everything I could carry of most value, that we would cross the river that night. After 12 o'clock we were ordered to the river, and after some time waiting on the bank were ordered to dismount, leave our horses and make our way across in the steamboat or flats; but our company concluded by whipping their horses into the river; they wanted to swim across, but in this we failed. I told our captain that as our horses would not swim because of the river being up, and the night dark, I would swim mine and break the way for the rest, and probably they would follow. I therefore stripped myself and horse, gave my clothes to the rest of the boys to guard and carry across on the boat; jumped on my horse and rode him in, but trying to turn his head up the river to keep him from the bushes, which were very thick, he got himself tangled in the bushes, threw me off and both swam to bank. I then put on my clothes, hitched my horse, took my blankets, etc., got on the steamer and crossed the river.[41]

By morning, Crittenden had been successful in extricating all of his men, and an empty camp lay before the Federals. Private James Baker of the 1st Ohio Battery recorded:

> The next morning, the 14th Ohio advanced under cover of our guns and found their camp entirely deserted. We advanced and took possession of their winter quarters on this side of the river and began to shell them on the other, but soon discovered that they were gone. I have heard of soldiers plundering an enemies [sic] camp, but now I know what it means. We, the artillery, took the center, the infantry the right and left wings, and in we went like a swarm of hornets, taking everything before us. We have annihilated an entire army, captured their camp, 14 pieces of artillery, a considerable amount of ammunition, 125 wagons loaded with baggage and about 1,500 horses and mules. Their army can never be collected again.... We have taken some of the nicest clothing I ever saw, broadcloth coats worth from five to twenty dollars a piece. I got a satin vest worth five dollars, a shirt worth a dollar and a half, and a silver handled stiletto, besides a number of other things. The amount number of killed and wounded I have not ascertained.[42]

In his official record, Thomas addressed the cost of the battle, and the losses inflicted on the enemy. Union casualties were placed at 29 killed and 208 wounded, for a total of 237. On the Confederate side, 192 had been slain, 309 were wounded, and 157 had been taken prisoner, adding up to 658. The Confederate threat to southeastern Kentucky had been thrown back, and the Union had received its first major victory of the war in the west. The South had lost two generals: Zollicoffer through his death, and Crittenden by virtue of his being disgraced because of his intoxication during the battle. The Southern force had been routed and dispersed throughout east Tennessee, and the Cumberland Gap was once more open to a vigorous campaign by the Federals. George Thomas had been the architect of the success, and was celebrated as a hero throughout the Northern press. He was not to enjoy the congratulations or appreciation of his superiors, however. Though four of his subordinates received their stars for their participation in the campaign, Thomas was not even mentioned by name in the official order of thanks from the War Department that was issued to the troops. No laurels were to be placed on his head by the administration, and no official demonstration of thanks was forthcoming. He would have to settle for finally winning the approval of Congressman Maynard, who declared, "You have undoubtedly fought the great battle of the war."[43]

Part of the reason for the apparent lack of appreciation shown Thomas by the administration may have come from his immediate superior. Buell believed that rewards to victorious commanders must be "treated with very great caution," since they tended to "produce jealousies and dissatisfaction in a regular army, and, composed as ours is, may lead to a most injurious condition of things." Because of this view of official praise, Buell counseled that battle rewards be "conferred exclusively by brevets," and his praise to an officer who he felt was merely doing his duty was indeed scant.[44]

General Crittenden tried in vain to assert that he had faced a Federal army that was superior to his by almost three to one, but rumors of his drunkenness filtered back to the Confederate capital. One Richmond diarist noted "It is already circulated here that he is very intemperate and that it was known when he was appointed. I fear it is too true." Allegations were made questioning his loyalty because of the fact his brother served under Buell, commanding a division in the Federal army. Jefferson Davis even came under attack from the media and political adversaries for his role in appointing him to command. In the end, there was little Crittenden could do but submit to the public censure. In October of 1862 he would finally succumb to the effects of his poor judgment at Mill Springs and resign his commission as major general in the Confederate army.[45]

Chapter Seven

Early Battles in the West

The victory at Mill Springs had destroyed the right flank of Albert Sidney Johnston's defensive line in Kentucky. On February 6, Brigadier General Ulysses S. Grant breached the left of the Confederate line when he captured Fort Henry, Tennessee, on the Tennessee River. Ten days later, Grant captured Fort Donelson, Tennessee, and its 16,000 man garrison, on the Cumberland River, and the left flank of Johnston's grand defensive line was unhinged. General McClellan had been prodding Buell to send Thomas on a thrust into east Tennessee in order to secure that region and achieve a pet project of the administration. With the recent developments, Buell saw the possibility that all of Tennessee might fall into his hands, and made no plans to order Thomas into the mountains at Cumberland Gap. Instead, he informed Thomas that General Stephen Carter's brigade would be sufficient to deal with the Confederates in East Tennessee. The bulk of Thomas's division was to cooperate with Buell in a campaign against General Johnston's position at Bowling Green. President Lincoln, however, was still pushing upon his commander the need to occupy east Tennessee and free the Unionist citizens there from the yoke of Confederate control. In a message to Buell, he asked "Could not a cavalry force under General Thomas on the Upper Cumberland dash across, almost unmolested, and cut the railroad at or near Knoxville, Tennessee?"[1] Buell remained unmoved. So far as he was concerned, the elimination of Johnston's army would accomplish all that the President desired by eliminating Confederate influence throughout the state.

As Buell consolidated his forces for a move on Bowling Green, Johnston, reacting to the disasters at Forts Henry and Donelson, anticipated his plans and acted accordingly. With the flanks of his line now in shambles, he decided to withdraw his army to Nashville, eliminating all threats to Kentucky, and leaving a large portion of Tennessee open to Union occupation. General McClellan altered his orders to Buell for a campaign against east Tennessee and directed him to march his army for a junction with Grant's Army of the Tennessee for a joint operation against Nashville. Once Johnston had been forced out of the city, the combined Union forces were then to fan out into Alabama and Mississippi, cutting the railroads and disrupting the enemy lines of supply and communication. By the time Thomas reported to Buell at Louisville, Brigadier General Ormsby Mitchell had already taken Bowling Green and was marching toward Nashville. The rest of Buell's army was already en route to join him, proceeding up the Cumberland River by flatboat.[2]

Jefferson Davis was also reacting to the crisis in the west. He dispatched General P.G.T. Beauregard to Johnston as his second in command. Beauregard first went to Jackson, Mississippi, where he gathered together 10,000 men from Braxton Bragg's forces at Mobile, Alabama, 5,000 men from Louisiana, Major General Leonidas Polk's command from Columbus, and

Major General William J. Hardee's command from Arkansas. Beauregard organized the army into four corps, with Polk commanding the 1st, Bragg the 2nd, and Hardee the 3rd. The 4th Corps was originally assigned to General Crittenden, but the charges of drunkenness at Mill Springs caused the assignment to go to John C. Breckinridge instead. Beauregard moved the army he was gathering from Jackson to Corinth, Mississippi, in anticipation of a junction with Johnston. In all, there would be some 44,000 men available to Johnston when he and Beauregard joined forces.[3]

Thomas's division was assigned to the rear of Buell's army when it moved out for Nashville, owing to the fact that it had already fought a battle at Mill Springs. The divisions of Nelson, McCook, Crittenden, and Wood would lead the way, in that order. By the time Thomas's men were embarking on vessels to make the trip to Nashville, word came that the city had fallen to Nelson's division without a fight on February 23.[4] Johnston considered the place to be indefensible, as it had never been fortified, and had retreated into Mississippi to join forces with Beauregard's army in the vicinity of Corinth. Thomas and the 1st Division finally reached Nashville on March 4, 1862. Buell had been spending his time since the fall of Nashville constructing fortifications and organizing his supply lines. Finally, on March 16, he was ready to undertake the next phase of the campaign, and join forces with Grant's army in a concerted push against Corinth. Once more, Nelson's division was in the lead and Thomas's was bringing up the rear. The rendezvous point was to be on the west bank of the Tennessee River, at a place called Pittsburgh Landing. The site was only twenty miles north of Corinth, and had been chosen by General Sherman, who was in command of Grant's advance. Despite the fact that they were in such proximity to the enemy, neither Grant nor Sherman thought of constructing earthworks or fortifying their position. Instead, they simply made camp and awaited the arrival of the Army of the Ohio.

Grant had only recently gotten back into the good graces of his superiors. Despite the fact that he had become a national hero after the fall of Forts Henry and Donelson, his immediate superior, Henry Halleck, had relieved him of command on March 3. Halleck stated his reason for doing so stemmed from Grant's misconduct, and cited rumors of drunkenness, and Grant's inability to provide him with information concerning the strength of his army as the primary factors in making his decision. Halleck did not state that he had been upstaged by a subordinate, or that he planned to assume command of the army himself before the next great battle so that he could garner the credit for the victory that was sure to come. Brigadier General Charles F. Smith was appointed by Halleck to replace Grant, but pressure from the administration forced Halleck to reinstate the hero of Fort Donelson to command on March 15.

Grant's Army of the Tennessee would have some 42,000 men spread out among the campsites at Pittsburgh Landing. Grant had not thought of erecting defensive works because "I regarded the campaign we were engaged in as an offensive one and had no idea that the enemy ... would take the initiative."[5] Besides, he was to be joined any day by Buell's Army of the Ohio, and the combined forces would give him a numerical superiority that Grant must have felt made it prohibitive for offensive operations on the part of the Confederates.

Buell's army was indeed on its way, but that was exactly the incentive that caused Johnston and Beauregard to initiate an aggressive campaign. General Mitchell had been sent on another independent mission. He had orders to make for Murfreesboro to repair the railroad at that place for use by Buell's army for supply purposes. He was then to proceed into Alabama in an effort to cut Johnston's supply lines from the east. Buell's main body made rapid progress toward reaching Grant until it arrived at Columbia, Tennessee. The Confederates had destroyed the bridge over the Duck River, which was then in flood stage, and Buell, having no pontoons or boats, was forced to wait for the flood waters to recede before he was able to cross his troops. After the opposite shore had been reached, the march was further delayed by heavy rains that turned the roads to quagmires and all but stopped the advance of the supply trains and artillery.

By April 4, the road ahead was once more clear, and the Army of the Ohio was prepared to make the final portion of the march toward Pittsburgh Landing. But Buell's was not the only army making a rapid march in the direction of Grant. Albert Sidney Johnston had begun his offensive on April 3, when he pointed his columns north and marched out of Corinth to try to redeem the failing fortunes of the Confederacy in the west. Johnston issued a battle order to the troops: "I have put you in motion to offer battle to the invaders of your country. You can but march to a decisive victory.... Remember the fair, broad, abounding land, the happy homes, and the ties that would be desolated by your defeat."[6]

By April 4, the Confederate army had reached a position within striking distance of Grant's army, and the Confederates went into camp with orders to launch a pre-dawn attack on the following morning. But the Southern offensive started to come unraveled when the troops attempted to assume their assigned places in the battle line. A heavy rain necessitated that preparations could not get under way until dawn. The corps of Bragg, Polk, and Hardee had become intermingled during the march, and further delays were experienced in deploying the troops. Precious hours were wasted sorting out the confusion and it was late afternoon before the army was finally in readiness to attack. The Confederates were now within two miles of the Union camp, and there had been sporadic firing between Rebel skirmishers and the Federal outposts. Beauregard was convinced that they had lost the element of surprise and the attack should be called off. He favored a return to Corinth, but Johnston overruled. "We will attack at daylight tomorrow," he said. "I would fight them if they were a million."[7]

Johnston launched his attack on the morning of April 6 and caught the Union forces completely by surprise. Grant was at his headquarters at Savannah, several miles away, so he was not even with the army when it was attacked. Sherman held the right of the Union line at Shiloh Church. To his left were the divisions of Brigadier Generals John McClernand, Stephen A. Hurlburt, and W.H.L. Wallace. In the center, and advanced from this line, was the division of Brigadier General Benjamin Prentiss. Johnston launched his attack by corps, with Hardee in the lead, followed by Bragg, Polk, and Breckinridge. The flanks of the Union army were driven from the field after bitter fighting, but Prentiss, reinforced by Wallace, held fast in the center, despite repeated attacks by Bragg's Corps. Prentiss's stand at the Hornet's Nest was buying time for Grant and Sherman to reform their lines and resist the further advance of the Confederates. At approximately 2:30 P.M., General Johnston was mortally wounded, and the command devolved upon Beauregard. It was 5:30 before the issue was decided at the Hornet's Nest, and the 2,000 Union survivors finally surrendered. Prentiss had held his position for seven hours, and had prevented the Confederates from driving the Army of the Tennessee into the river for which it was named.

By the time Beauregard had dispensed with Prentiss and renewed the advance, the Federals had put together an improvised line with the Tennessee River to their backs. Grant had posted 53 pieces of artillery, and was supported by the fire of Union gunboats in the river. Grant had also received much-needed reinforcements: Buell's army was finally on the scene, and Nelson's division had been ferried across the river and placed on Grant's left flank. The division of Major General Lew Wallace, which had become lost on the field and had taken no part in the battle thus far, had also recently returned to the fold and was positioned on the Union right flank. Beauregard's men were exhausted and intermingled by the time the final push was made against the Union line, and it sputtered out as darkness brought a close to the fearful day of combat.

During the night, Buell's army continued to cross the river, and by the morning of April 7, Grant had 39,000 effectives with which to face Beauregard's battered and bloodied army. The Federals surged forward, sweeping the gray-clad lines before them, and regained all of the ground that had been lost the previous day. In the middle of the afternoon, Beauregard made one last attempt to reverse the fortunes of the battle when he counterattacked at White Oaks Pond. When this attack was repulsed, Beauregard ordered a general withdrawal of his entire army, and retired in the direction of Corinth.[8]

Thomas and his 1st Division had missed the battle, being kept in reserve on the Kentucky side of the river. His command had not been bloodied by the fighting that was the most severe ever witnessed on the North American continent up to that time. More men had fallen during these two April days than had been lost in the eight years of the American Revolution. Casualty rates amounted to about 25 percent of the total number of men engaged, a staggering figure by any standard. The Union suffered a total of 13,573 casualties in securing the victory. The Confederates sustained 10,699 casualties in suffering the defeat.[9]

Beauregard was allowed to withdraw his battered army from the field unimpeded by the victorious Federals. Grant felt his own army too badly used to mount a pursuit, and allowed the men two days to rest before taking up the chase. Finally, on April 8, Sherman's division spearheaded the pursuit of the fleeing Confederates, but the advance was called off when Sherman ran into the Confederate rear guard, under the command of Lieutenant Colonel Nathan Bedford Forrest, at Fallen Timbers.[10]

Thomas's division was finally brought across the river two days after the battle. His men stacked arms on the field and pitched in to help with the gruesome task of gathering the dead and wounded. Sherman observed, "Dead bodies of men in blue and gray lay around thick, side by side." McClernand said, "Within a radius of 200 yards of my headquarters tent the ground was literally covered with dead." A newspaper correspondent counted 200 dead Confederates in a one acre field, and in another area measuring fifty feet square were found thirty dead men and thirty dead horses from a Southern battery. Beauregard had sent a message to Grant on April 8 requesting permission to bury his dead, but had been informed by the Union commander that the task had already been completed, owing to the warm temperatures and rapid decomposition of the bodies. In truth, the job of burying the dead would not be finished until April 11. The dead Confederates were buried in numerous long trenches, with as many as 147 soldiers to a common grave. The Union dead were treated with more care, though they were also buried together in mass graves. One Union soldier assigned to burial detail wrote his parents, "I dread tomorrow. Burying those unfortunate Rebel dead. They are swollen and smell so awful bad and terrible many of them. I do not see how I can stand it."

Conditions for the wounded were little better. Some 8,400 Union wounded and 1,000 captured Confederate wounded endured pain and privation almost beyond the limits of human endurance. Doctors were in short supply, medicines were almost nonexistent, and food and shelter were almost impossible to obtain. Many wounded were forced to lay in the mud caused by rains that came on April 8 and 9, without medical attention, and with nothing to eat or drink since before the battle. Thomas's men assisted the rest of the army in trying to bring order out of this chaos, and in doing what they could to alleviate the suffering of their wounded comrades.[11] One officer in Thomas's command noted, "None who participated in it or witnessed it will ever forget it."[12]

General Halleck did not arrive at Pittsburgh Landing until after the Battle of Shiloh had already been fought. One of the first orders of business for Halleck was the promotion of officers he felt worthy of commendation for their contributions to the victory. He forwarded his recommendation that both Sherman and Thomas be elevated to the rank of major general of volunteers, even though Thomas had taken no part in the battle. On April 25, 1862, Thomas was duly approved to receive the rank of major general, and Halleck placed him in command of the right wing of his combined army, with Grant being assigned as his second in command. The reasons for this situation were numerous. Thomas was obviously receiving a tardy recognition for his victory at Mill Springs, as he had contributed nothing to the Shiloh campaign. Halleck was taking the opportunity of issuing a reprimand to Grant because of his lack of caution in allowing Johnston's army to surprise him at Shiloh. He was also punishing the general over allegations that he had "resumed his former bad habits" and had been drinking heavily. Halleck saw an opportunity to replace Grant with Thomas and he did not hesitate to do so. Thomas would act as Grant's superior when Halleck marched the army forward to challenge the Confederates at Corinth, and this embarrassment, though not of Thomas's making, would stick with Grant for the remainder of the war.[13]

Henry Halleck was considered by many of his contemporaries to be a textbook general, and not a leader of men. Indeed, he had authored a standard military text at the age of thirty-one. It was one of the reasons for the high esteem with which he was held by the administration. With his soldiers, however, he was commonly known as "Old Brains," a nick-name that was used derisively in referring to his lack of competence as a field commander. Halleck gathered to himself every available Union unit that could be spared from his sphere of influence. By the time he was done, an impressive army of some 120,000 men had been brought together to face a Confederate army of less than half that size at Corinth. Halleck divided his army into four parts: the right wing under Thomas, the center under Buell, the left under Brigadier General John Pope, and the reserve under McClernand. Even with this massive force, Halleck seemed hesitant to bring the Confederates to battle, and it was not until May 6 that he finally ordered Thomas's wing forward on the 25 mile march to Corinth. Halleck cautioned Thomas to be on guard for any offensive movements by the enemy, and was so fearful himself of a Confederate counterstroke that he pushed his army forward at a snail's pace. Short distances were covered each day, followed by extensive digging of field fortifications each evening. So slow was Halleck's advance that it took him almost three weeks to traverse the distance of 25 miles between his starting point and the Confederate works. The officers and soldiers under his command took notice of the manner in which they were being led and cried out against the timidity of Halleck's actions. One disgusted officer observed Halleck "jogging along the lines with a tall army hat on, minus cord and tassel, his head thrown forward, his shoulders up and jerking about; if he had only a pair of saddle bags, 'Old Brains' would have been the beau ideal of a country doctor."[14]

The Confederates had been keeping a close eye on the agonizingly slow movements of the Federal juggernaut headed their way. The disparity in numbers between the opposing armies dictated that they could do little more than harass the irresistible invading force, but this was sufficient to keep Halleck in a cautious, hesitant state of mind. Beauregard had been able to replace his losses from Shiloh through the addition of the commands of Earl Van Dorn and Sterling Price, but that still left him with only 50,000 men, of all arms, with which to face Halleck's overwhelming force. There was really little for Beauregard to do. If he remained in Corinth he risked the possibility of being surrounded and losing his entire army in a siege. That eventuality would mean that two-thirds of all the effective military manpower in the region would be taken off the board, leaving an area from Knoxville to Louisiana to be defended by a force smaller than any one of Halleck's four wings.

On May 25, Beauregard held a council of his officers to discuss the situation and seek their opinions about the future movements of the army. All present agreed with their commander that the only sensible thing to do was to evacuate the town and withdraw the army fifty miles south, to Tupelo, Mississippi. From that date to May 29, the Confederates stealthfully slipped out of Corinth without alerting the Federals as to their intentions. Beauregard was able to convince Halleck that he was preparing for an offensive using elaborate ruses, like running empty trains into the town, and having the men cheer as if they were being reinforced. The deceptions worked so well that General Pope reported to Halleck that he expected to be attacked on the morning of May 29, the very day the evacuation of Corinth was complete. Halleck did not pursue Beauregard to Tupelo. Corinth had been his objective, not the Confederate army, and "Old Brains" was quite content to claim a tremendous victory because of his capture of the town. Instead of initiating an active campaign to capture Vicksburg, Mississippi, or secure the whole of Tennessee for the Union, he occupied himself by constructing intricate defensive fortifications around Corinth. One positive result that came from the campaign was the fall of Memphis, Tennessee. Beauregard felt the city to be untenable once his army withdrew to Tupelo, and he ordered it evacuated. Memphis and Fort Pillow fell into Federal hands, opening the navigation of the Mississippi River as far south as Vicksburg.[15]

Once the army was safely in Tupelo, Beauregard, who had been suffering the effects of ill health for some time, decided to take a sick leave to Bladon Springs, Alabama, to recover his health. President Davis viewed his departure from the army to be akin to desertion and replaced him with Braxton Bragg as commander of the Army of Tennessee. When Beauregard learned of his replacement he wrote to his aide, "If the country be satisfied

General Henry Halleck. During the Corinth campaign, he relieved Grant from army command and replaced him with Thomas. Though Grant was eventually reinstated, the incident caused him to harbor a grudge against Thomas for the remainder of the war (United States Army Military History Institute).

to have me laid on the shelf by a man who is either demented or a traitor to his high trust—well, let it be so. I require rest & will endeavor meanwhile by study and reflection to fit myself better for the dark hours of our trial, which, I foresee, are yet to come. As to my reputation, if it can suffer by anything that living specimen of gall & hatred can do—why it is not then worth preserving.... My consolation is, that the difference between 'that Individual' and myself is—that if he were to die today, the whole country would rejoice at it—whereas, I believe, if the same thing were to happen to me, they would regret it."[16] When the Federal forces did finally move out of Corinth, they would be facing the third Confederate commander in as many months.

President Lincoln was responsible, at length, for stopping the digging around Corinth and setting in motion a campaign designed to actually help end the war. The president requested that Buell's army be sent to east Tennessee to secure Knoxville and Chattanooga. The Confederates kept one step ahead when President Davis ordered Braxton Bragg to occupy the strategic city of Chattanooga with his army before Buell could arrive. General Halleck was promoted to General-in-chief, to replace General McClellan, and was called away to Washington. He left George Thomas in command of the portion of the army that remained at Corinth. Thomas did not relish his post and requested to be relieved of command there. On June 10, his request was granted, and command of the Army of the Tennessee reverted back to U.S. Grant. General Pope was also sent east, and command of his Army of the Mississippi went to Major General Edward O.C. Ord. Within two weeks' time, Thomas was back at the head of his own 1st Division, serving under Buell. His first assignment was to fortify the city of Tuscumbia, Alabama, followed by repair work on the Memphis and Charleston Railroad. His troops were occupied with the railroad duty for about a month until they were relieved by a division of E.O.C. Ord's army in late July.[17]

Thomas marched his division to Dechard, Kentucky, where he reported for duty to Buell on August 7, 1862. He found his commander faced with numerous situations demanding his attention. Major General Edmund Kirby Smith was operating against Carter's force at Cumberland Gap. Brigadier General Nathan Bedford Forrest and Colonel John Hunt Morgan were active in the state with their cavalry detachments, destroying bridges in Buell's rear and threatening Nashville. Bragg was at Chattanooga with his army, and Buell had no idea what his intentions were, or where he intended to lead his army. Though Buell had more than enough men in his army to effectively deal with Bragg, he seemed more than willing to allow the Confederate commander to dictate the action, instead of forcing the issue himself by attacking the Confederate army, wherever it might be. Part of the reason for this was the need commanders felt to protect lines of supply and communication. Forrest's and Morgan's forays into the state served to paralyze the Union commander from assuming the offensive and taking the war to Bragg's army.

Governor Andrew Johnson had become so disillusioned by Buell's lack of action that he was advocating a change in command, and supported Thomas for the job. When Thomas reached Dechard, Buell handed him a letter from Johnson expressing his conviction that a change be made. Thomas read with horror what he perceived to be a slight against his immediate superior. Always loyal to a commander he felt was trying to do his duty, Thomas took pen in hand and wrote a response to Johnson: "... I most earnestly hope I may not be placed in the position, for several reasons. One particular reason is that we have never yet had a commander of any expedition who has been allowed to work out his own policy, and it is utterly impossible for the most able General in the World to conduct a campaign with success when his hands are tied, as it were by the constant apprehension that his plans may be interfered with at any moment.... I confidently assure you that Gen. Buell's dispositions will eventually free all Tennessee and go very far to crush the rebellion entirely."[18] What Thomas did not know at the time of his writing to Johnson was that his commander would vacillate for almost two months before engaging Bragg's army, and even then he did so only in response to Confederate actions.

Part of Buell's inactivity stemmed from misinformation deliberately given to him by the enemy. On July 12, Colonel Philip H. Sheridan visited some friends in the Confederate camp between Rienzi and Guntown, Mississippi. He was greeted by Colonel Joseph Wheeler;, Colonel E.D. Tracy, of the 19th Alabama Infantry; Captain T.M. Lenoir, a staff officer on General Bragg's staff; and Captain F.H. Robertson, of the Southern artillery. The group discussed a wide range of subjects, and the Confederates displayed a tendency to have loose tongues in regard to military affairs. They informed Sheridan that Bragg had no intention of undertaking offensive operations until after the harvest had been made, as the army was in need of sustenance for both men and horses. They told Sheridan that when the Southern army did move, it would go west, toward Holly Springs, Mississippi, and west Tennessee. Sheridan had no idea that this information was being deliberately planted with him, in hopes that the high command of the Union army would be deceived as to the real intentions of the Confederates.[19]

Bragg had already settled upon a plan of campaign that Buell should have anticipated, had he taken the time to look at a map and speculate upon his options based on the placement of Union forces. Grant, still at Corinth, had too strong an army for Bragg to attack in its fortified position. If he were to invade west Tennessee, as he led Buell to believe he would, Alabama and Georgia would be left open for Union invasion. A campaign against Nashville would place his army between Grant's and Buell's forces, either of which was stronger than his own. The only viable option Bragg had left to him was an invasion of central Tennessee, possibly resulting in a drive into Kentucky. Colonel Morgan's raids through his native Kentucky convinced the cavalry commander that the Bluegrass State was ready for the picking, and that its citizens would rise up to support a liberating Confederate army. He was able to successfully argue to Bragg that large numbers of recruits would rally to the Southern banner if he would only lead his army into Kentucky.[20] A victory in Kentucky could have the benefits of removing the seat of war from Tennessee, threatening the Northern state of Ohio, increasing the ranks of the Confederate army, and provisioning that army from the vast larder of Kentucky. But Buell was convinced that Bragg's main force was destined for west Tennessee, and could not be induced to alter his impressions even after E. Kirby Smith invaded eastern Kentucky with an army of some 15,000 men on August 14.[21] Buell considered Smith's movement to be nothing more than a feint, designed to draw his attention away from Bragg, and allowing that officer to operate freely in western Tennessee.

Thomas was not deceived by the planted information or by the actions of Kirby Smith. He had questioned some loyal residents and Negroes in McMinnville, Tennessee, and had divined Bragg's true intentions. He advised Buell, "The demonstration in this direction [Smith's] is to cover the advance of the enemy toward Kentucky."[22] Thomas suggested that the army be concentrated at McMinnville, the best possible position from which an advance into central Tennessee and Kentucky could be thwarted by the Federals. But Buell was in no mood to accept advice from his subordinate. He envisioned an attack from General Van Dorn's army in Alabama, in concert with a movement by Bragg, and he accordingly ordered Thomas to march his division to Altamont to guard against such an eventuality. Upon reaching his assigned position, Thomas notified Buell that Altamont did not contain the water and forage to subsist his division for one day. He informed his superior, "I deem it next to impossible [for Bragg] to march a large army across the mountains by Altamont," and reiterated that "The occupation of McMinnville, Sparta & Murfreesboro will in my opinion secure the Nashville & Chattanooga Railroad." If Thomas's dispositions had been adopted, Bragg could not have passed by Sparta without being forced to fight a battle at a disadvantage to himself.[23] Thomas returned to McMinnville but on August 30 he received orders to proceed to Murfreesboro. Thomas voiced the opinion that Buell was playing into Bragg's hands by uncovering the most direct route for an invasion of Kentucky, but he dutifully obeyed his orders. He had no sooner arrived at Murfreesboro than new orders directed him to march to Nashville to calm the fears of Governor Johnson, who also feared a Confederate thrust in that direction.

On the same day that Thomas was ordered to Murfreesboro, General E. Kirby Smith was scoring a singular victory over the Federal forces in Kentucky. He had marched his army into the eastern portion of the state on August 14 as part of a two-pronged attack. Bragg did not get his force in motion until a week later, when he marched toward Sparta, exactly as Thomas had predicted he would. Smith had bypassed the Union stronghold at Cumberland Gap. By August 29, his forces had reached Kingston, five miles south of Richmond, Kentucky. Confederate cavalry reported a strong force of Union infantry at the latter place, drawn up in line of battle and intending to make a stand. These were the brigades of Brigadier Generals Mahlon Manson and Charles Cruft, under the overall command of Manson.

On August 30, Smith advanced his army to attack the Federals at Richmond. As he was preparing his lines for the assault, General Manson took the initiative by attacking the right flank of Smith's vastly superior force. The Confederates held, and then counterattacked against the Union center, breaking the Union line and forcing them back:

> After driving the Federals some three or four miles, they made another stand. When we came up to where they were, the order to charge was again given, they staying long enough to give us only a volley or two, when they precipitately and in great disorder retreated again. We killed, wounded, and captured a great many of them, while they killed and wounded some of us. As fast as we could we followed them up.... It must have been about three o'clock in the afternoon when the Federals made their third and last stand, the spot they had selected for that purpose being in the little cemetery just at the outskirts of the town of Richmond, Ky. They sheltered themselves behind the tombstones. We had to approach them through a field of corn which was very tall and in full ear and was enclosed by a high rail fence.... The Federals showed strong and stubborn resistance; but seeing that we steadily advanced toward them, after giving us two or three rounds, they broke into a deep run, showing that they were in a wild and ungovernable panic. Then it was that we charged them with a double-quick, killing, wounding, and capturing many of them.[24]

General Manson attempted to retreat from the field, but Kirby Smith had ordered his cavalry to block off their escape route. Manson could not cut his way through the cavalry screen and was forced to surrender, along with approximately 3,000 men who were still with him. General William Nelson, the overall Union commander of the region, had arrived at Richmond during the Federal retreat, but there was nothing he could do to stay the disaster. He received a painful leg wound before gathering up what remnants of Manson's force he could find and retiring back to Lexington. The battle had been one of the most lopsided victories of the war for the Confederates. Smith's army had suffered casualties of only about 750 men, while it had inflicted losses on the Federals of 1,050 killed and wounded and 4,303 captured. The Confederates had also captured nine pieces of artillery, 10,000 stand of small arms, and a huge quantity of military stores.[25]

General Buell still failed to see the logic of Thomas's advice to guard against an invasion by Bragg's forces in central Kentucky. Though he was convinced that Smith and Bragg were working together in this campaign, he believed that Smith's purpose was to lure the main Federal army into chasing after him, leaving Bragg free to conduct operations against Nashville or in western Kentucky. On September 5, Bragg's army marched through Sparta and reached the Kentucky state line. As they passed over into the Bluegrass State, the men were greeted by a sign that had been nailed to a tree by members of the pioneer corps: "You now cross from Tennessee to Kentucky."[26] For the first time, Buell's eyes were opened to see the reality of the situation before him. Bragg had no intention of marching against Nashville, and was headed for the heart of Kentucky, just as Thomas had predicted.

Buell got his army in motion, cautiously shadowing the movements of the Confederates while he decided upon his own course of action. Governor Johnson, back in Nashville, was still not convinced, however. On September 14, two days after Bragg's army had arrived in Glasgow, Kentucky, Johnson sent the following message to Buell:

> It is all important that Major-General Thomas and his forces, as now assigned, should remain in Nashville. There is the utmost confidence in his bravery and capacity to defend Nashville against any odds. I am advised that, including your division of the army, there is not less than 75,000 men in Kentucky and the number increasing, so you will be enabled to meet Smith and Bragg successfully. I was reliably informed on Yesterday that a portion of Bragg's force were lingering about Carthage and the Cumberland River. Bragg, no doubt with them, daily informed as to the number of our forces passing into Kentucky and the force left here. If our strength is much reduced at this point they will be induced to attack Nashville as a matter of course. In conclusion I express the strong and earnest hope that the present assignment of forces under General Thomas for the defense of Nashville may not be disturbed.[27]

Buell appeased Johnson by leaving Thomas in Nashville for two weeks, during which time significant work was done to strengthen the fortifications. Thomas then detached Brigadier General James S. Negley, with 6,000 men, to remain in the city, while he marched to meet Buell with the remainder of his force. He finally caught up with his commander at Prewitt's Knob, Kentucky, several miles below Mumfordville, on September 24. Bragg had scored another lopsided victory at the latter place a little more than a week earlier, when he captured Colonel John T. Wilder's garrison force of 3,566 men, while sustaining only 714 casualties of his own.[28]

Both armies seemed to be headed in the direction of Louisville, but when Bragg veered off at Sonora on a course for his true destination of Frankfort, he left Buell an open road to march to Louisville. Thomas arrived there on September 27, and was greeted by serious denunciations of his superior. Governor Levi Morton of Indiana was in Louisville with several companies of newly recruited soldiers. He openly declared that his Indiana men would never serve under the likes of Buell. Grumbling also came from the men in the ranks, who had lost confidence in their commander and despaired of his leadership in the coming battle. The final straw seemed to come when General Nelson became embroiled in an altercation with Brigadier General Jefferson C. Davis that resulted in Davis's shooting Nelson dead in a Louisville hotel. Governor Morton exerted his influence to prevent Buell from prosecuting Davis, and it seemed to all that he had lost control of his army. Buell had certainly lost the support of a large number of citizens throughout the land. He was particularly vilified in Indiana, where the *Indianapolis Journal* ran an editorial enumerating Governor Morton's complaints against him, and outrageously going so far as to counsel Indiana troops to kill him if possible.[29]

The assassination of General William Nelson by General Jefferson C. Davis. Nelson's death caused a void in Union command and necessitated the appointment of a new corps commander for the Army of the Ohio (United States Army Military History Institute).

The War Department had been closely monitoring the situation in Kentucky, and Secretary Edwin Stanton acted on September 29, when he sent orders to Thomas directing him to relieve Buell and assume command of the army. This Thomas declined to do. According to Buell:

> In a little while General Thomas came to my room and stated his intention to decline the command. I answered that I could not consent to his doing so on any ground that was personal to me, and that if his determination was fixed I must be allowed to see the message he proposed to send. He then prepared the following dispatch to General Halleck: "Colonel McKibben handed me your dispatch placing me in command of the Department of the Tennessee. General Buell's preparations have been completed to march against the enemy, and I therefore respectfully ask that he may be retained in command. My position is very embarrassing, not being well informed as I should be as the commander of this army, and on the assumption of such a responsibility." I could make no personal objection to his reasons, but I encouraged him to accept the duty assigned to him, saying that nothing remained to be done but to put the army in motion, and that I would cheerfully explain my plans to him and give him all the information I possessed. He persisted, however, and the message went off.

Halleck responded that he had not issued the order, and had no power to revoke it. However, he would suspend its implementation while the question was being submitted to the War Department. Buell had received a stay of execution, and he used the time to initiate offensive operations intended to bring Bragg's army to battle.[30]

Thomas's refusal to assume command of the army raises many points to discuss. He was certainly well acquainted with the strength and disposition of the Federal army. He was also well informed as to the strategic situation that then existed in the state, as evidenced by the advice he had been giving Buell all along. In fact, events had proven that he had a much firmer grasp of the situation than his commander, and was better suited to react to the movements of the enemy. Thomas never questioned his own ability to lead the army, and he was more than qualified to do so. Why then did he decline to accept his appointment as army commander? The answer to this question can only be found in the character of the man. Thomas was loyal beyond question to any superior he felt was trying to do his duty, regardless of whether that officer's actions were contrary to the opinions he himself held. That, combined with his constant indulgence to guard against the unnecessary impugning of a brother officer's reputation, made it impossible for Thomas to accept the command, as a point of honor. He could take no part in destroying Buell's reputation, even if he had previously disagreed with his actions, because he was honor-bound to support his superior. Some years after the event, Thomas explained that he could not permit himself to be used "to do Buell an injury."[31] He had exhibited the same qualities when reporting on General Patterson's campaign in Virginia, though he had also disagreed with the actions of that officer. In Thomas's mind, his advancement could only come as a result of his own accomplishments, and not by climbing over the heads of his superiors. He was also unwilling to participate in anything he viewed to be political in nature, a stance he had taken ever since witnessing the unfair treatment General Taylor had received during the Mexican War. As such, he stood in sharp contrast to many of the officers he served with, and some he would later serve under.

When Buell marched his army out of Louisville in search of Bragg, Thomas was assigned the position of second in command of the Federal army. This effectively relegated him to a negligible role in the campaign, and denied him a field command. Buell's army of approximately 60,000 men was organized into three corps, commanded by Major Generals Alexander McCook, Thomas L. Crittenden, and Charles C. Gilbert. Gilbert was a newcomer to the army, and had been promoted by Major General Horatio Wright from captain in the inspector general's department to major general in command of General Nelson's old corps. The only problem was that Wright did not have the authority to grant such a promotion. President Lincoln informed him as such when he learned of the situation, but consented to grant Gilbert the rank of brevet brigadier general, pending the approval of Congress. Congress refused to act on the nomination, however, declining to approve Gilbert's promotion. When Buell's army reached Louisville, he found Gilbert dressed in the uniform of a major general, and assuming the responsibilities of that

General Charles Gilbert. The appointment of Gilbert to Corps command, despite the fact that his commission as a general officer was never confirmed by the Senate, was a source of embarrassment to the government (United States Army Military History Institute).

rank with Nelson's old corps. Having no reason to question the authenticity of his rank, Buell had taken him along on the march to engage Bragg as one of his corps commanders. Though Buell was unaware that Gilbert was impersonating a corps commander, Gilbert was certainly informed that his commission as a major general had been refused and that he was not entitled to occupy that position. This corps should rightly have been assigned to General Thomas, and the deception of Gilbert, and the resulting failure to assign Thomas to his place, would have terrible consequences in the upcoming battle.[32]

By October 8, 1862, Buell's army had made contact with the Confederates at Perryville, Kentucky. Buell issued orders not to bring on a general engagement until all of the Union army was up and in position. He planned to assume the offensive on October 9. But Bragg was not content to sit by and await Buell's attack. Kirby Smith's army had failed to join him, leaving him in the position of being outnumbered almost three to one, but Bragg nonetheless chose to be the aggressor on the field. On the afternoon of October 8, he threw his army against General McCook's corps, holding the left flank of the Union line. Gilbert's corps was to the right of McCook, holding the center, with Crittenden's corps serving as the right flank of the army. The impetus of the Confederate attack fell full-force upon McCook's men. The division on the far left, under the command of Brigadier General James S. Jackson, was severely mauled and driven back, with Jackson and one of his brigade commanders, Brigadier General William R. Terrill, being killed. Brigadier General Lovell H. Rousseau's division was next in line to Jackson's, and was also severely handled. They were still in the fight, but had suffered approximately 32.5 percent casualties in some of the most savage fighting to take place during the entire war.[33]

McCook was left to face the full wrath of the Confederates alone for two reasons. First, there was an atmospheric condition known as an acoustic shadow that prevented Buell from hearing the sounds of the battle, even though his headquarters was only four miles distant from the scene of the fighting. McCook, fighting for his life on the Federal left, did not bother to send a messenger to Buell requesting aid because he was sure that his commander would ride to the sound of the guns with relief for his corps. But owing to the acoustic shadow, Buell had no idea that his

General Don Carlos Buell. Because of an atmospheric oddity known as an acoustic shadow, Buell did not even know the Battle of Perryville was being fought until it was almost over, even though his headquarters were only a few miles removed from the field of engagement (United States Army Military History Institute).

army was being engaged, even though the sounds of the struggle could be heard clearly in Louisville, 70 miles away. It was not until 4:00 P.M., nearly three hours after the battle had commenced, that Buell was made aware of the desperate situation on his left flank and ordered Colonel Michael Goodling's brigade of Mitchell's division to the support of McCook's battered corps. Once apprised of the danger, he immediately sprang to action, but the situation was almost beyond his control by the time he became involved.[34]

The second reason McCook was allowed to face the Confederate army alone was the inaction of the corps commander who occupied the position in line to his immediate right. Gilbert became paralyzed by the Confederate attack because he feared an assault upon his own lines, and he therefore declined to come to McCook's assistance. His corps was reduced to the role of spectators to the battle, as the men in his battle line watched their comrades being slaughtered. A soldier in the 36th Illinois Infantry spoke for most of the men in Gilbert's corps when he said: "When Rousseau's line was broken, and the enemy's hosts were surging over the field, their advanced line fringed with fire, every glass was directed thitherward, and when our lines went down before the irresistible charge, many a prayer went up to heaven, 'God help our poor boys now!'"[35]

Gilbert's officers were pressing upon him to assist McCook, but the corps commander was unmoved. Colonel Nicholas Greusel was watching the carnage from Gilbert's line, unable to render much-needed support, when he turned to Captain Henry Hescock, in command of a battery of Missouri Light Artillery. "Captain Hescock," he said, "those fellows over yonder are using McCook's boys rather roughly. Can't you reach them with your shot?" Hescock elevated his cannon and attempted to get the range. Soon his shells were bursting amidst the advancing gray lines of the Confederates, tearing huge holes in their ranks with each explosion, amid the cheers of Gilbert's men. Greusel and Hescock acted on their own initiative, without orders from Gilbert, and were providing McCook with the only support he was to receive from Gilbert's corps. Hescock's fire proved to be highly effective, however, as 430 Confederate dead and wounded were later counted in the area he had been shelling.[36]

It can only be speculated what would have been the effect on the battle had Thomas been in command of the center corps in the line, instead of being attached to Crittenden's corps on the far right, and well removed from the scene of action. Based on his previous and subsequent actions, it can be readily assumed that he would have supported McCook with all his available force, however, and would have overpowered Bragg's attacking army. As it was, the imposter Gilbert remained frozen in place, allowing the Confederates to fight a battle of numerical equality in which they were driving McCook's Federals and threatening to capture the supply train for the entire Union army.

Major General Benjamin F. Cheatham, commanding the right of Bragg's army, threw his brigades forward to deliver the knock-out blow that would drive the remnants of McCook's corps from the field and seal the victory for the Confederates. Colonel John C. Starkweather's Union brigade was all that stood in the way of a rout of the Federal left. Starkweather's men occupied a strong defensive position on top of a hill. When the Confederates fired their first volley, Starkweather's men "wavered a little, but McCook was there watching the progress of the fight, cheering and encouraging the men. Pride and discipline at length asserted its way over the troops, every man moved forward to his former position and inflexibility held the line.... For half an hour wave after wave of Southern valor dashed against Starkweather's Brigade, to be hurled back, their ranks bleeding and discomfitted [sic], followed by wild, irregular cheers." Starkweather's men were holding firm, but they were paying a terrible price for doing so. The brigade would suffer 756 casualties in making their stand. Owing to the close quarters in which the battle was raging, 109 of those casualties would be listed as captured prisoners.[37] Private Sam Watkins of the 1st Tennessee Infantry remembered the fury of the fighting: "The guns were discharged so rapidly that it seemed the earth itself was in a volcanic uproar. The iron storm passed through our ranks, mangling and tearing men to pieces. The very air seemed full of stifling smoke and fire, which seemed the very pit of hell, peopled by contending demons."[38]

Late in the afternoon, as Brigadier General S.A.M. Wood's Confederate brigade was advancing to exploit a breach in the Union line, Brigadier General Michael Goodling's brigade finally appeared on the field. It was now close to 5:00 P.M., and darkness was already gathering in the October sky. If the Confederates were to drive the enemy from the field, it must be done quickly. Wood hit Goodling with such ferocity that the Union commander thought that he was facing a force several times its actual number. "The battle now raged furiously," Goodling wrote.

> One after another of my men were cut down, but still, with unyielding hearts, they severely pressed the enemy, and in many instances forced them to give way. Here we fought alone and unsupported for two hours and twenty minutes, opposed to the rebel General Woods entire division, composed of fifteen regiments and a battery of ten guns. [In reality, Wood had only four regiments and a battalion of sharpshooters.] Fiercer and fiercer grew the contest and more and more dreadful became the onslaught. Almost hand-to-hand they fought at least five times their own number, often charging upon them with such fiercelessness [sic] and impetuosity as would force them to reel and give way, but as fast as they were cut down their ranks were filled with fresh ones. At one time the Twenty-second Indiana charged on them with fixed bayonets and succeeded in routing and throwing them from their position on our right, but at the same time they brought in a reserve force on our left.

General Polk, seeing the opportunity, had added the brigade of Brigadier General St. John R. Liddell to Woods's assault. Goodling "advanced to ascertain if possible the position of the enemy [Lidell's Brigade]. As I advanced down the line we were greeted with a heavy volley of musketry, which plainly enough told me the direction of the enemy. With shouts and exclamations my men again rallied to the

General Braxton Bragg. A favorite of President Jefferson Davis, Bragg's Kentucky campaign met with failure, in part because his army was not vigorously sustained or supported by the people of Kentucky (United States Army Military History Institute).

onset." But the addition of Liddell's men was having the desired effect for the Confederates. Goodling's line was being forced back, and the Union left was coming unhinged. Goodling himself was captured and "conveyed from the field" as darkness settled over the countryside.[39]

Bragg's army had succeeded in accomplishing its purpose. The left flank of the Union army had been shattered and driven from the field. But the Confederates had accomplished the feat too late in the day to take any advantage of it. Nightfall brought an end to the fighting as it was impossible to distinguish friend from foe in the smoky darkness. Just as dusk was covering the landscape, Brigadier James B. Steedman's brigade arrived on the field and was placed in position to defend the Federal left. A great opportunity had slipped through Bragg's hands, due mostly to the heroic stands made by Starkweather's and Goodling's men.

Bragg had inflicted 4,348 casualties on the Federal army, but he had sustained about 7,000 of his own in the process.[40] Daybreak on October 9 found both armies still facing one another, with neither willing to initiate a resumption of the fighting. Bragg realized that he was facing Buell's entire army, and at midnight he pulled his regiments out of line and began a retreat toward Harrodsburg. Buell did not pursue the Confederates until October 11, and though he took in a large number of stragglers from the Rebel ranks, he never did catch up to Bragg and bring him to battle. In the end, the Confederates were allowed to slip back into Tennessee, where they prepared to fight another day. By the time Buell decided to call off the pursuit of Bragg's forces, he finally received official confirmation that Charles Gilbert was not a major general in the Federal service. Gilbert was summarily dismissed from command, but Buell did not take the opportunity of placing Thomas in his stead. Gilbert's regiments were divided between McCook's and Crittenden's corps.

Buell would single out Thomas for complimentary mention in his official report of the Perryville campaign, citing him for "the most valuable assistance." In truth, Thomas had done almost nothing to affect the outcome of the campaign, and the course of the battle would probably have been unchanged if he had not even been present with the army. This situation was not of Thomas's making, as Buell had relegated him to obscurity by assigning him as second in command of the army, a position that carried an impressive title but no real authority. His placement with Crittenden's corps on the far right of the Union line had also served to keep him out of the fight. Perryville would be the only battle of the Civil War where Thomas's presence would bear no outcome on the result of the fighting. The escape of Bragg's army ensured that there would be more fighting ahead, however, and Thomas would take a conspicuous part in all of it.

Chapter Eight

Savior at Stones River

The conclusion of the Perryville campaign brought with it a storm of controversy directed at the commander of the Army of the Ohio. Soldiers in Buell's own army were disgusted that Bragg's army had been permitted to leave Kentucky without being destroyed by the superior numbers the Federals had at their command. The troops felt that the problem lay in leadership, and placed the blame squarely at Buell's feet. The rumor was even rampant within the army that Bragg had been allowed to make his way safely back to Tennessee because he and Buell were brothers-in-law.[1]

Buell also found few friends within the government. Andrew Johnson had been one of his chief antagonists, and had actively campaigned to secure his removal from high command. Johnson had gone so far as to urge the governors of Illinois, Indiana, and Ohio to join with him in demanding Buell's replacement, and petitions from these political leaders were instrumental in prodding the War Department into action.[2]

Thomas was naturally one of the top candidates to replace Buell. After all, he had been offered the command immediately prior to the Battle of Perryville. Thomas also enjoyed the support of Secretary Stanton and Andrew Johnson. But Treasury Secretary Salmon P. Chase was a supporter of Major General William Starke Rosecrans for the command. Rosecrans was from Ohio, as was Chase, and political partisanship was coming into play. President Lincoln voiced the opinion that he was not in favor of replacing one Southern-born commander for another, as Buell and Thomas were both sons of slave states. Rosecrans's appointment would ensure that a Northerner commanded the army. It would also serve to help the Republican image in the upcoming November congressional elections. Rosecrans was a Catholic, and his brother was the Catholic curate Sylvester Horton Rosecrans. Most Catholics in the North had become disaffected with both the war and the Republican Party. They viewed the conflict as nothing more than a war of New England Yankees and Puritans that they had no stake in. The appointment of a fellow Catholic to such an important command might increase support of the church for the war effort and sway Catholic votes to the Republicans in the coming election. By means of rationalization, it was stressed that Thomas had already been offered the command and had declined it. He had also been second in command at the Battle of Perryville and was forced to shoulder some of the responsibility for the failure on that field. Lincoln decided the issue when he said, "Let the Virginian wait, we will try Rosecrans."[3]

William S. Rosecrans was an intimate of Thomas's, having been two years his junior at West Point. In fact, it was Rosecrans who was responsible for tagging Thomas with one of his first nick-names, "George Washington," out of respect for his sterling character and deportment. After graduation in 1842, Rosecrans served for ten years in the Engineer Corps. He missed the Mexican War, and therefore endured the slow advancement rate prevalent in the army at that time. In 1853, after eleven years of service, he received his first promotion to the rank of 1st lieutenant. In 1854, he resigned his commission to become a civilian architect and engineer in Cincinnati. The outbreak of the Civil War found him running an unsuccessful kerosene refinery.

Seven days after the firing on Fort Sumter he was given an appointment as colonel and assigned to the staff of George B. McClellan. In June of 1861 he was promoted to the rank of brigadier general. Rosecrans led a brigade at the Battle of Rich Mountain, and when McClellan was promoted to command of the Army of the Potomac, he remained in western Virginia, where he conducted a successful campaign against Robert E. Lee that resulted in the Confederates' being driven out of that portion of the state. May of 1862 found him in command of the left wing of General John Pope's Army of the Mississippi in Halleck's campaign against Corinth. Rosecrans rose to command of that army when Pope was called east to command in Virginia. In October of 1862, while Buell was facing Bragg in Kentucky, Rosecrans fought the Battles of Iuka and Corinth in Mississippi.

On September 17, 1862, he was given a commission as major general of volunteers. On October 25, 1862, he was reappointed to the rank of major general, but this time the date of commission was pre-dated to March 21, 1862, in an effort to make his date of commission senior to many of the other major generals in the army. He was to be appointed to command of the Army of the Ohio, redesignated as the Army of the Cumberland, and the earlier date of his commission would avert possible dissension from his corps commanders who would otherwise have been senior to him. On October 27, he assumed command of the army, and a new era for the Cumberlanders began.[4]

Prior to his dismissal from command, Buell had left the army and gone to Louisville seeking treatment for a leg injury he had suffered when his horse fell on him during the Perryville campaign. The army was left in General Thomas's capable hands, and he marched it to Bowling Green, on the way back to Nashville. The troops in the ranks seemed to be relieved that Buell was no longer with them, and hoped that Thomas's

General William S. Rosecrans. His drawn battle at Stones River was heralded as a major victory in the North and cast Rosecrans as one of the leading Union generals of 1863. Before the year was over, the Battle of Chickamauga would destroy his reputation and cause his dismissal as commander of the Army of the Cumberland (United States Army Military History Institute).

temporary assignment could be made permanent. Buell received notification of the change in command while he was seeking medical attention in Louisville. In what was obviously an intended slight, neither Secretary Stanton nor General-in-Chief Halleck contacted him with any advance notice of the decision that had been made. Instead, General Rosecrans carried with him a message from Halleck informing Buell that the bearer was to be his replacement. "General: The President directs that on the presentation of this order you will turn over your command to Maj. Gen. W S Rosecrans, and repair to Indianapolis, Ind., reporting from that place to the Adjutant General of the Army for further orders."[5] Buell's response to his dismissal was: "Under the circumstances I am sure I do not grieve about it."[6]

Rosecrans attempted to soothe any possible breach between himself and Buell caused by the uncomfortable situation in a letter written on October 30, 1862:

> I know the bearer of unwelcome news has a "losing office," but feel assured you are too high a gentleman and too true a soldier to permit this to prejudice any feelings of personal unkindness between us. I, like yourself, am neither an intriguer nor newspaper soldier. I go where I am ordered; but propriety will permit me to say that I have often felt indignant at the petty attacks on you by a portion of the press during the past summer, and that you had my high respect for ability as a soldier, for your firm adherence to truth and justice in the government and discipline of your command. I beg you, by our common profession and the love we bear our suffering country, to give me all the aid you can for the performance of duties of which no one better than yourself knows the difficulties.[7]

Such an appeal from a fellow West Pointer would be almost impossible for a professional soldier such as Buell to ignore. The olive branch that Rosecrans was offering acknowledged the difficulties Buell had experienced with the administration, and was as close as he would come to receiving vindication for his service to the country. He reported to Indianapolis for instructions that never came. After more than a year awaiting orders, he was mustered out of the volunteer service in May of 1864. On June 1 of that same year, Buell resigned his commission in the regular army and quietly retired to civilian life. General Grant would later recommend his reinstatement to command, but the government declined to act on the recommendation.[8]

When Thomas received news of the change in command it prompted him to write a letter of protest to Halleck. Thomas knew that Rosecrans's commission as a major general was junior to his own, but he was unaware, at the time he wrote the letter, that Rosecrans had been recommissioned at that grade so that the rank could be pre-dated.

> Soon after coming to Kentucky in 1861 I urged the Government to give me 20,000 men properly equipped to take the field, that I might at least make the attempt to take Knoxville and secure East Tennessee. My suggestions were not listened to, but were passed by in silence. Yet, without boasting, I believe I have exhibited at least sufficient energy to show that if I had been entrusted with the command of that expedition at that time [October 1861] I might have conducted it successfully. Before Corinth, I was entrusted with the command of the right wing of the Army of the Tennessee. I feel confident that I performed my duty patriotically and faithfully and with a reasonable amount of credit to myself. As soon as the emergency was over I was relieved and returned to the command of my own division. I went to my duties without a murmur, as I am neither ambitious nor have any political ambitions.
> On the 29th of last September I received an order through your aide, Colonel McKibben, placing me in command of the Department of Tennessee, and directing General Buell to turn over his troops to me. This order reached me just as General Buell had by most extraordinary exertions prepared his army to pursue and drive the rebels from Kentucky. Feeling convinced that great injustice would be done him if not permitted to carry out his plans I requested that he

might be retained in command. The order relieving him was suspended, but to-day I am officially informed that he is relieved by General Rosecrans, my junior. Although I do not claim for myself any superior ability, yet feeling conscious that no just cause exists for overslaughing me by placing me under my junior, I feel deeply mortified and aggrieved at the action taken in this matter.[9]

Thomas did not resent having another officer placed over him. He had almost constantly subordinated himself to others ever since the war had begun. Being a stickler for military protocol himself, he could not bear silently what he perceived to be an official disregard for proper procedure. It was nothing personal against Rosecrans, an officer Thomas was familiar with, even if he was a stranger to the Army of the Cumberland, or, until recently, a civilian who had been out of the service for seven years. What Thomas rejected was the humiliation felt by a man of honor at being forced to subordinate himself to an officer of lower rank, especially when he felt that he had done nothing to deserve such a rebuke from the government. The curiosity in all this is the act of recommissioning Rosecrans so that his commission pre-dated Thomas's. President Lincoln, as commander in chief, had the authority to make any command decisions he deemed necessary, and was not bound to acknowledge the military's code of seniority. If he wanted Rosecrans to command the army, it was totally within his authority to appoint him to that post, regardless of whether he was junior to any of his corps commanders or not. Did Lincoln feel that he could slip one past Thomas, or, knowing the character of that officer, did he believe that his unyielding adherence to military protocol would compel him to accept the situation once he found out about the change of dates, irregular as they might have been?

On November 15, 1862, General Halleck responded to Thomas's protest:

Your letter of October 30 is just received. I cannot better state my appreciation of you as a general than by referring you to the fact that at Pittsburgh Landing I urged upon the Secretary of War to secure your appointment as major-general, in order that I might place you in command of the right wing of the army over your then superiors. It was through my urgent solicitations that you were commissioned.

When it was determined to relieve General Buell another person was spoken of as his successor and it was through my repeated solicitations that you were appointed. You having virtually declined the command at that time it was necessary to appoint another, and General Rosecrans was selected.

You are mistaken about General Rosecrans being your junior. His commission dates prior to yours. But that is of little importance, for the law gives to the President the power to assign without regard to dates, and he has seen fit to exercise in this and many other cases.

Rest assured, general, that I fully appreciate your military capacity, and will do everything in my power to give you an independent command when an opportunity offers.

It was not possible to give you the command in Tennessee after you had once declined it.[10]

It seems that both Stanton and Halleck truly supported Thomas as the rightful successor to Buell, but they were overruled by the wishes of Lincoln. When Secretary Stanton returned to his office from the meeting in which Rosecrans had been selected, he was heard to grumble "Well, you have your choice of idiots, now look for frightful disaster."[11]

If Lincoln was playing to Thomas's sense of military propriety when he pre-dated Rosecrans's commission, his estimation of the man was perfectly correct. Upon receiving Halleck's message, Thomas immediately replied with a humble and recanting posture. He thanked Halleck for the kindness of his words and told him "I should not have addressed you in the first place if I had known that Rosecrans' commission dated prior to mine. The letter was written not because I desire a command but for being superseded as I supposed, by a junior in rank when I felt there was no cause for so treating me. I have no objections whatever to serving under General Rosecrans now that I know his commission dates prior to mine, but I must confess that I should feel very deeply mortified should the President place a junior over me without just cause, although the law authorizes him to do so should he see fit."[12]

Officers in the army were well aware of their standing in relation to their peers, and it can be reasonably assumed that Thomas had complete knowledge of who was superior to him and who was not. He wrote his letter of protest to Halleck because of this knowledge. Thomas was not duped by the pre-dating of Rosecrans's commission. That action had merely given him the opportunity to serve under Rosecrans without feeling that his honor had been insulted. As with other true gentlemen of the period, Thomas felt that honor must be protected above all else. Honor had been the basis for his decision to remain with the Union. It had caused him to alienate himself from family and friends, to endure the wrath of the people of his region, and to turn his back on his native Virginia. That same honor would not allow him to suffer in silence the indignation of being publicly humiliated by being passed over for a junior when he had done nothing to deserve such a slight. Honor would not have allowed him to retreat from the stance he had taken in his original letter to Halleck, and there is little question but that he would have requested to be relieved of his duties with the army had it not been for the pre-dating of Rosecrans's commission. That circumstance, fraudulent as it might have been, gave Thomas the means to back down from the stance he had taken with his honor intact, and the officer availed himself of the opportunity.

Rosecrans began to organize his army and make himself familiar with his officers, but the administration was impatient for active campaigning. Within a month, he was already enduring the same sort of official harassment that he had told Buell caused him indignation on behalf of that officer. On December 4, Halleck wrote him, "The President is very impatient at your long stay in Nashville. The favorable season for your campaign will soon be over. You give Bragg time to supply himself by plundering the very country your army could have occupied. From all information received here, it is believed that he is carrying large quantities of stores into Alabama, and preparing to fall back partly on Chattanooga and partly on Columbia, Miss. Twice have I been asked to designate someone else to command your army. If you remain one more week at Nashville, I cannot prevent your removal. As I wrote you when you took the command, the Government demands action, and if you cannot respond to that demand someone else will be tried."[13]

Halleck obviously had selective memory when it came to his own glacial advance on Corinth some six short months before. Rosecrans's response showed both courage and character.

> Your dispatch received. I reply in few but earnest words. I have lost no time. Everything I have done was necessary, absolutely so, and has been done as rapidly as possible. Any attempt to advance sooner would have increased our difficulty both in front and rear. In front, because of greater obstacles, enemies in greater force, and fighting with better chances of escaping pursuit, if overthrown in battle. In rear, because of insufficiency and uncertainty of supplies, both of subsistence and ammunition, and no security of any kind to fall back upon in case of disaster.... Many of our soldiers are to this day barefoot, without blankets, without tents, without good arms, and cavalry without horses. Our true objective now is the enemy's force, for if they come near, we save wear, tear, risk, and strength.... If the Government which ordered me here confides in my judgment, it may rely on my continuing to do what I have been trying to do — that is, my whole duty. If my superiors have lost confidence in me, they had better at once put some one in my place and let the future test the propriety of the change. I have but one word to add, which is,

that I need no other stimulus to make me do my duty than the knowledge of what it is. To threats of removal or the like I must be permitted to say I am insensible.[14]

Part of the organizational duties that Rosecrans was addressing was the command structure of the Army of the Cumberland. In his initial meetings with Thomas he had offered him the position of second in command for the army, a post that would recognize his previous accomplishments and grant him a title commensurate with his record. Thomas was not in accord with this arrangement, however. He had tasted the role of top subordinate under Buell, and it had left a sour taste in his mouth. What he desired was the opportunity to stand or fall on his own merits, and that could only be accomplished through holding a well-defined command, in direct charge of troops on the battlefield. Rosecrans assented to Thomas's wishes and, on November 5, assigned him to command of the center of the army. General McCook commanded the right and General Crittenden the left. In essence, Thomas had been assigned to the corps that had been led by Gilbert at Perryville, though there had been some shifting of commands within the corps structure.[15] Among the commanders of the five divisions assigned to him were Brigadier Generals Lovell Rousseau, John J. Reynolds, Robert B. Mitchell, James S. Negley, and Speed S. Fry.

Rosecrans also reorganized his mounted arm and appointed Brigadier General David S. Stanley to be his cavalry chief. Instead of parceling out the regiments of horse among the infantry units, Rosecrans had them brought together into brigades, creating a more efficient and powerful military body, one that could better deal with the likes of Joe Wheeler or Nathan Bedford Forrest once the campaign was underway.[16]

By all accounts, Rosecrans was a diligent and dutiful commander. He was said to be the first officer out of his cot in the morning and the last to go to bed at night. His watchful concern for the care of the troops under his command quickly won them over, and greatly complemented that shown by Thomas. Indeed, Rosecrans consulted regularly with his ranking major general on topics concerning the administration of the army, and in most cases adopted his suggestions. The personalities of the two men complemented one another. Rosecrans was outgoing, effusive, and demonstrative in all things, while Thomas was steadfast, dependable, but most of all, reserved. Though their personalities were diametrically opposed, both officers kept the best interests of the men foremost in their actions, and the ranks responded with loyalty and affection. When Thomas approached his superior with advice concerning the removal of some of the drunken or incompetent officers in his command Rosecrans responded by having them relieved, including Brigadier General Ebenezer Dumont, a division commander in the center corps. Rosecrans showed such deference to Thomas that, in addition to commanding the center of the army, he actually performed the duties of chief of staff for the army as well.

Both men were very detail-oriented when it came to the men under their command. No item was too trivial to escape Rosecrans's attention, and he personally addressed questions of training and equipment normally delegated to subordinates. Thomas had always exercised exactly the same approach in dealing with his men, and that is a major reason why he had been a favorite in the Army of the Cumberland ever since he had come west from Virginia. "Keep everything in order," he had once told an artillery officer. "The fate of a battle may turn on a buckle or a linch-pin."[17]

Thomas supported Rosecrans in his refusal to be bullied into moving his army against the enemy before it was properly prepared to do so. Thomas's corps was in readiness by the middle of December, but he was called to Nashville on December 18 to testify before a commission that had been convened to gather information regarding Buell's conduct in the Perryville campaign. For two days, he testified and answered the questions of the members of the panel. When he told the members that he had recommended that the army make a stand at McMinnville and Sparta instead of falling back to Nashville, Buell challenged his testimony. Thomas promptly produced copies of the telegrams he had sent to Buell which contained verification of his statements, and Buell was forced to concede the point that he had disregarded Thomas's sound advice, and that his actions had led to the invasion of Kentucky by an enemy force.[18] The Virginian was not attempting to discredit his former commander; he was merely telling the truth. To be sure, he had sustained Buell on the eve of Perryville even though his advice had been ignored by that officer.

After fulfilling his obligation to testify before the commission, Thomas returned to his corps, then located in the vicinity of Gallatin, Tennessee. On December 22, he left Reynolds's division and all but one brigade of Fry's division at Gallatin and marched the remainder to Nashville. At that place, General Robert Mitchell's division was detached from his corps to serve as a garrison force for the city. This left Thomas with only two full divisions, plus one brigade, or 13,400 men, for active campaigning. McCook had 16,000 men in his corps, and Crittenden's corps contained 13,200. Stanley's cavalry accounted for some 4,000 troopers, bringing the total of Rosecrans's effectives to approximately 47,000 men. (Reports would place Rosecrans's effective strength at between 43,000 and 44,000 at the time the battle was fought.) Within the next few days, the Federal army would assume the offensive and quiet the harassment its commander had been enduring from the government in Washington.

On December 26, Rosecrans started his columns forward on three different roads in the direction of Braxton Bragg's army, which was then in the vicinity of Murfreesboro, Tennessee. Rosecrans cautioned his corps commanders, "We shall begin to skirmish probably as soon as we pass the outposts. Press them hard. Drive them out of their nests. Make them fight or run."[19]

As the army marched out of Nashville for the thirty mile journey southeast to Mufreesboro, rumors abounded among the men in the ranks. It was said that scouting reports placed the size of Bragg's army between 50,000 and 70,000 men. Camp gossip had also given credence to the rumors that Bragg was being reinforced by divisions arriving from Robert E. Lee's army in Virginia.[20]

Bragg's Army of Tennessee, some 37,000 strong, was formed in a 32-mile crescent centered on Murfreesboro and facing Nashville. Major General William J. Hardee commanded the left of the line, in the vicinity of Triune, about 14 miles to the west. Major General Leonidas Polk's corps held the center of the line, arched around Murfreesboro. The right of the line stretched 12 miles east, to Readyville, and was held by a division of Hardee's corps under the command of Brigadier General John McCown. The cavalry of Brigadier General Joseph Wheeler was assigned the responsibility of patrolling the country between the Confederate lines and Nashville to keep an eye on any Federal movements.[21] Wheeler would imitate the feat accomplished by J.E.B. Stuart in Virginia when he rode completely around Rosecrans's army, gathering valuable information for Bragg.

A soldier in the 36th Illinois Infantry, in McCook's corps, described the beginning of the march:

> Called at six, with orders to march at seven; all in hurry and confusion. The shelter tents were issued; the men had threatened they would not receive them, considering it an imposition to have them substituted for regular tents.... This morning many refused them, preferring to be without

any, as all the large tents were ordered back to Nashville.... We had not gone far before it was evident to all that this was a movement in force.... It became a certainty that we were now advancing on the enemy, and were about to have war in earnest.... We had not gone far before it began to rain, and soon to pour, making the road tedious to the men.... The skirmishers soon came upon a band of the enemy's cavalry, and a brisk firing was kept up for some time. Our regiment being on the advance, we were very near. Our skirmishers were very much exhausted by tramping through the muddy corn and cotton-fields and trailing through the brush.

Rosecrans had been correct in assuming that his army would encounter the enemy as soon as it marched out of Nashville. When the 36th Illinois stopped that night at Nolansville, Tennessee, many soldiers found themselves with no shelter. "The ground was thoroughly drenched with rain.... The boys began to put up their shelter tents, and then it appeared as though those who had refused them were not wise.... During the night the rain began to pour down in torrents, and it was sad to think that so many of our boys were sleeping out in their blankets, and must in veritably be made sick."[22]

All three of Rosecrans's columns were experiencing similar scattered resistance from Confederate skirmishers as Bragg's army consolidated itself around Murfreesboro. On December 30, the Army of Tennessee was put into line of battle at Stones River, on the west bank. Polk's Corps was on the right, and the majority of Hardee's Corps was formed up on his left flank. One of Hardee's divisions, under the command of John C. Breckinridge, was left on the east bank to guard against a reported advance from the north, by a portion of the Federal army on the Lebanon Road. That night, the two armies were within two miles of one another, and each commander made plans for battle on the following morning. As the soldiers bedded down for the night they were serenaded by a battle of the bands as Yanks and Rebs vied for control of the night. Each side tried to drown out the other with renditions of their own patriotic airs. Finally, a band began to play "Home Sweet Home," and all the musicians, both North and South, took up the notes of the nostalgic song.[23]

The Union army was in line with Crittenden on the left, Thomas in the center, and McCook on the right. An ironic twist of circumstance witnessed both commanders adopting exactly the same strategy. Both Bragg and Rosecrans opted to hold with their right and attack with their left. If the attacks were launched simultaneously, the effect would be that of a clockwise-turning pin-wheel. But Bragg beat Rosecrans to the punch on the morning of December 31, when he threw 13,000 men of Polk's and Hardee's Corps against Thomas and McCook. For the second time in as many major battles, McCook would be holding a flank that was the focus of a massed enemy assault. But this time, Thomas, not Gilbert, would be in command of the center.

McCook's Corps was bent back like the blade of a closing jackknife and driven three miles. Brigadier General August Willich, a brigade commander in Richard Johnson's 2nd Division of McCook's Corps, was captured, and his men fled from the field. Many of them did not arrest their flight until they reached Nashville. The divisions of Jefferson C. Davis and Philip Sheridan were thrown back upon Negley's Division of Thomas's Corps, forcing Thomas's line to bear the brunt of the Confederate assault. When Negley was flanked and almost surrounded, Thomas ordered him, "Cut your way out." Arthur MacArthur of the 24th

Opposite: Maps showing the battlefield positions of the opposing armies at Stones River from December 30, 1862, to January 1, 1863. From *The History of the Civil War in the United States*, by Samuel Schmucker. Published by Jones Brothers & Co., Philadelphia, Pa., in 1865.

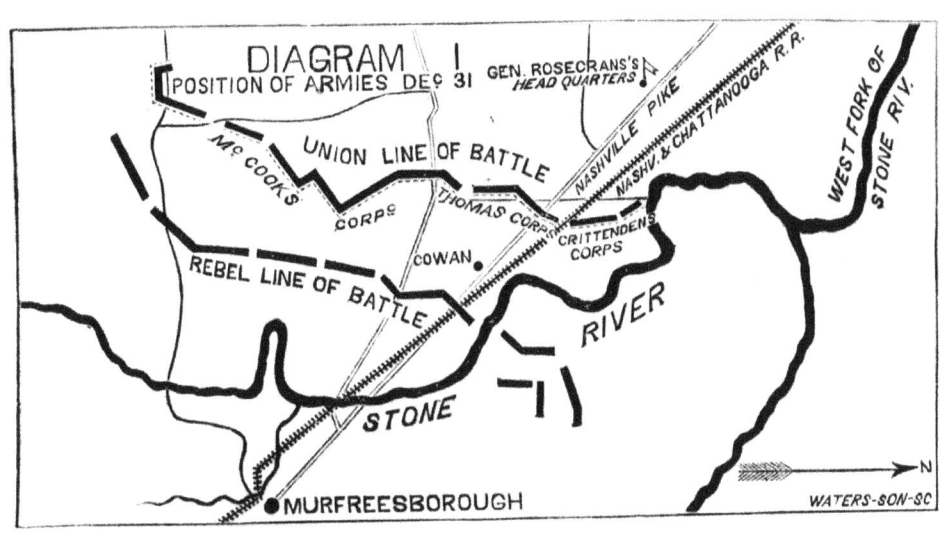

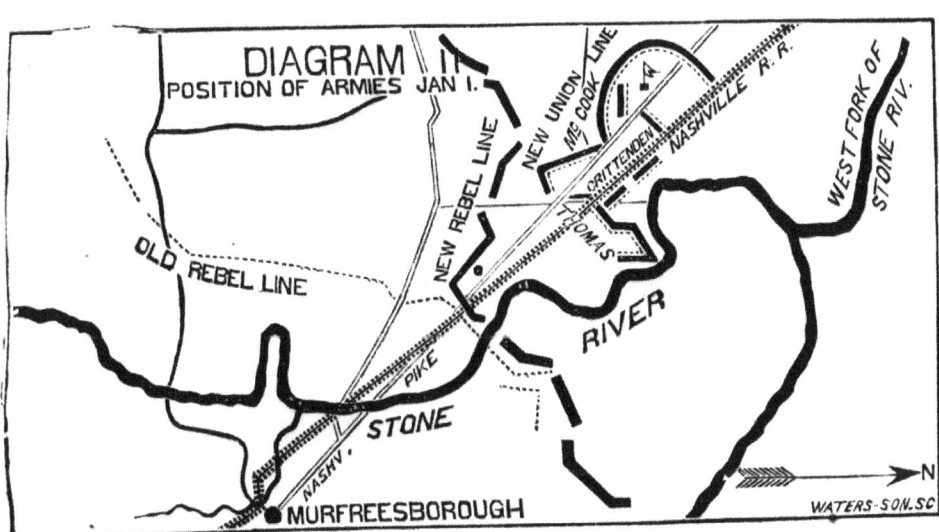

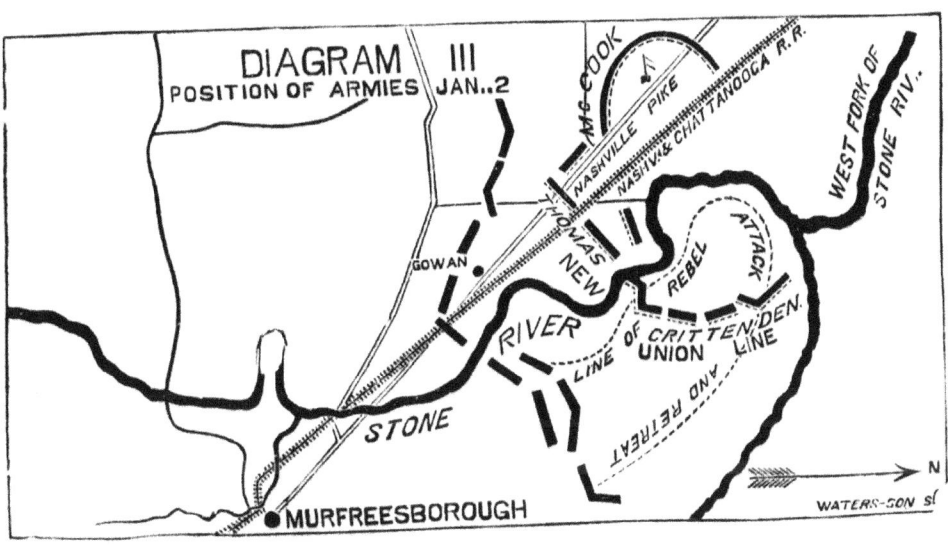

General Alexander McCook. His corps was roughly handled at Stones River, but was able to rally on Thomas's steadfast line (United States Army Military History Institute).

Wisconsin Infantry, part of McCook's Corps, described the frightful struggle that was being waged on the Union right flank: "The bullets seemed to be passing around my ears in perfect showers, similar to a heavy hail storm. Then cannon shell, grape, cannister [sic] and solid shot began to fly." Another soldier related, "The bullets came zip around me on all sides, over my head, and now to look back on it, it seems to me a perfect miracle that I escaped without a scratch." He went on to state that there was "Hardly a man in our company but what had Bullet Holes in some part of his clothing, or else in his Blankets."[24] The pressure was too great for the Union men to withstand, and the right crumbled under the massive pounding of Rebel arms.

Brigadier General Philip Sheridan's division was on the far left of McCook's line, next to Thomas's command, and bent back upon Negley. The Rebel attack was threatening to sever the two corps, but Sheridan fought a bloody delaying action that blunted the gray tide and bought time for the Federal army. He had appealed to Thomas for support, but Thomas initially declined to detach any men from his hard-pressed line without orders to do so from Rosecrans. As soon as he received that approval, he immediately sent two brigades to Sheridan to help him hold his own. By noon, the Union line was bent back upon itself, and was holding on only by extreme effort. Along Thomas's line the troops were drawn up in the shape of an open rectangle. Negley's Division held the front line, with Sheridan's Division formed perpendicular to his right and Rousseau's Division perpendicular to his left.[25] Rosecrans was everywhere along the line, encouraging the troops, and instilling the confidence for them to hold on. Thomas was also doing his part to steady the men. A fellow officer observed him as being "calm, inflexible, from whose gaze skulkers shrank abashed."[26]

At one point in the battle, when Rousseau and Negley were retiring from the field, Thomas ordered Colonel O.L. Shepherd, in command of a brigade of United States Regulars, to cover the withdrawal. "Take your brigade over there and stop the Rebels," he directed Shepherd. According to Thomas, Shepherd's and two other brigades lost nearly half their numbers, but the mission was accomplished and the line was held. This was a turning point of the battle. If Thomas's line gave way, Crittenden would be isolated and possibly destroyed. The main Confederate pressure was now exerted against the divisions of Rousseau, Negley, and Palmer. Negley's and Rousseau's flanks were exposed, and all three commands were virtually surrounded. Palmer's division was fighting off attacks from the Federal rear, while Rousseau's men faced in several different directions to face their assailants.

General Thomas knew that the only way to save his corps, and the entire army, was to establish a new line holding on tightly to Crittenden's right, while he gathered together the scattered portions of McCook's Corps on his right. He first established a temporary line to cover his movements while he massed his artillery on high ground to the rear that had been selected for a permanent line. Then he moved part of his infantry to the low ground, in front of the batteries, where they could add their fire to the effort to stop the advancing enemy. When the Confederates swept forward against his improvised line, they were greeted with combined musketry and artillery that stopped them cold in some of the bloodiest fighting to take place on the field that day. As one Union veteran remembered, the Confederates were mowed down like "chaff which the wind driveth away."[27] The stand made by Thomas's Corps prevented the rout of the center, and saved Crittenden from being cut off and surrounded by Bragg's entire army. "Old Dependable" had held, and the Army of the Cumberland would live to fight another day.

Thomas now massed his regiments into a strong defensive position while he clung to Crittenden's Corps.[28] The hinge of the Federal position was at a place called Round Forest, where Crittenden's right joined Thomas's left. The fighting that would take place there would lead soldiers of both sides to rename it Hell's Half Acre. Bragg was insistent on driving the Union army from the field, and he ordered Breckinridge to bring his division across the river and launch an attack on Hell's Half Acre.[29]

Breckinridge, commanding the largest division in Bragg's army, protested against making the attack, feeling that the Union line at that point was too strong to assail. His concerns were ignored by his commander, and his four brigades were thrown piecemeal upon the hinge of the Union line. The order for the attack only intensified the hatred already existing between Breckinridge and Bragg. For his part, Bragg was nursing a grudge against not only Breckinridge, but all Kentuckians, as a result of the failed Perryville campaign. Bragg felt that the Kentuckians dabbled too much in politics and not enough in soldiering. He was personally offended when the Confederate Congress voted him a message of thanks for the Kentucky campaign that was prevented from being a unanimous gesture only by the dissenting votes of the two members of that house from the Bluegrass State.

His vindictive nature may have been what prompted an episode that took place a few days before the battle that threatened to tear apart his army. A corporal in the 6th Kentucky Infantry had left the ranks to help his widowed mother prepare for the winter. General Bragg hired bounty hunters to go after him and bring him back to the army. Once he was returned, the Kentuckian was tried before a court-martial, found guilty of desertion, and sentenced to death. On December 20, Bragg approved the findings of the court and ordered the condemned man to be shot to death the day after Christmas. He further ordered that the firing squad be made up of men from his own outfit, and that the entire Kentucky Brigade be present to witness it. Breckinridge and other officers from the Kentucky Brigade pleaded with Bragg to commute the sentence, but the commander refused, avowing that he would shoot every Kentuckian in the army if that were what it took to bend them to his will. Breckinridge screamed at Bragg that this was murder, and he would not stand to have his men treated like animals. The confrontation between the two officers became so heated that members of a few Kentucky companies in the immediate vicinity ran to retrieve their stacked muskets, intent on resisting Bragg's order by force, if necessary. Breckinridge was able to restore order short of all-out mutiny, and, for the good of the service, reluctantly carried out the order for the execution. When the Kentuckians went forward to the attack at Hell's Half Acre, it is questionable whom they hated more; the Yankees to their front, or their own commander in their rear.[30] Brigadier General Roger W. Hanson, commander of the Kentucky Brigade, felt that Bragg was deliberately sending his men to their deaths, and he proposed to go to Confederate headquarters to kill the commander himself.[31]

Crittenden's Corps had been involved in the fighting since the opening of the battle, but it was now, along with Thomas's Corps, to become the focal point of the Southern attack. Breckinridge's 4,500 men formed the left of the Southern line of attack. A brigade of Tennessee troops under the command of General Gideon J. Pillow was on their right. The brigades of Colonel Randall Gibson and Brigadier General William Preston were in reserve, 200 yards to the rear. The Union line had been roughly handled during the morning, and had almost been broken. It had been holding on to its ground since noon, but Bragg felt that one more determined push would put it to flight again. Unknown to Bragg, the Federals were well aware of his preparations. The Confederate movements were clearly visible to the men of Brigadier General Horatio P. Van Cleve's Division, under the command of Brigadier General Samuel Beatty since Van Cleve had been wounded earlier in the day. Crittenden and Rosecrans began calling for reinforcements. The divisions of Jefferson C. Davis and Milo S. Hascall were brought in to bolster the line, as were the brigades of William P. Hazen and Charles Cruft, from Negley's Division. Federal artillery was massed on a hill across the river from the infantry, as Crittenden's chief of artillery, Major John Mendenhall, collected 58 pieces of ordnance together.[32] General Hanson may

General John C. Breckinridge. Breckinridge and his fellow Kentuckians developed a hatred for Braxton Bragg at Stones River, feeling that their commander was needlessly sacrificing their lives (United States Army Military History Institute).

have been wrong about Bragg's intention in ordering the attack, but his impression that it would be suicidal was borne out by the strength of the Union line.

At 4 P.M. on New Year's Eve, amid the rain and sleet that had been falling all day, General Breckinridge gave the order, "Up, my men, and charge!" and the gray-clad line surged forward. They were instantaneously met by a withering fire from Beatty's infantry and Mendenhall's big guns that tore gaping holes in their lines. But on they came, at the quick-step, determined to cross the 600 yards that separated them from the enemy. Orders had been given for the first line to fire but one volley, followed by a bayonet charge. Breckinridge ordered the line to stop when it had reached a point halfway to the Union line. He had noticed that the Federals overlapped his right flank, and reformed so that his second line of infantry was extended to the right. He also brought up a battery of artillery to support the flank.

With these dispositions completed, the attack was resumed. As the Confederates closed on the Union line, Federal artillery was compelled to withhold their fire, out of fear of hitting their own men. Beatty's men were also holding their fire, creating an eerie calm before the storm. When Hanson's Brigade was within 150 yards of Beatty's position, they were greeted by a volley of musketry. Though their ranks were thinned, the Kentuckians let loose with a Rebel yell, returned the volley, and charged with bayonets. The Federals fired another volley, but the Confederate wave was not to be stopped. All along the line, they gained the crest of the Federal line and pushed the defenders back. The battle became a confused scene of hand-to-hand fighting as the Union troops vainly attempted to hold their position. For half an hour, the struggle continued, until the Federal line finally broke and ran. Breckinridge's men had accomplished what few in their ranks thought possible: they had sprung the hinge at Hell's Half Acre, and were on the verge of winning the day.

But the tide of battle was beginning to turn. As Breckinridge's men crested the Union works and began to pursue the fleeing Federals, they came under the full fire of Mendenhall's batteries. Federal gunners punished the attacking enemy, firing at a rate of 100 rounds per minute. Gaping holes appeared in the Confederate lines, and one Union soldier observed that the Rebels must have thought they "opened the door of Hell, and the devil himself was there to greet them."[33] Smoke from the cannon mixed with that from the muskets, and was held close to the ground by the dampness caused by the cold rain and sleet. It was impossible to see clearly for more than a few yards, but the artillerists continued to ram home their charges and fire blindly into the hazy curtain of smoke that concealed the attacking Southerners.

The Federal gunners brought the Confederate pursuit of their fleeing comrades to a halt. The attackers were simply being blown apart by the massed fire of the big guns. At first, they clustered together in the Union works and on both sides of the river, but the continued barrage eventually caused them to fall back in retreat. Colonel John F. Miller, a brigade commander in Thomas's Corps, saw the Confederates wavering and, without orders, pushed his men forward in a counterattack. They charged across the river, sweeping the remnants of Hanson's and Pillow's Brigades from their front. Rosecrans observed Miller's actions and knew that the Confederates were spent. He ordered the counterstroke supported by regiments of General Stanley's cavalry, as well as units from both Negley's and Palmers Divisions. Southern officers tried in vain to rally their men and make a stand, but Miller's regiments were not to be stopped. By 4:45 P.M., Bragg realized that the situation on the field could not be reversed, and he ordered Brigadier General Patton Anderson's Brigade to help cover the retreat of the Confederates back to their original lines. The late December sky was beginning to darken, and both sides were content to end the fighting. When Breckinridge reviewed his mangled regiments, he was reported to be "raging like a wounded lion as he passed the different commands from right to left. Tears broke from his eyes when he beheld the little remnants of his own old brigade." He cried out, "My poor Orphans! My poor Orphans! My poor Orphan Brigade! They have cut it to pieces."[34]

The freezing rain that had tortured the soldiers of both sides ended with the gathering dusk, but resumed when full darkness covered the field. The firing died down, and both armies beheld a "dreadful field with its burden of mutilation and death." A strong wind added to the falling temperatures and froze the ground. Some of the wounded were actually trapped in their misery when their own blood froze solidly to the earth.[35] Both armies were badly mauled, and the men were completely used up. It had been one of the bloodiest days of the war, with neither side emerging victorious. The opposing soldiers rested as best they could, as each side wondered if the following day would bring a resumption of the savagery just concluded.

The address Rosecrans drafted for the troops on the night of the battle to be distributed the following morning sounded like he had every intention of continuing the contest at the earliest possible convenience:

> The General Commanding desires to say to the soldiers of the Army of the Cumberland that he was well pleased with their conduct yesterday.... He now feels perfectly confident with God's grace and their help, of striking this day a blow for the country, the most crushing, perhaps, which the rebellion has yet sustained. Soldiers! the eyes of the whole nation are upon you; the very fate of the nation may be said to hang on the issues of this day's battle. Be true, then, to yourselves, true to your own manly character and soldierly reputations; true to the love of your dear ones at home, whose prayers ascend this day to God for your success. Be cool. I need not ask you to be brave. Keep ranks. Do not throw away your fire. Fire slowly, deliberately — above all, fire low, and be always sure of your aim. Close readily in upon the enemy, and when you get within charging distance, rush upon him with the bayonet. Do this, and victory will certainly be yours. Recollect that there are hardly any troops in the world that will stand a bayonet charge, and that those who make it, are sure to win.[36]

A gathering of the primary generals of the Army of the Cumberland was held at General McCook's headquarters on the night of December 31. General Thomas found an improvised seat and rested his weary body as the officers discussed the events of the day, and is reported to have nodded off several times during the course of the conversation. Rosecrans inquired of Surgeon Eban Swift if he had enough transportation to remove the wounded from the battlefield. Swift responded that there were five or six thousand wounded, but he felt that a large enough number of them were ambulatory so as to make his transportation adequate to remove the badly wounded. Rosecrans then asked Thomas, "Will you protect the rear on the retreat to Overall's Creek?" Thomas emphatically replied that "This army can't retreat!" General Phil Sheridan strongly voiced his support of Thomas's stance, joined by General Crittenden.[37] The theme of Rosecrans's conversation had left the impression with all present that he had been inclined to withdraw the army from Murfreesboro as soon as possible. Just as he had done during the battle, Thomas now anchored the line, preventing another retreat from the field. John L Yaryan, a junior officer present in the room, noted, "If there was a cheerful expressioned face present I did not see it." But in Thomas he saw the qualities that always inspired confidence in those under his command. He was "as always ... calm, stern, determined, silent and perfectly self-possessed, his hat set squarely on his head. It was a tonic to look at the man." Several versions of the officers' meeting exist, but in each one Thomas is portrayed as strongly opposing any thought of surrendering the field to the enemy. One account of the meeting has him stating, "I know of no better place to die than right here," and punctuated his statement by walking out of the room.[38] In all of the versions, the question was decided. There would be no retreat.

So the army would stay and fight it out. New Year's Day of 1863 dawned clear and cold. The rains of the previous night had ceased. The efforts of the previous night to strengthen the Union works paid dividends almost immediately. Bragg sent Nathan Bedford Forrest's cavalry out to probe the Federal lines, searching for a weak spot. Forrest reported back to his commander that no such spot was to be found. Both armies were exhausted from the fighting of the previous day, and neither commander was willing to initiate further action on the day President Lincoln would sign the Emancipation Proclamation into law. Sporadic, random firing between pickets let both sides know that an enemy was nearby, but the majority of the soldiers were able to rest and regain their strength, unmolested by the foes who lurked just beyond their lines. General Joe Wheeler's command was one of the only units to be active during the day. His troopers captured a large wagon train, filled with supplies for Rosecrans's army; this was about the only major event to take place before nightfall covered the land.[39]

Dawn of January 2 found both armies still somewhat stunned from the carnage of New Year's Eve. Sporadic firing from the picket lines dominated the activity of the morning and early afternoon, as each commander waited for the other to make the first move. During the late afternoon, General Crittenden ordered Beatty's Division to occupy a hill on the east bank overlooking two fords of the river on the Federal right flank. General Bragg was concerned that Beatty's men posed a threat to General Polk's position, and ordered General Breckinridge to attack the Federals and drive them back. Breckinridge once more protested his assignment, feeling the Union position too strong to assault. He met with General William Preston for the purpose of making a death-bed declaration: "General, this attack is made against my judgment and by special orders of General Bragg. Of course we all must try to do our duty and fight the best we can; but if it should result in disaster and I be among the killed, I want you to do justice to my memory and tell the people that I believed this attack to be very unwise and tried to prevent it."[40]

General Crittenden was riding with Major Mendenhall on the Nashville Pike at about 4 o'clock P.M. when he saw Breckinridge putting his men in line of battle to make the assault. The Confederates, some 4,500 strong, were placed in two lines, with fixed bayonets. Just as with the attack on Hell's Half Acre, the first line was instructed to fire only one volley before closing on the enemy with cold steel. Mendenhall immediately rode off to concentrate all the artillery he could at McFadden's Ford, on the west side of Stones River, in support of Beatty's line. Fifty-eight guns were massed at this point. When Breckinridge's men surged forward, Beatty's troops were obliged to give ground and were driven to the bank of the river. It was at this time that the Federal gunners roared into action. According to Crittenden, he turned to Mendenhall and said: "'Now, Mendenhall, you must cover my men with your cannon.' Without any show of excitement or haste, almost as soon as the order was given, the batteries began to open, so perfectly had he placed them. In twenty minutes from the time the order was received, fifty-eight guns were firing upon the enemy. They cannot be said to have been checked in their advance — from a rapid advance they broke at once into a rapid retreat. Reinforcements soon began to arrive, and our troops crossed the river, and pursued the fleeing enemy till dark."[41]

Breckinridge's first line was thrown back by the discharge of the guns, but his second line, reinforced by some of the rallied units of the first, tried to press the attack home. They were in turn forced to retreat by the furious fire of the Union gunners. As the second line was retreating, pursued by elements of Beatty's command, Thomas noted that the Union regiments had become intermingled. He sent orders to General Negley to advance his command in support of Beatty. Negley was not in the immediate vicinity of his troops when Thomas's orders arrived, so Colonel John F. Miller took the initiative to carry out the orders by attacking Breckinridge's men with seven regiments that were nearby. General Davis moved his division in support of Miller, with the result of driving the Confederates beyond a key position on their line, which the Federals quickly fortified. This movement made Bragg's line at Stones River untenable, and he was forced to order the retreat of his army to Murfreesboro. The rains returned that night, making a pursuit by Rosecrans impossible, since Stones River rose to almost flood stage, and the muddy fields were made impassable for his artillery.[42]

Bragg left his wounded at Murfreesboro, while he led the rest of his army to Tullahoma, 40 miles distant. The Stones River campaign was ended. It was one of the hardest-fought battles to take place during the course of the war, and, in terms of the number of men engaged, one of the bloodiest. Rosecrans lost 31.5 percent of his command, or 13,230 men. Bragg's casualties were somewhat lower, with the Confederates sustaining losses of 28 percent, or 10,306 men. As such, the combined casualties almost equaled the terrible carnage at Shiloh.[43] Most historians rate Stones River to be a drawn battle, but President Lincoln and the Northern public embraced it as a hard-fought victory. One can only imagine the effect on Northern war weariness had a defeat at Stones River followed so closely upon the heels of the disaster Union arms had suffered at Fredericksburg, Virginia, in the middle of December. As it was, the people of the North felt that they had won the first major engagement to be fought in the new year, and Lincoln's Emancipation Proclamation was issued from a position of strength, not of defeat.

Thomas had been instrumental on the battlefield and in the council of war, exhibiting at all times the solid and unshakable characteristics that had already made him a pillar of the Army of the Cumberland. His grasp of the battle on the first day's fighting had prevented what might have been a terrible reverse to the Union war effort in the west, and his deployment of Negley's men on January 2 decided the issue in favor of Union arms. He had been an anchor for the army on the banks of Stones River, a role he would play repeatedly in the upcoming months and years.

Chapter Nine

The Tullahoma Campaign

Following the battle, the Army of the Cumberland performed the all-too-familiar task of burying the dead and caring for the wounded. On January 5, 1861, it marched into Murfreesboro and took possession of the town. Though most historians feel that Stones River was a drawn battle, the administration and the Northern public hailed it as a great victory. Rosecrans was the hero of the hour, and his Army of the Cumberland took center stage. The soldiers in that army could take great pride in their accomplishments. They had been victorious at Mill Springs, had turned the tide at Shiloh, captured Corinth, repulsed the invasion of Kentucky, and now had driven Bragg from central Tennessee. The Army of the Potomac may have been getting the worst of it in almost every encounter with Robert E. Lee's Army of Northern Virginia, but the Cumberlanders were coming to regard themselves as a force to be reckoned with in the west.

Indeed, the battle held more serious ramifications for the North than merely a victory on the battlefield. Few men in the ranks realized just how important their victory had been. In the fall of 1862, France and England were both poised to formally recognize the Confederacy and welcome it into official status among the world's nations. Along with this recognition came the implied promise of foreign aid in fighting against the North. Most certainly, steps would be taken to eliminate the hated Federal blockade, which was strangling the South. Both European powers waited only for some sign that the South was destined to win the war before making the diplomatic step and aligning themselves with the Confederacy. The invasion of Maryland by Robert E. Lee, and the corresponding invasion of Kentucky by Braxton Bragg, seemed to be just the sort of vindication England and France were looking for. If the Confederate armies could win a significant battle on Northern soil, it would be proof positive that the Federal government was not going to be able to coerce the South back into the Union. When both invasions were crowned with failure, the foreign powers hesitated, but still clung to the policy. William E. Gladstone, a member of the British Cabinet and a future prime minister, voiced the sentiments of his government when he stated three weeks after Antietam: "We know quite well that the people of the North have not yet drunk of the cup — they are still trying to hold it far from their lips — which all the rest of the world see, they nevertheless, must drink of it. We may have our own opinions about slavery; we may be for or against the South; but there is no doubt that Jefferson Davis and other leaders of the South have made an army; they are making, it appears, a navy; and they have made, — what is more than either, — they have made a nation. We may anticipate with certainty the success of the Southern States, so far as their separation from the North is concerned."[1]

The issuance of Lincoln's Emancipation Proclamation posed a problem for European leadership. The vast majority of the common people in both Britain and France strongly objected to slavery, and Lincoln's assertion that this was to be a war to free the slaves struck a chord with them. The politicians of England and France were little influenced by the will of the people they represented, however, for they felt that the Emancipation Proclamation was a moot point. The North would never be able to abolish slavery so long as the Confederacy remained an independent nation, and therefore, diplomatic relations with them must be opened. Lee's crushing victory over the Army of the Potomac at Fredericksburg, Virginia, in December of 1862 served to justify the British and French opinions about the state of affairs in America. They watched and waited for news of further Confederate victories, victories that would have spurred the European politicians to action.

Then came Stones River. The defeat of Bragg's army caused England and France to take a step backward and re-evaluate the situation. The Union victory added an exclamation point to Lincoln's issuance into law of the Emancipation Proclamation on January 1, 1863, and showed to the world that the Union was not yet finished in trying to impose its will on the South. Both England and France sought to be on the winning side in the conflict, and neither country wished to bear the embarrassment of backing the losing horse. Both countries adopted a wait-and-see attitude. Both were poised to grant formal recognition and aid, but only once the Confederacy had proven that they no longer needed it, and could stand on its own. Future events would dictate that England and France would continue to ride the fence until the tide of the war turned against the South and all hope of recognition was lost. The Battle of Stones River was a crucial factor in determining the foreign policy of both England and France, and of effectively keeping them out of the war.

Back in Murfreesboro, General Rosecrans was busy reorganizing his army and seeing to issues of equipment and supply. He began to petition the government for more cavalry, more artillery, and replacements for the men he had lost at Stones River. In addition, he asked the War Department to officially designate the wings of his force as corps in the army. This request was readily granted, and Thomas's center wing was designated the 14th Corps, McCook's right wing became the 20th Corps, and Crittenden's left wing became the 21st Corps. In addition, some 14,000 men were added to the Army of the Cumberland when Major General Gordon Granger's force, temporarily designated as the Army of the Kentucky, was folded into it as the redesignated 4th Corps.[2]

Secretary Stanton was happy to perform any service for his victorious general. He told Rosecrans, "There is nothing within my power to grant to yourself or your heroic command that will not be cheerfully given."[3] Rosecrans began by asking for items like 1,000 horses and 2,000 short rifles for his cavalry, but he quickly pressed Stanton to the limit with his requests. The topper came when he requested that his commission as major general be once more pre-dated, from March 21, 1862, to December 21, 1861. This move would have made him the senior major general operating with any army in the field. Stanton categorically refused to take part in this scheme, but the requests from Rosecrans kept coming in to the War Department. In fact, they became such a burden that General Halleck finally sent a message to Rosecrans, scolding him for the expense incurred by the government for the telegrams he was sending, and telling his that no other commander in the field sent nearly so many.[4]

Relations between Rosecrans and the administration were already becoming strained. Ever since the victory at Stones River, the War Department had been nudging the general to initiate a campaign against Bragg's army. Rosecrans had declined to do so, spending the late winter and early spring months reorganizing and refitting his army. He also issued liberal furloughs for his men to go home during this period.

A military train. Rosecrans's army depended on the railroad to supply its needs during the Tullahoma campaign. General Thomas put the trains to further use by turning railroad cars into mobile hospital units, ensuring that his men would receive the fastest and best medical treatment possible (United States Army Military History Institute).

In the meantime, Bragg had been using the time to establish a formidable line of defense that centered on Tullahoma. On the left, it stretched to Shelbyville, under General Polk. The right, under the command of General Hardee, was extended to Wartrace. The total length of the line was some 75 miles. Although he had lost the services of General Breckinridge and his 10,000 men when that officer was reassigned to General Joseph E. Johnston's command, reinforcements continued to come in, until his command numbered some 44,000 men. The position Bragg had assumed was strictly defensive in nature. The men had dug earthworks all along the line, and had felled trees and inserted rows of sharpened stakes for a distance of 600 yards to their front, in an effort to impede any attacks by the enemy.

While he kept his infantry and artillery placed in their fortified stronghold, Bragg loosed his cavalry to create havoc in Rosecrans's lines of communication and supply. Brigadier General John Colburn had a brush with the troopers of Nathan Bedford Forrest and Earl Van Dorn at Franklin, eighteen miles south of Nashville, and the result was a loss of 1,300 men to Colburn's command. Forrest then took some 800 Union prisoners at Brentwood. The worst reverse to Union arms came when Rosecrans directed Colonel Abel Streight to make a foray behind Bragg's line, into northern Alabama. There weren't enough horses to properly mount Streight's command, so the men were issued mules instead. Forrest's command caught up with Streight and inflicted 1,800 losses.[5]

Even with these losses, the ranks of the Army of the Cumberland were swelling with each passing day. The largest portion of the new recruits were assigned to Thomas's 14th

Members of the 21st Michigan Infantry Regiment. Steady and self-reliant westerners like these made up the bulk of Rosecrans's Army of the Cumberland (United States Army Military History Institute).

Corps, and the general spent the majority of his time seeing to their training and discipline. By the time Rosecrans's organization of the army was complete, Thomas's Corps would contain some 26,000 men, the largest of any in the army, including the reserve. Rosecrans's total force now totaled some 97,000 men. Many of these would have to be detached for garrison duty at the various points occupied by the Federals, but this would still leave the general with a field command that could top 60,000 men. The administration felt that this was more than enough to engage Bragg's inferior army, and Rosecrans began to receive pointed barbs from the War Department to get his army moving and back into the war by early June. After all, Grant's army was operating against Vicksburg, Mississippi, and the Army of the Potomac had already conducted a campaign in Virginia, failure though it was. The administration desired to have the Confederate armies pressed from all fronts, in order to deprive them of the advantages of mobility afforded by their interior lines of communication. But from Rosecrans's point of view, the Confederate position at Tullahoma was still too strong to assault with the force he then had on hand, and he would not allow himself to be prodded into action before he felt his army was prepared.

On June 8, 1863, he distributed a survey to his corps and division commanders, seeking their opinions of initiating an immediate campaign against the Confederates. There were three questions he desired them to answer:

1. From the fullest information in your possession do you think the enemy in front of us has been so materially weakened by detachments to Johnson or elsewhere that this army could advance ... at this time with strong reasonable chances of fighting a great and successful battle?
2. Do you think an advance of our army at present likely to prevent additional re-enforcements being sent against General Grant by the enemy in our front?
3. Do you think an immediate or early advance of our army advisable?[6]

Thomas, McCook, and Crittenden all answered "no" to the final question on Rosecrans's survey. The consensus of the vast majority of the corps and division commanders was that such an advance should not be made at this time.

One of the few dissenting votes came from Brigadier General James A. Garfield, who felt that Rosecrans's "general movement has been wisely delayed until now till your army could be massed and cavalry mounted." But with those details finally accomplished, Garfield felt that the time had come to put the army in motion and decide the issue in Tennessee.[7] The corps commanders were not convinced. They were operating under the assumption that Rosecrans intended to make a direct frontal assault on the strong Rebel fortifications at Shelbyville. To Thomas's mind, this would be folly. He wrote that even should such an attack be successful, the Confederates would "draw us away from our base, attack and destroy our communications, or threaten them so strongly as to greatly weaken our main force, and then send re-enforcements of artillery and infantry to Johnson."[8]

Rosecrans omitted the views of Garfield when he sent a summary of the survey answers to General Halleck, in an effort to defend the hesitation of his actions. On June 16, he received a terse response from the general-in-chief: "Is it your intention to make an immediate movement forward? A definite answer, yes or no, is required." Rosecrans still vacillated. "If 'immediate' means tonight or tomorrow, No. If it means as soon as all things are ready, say five days, yes."[9]

The delay would also give Rosecrans time to develop a new plan of campaign, as the majority of his commanders felt it would be a mistake to advance against Bragg's strongly posted left wing. At length, he settled upon the strategy of marching his army against the Confederate right flank. This plan would call for a portion of the army to travel through the mountainous passes north of Tullahoma, but it would provide the Federals with a better chance of maneuvering the Confederates into the open, instead of throwing their battle lines upon Bragg's prepared positions. General David Stanley described a meeting of Rosecrans with his corps commanders a few nights before the intended campaign was begun. All the officers "met at headquarters to discuss the routes and parts assigned to each. The discussion lasted almost until daylight next morning. One of the most noted members of this council and who afterwards commanded the same army, [Thomas] went to sleep in his chair and slept the sleep of innocence for several hours whilst the others discussed the prospective bloody campaign."[10]

On June 24, the marching orders were issued, and the Army of the Cumberland got underway. Thomas had ordered his men to pack eight days' rations in their haversacks, and to make sure they had a full forty rounds in their cartridge boxes.[11] John M. King, a soldier in the 92nd Illinois Infantry of Thomas's command, noted in his diary that "it was evident that a tremendous campaign had been planned and that the armies on both sides were keen for war to the hilt.... We pulled up stakes on the 23rd, knowing as we believed that the campaign had opened in dead earnest."[12]

Rosecrans attempted to freeze Hardee's Corps in place on the Confederate left by means of a ruse perpetrated by General Stanley's cavalry. Stanley was ordered to advance against Shelbyville on June 24 and make a bold demonstration against Hardee's lines. That night, he was to have his men build numerous campfires throughout the countryside, in the rear of his position, to give Hardee the impression that he was supported by a large force of infantry. If the deception worked, it would make Hardee think that he was about to be attacked by the entire Federal army, while Rosecrans stole a march against his real objective, the Confederate right.[13] General Stanley's troopers drove the Confederate cavalry skirmishers through Eagleville and Unionville and pressed them back upon Hardee's main line at Shelbyville. Stanley recalled, "In a severe skirmish on that day, one of the ridiculous things that sometimes happen to

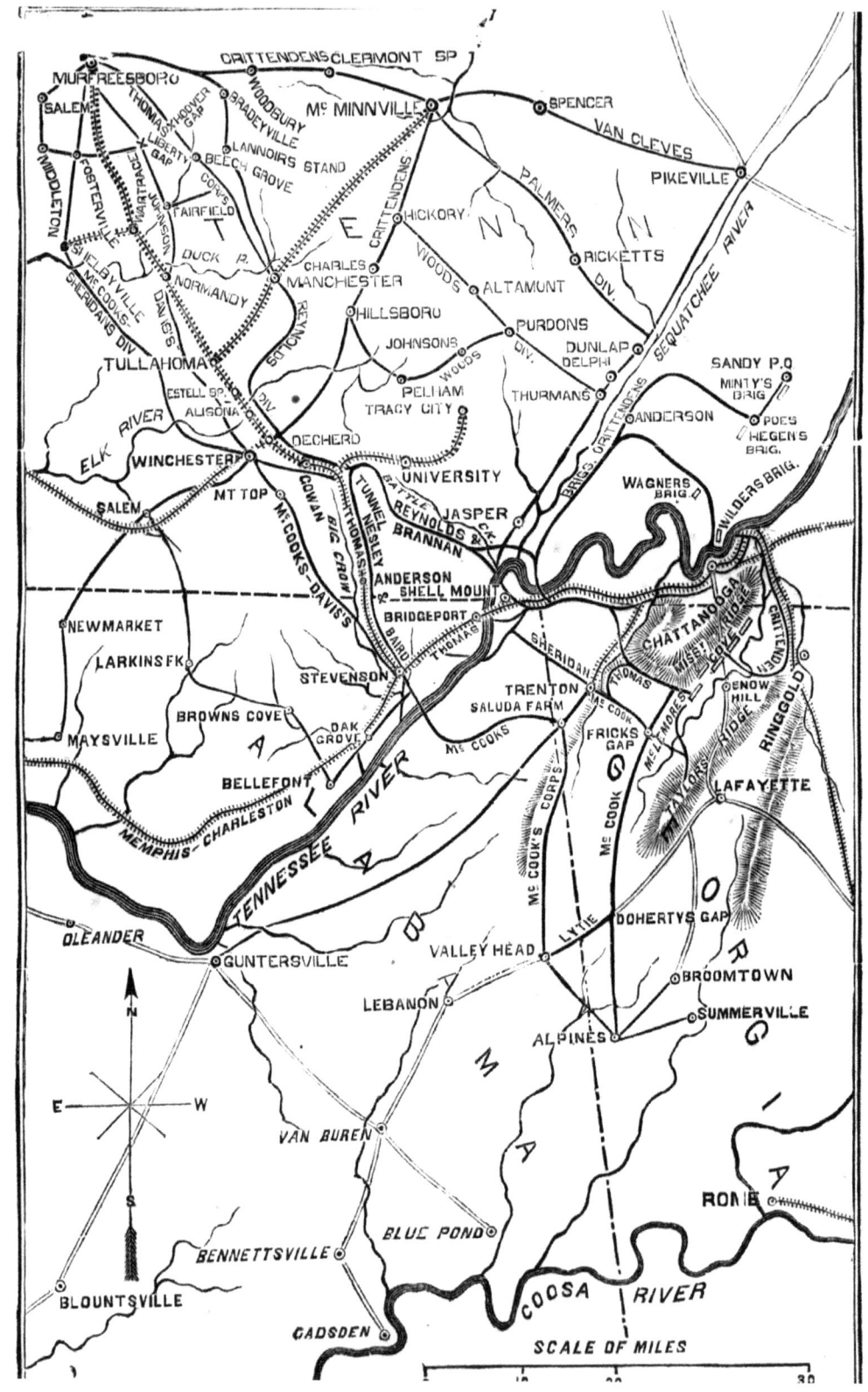

lighten up the death roll, occurred. The Confederates made a charge on our line of skirmishers, but recoiled when they met a brisk fire. One trooper continued to charge straight down our lines. As he passed along the line of skirmishers of the 1st Tennessee cavalry [Union] every man took a shot at the bold horse soldier. He dashed into our lines with his gray clothes full of bullet holes but with a whole skin, when it was discovered that a bullet had cut both reins, and it was the horse that did the charging, the trooper being an unwilling participant."[14] Stanley's feint proved effective, and Hardee prepared to defend his position against the massed assault he was sure would come on the following morning.

Rosecrans's main body marched against the Confederate right, under Polk. Polk's positions were screened by a range of hills that ran roughly east to west, and separated Duck River from the headwaters of Stones River. A series of gaps through the mountains were held by strong pickets from the divisions of Major Generals Patrick Cleburne and Alexander P. Stewart. Stewart guarded Hoover's Gap, just north of Wartrace, and Cleburne was in charge of Liberty and Guy's gap, closer to Tullahoma. Colonel John T. Wilder, in command of a brigade of mounted infantry, was ordered by Rosecrans to spearhead the advance toward Hoover's Gap, with Thomas's Corps following closely behind. Wilder was instructed to vigorously push the Rebel pickets. This he accomplished with expediency, driving them back upon their reserves, which were, in turn, driven back upon Stewart's main body, four miles south of Tullahoma. Wilder had advanced so rapidly that Thomas's infantry support was still six miles in his rear by the time he hit Stewart's main line. When Brigadier General Bushrod Johnson's Confederate brigade was thrown forward to push back the Union troopers, Wilder's men made good use of their Spencer repeating rifles to hold their ground until Thomas's leading units began to arrive in the vicinity. When Thomas arrived, he took Wilder by the hand and exclaimed: "You have saved the lives of thousands of men by your conduct today. I didn't expect to get this gap for three days."[15]

Upon discovering that this was a general advance of the entire Union army, and knowing that the gap he was assigned to defend was already lost, Stewart gave the order for his division to withdraw back to Bragg's main body. McCook's Corps, following Thomas, captured Liberty Gap, southwest of Hoover's Gap, and assumed the lead of the advance, toward Manchester. By nightfall, both corps were camped two short miles from Tullahoma. Crittenden's Corps had been sent on an end run around the Confederate right, with its objective being Woodbury. From this point, Crittenden would be on the Confederate right flank and rear, placing Bragg's entire line in jeopardy. But heavy rains made the roads almost impassable, and forced Crittenden's march to slow to a snail's pace. His corps took four days to cover the seventeen miles required to arrive at Woodbury, four miles in the rear of the Confederate army. Upon arrival, however, Crittenden discovered that the fields to his front contained numerous patches of quicksand created by the rains, making it almost impossible for him to advance.

By this time, Bragg had divined the true intentions of Rosecrans's army. Knowing that his line was already turned, and not willing to stand and fight at such an obvious disadvantage, Bragg opted to vacate the current position and withdraw his army to the south, where it could be placed to guard the strategically important city of Chattanooga. The Confederates

Opposite: Map of Murfreesboro to Chattanooga, encompassing the area contested during the Tullahoma campaign. From *The History of the Civil War in the United States*, by Samuel Schmucker. Published by Jones Brothers & Co., in Philadelphia in 1865.

crossed the Tennessee River and eventually retired toward the southeast corner of the state. Rosecrans had successfully dislodged the enemy from their formidable lines and had sustained only minimum losses in the process. Union casualties were comparatively low at 570 men. Confederate casualties were never fully reported, and the total remains unknown.[16] The Union army had been spared the blood bath that must surely have occurred if Rosecrans had stuck to his initial plans for a frontal assault against the Confederate left. By adopting the judgment of Thomas and the other corps commanders, he had achieved his objective through maneuver and now had the Confederates out in the open, where a battle could be fought at more advantage to the Union.

General David Stanley noted, "After one year, marching and several bloody battles, the two armies stood where they had started a year before, but the relations were different. The Union soldier had gained in tone; the Confederate had lost in hope and spirit." He went on to praise Rosecrans's campaign, saying that "No better example of strategy was carried out during the war."[17] Thomas considered Rosecrans's campaign to be a masterful stroke, all the more because of the low number of casualties. Following the evacuation of the Confederate lines, he met with Rosecrans and, taking his commander by the hand, let loose with a rare instance of unbridled enthusiasm. "This is the grandest campaign of your career!" he exclaimed. The soldiers in Thomas's Corps were equally heartened by their recent success. "We called him out and cheered him [Thomas] until he had to talk," an officer remembered. "He raised his hand ... and said: 'Soldiers, when I saw the gallant charges and assaults you made that drove the enemy out of Hoover's Gap, I felt proud of my corps.' And we cheered him till it echoed through the woods."[18]

The desired result, the entrapment of Bragg's entire force, failed only because of inclement weather and bad roads, which delayed Crittenden from getting into position to cut off the Confederate retreat. Still, the campaigning had been a great success thus far, and the prospect of eliminating Southern control from all of Tennessee seemed well within the grasp of the Federals. Rosecrans began the pursuit of Bragg's army on June 30, the day Bragg ordered his gray-clad legions south. General U.S. Grant had Lieutenant General John C. Pemberton's Confederates trapped at Vicksburg, Mississippi, and the fall of the Southern bastion was expected daily. If Rosecrans could win a decisive victory over Bragg's army, the issue of the war in the west could well be decided before the summer was over.

Secretary Stanton was pushing for just such aggressive action from the Army of the Cumberland. In his dispatch to Rosecrans announcing Grant's capture of Vicksburg, the secretary made no mention of the accomplishment of his army in ridding central Tennessee of Confederate influence. Instead, his tone implied that it was time for the Army of the Cumberland to contribute to the war effort. "You and your noble army now have the chance to give the finishing blow to the rebellion," he said. Rosecrans, always quick to take offense to a slight, real or imagined, shot back an immediate response. "You do not appear to observe the fact that this noble army has driven the rebels from Middle Tennessee, of which my dispatches advised you," he replied. "I beg in behalf of this army that the War Department may not overlook so great an event because it is not written in letters of blood. I have now to repeat that the rebel army has been forced from its strong intrenched positions at Shelbyville and Tullahoma, and driven over the Cumberland Mountains."[19] Stanton failed to acknowledge Rosecrans's plea for an official commendation to the army from the War Department. To his mind, Chattanooga was the prize, and the Army of the Cumberland had only begun a campaign, not finished one. Praise for Rosecrans's brilliant maneuvers would be reserved until such time as they resulted in the hoisting of the flag of the United States over the captured city of Chattanooga.

Bragg fell back to Chattanooga, reaching that place on July 7. As Rosecrans planned the next phase of his campaign, the capture of Chattanooga, he discussed his strategy with Thomas. Rosecrans proposed to outflank Chattanooga in much the same way as he had operated against the Tullahoma line. He would march his army by three separate routes, through as many passes of the Cumberland Mountains, arriving at a place south of Chattanooga, in Georgia, where he would be in position to cut the Confederates off from supplies and reinforcements. Bragg must then be compelled to either give up Chattanooga or come out of his defenses and offer battle on ground of Rosecrans's choosing.

Thomas must have surprised his commander when he disagreed with the proposed plan of campaign. A quick look at the map revealed inherent danger to Thomas's mind, and he pointed out that the passes were two, twenty-six, and forty-two miles south and southwest of Chattanooga. The distance between them meant that the Union army would be widely separated, and the corps would not be within supporting distance of one another. Should Bragg suddenly take the initiative, he could easily attack and destroy the army in piecemeal fashion while it was thus deployed. Thomas suggested that the army be kept well in hand, and that the flanking movement be made much further south, cutting the East Tennessee and Georgia Railroad between Rome and Atlanta. He argued that this route would have the same effect on Bragg's forces at Chattanooga without putting the Union army in any danger of being attacked in detail. While all this was going on, Major General Ambrose E. Burnside, who had recently arrived in east Tennessee with the Army of the Ohio, could threaten Chattanooga from the north, operating out of Knoxville. Whether or not Rosecrans seriously considered Thomas's suggestions is a matter for speculation. It is certain that he did not adopt them into his campaign strategy, opting instead to follow the course he had previously laid out.[20] Perhaps he was influenced by the relative ease with which he had been able to pry Bragg out of his Tullahoma defenses. It should be remembered, however, that the flanking movement at Tullahoma had come about as a result of Thomas's disapproval of Rosecrans's original plan to mount a frontal assault at Shelbyville. He had been correct on that occasion, and history would prove that he was right in opposing the repetition of that maneuver south of Chattanooga.[21]

Though having a population of only about 2,500 residents, the city of Chattanooga was strategically important as the Confederate main base of railroad transportation, supply, and communication for the entire region. More than any other city in the South, Chattanooga served to tie the Confederacy together into a nation. Its fort-girded defenses also served as the protecting bastion for northwestern Georgia, the roadblock on the route to Atlanta. Both sides recognized the immense importance of the city, and each braced themselves for the struggle they believed would fought for possession of it. The anticipation of the cost in lives that ownership of Chattanooga would demand was akin to that experienced fourscore years later during World War II, when amphibious operations were mounted to wrest away from the Japanese their island strongholds in the Pacific.

Back in Washington, the War Department was watching Rosecrans' actions with keen interest. The commander of the Army of the Cumberland was receiving a steady flow of messages from Stanton and Halleck prodding him to make an immediate campaign against Bragg's army. The administration waited impatiently for word that the impending campaign was about to be underway. Finally, in the middle of August, Rosecrans had sufficiently prepared himself, and Washington saw signs that the army was preparing to move. Secretary Stanton desired to have a direct pipeline from which to receive information concerning the campaign, and he ordered Charles A. Dana, one of his assistant secretaries of war, to report to Rosecrans in person. Dana carried with him a letter of introduction from Stanton to Rosecrans: "General: This will introduce to you Charles A. Dana, Esq., one of my assistants, who visits your command for the purpose of conferring with you upon any subject which you may desire to have brought to the notice of the department. Mr. Dana is a gentleman of distinguished character, patriotism, and ability, and possesses the entire confidence of the department. You will please afford to him the courtesy and consideration which he merits, and explain to him fully any matters which you may desire through him to bring to the notice of the department. Yours truly, Edwin M. Stanton."[22] Far from crediting Rosecrans or his army with the accomplishment of a great deed in expelling the Confederates from middle Tennessee, the War Department was embedding a spy in headquarters to keep an eye on the activities of the Army of the Cumberland and make reports to Stanton.

On August 5, Halleck, on behalf of Stanton, had ordered Rosecrans to engage the Confederates, regardless of whether or not his army was prepared for such a move. One of Rosecrans's chief concerns was the fact that a substantial amount of food must be collected to subsist the army during its campaign. He estimated the need to be twenty days' rations, and advised that the march not be undertaken until such time as the corn had matured sufficiently to provide food for both men and animals. Rosecrans enjoyed the complete support of his subordinate commanders in delaying the march until after the problems of supply had been addressed. Thomas spoke for the officer corps when he told his superior, "That's right! Stand by that, and we will stand by you to the last."[23] Despite continual harassment from Washington, Rosecrans stuck to his own decision and delayed the advance until all was in readiness to do so. As the middle of August approached, his arrangements were finally completed, and marching instructions were issued to his commanders. The assistant secretary of war was en route to join the army, but that army was now underway.

Dana would not reach the army until after the final phase of the campaign was completed. Rosecrans was now ready to put the army in motion, much to the delight of the administration, and Stanton may have thought Dana's assignment to be unnecessary by the time he embedded himself with the Cumberlanders. Crittenden's Corps was sent to the Sequatchie Valley, across the river from Chattanooga, to provide much the same sort of feint that Stanley had effected at Shelbyville. Crittenden was to occupy Bragg's attention by making him think that the Union forces intended to attack by means of a river crossing, in much the same manner as had been done at Fredericksburg the previous December. Crittenden's artillery shelled the town from across the river, and four brigades were detached to deceive the Confederates into thinking that a crossing was imminent. The Yankees floated logs and pieces of lumber down past the enemy defenses, and slapped boards together, giving the impression that a pontoon bridge was under construction.

John King of the 92nd Illinois was with Crittenden's command, and described the actions of his regiment at this time. "The first time the regiment struck the Tennessee River they deployed into skirmish line up and down the river, every man concealing himself behind some object, such as a tree, stump, stone, hummock, or tuft of grass or brush, and each man tried his hand at rebel heads at long range, and kept it up until the novelty wore off, when they withdrew, went into camp, got supper, and went to bed."[24]

While Bragg's attention was thus diverted, Rosecrans got Thomas's and McCook's Corps underway toward the real objective. Two pontoon bridges were constructed across the Tennessee River, one three miles from Stevenson, Alabama, measuring twelve hundred fifty feet, and another at Bridgeport, Alabama, measuring twenty-seven hundred feet. Thomas's and McCook's Corps were marched to the Confederate side of the river without the loss of a single man or animal. Thomas's Corps marched south from Bridgeport, for a distance of fifty-one miles, to the mouth of Steven's and Cooper's Gaps, in the Lookout Valley. This placed the corps twenty-six miles south of Chattanooga. McCook's Corps marched forty-nine miles, over Raccoon Mountain and Sand Mountain, through Valley Head, then over Lookout Mountain to Broomtown Valley. From here, he was forty-two miles from Chattanooga, and sixteen miles from Thomas. Crittenden, his feint in front of Chattanooga complete, followed Thomas's Corps, and then turned east, crossing the brow of Lookout Mountain and heading for Chattanooga.

By this time, Bragg had discovered the movements of the enemy and had determined that the city had become indefensible. On September 8, as Crittenden's soldiers stood on Lookout Mountain they observed a dust cloud trailing south from the city. Bragg had determined that the city was untenable, and sought to avoid subjecting his army to a siege, like the one that had ended so disastrously for the defenders of Vicksburg two short months before. It was correctly deduced that the Confederates were abandoning the town, and Crittenden pushed forward to seize the prize for which the campaign had been waged. On September 9, his forces entered Chattanooga, and the United States flag was raised over the captured city.[25]

Bragg's army had been driven out of Tennessee and was in full retreat into Georgia. Chattanooga was in Union hands, and with Burnside at Knoxville, the Unionist sympathizers in east Tennessee were once more firmly under Federal control. Thus for the Tullahoma campaign had been a spectacular success. It had accomplished more, with fewer losses, than any campaign that had thus far been conducted in the war. The nation had steeled itself for a blood-bath in front of Chattanooga, but Rosecrans had captured the city without having to fight a desperate battle. In fact, he had lost far fewer than 1,000 men in prying the Confederates out of two different fortified lines. Grant's capture of Vicksburg, and the 30,000 Confederate prisoners who were surrendered when that city capitulated, had been getting the lion's share of the press in the east, but Rosecrans's relatively bloodless victories were now receiving the credit they deserved. The commander of the Army of the Cumberland was being hailed as a military genius, and his name was being circulated for everything from general-in-chief of the Union armies to a possible presidential candidate in the 1864 election. Indeed, Rosecrans had reached the apex of his military career. He had attained his objectives and had done so in brilliant fashion. Rosecrans received information from local loyalists that Bragg's army was in full flight and, if pushed, would not stop retreating before it reached Atlanta. He notified Thomas of the current state of affairs: "A dispatch is just received ... Chattanooga is evacuated by the rebels. The general commanding desires you to call on him at once to consult in regard to arrangements for the pursuit.... Order your whole command in readiness to move at once."[26]

Thomas was fearful of the content of Rosecrans's message, as it indicated that the commanding general intended to push forward immediately, without taking time to consolidate his position at Chattanooga and perfect his lines of supply and communication with Nashville and Bridgeport. Thomas argued for just such a plan when he met with Rosecrans, but the commander would hear nothing of delays. He was convinced that the Confederates were thoroughly demoralized, and that all that was needed was a forceful push from his army to keep their retreat going, and possibly turn it into a rout.[27] Then again, there was the constant harassment he had been receiving from Halleck and Stanton. He had been receiving daily criticism from the War Department for his inactivity, and was not about to subject himself to further abuse at the hands of the politicians in Washington. He determined to chase the Rebels into the heart of Georgia, win the decisive battle of the campaign there, and prove his critics wrong, once and for all. He telegraphed a message to General Halleck that served to redeem his injured pride and proclaim his own judicious actions: "Chattanooga is ours without a struggle and East Tennessee is free."[27]

To the men in the Army of the Cumberland, it must have seemed as if they were on the verge of momentous events that would finally bring the war in the west to a successful close in favor of Union arms. Little did they realize that the fateful battle for the control of Chattanooga was yet to be fought. Braxton Bragg's army was in retreat, but it was far from being beaten. In fact, it was growing stronger and more dangerous with each passing day. Thomas's unheeded advice would come back to haunt Rosecrans, resulting in his subsequent fall from grace, and the elevation of Thomas as one of the greatest Union heroes of the war.

Chapter Ten

The Rock of Chickamauga

Rosecrans's strategic movements served as an alarm for the entire Confederacy, as Bragg's army relinquished its control over Tennessee. The gateways into Georgia and Alabama seemed open to the Federals, signaling a potential crisis to the Southern military and government alike. Leaders from all over the South took immediate steps to meet the danger and counter the success the Federals were thus far enjoying.

The changes in Bragg's army had begun as soon as July 13, 1863, when the command structure of the Army of Tennessee began to be addressed. Like Breckinridge, General Hardee had lost confidence in Bragg and requested to be assigned to duty outside of the sphere of Bragg's influence. His request was granted, leaving his corps without a commander. Hardee's replacement was found in the person of Major General Daniel Harvey Hill, "Stonewall" Jackson's brother-in-law, and a hard-fighting division commander in the Army of Northern Virginia, who had most recently been defending Richmond during the Gettysburg campaign. Jefferson Davis approached Hill, telling him, "Rosecrans is about to advance upon Bragg; I have found it necessary to detail Hardee to defend Mississippi and Alabama. His corps is without a commander. I wish you to command it." Hill protested, on the grounds that General A.P. Stewart, as his senior, was rightfully entitled to the command, and he did not wish to slight that officer. Davis responded, "I can cure that by making you a lieutenant-general. Your papers will be ready to-morrow. When can you start?" As promised, Hill's commission as lieutenant-general was approved, dated for July 11, 1863.[1] Hardee's departure from the army would also be compensated by the return of Breckinridge. Following the fall of Vicksburg, that officer had been ordered back to the Army of Tennessee, and subordinated once more to a commander he despised almost as much as he did the Yankees.

But General Hill was just the beginning of the aid that President Davis planned to send to the beleaguered Confederates under Bragg. The Army of the Potomac was back in Virginia, but Major General George Gordon Meade showed no inclination to pursue an aggressive campaign against Lee's Army of Northern Virginia following his victory at Gettysburg. With the situation in Virginia being static, Davis saw an opportunity for Lee's army to assume a defensive posture, allowing reinforcements from the eastern army to be sent to Bragg to decide the issue in the west. Lieutenant General James Peter Longstreet, along with two of his divisions under Major Generals John Bell Hood and Lafayette McLaws, was ordered to northwestern Georgia. Longstreet himself had advised such a reinforcement prior to the battle of Gettysburg, with a view to overwhelming Rosecrans, then marching on Grant to relieve the pressure on Vicksburg. On August 15, 1863, while the Tullahoma campaign was in progress, he had written directly to Confederate Secretary of War James Seddon to once more forward the suggestion.

General Lee was opposed to a division of his army. He was called to Richmond to consult with Davis on August 29, during which time he proposed to undertake offensive operations against Meade's army. This plan was overruled by Davis, who recognized that the loss of Chattanooga was tantamount to the Union's holding a knife at the heart of the South. The city must be recaptured and the lost territory recovered. He accordingly issued orders for the transfer of Longstreet and his two divisions to Georgia. On September 9, the first trains began to arrive at Orange Court House and Louisa Court House to transport Longstreet's men south. The most direct line from Longstreet's camps on the Rapidan River to Chattanooga was a distance of 540 miles. Owing to Burnside's presence at Knoxville, the Confederates were compelled to take a round-about route, which was 925 miles in length.[2]

Longstreet did not himself entrain for Georgia until September 14. Before leaving, he had written a letter to General Lee which expressed his feelings about the mission he was about to embark upon: "If I can do anything there, it shall be done promptly. If I cannot, I shall advise you to recall me. If I did not think our move a necessary one, my regrets at leaving you would be distressing to me, as it seems to be with the other officers and men of my command. Believing it to be necessary, I hope to accept it and my other personal inconveniences cheerfully and hopefully. All that we have to be proud of has been accomplished under your eye and your orders. Our affections for you are stronger, if it is possible for them to be stronger, than our admiration for you."[3] Longstreet's comments are especially relevant when one considers that he had so recently been in command of the famed assault at Gettysburg that would forever be known as Pickett's Charge. In Georgia, he would direct another attack on a Union line of battle. This one would not be so famous, but it would be equally desperate and bloody, and, because of the defensive exertions of George Henry Thomas, it would also fail in achieving its objective.

Bragg was well aware of the fact that heavy reinforcements were on the way to his army. The rapid retreat that heartened Rosecrans was actually a strategic withdrawal with a view to organizing his forces for a counterstroke against the overextended Federals. By the time the concentration was complete, Bragg would have 71,551 effectives in his army with which to oppose the 56,965 men in the Army of the Cumberland.[4] It would be one of the few times during the course of the war that the Southern forces would outnumber the enemy on the field of battle. The Confederacy was mounting a supreme effort to redeem its fortunes in the west, and was staking all on this endeavor to retake Chattanooga.

Completely unaware of the massive force that would soon be assembled in his front, Rosecrans disregarded Thomas's cautious advice and adopted a speed and vigor heretofore unknown in the campaign. On September 9, the day Chattanooga fell into his hands, he issued orders to press the pursuit with all haste. "Major General Thomas, Commanding Fourteenth Army Corps: The General commanding has ordered a general pursuit of the enemy by the whole army. General Crittenden has started to occupy Chattanooga and pursue the line of Bragg's retreat.... General McCook has been ordered to move at once on Alpine and Summerville. The General commanding directs you to move your command as rapidly as possible to Lafayette and make every exertion to strike the enemy in flank, and if possible to cut off his escape."[5]

General John B. Turchin could not believe that the Federal government was not vigorously supporting Rosecrans's army with substantial reinforcements. Turchin felt that the independence of military departments was "the essence of military absurdity," and could not understand why "Grant on the Mississippi had nothing to do with Rosecrans in Middle Tennessee, and Burnside in East Tennessee had nothing to do with either Rosecrans or Grant; while Middle Tennessee and East Tennessee lay in the same theater of war."[6]

At this point in time, Rosecrans was still operating under the assumption that Bragg's army was intending to continue its retreat to Rome and beyond. As he had done with Buell prior to the Perryville campaign, Bragg had intentionally planted false information with the Union commander to conceal his true intentions. He sent scouts, posing as Confederate deserters, into Rosecrans's lines with stories detailing the demoralization of the Southern army, and reports of its precipitate retreat toward Rome. Rosecrans was quick to credit the tales being told by the bogus deserters. Feeling that he had put the Confederates to flight, he reasoned that a push by his army would be all that was needed to induce the Confederates to fall back into central Georgia and open the road to Atlanta. Furthermore, Rosecrans was still operating under the belief that he was facing only 35,000 to 40,000 Confederates. He had no idea that Bragg's army was being heavily reinforced.

Back in Washington, General Halleck, Secretary Stanton, and the rest of the administration were well aware that steps were being taken to strengthen the Army of Tennessee, but for unknown reasons, this information was not passed along to Rosecrans.[7] Possibly the War Department felt that providing Rosecrans with that information might induce him to hesitate in making any further forward movements. The administration was anxious for a push into Georgia, which would result in dividing the Confederacy in two, separating Virginia and the Carolinas from the Gulf States. Such a move could not help but be a death blow to the Southern nation, and bring about a speedy conclusion to the war.

The demoralized condition of the Confederate army was precisely the impression Bragg wished for his counterpart to have. Far from being in head-long flight, the Army of Tennessee halted at Lafayette, Georgia, to regroup and reorganize. As reinforcements began to arrive, Bragg studied the maps and planned for a counteroffensive that would break the back of the Army of the Cumberland once and for all. It was as readily evident to him as it had been to Thomas that Rosecrans had committed a grave error in allowing his army to become separated. The Federals were spread out on a line sixty miles in length, from Crittenden's left, near Chattanooga, to McCook's right, near Alpine, Georgia, and were in a precarious situation. By quick movements, Bragg could crush each of three Union corps in detail before they could be supported by the rest of the army.

The Union center, under Thomas, was the nearest to both Lafayette and the gathering Confederate army. Rosecrans's orders for the 14th Corps to push forward to Lafayette to cut off the retreat of the Rebels, or to attack them in flank as they withdrew, was actually playing precisely into Bragg's hands. Thomas's corps would be advancing alone against the entire Confederate army. Neither Crittenden nor McCook would be within supporting distance of the Union center. McCook was the furthest away, a distance of some fifty miles, but four or five days' march through the mountain passes they would have to take to reach Thomas. Bragg observed the movements of Thomas's corps and made plans to crush it and drive a wedge between Crittenden and McCook. On September 9, he issued orders for a general assault to be made on the following morning.

On September 9, General James Negley's Division, the advance of Thomas's Corps, began marching through Steven's Gap of Lookout Mountain into McLemore's Cove. The cove was six to nine miles wide, and crossed over Chickamauga Creek on the way to Dug Gap, a pass through Pigeon Mountain to the southeast. Thomas had planned to pass through Dug Gap to get to Lafayette, where he would attack whatever Confederates still remained at that place. Negley and his staff rode in front of the column as it marched through the cove. Since intelligence from the Federal high command advised that the Rebels were in full flight, little caution was exercised by Negley or his men, and the regiments advanced in column of march, without throwing out skirmishers or flankers. When Negley and his officers approached Dug Gap, they were suddenly fired upon by a Confederate skirmish line posted in front of the gap. Beating a hasty retreat, Negley and his officers galloped to the 78th Pennsylvania Infantry, the first regiment in line of march, and ordered the colonel to get his men into line of battle immediately. The Pennsylvanians advanced across the cove, crossed Chickamauga Creek, drove the Rebel skirmishers back into Dug Gap, and ascended a road leading up the valley from Crawfish Springs that allowed the men a view of the surrounding countryside. Chickamauga was an Indian word meaning "river of death." The Pennsylvanians were appalled by what they saw, and if any of them knew what the name of the creek meant, they must have thought it quite appropriate. The Confederates at Dug Gap were not part of a rear-guard action. Instead, they were the vanguard of Bragg's entire army. Negley's Division had walked right into a trap, and was nearly surrounded by a vastly superior force. The division stood alone, beyond supporting distance of the remainder of Thomas's Corps, and almost out of reach of the rest of the Union army.[8]

Thomas's Corps, well to the rear of Negley, was lumbering forward. It was slowed by the encumbrance of 400 badly needed supply wagons. Also, there were the roadblocks of felled trees and boulders that the Confederates had placed in the roads to slow his progress. Thomas was further hampered by a total lack of any cavalry to clear his line of march, reconnoiter the enemy, or verify information. When Rosecrans chided him for not moving Negley forward quickly enough, Thomas replied: "I do not see how it was possible for him to advance further or more rapidly than he has. If I had Wilder's cavalry I am satisfied Lafayette would have been in our possession as with it [the cavalry] I could have prevented the enemy from blockading the road."[9] Neither Thomas nor Rosecrans realized at this time how lucky Negley and the rest of the 14th Corps were that the pursuit was not as rapid as the commanding general desired.

Braxton Bragg was also exhibiting impatience over the delays that were taking place in the vicinity of Chickamauga Creek. He had ordered General D.H. Hill to advance with the divisions of Generals Thomas C. Hindman, Patrick R. Cleburne, and John C. Breckinridge and attack Negley's isolated division. The assault was to have taken place on the morning of September 10, but Bragg waited in vain to hear the sound of musketry coming from McLemore's Cove and Dug Gap. Hill hesitated due to a lack of knowledge of the roads and the enemy's position. He also told Bragg that Cleburne was indisposed because of illness, though Cleburne later denied that he had been sick. General Hindman was reluctant to throw forward his men because Negley had taken a bold stance in deploying his division for battle once the Confederates in Dug Gap had been detected. Negley's determination to hold his position led Hindman to believe that the force in his front consisted of more than a single Union division. Bragg was furious and would later place Hindman under arrest for his timidity on the field of battle. In the end, a golden opportunity was lost, and September 10 was allowed to close without the Confederates' being able to take advantage Negley's precarious

Opposite: Maps showing the relative positions of the Union and Confederate forces on the Chickamauga battlefield. From *The History of the Civil War in the United States,* by Samuel Schmucker. Published by Jones Brothers & Co., in Philadelphia in 1865.

N
S
RIDGE
GAP
STEEDMAN
NEGLEY
WOOD
VAN CLEVE
2 BRIGS. 1 BRIG.
BRANNAN
REYNOLDS
JOHNSON
PALMER
BAIRD
THOMAS' LAST POSITION
THOMAS' 2ND POSITION
SHERIDAN
BRANNAN
NEGLEY 2 BRIGS
DAVIS 1 BRIGADE
THOMAS' 1ST POSITION
Mc COOK. CRITTENDEN. THOMAS
MISSIONARY
CAVALRY
MINTY
WILDER
FIRST REBEL POSITION
POLK
EWELL
JOHNSTON
LONGSTREET
WEST CHICKAMAUGA RIVER
READS FORD
WATERS SON. N.Y.

DIAGRAM I.

TO KNOXVILLE AND CLEVELAND
E. TENN. VIRG. R.R.
CHATTANOOGA
TENN RIVER
CHICKAMAUGA
NASHVILLE-CHAT. R.R.
LOOKOUT CK.
LOOKOUT MOUNTAIN
MISSIONARY RIDGE
T E N N.
WESTERN & ATLANTIC R.R.
ROSSVILLE
JOHNSON
EAST CHICKAMAUGA R.
CHICKAMAUGA RIVER
GRANGER'S RESERVED CORPS
RIDGE
CHATTANOOGA CREEK
G E O R G I A
REBELS
REBEL LINE
KELLEY
WOOD
BRANNAN
BAIRD
JOHNSON
PALMER
VAN CLEVE
REYNOLDS
READS FORD
RINGGOLD
HOSPITAL
WILDERS CAV.
MISSIONARY
ROSECRANS H'QS
WIDOW GLENN
DAVIS
WOOD
CORDONS MILL
SNOW HILL
SHERIDAN
TO LAFAYETTE
NEGLEY
CRAWFISH
WEST CHICKAMAUGA
PEA VINE CREEK
N
S
E
W
TO ATLANTA

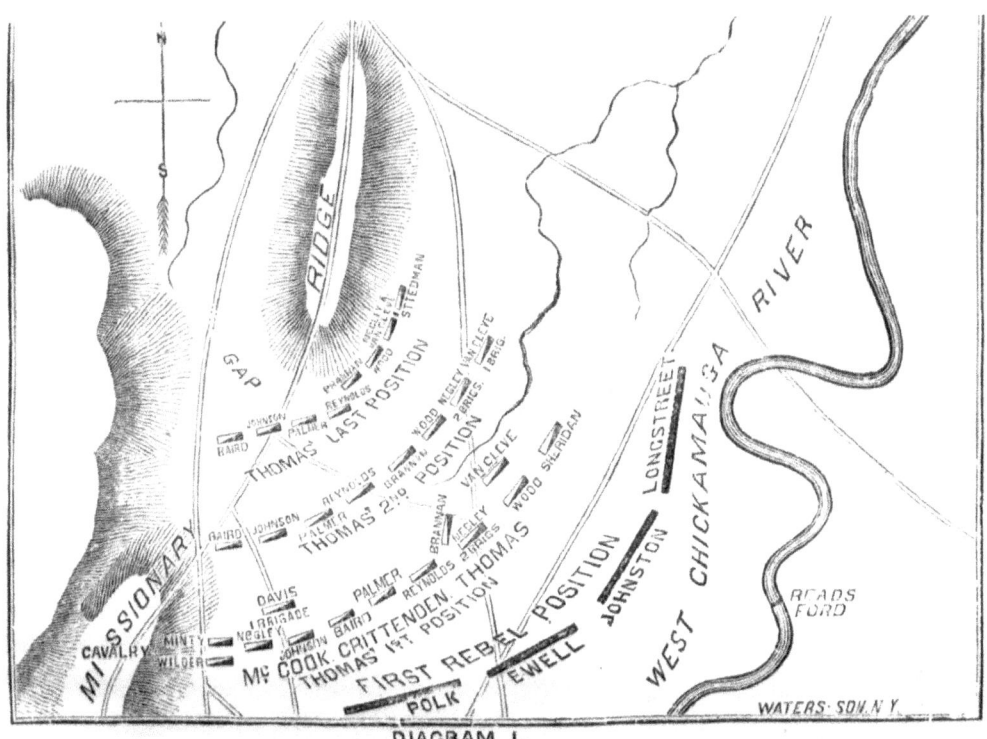

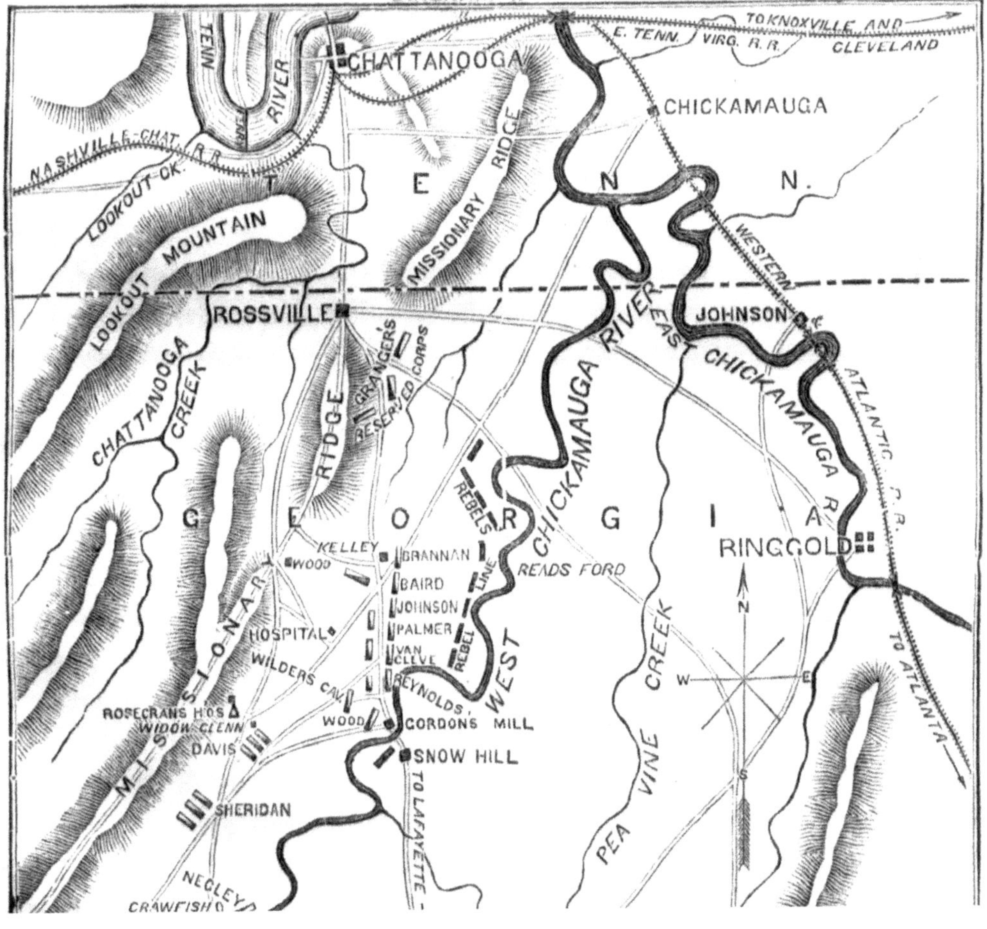

situation. Help was on the way, and the morning of September 11 would witness somewhat altered circumstances for both sides.[10]

During the 10th, Negley had withdrawn his line to a patch of woods west of the road to Crawfish Springs, near the Widow Davis house. He changed his battle line to face north, in response to the proximity of the Confederates on his flank, and prepared to hold his ground regardless of the odds. Negley had immediately sent to Thomas for assistance upon discovering the true state of affairs. "Old Reliable" responded by ordering Brigadier General Absalom Baird's division, the closest to Negley, to make a forced march to relieve the isolated division. Soldiers in Baird's Division remembered the march as the hardest they had made during the war, as they trudged through the night, over mountain roads, to the scene of danger.

Thomas informed Rosecrans of Negley's contact with a superior force, but the army commander was obviously still operating under the delusion that the Confederates were in head-long retreat. At 10:00 P.M. on the night of September 10, Rosecrans sent Thomas the following message: "The commanding general directs me to say that General Negley's dispatch forwarded by you at 10:00 A.M. is received. He is disappointed to learn from it that his forces move tomorrow morning instead of having moved this morning, as they should have done, this delay imperiling both extremes of the army. Your movement on Lafayette should be made with the utmost promptness. You ought not to encumber yourself with your main supply train. A brigade or two will be sufficient to protect it. Your advance ought to have threatened Lafayette yesterday morning."[11] At 10:30 P.M., Thomas provided Rosecrans with further information concerning Negley's findings of the day. More information was sent at 4:00 A.M. Thomas warned Rosecrans, "All information goes to confirm that a large part of Bragg's army is opposed to Negley," but the commander still failed to see the impending danger. Instead, he caustically replied that "Your desperate dispatches of 10:30 last night and of 4 this morning have been received. After maturely weighing the notes, the General commanding is induced to think that General Negley withdrew more through prudence than compulsion. He trusts his loss is not serious."[12] Rosecrans's tone implies that he felt Thomas to be an alarmist, and his reply is akin to a parent addressing a child who was overreacting to a situation. Rosecrans proceeded as if he felt the force Negley ran across to be nothing more than a rear guard, certainly nothing worthy of the caution his senior corps commander was now exhibiting.

On the morning of September 11, Baird's Division arrived in McLemore's Cove, at the base of Lookout Mountain. Baird allowed the troops a short rest before marching the nine miles down the cove that separated him from Negley. He found Negley drawn up in line of battle and placed his men on the left of this line, throwing out skirmishers. The Federals now had 10,000 men on the field, and the situation looked somewhat more promising than it had the previous day. The Union forces were still seriously outnumbered, however, as Bragg had 30,000 men confronting them. Thomas's other two divisions, under Brigadier General John M. Brannon and Major General Joseph J. Reynolds, were still west of Lookout Mountain and not in supporting range, but they were on the march and closing the gap between themselves and their isolated comrades.

Rosecrans was not yet convinced of the danger facing his army, but Negley, Baird, and Thomas were fully aware of the need for immediate and prudent action. Once Negley's and Baird's Divisions had formed a junction, it was felt that the combined Union force was now sufficient to execute a withdrawal in the face of the enemy, without being gobbled up as

Negley's sole division might have been had he attempted to exercise such a movement without Baird's supporting force. By 8:00 A.M., the Federals began to evacuate the valley, retracing their steps through Steven's Gap, and marching toward a junction with the remainder of the 14th Corps. The withdrawal would take most of the day, and the Northerners would still be in danger of being assaulted until they were all safely west of Lookout Mountain.[13]

Bragg lost another opportunity to destroy the Federals during the withdrawal. For a second day, he was unable to coordinate an attack by his subordinate commanders, though Cleburne did make a pursuit with his division. The Confederates were slowed by their crossing of Pigeon Mountain, which required men to drag the cannon and wagons over the rocky height. Brigadier General S.A.M. Wood's Brigade was in the advance, but was only able to engage the rear-guard skirmishers of the Federals after crossing Chickamauga Creek. It was nightfall before Cleburne's men reached the base of Lookout Mountain, and by that time, the Federals were safely through Steven's Gap and on the west side of the mountain. The Confederates could hear the sounds of the Union wagons and artillery making their way up the road, but the trap was sprung, and the Federals had eluded it. Lieutenant-Colonel Archibald Blakeley, commanding the 78th Pennsylvania, later wrote, "The extrication of our division from the environment of Dug Gap by General Negley was to my mind the most masterly piece of generalship I saw during the war."

On September 12, Thomas arrived at Steven's Gap in person, and established his headquarters as the rest of his corps consolidated at that spot.[14] Thomas was joined here by Rosecrans and Assistant Secretary of War Charles Dana. Dana's comments at this time reveal that neither he nor the commanding general were yet convinced that the Confederates were prepared to offer battle to the still widely separated Army of the Cumberland: "I left Chattanooga with Rosecrans and his staff for Thomas' headquarters. We found everything progressing favorably there. The movements for the concentration of the three corps were going forward with energy. Scouts were coming in constantly, who reported that the enemy had withdrawn from the basin where our army was assembling; that he was evacuating Lafayette and moving toward Rome. It seemed as if at last the Army of the Cumberland had practically gained a position from which it could effectively advance upon Rome and Atlanta, and deliver the finishing blow of the war."[15]

Thomas held quite a different view. To his staff he confided, "Nothing but stupendous blunders on the part of Bragg can save our army from total defeat." Negley and Baird had been extricated from McLemore's Cove, "and I believe I may be able to save this corps. But Bragg is also in position to strike McCook and Crittenden before they have a chance to extricate themselves."[16]

Luckily for the Federal army, the blunders of which Thomas spoke came to pass. By this time, Rosecrans had come to realize that his army was in a dire situation, and he took steps to meet the danger with all possible haste. McCook and Crittenden were ordered to concentrate on Thomas's position at Steven's Gap as soon as possible. McCook advised Thomas that the enemy were in his front, to which Thomas responded by ordering him to retrace his steps to the southern end of Lookout Mountain, and proceed north through Lookout Valley. This would require a march of 60 miles, instead of the 25 that currently separated the two corps. The added miles would cause a delay that irritated Rosecrans, but once again, his senior corps commander's judgment was proven correct. Had McCook advanced by the shortest and most direct route he would have marched straight into Bragg's waiting army, and could not possibly have avoided a disastrous defeat. It would take McCook several days to reach Thomas, but he would arrive intact, and ready to meet the Confederate menace.

Crittenden was also experiencing difficulties in effecting a junction with Thomas. With McCook now safely beyond the Confederates' reach, and Thomas massed behind the defensible position at Steven's Gap, Crittenden's Corps found itself the object of Bragg's attention. Crittenden had pulled his corps back from its furthest advance, at Ringgold, Georgia, and had concentrated across the Chattanooga-Lafayette Road, just north of Lee and Gordon's Mill, some twelve miles from Thomas. On the night of September 12, Bragg issued orders to Lieutenant General Leonidas Polk to spearhead an attack on Crittenden with his corps. Polk was to be supported by the corps of Major Generals W.H.T. Walker and Simon B. Buckner. Bragg sent Polk three follow-up messages that night, in an effort to ensure there were no misunderstandings concerning the planned assault. Too many chances had already slipped through his fingers, and the Confederate commander wanted to make sure this attack was carried out exactly as he planned it. But Polk balked at his orders to initiate the action. For some reason, he became timid and informed Bragg that he did not have enough men to make the attack. Though he would already enjoy a three-to-one advantage over Crittenden, he told Bragg that he must have additional force to "make failure impossible."[17] September 13 was permitted to come and go without an attack on Crittenden's Corps. Bragg was exasperated almost beyond the limit of human endurance.

Rosecrans was not the only high-ranking officer recently convinced of the peril of the Army of the Cumberland. General Halleck took up the alarm, hurriedly sending messages to Burnside at Knoxville, Grant at Vicksburg, and General Stephen A. Hurlburt at Memphis to rush whatever help they could to Rosecrans. These reinforcements would not arrive until after the expected engagement had already been fought. Rosecrans would have to meet the threat with the forces he presently had at hand. The only reinforcements that would reach Georgia in time to affect the outcome of the campaign would be wearing gray.

Bragg was severely disappointed by the failure of Polk to initiate the engagement with Crittenden prior to the latter officer's making contact with the center, under Thomas. By nightfall of September 16, Crittenden's Corps had made contact with Thomas at McLemore's Cove, with the bulk of his men holding a good defensive position at the southern spur of Missionary Ridge. McCook's Corps was still marching toward Thomas, and would arrive the following day. By September 17, the Federal army would be concentrated and all three corps would be within supporting distance of one another. The Confederates had squandered an opportunity to defeat the Federals while they were widely dispersed and vulnerable. Thomas's stand at Steven's Gap had provided a rallying point for the entire army, and though the situation still favored the Southern army, Bragg's prospects of success were now considerably diminished.

Elements of Longstreet's Corps began to arrive during September 17, and would continue to roll in throughout the next two days. Longstreet himself would not reach the scene of combat until September 19. Even so, the Confederate commander made plans to engage Rosecrans with the force he had at hand. The majority of Longstreet's men would be on the field on the 18th, and Bragg, irritated by the previous failures of his subordinate commanders to press their advantage, determined to launch his offensive at the earliest possible opportunity.[18] On the night of September 17, Bragg issued orders to his commanders to initiate the battle at 6:00 A.M. on the morning of the 18th:

> 1. Johnson's column [Hood's] on crossing at or near Reed's Bridge, will turn to the left by the most practicable route and sweep up the Chickamauga toward Lee and Gordon's Mill.
> 2. Walker, crossing at Alexander's Bridge, will unite in this move and push vigorously on the enemy's flank and rear in the same direction.

3. Buckner, crossing at Thedford's Ford, will join in the movement to the left, and press the enemy up the stream from Polk's front at Lee and Gordon's Mills.
4. Polk will press his forces to the front of Lee and Gordon's Mills, and if met by too much resistance to cross will bear to the right and cross at Dalton's Ford, or at Thedford's, as may be necessary, and join in the attack wherever the enemy may be.
5. Hill will cover our left flank from an advance of the enemy from the cove, and by pressing the cavalry in his front ascertain if the enemy is reinforcing at Lee and Gordon's Mills, in which event he will attack them in flank.
6. Wheeler's cavalry will hold the gaps in Pigeon Mountain and cover our rear and left and bring up stragglers.
7. All teams &c, not with troops should go toward Ringgold and Dalton, beyond Taylor's Ridge. All cooking should be done at the trains. Rations, when cooked, will be forwarded to the troops.
8. The above movements will be executed with the utmost promptness, vigor, and persistence.[19]

General Thomas had begun his day on September 17 at 3:30 A.M. by overseeing the battle readiness of his men. Rosecrans had ordered him to close up on Crittenden's Corps by advancing his position to Chickamauga Creek. Thomas dictated orders to his division commanders to "See that the men are provided with 20 rounds of ammunition in their pockets in addition to the cartridge boxes being full."[20] Thomas perceived that an attack was close at hand, and, as usual, was taking steps to ensure his men were fully prepared to meet any contingencies that might arise. After breakfast, Thomas got his corps in motion, and marched all day. By 10:20 A.M. on September 20, he had reached Alley's Spring, where he put three divisions into line, connecting on the left of Crittenden's position and interposing himself between Bragg's army and Chattanooga. Reynold's Division had been left behind to guard Dug Gap until the arrival of McCook's Corps, which was then to form on Crittenden's right.[21]

Bragg's orders for battle were issued with the assumption that Crittenden's Corps formed the left flank of the Union army. It was his intention to roll up this flank and sweep it back upon the mountains and the center of the Federal army. But Thomas had extended Crittenden's line, and it was he who now held the left flank. The change in the Federal alignment bore little importance in the events of September 18, however, for Bragg's plan of battle once more came to naught. Though there were several clashes of cavalry along the lines, the general movement of the Confederate army that Bragg had ordered was delayed until the following day. As night fell, the bulk of the Rebel army was still occupying positions on the far side of Chickamauga Creek.

During the night, the divisions of Alexander P. Stewart, William Preston, Benjamin Cheatham, and William H.T. Walker, and part of John Bell Hood's, crossed the Chickamauga Creek and got into battle line by 7:00 A.M. Dawn of September 19 found a large portion of Bragg's army on the west side of the creek, a fact that was not readily evident to the Federals. In fact, General McCook had met with Thomas early that morning to discuss what he thought to be an isolated Confederate brigade that was trapped on the Union side of the creek. Reed's Bridge had been ordered burned by Union cavalry on the 18th, but Forrest's cavalry had prevented its destruction. Both McCook and Thomas were unaware that the demolition of the bridge had not been successfully carried out, causing them to think that the Confederates on the western side of the creek were trapped. Thomas took McCook's suggestion and ordered General John Brannon to take two of his brigades and attack this Confederate force, which he believed to be only of brigade strength, at 8:00 A.M. One brigade was to be left behind to guard the road to Alexander's Bridge.

When Brannon made contact with the Rebels, he soon discovered that he was not facing a sole brigade, but rather a vastly superior enemy force. The story is told that when the brigades of Colonels Ferdinand Van Derveer and John T. Croxton engaged with the enemy, Croxton sent a message back to Thomas requesting clarification as to which of the five or six enemy brigades in his front was the one the general desired him to engage and capture.[22] Both Rosecrans and Bragg had planned their strategy for the day, but Thomas's movement, based on McCook's information, would force both commanders to react to conditions on the battlefield instead of directing the action as they had intended. The Battle of Chickamauga was to be opened not by the execution of well-thought-out strategy. Instead, it would be brought about by chance, the great equalizer in war. Despite all of Bragg's efforts to be the aggressor in this battle, Thomas and the Federals were the ones to fire the opening shots.

The force Brannon's three brigades were encountering were the three dismounted brigades of Nathan Bedford Forrest's cavalry, supported by two additional mounted brigades. Walker's infantry division was not yet on the field, but was marching from the south to join in the fray. Thomas quickly ascertained that the situation in his front was much changed from the impression given to him by McCook and immediately ordered Baird's Division forward in support of Brannon. He further directed that the brigade commanders form their lines into hollow squares to resist attack from all sides, and ordered that all commanders hold their ground. Shortly before noon, Walker's Confederate infantry arrived on the scene, and the pressure to the Union left became so acute that General Baird despaired of being able to hold his position. A *Chicago Journal* correspondent with the army said that the Confederates "bore down upon Brannon like a mountain torrent, sweeping away a brigade as if it had been driftwood."[23]

Croxton, who had previously been permitted to withdraw from the field to replenish his ammunition, returned at this critical time and helped to stay the impending disaster. Thomas found more support in the form of Richard W. Johnson's Division, of McCook's Corps, which Rosecrans had ordered forward. Johnson's men were thrown into the fight with fixed bayonets. They recaptured a Union battery that had been lost, and for a while they stabilized the Federal line. More support was on its way to Thomas. General Joseph Reynolds's Division, of Thomas's Corps, had been relieved of its duty at Dug Gap, and was marching to rejoin the rest of the 14th Corps. Reynolds had somehow gotten behind Major General John M. Palmer's Division of Crittenden's Corps on the line of march, but they were near at hand and available for support.[24]

Thomas Berry, an officer in Forrest's cavalry, described the intense struggle taking place during the initial phases of the battle. "Neighing horses, wild and frightened, were running in every direction, seething crackling bullets, the piercing screaming fragments of shells, the whirring sound of shrapnel and the savage shower of canister, mingled with the fierce answering yells of defiance, all united in one horrible sound. The ghastly, mangled dead and horribly wounded strewed the earth for over half a mile up and down the river banks. The dead were piled upon each other in ricks, like cordwood, to make passage for advancing columns. The sluggish stream of Chickamauga ran red with human blood." This officer attested to the ferocity of the fighting by stating, "I had been in 60 battles and skirmishes up to this time, but nothing like this had I ever seen. Men fought like demons."[25]

The divisions of both armies were now stacking up in the vicinity of Thomas's Corps, and as new units came onto the field they were quickly funneled into the fight. Johnson's Division had successfully thrown back Walker's Confederates. Palmer arrived to bolster the Union position, but Benjamin Cheatham's Division launched a furious attack that breached the lines of both Johnson and Palmer. Sergeant J.K. Young, a soldier in the 89th Illinois Infantry of Johnson's Division, related, "The line in front of us stalks grimly into the smoke. Men cheer but in that awful roar the voice of a man cannot be heard 10 feet away. Men fall to the right and left. The line stumbles over corpses as it hurries on. There are flashes in the smoke cloud, terrible explosions in the air, and the men are stepped on or leaped over as they throw up their arms and fall upon the grass and scream in the agony of mortal wounds."[26] Reynolds took position on the Federal right, just in time to meet a thrust by A.P. Stewart's Division. The ebb and flow continued throughout the afternoon, as the divisions of Confederate Generals St. John Liddell and Bushrod R. Johnson were thrown into the fray.

By 1:00 P.M., Rosecrans had determined to relocate his headquarters from Crawfish Springs in order to be nearer the scene of fighting. He selected the house of a young widow, Eliza Glenn, which was located immediately behind Thomas's right flank. Charles Dana accompanied Rosecrans, and wrote, "Although closer to the battle, we could see no more of it here than at Crawfish Springs, the conflict being fought altogether in thick forest, and being invisible to outsiders. The nature of the firing and the reports from the commanders alone enabled us to follow its progress." Even so, Rosecrans was able to keep well informed about the progress of the battle by using the telegraph that he had had installed at the Widow Glenn house. Reports came in constantly, and were in turn forwarded to Washington. Dana sent eleven different messages to the War Department throughout the day, keeping the government apprised of the situation as it transpired.[27]

By 4:00 P.M., John Bell Hood's Division from the Army of Northern Virginia was on the field and was quickly sent into the melee. Hood advanced with his crippled arm in a sling, from the wound he had received less than three months before while leading the charge of the second day at Gettysburg. William A. Fletcher, a soldier in Hood's Division, recounted how the Federals had to their rear a "high well-built worm rail fence.... I suppose it was the least of their thoughts of having to return that way, or they would have had it torn down to clear their rear." Hood's men pushed the Federals so rapidly that they did not have time to climb or push down the fence, and the Confederates at this point shot into what became a fleeing and fearful mob.[28] Though bloody and brutal, the fighting was producing no clear advantage for either side. More and more Confederate divisions had been added to the assault, but Thomas was able to parry each new thrust and maintain his position. The five divisions he had at his disposal had held their ground against the weight of seven divisions of Confederate infantry, supported by five brigades of dismounted cavalry.

As evening came on, Thomas looked to the next day and the resumption of hostilities he was sure it would bring. He ordered Baird and Johnson to pull back from their current line, to higher ground to their rear. Then, he found Palmer and Reynolds and ordered them to move their corps five hundred yards to a spot east of the Lafayette Road. Though night attacks were extremely rare during the Civil War, Thomas anticipated that the fighting was not yet concluded for the day and cautioned his commanders to be alert for another Confederate thrust. Before the corps commanders could execute his orders, however, Patrick Cleburne used the waning daylight to launch a determined assault upon Johnson and Baird.

The 77th Pennsylvania Infantry was in the first line of battle, and Cleburne's men completely annihilated the Pennsylvanians. One observer stated that the regiment was "lapped up like a drop of oil under a flame."[29] The Confederate attack, combined with the gathering darkness, served to create confusion in the Federal ranks, causing one of Baird's brigades to mistakenly fire on one of Johnson's brigades. Johnson's men returned the volley before realizing the error, as scores of Union troops were felled by friendly fire. The Confederates had captured three cannon and almost 300 prisoners, and had driven the Union troops for about a mile. Cleburne did not realize the consternation he was creating among the Federal troops and failed to press his advantage, however. In the darkness, he called off the attack and disengaged his division for the night.

Cleburne's troops bedded down for the night right where they were, among the dead and wounded that littered the battlefield. The night turned bitterly cold, causing great suffering among the soldier of both sides, especially the wounded who lay thick between the contending lines. One veteran of the day's fighting recalled, "The cries and groans from these poor fellows is perfectly awful. They are more dreadful than the storm of bullets that showered on us all day — friend and foe lying side by side, the friends of each unable to assist in the least. It was the hardest part of the battle to lie within hearing and not be able to assist them."[30]

The fighting of the first day at Chickamauga had not gone according to any plans that Bragg or Rosecrans might have intended. Thomas had initiated the battle when he acted upon McCook's faulty information regarding the Confederate brigade that had supposedly become isolated on the Federal side of the Chickamauga. From that point on, both sides reacted to events dictated by the fighting. Bragg had failed to mass his forces for a knock-out blow against the Federals, and had funneled his troops into the fight in piecemeal fashion. D.H. Hill would later equate his commander's actions that day to "the sparring of an amateur boxer as opposed to the crushing blows of the trained pugilist."[31] Thomas had been in tactical command of all of the Union forces engaged on the 19th, and, as usual, had fought his men with competence and determination. The Confederates had been unable to force Thomas from the field, despite the superior force that had been thrown at him. The following day would witness the arrival on the field of the remainder of Longstreet's 14,000 men from the Virginia Theater, and a resumption of the efforts to dislodge the Union army from its position. Thomas could not know it as the smoke cleared over the battlefield on the night of September 19, but before another day was over he would face the majority of Bragg's army in a desperate struggle that would win him everlasting fame and glory.

At midnight on September 19, Rosecrans called a council of his officers at his headquarters at the Widow Glenn's house. Reports had come in all day concerning the fact that Bragg's army had been heavily reinforced. Captured prisoners from Longstreet's Corps and Joseph E. Johnston's army in Mississippi confirmed the reports and caused Rosecrans to adopt a strictly defensive posture, thinking himself to be greatly outnumbered by the enemy. To be sure, Bragg heavily outnumbered Rosecrans on paper, but not all of the reinforcements being sent to him would arrive in time to take part in the battle. Four full brigades of Longstreet's Corps would not make it to Chickamauga in time to have any effect on the fighting. The fact was that Bragg held only a slight advantage over Rosecrans on the field, but the Federal commander had been fully convinced of his inferiority, and his future actions were to be based upon this assumption.

When Rosecrans's commanders gathered at his headquarters the events of the day were discussed. Disregarding the Reserve Corps, all but two brigades of the Union army had been engaged in the fighting that took place that day. Thomas expressed his conviction that he could hold his position on the left against anything the Confederates might throw against him, but suggested that Rosecrans pull back his right and center to the east slope of Missionary Ridge and the hills west of the Lafayette Road. He felt that this move would place the

Federal army on ground that was more easily defended, while at the same time guarding all but one of the routes leading to Chattanooga. The other main road to Chattanooga, the Rossville Road, was where the army's Reserve Corps, under Major General Gordon Granger, had been posted. Thomas's judgment was sound, but Rosecrans refused to accept it, citing as his reasons that such a move would require him to abandon his headquarters and the field hospitals that had been established near Crawfish Springs. Thomas was much fatigued by the events of the day, and the late hour of the council of war finally took its toll on him. He is reported to have dozed off during the remainder of the war council. Whenever he was awakened, he would mutter "Strengthen the left," and then nod off again.[32] Rosecrans, Crittenden, and McCook continued to discuss plans for the next morning.

By 1:00 A.M., the meeting was ended. It was decided that Thomas would maintain his current position, maintaining Johnson's Division from McCook's Corps, and Palmer's Division from Crittenden's. McCook's two remaining divisions were to extend Thomas's line to the right. Crittenden, with his two remaining divisions, was to position himself to the rear of the main line, at the junction of Thomas's and McCook's Corps, and was to act as the army reserve, responding to circumstances as they arose on the main line of battle. All present felt that the Confederates would make their main effort against Thomas's position. The placement of the troops was completed before daylight, as the men in the ranks steeled themselves against the slaughter that they knew would come with the rising sun.[33]

Bragg conducted a more informal council with his officers on the night of September 19. He announced his intention to reorganize the Army of Tennessee into two wings. Lieutenant General Leonidas Polk would command the right wing, consisting of his own corps, along with those of Hill and Walker. The left wing was assigned to Lieutenant General James P. Longstreet, and would be made up of Longstreet's Corps and Buckner's Corps. Bragg made this realignment even though Longstreet and the bulk of his men had not yet reached the army. Reports had been received at Confederate headquarters that Lee's Old War Horse had arrived in Georgia, and was in the general vicinity of Bragg's forces, but he was still en route when the Confederate commander issued his orders.

Longstreet spent most of the day of September 19 searching for his new superior. He arrived at the railroad station at Ringgold, Georgia, at 2:00 P.M. of that day. Much to his surprise, Bragg had sent no one to meet him to let him know where Confederate headquarters were located. It was 4:00 P.M. before Longstreet's staff and horse arrived on another train. The small party then set out, following the sounds of battle in the unfamiliar landscape, and hoping it would lead them to their desired destination. Once they encountered the stragglers and wounded of the army, all making their way to the rear, they inquired as to the location of Bragg's headquarters. But confusion ruled the day, and Longstreet and his party were almost captured when they inadvertently wandered into Federal lines in the gathering darkness. It was not until 11:00 P.M. that they finally found Bragg, asleep in bed. Bragg awoke and talked with Longstreet for about an hour. His plans for the following morning were quite simple. He planned to once more assail the Federal left and drive it into McLemore's Cove, where the whole Union army could then be destroyed. Polk's right wing would initiate the fighting at daylight, followed by Longstreet's left wing.[34]

Bragg's plan of attack called for Hill to launch the attack from the far right of the Confederate line. Somehow, Hill's division commanders received the orders, but Hill himself was never notified. His corps occupied a position on the far left of Polk's line, and would have to march to the other extreme of the Southern position, but it was not until about dawn, when his men should have been pressing their attack forward, that Hill learned from his subordinates of the orders. Once more, Bragg's battle plans were being delayed. The sun rose over the horizon, and hours passed, as Hill leisurely got his corps into position. An eerie silence enveloped the battlefield, as the anticipated battle failed to materialize. Bragg's rage knew no bounds, as he cursed Polk, Hill, and the rest of his generals. He issued orders for the attack to be gotten underway at once, but it was not until 9:45 A.M. that Breckinridge's Division marched around the end of Thomas's line, on the far left, and threw themselves upon the flank of Negley's Division.[35]

Negley was just arriving on the Union left when he was assailed by Hill. During the night, Thomas had received word from Baird that his line did not quite extend to Lafayette Road, and that he could not extend his line to cover it without severely weakening his position. Thomas sent word to Rosecrans of the situation and requested that Negley's Division be forwarded to lengthen his line to the left. Negley's orders were issued at 6:00 A.M., and it was only because of Hill's tardiness in making his attack that Negley was even able to reach the vicinity of Thomas's left in time to play a part in the opening of the battle. Thomas had ordered his men to construct strong log breastworks during the night, but Negley's men had not had time to build any defensive structures before Breckinridge's men fell upon them.

John Beatty's Brigade had been the first of Negley's men to reach their position, and after an hour of savage fighting his line was shattered. Forrest's Southern cavalry worked its way around to the rear of the Union line, and for a moment it seemed that the Federal left was on the verge of giving way. But Thomas gathered up reserves and flung them into the fight, bolstering the line and regaining the lost ground. Negley's other two brigades were not yet in position because their place in their old line had not yet been filled by a replacement from McCook's Corps. Major General Thomas J. Wood had been ordered to relocate his division to Negley's position, but had been tardy in doing so.

Upon discovering that Wood was not posted in the position he had been ordered to, Rosecrans went in search of that officer. When the Federal commander caught up with his subordinate, he cursed him violently in front of all of his officers and men. One version of the meeting between the two officers, from which most of the profanity was removed, had Rosecrans screaming: "What is the meaning of this, sir? You have disobeyed my specific orders! By your damnable negligence you are endangering the safety of the entire army, and, by God, I will not tolerate it! Move your division at once, as I have instructed, or the consequences will not be pleasant for yourself!" Though Wood's blood must have boiled at being the target of such a public reprimand, he simply saluted and went off to get his brigades in motion. Rosecrans could not know it at the time, but this incident with Wood would bear dire consequences later in the afternoon.[36]

Bragg's divisions assaulted the Federal line en echelon, from north to south, or from the left to the right of the Union line. Pressure was mounting against Thomas's position, but the Confederates were finding it impossible to breach his forbidding log breastworks. Though the works were charged by the divisions of Breckinridge and Cleburne, the attacks were thrown back with heavy loss. Thomas was requesting reinforcements, and Rosecrans obliged as quickly as he could free units from the right flank. At about 10:30 A.M., Captain Sanford Kellog came into Thomas's headquarters with news that there was a gap in the Union line between Wood's and Reynolds's divisions. In actuality, no gap existed. Kellog had ridden along the Federal line and had seen a patch of heavy woods with no troops in front of it, and had assumed that the place was undefended. In reality, Brannon's entire division was concealed in those woods, connecting Woods's line with that of Reynolds.

Thomas passed along Kellog's observations to Rosecrans. The commander accepted the information as being factual without bothering to check it out. He subsequently sent orders to General Wood: "The general commanding directs you to close up on Reynolds as fast as possible and support him." Woods was aware that Brannon's Division was posted on his left, and the order made no sense to him. Literally taken, he was being ordered to close his left flank to Reynolds's right, but Brannon was in the way. The word "support" implied that he was to take position behind Reynolds. To Wood, the order was utter nonsense. He would be pulling his division out of line and marching it to a place where it would not be needed. In the process, he would be creating a hole in the line where none had previously existed. Had he not been the victim of Rosecrans's public rage only about an hour before, Wood most probably would have ridden to headquarters to seek clarification of the orders, and the mistake would have been discovered. As it was, Wood promptly obeyed the peremptory orders, not willing to bring himself in line for another public tirade from his superior. He marched his men toward Reynolds, vacating a quarter-mile section of the line, and creating a huge gap between Thomas and McCook.[37]

Wood of course realized that the removal of his division from the line would create a dangerous gap. In speaking of his orders from Rosecrans, he said, "General McCook was with me when I received it. I informed him that I would immediately carry it into execution, and suggested that he should close up his command rapidly to my right to prevent the occurrence of a gap in our lines. He said he would do so and immediately rode away."[38] Despite his intentions, McCook failed to move his men into position in an expedient manner, and the gap Wood foresaw came to be a reality.

Rosecrans ordered two of Philip Sheridan's brigades, which had been positioned to the right of Wood's old place in line, to the support of Thomas. Jefferson C. Davis, from Crittenden's Corps, was instructed to move his division forward to fill the ground evacuated by Wood and Sheridan. The time was now about 11:30 A.M. The sequential assaults of Bragg's divisions, from right to left, had been progressing down the line all morning. Polk's entire wing was now engaged, and Longstreet's wing was preparing to enter the fray. As luck would have it, Longstreet had assembled the divisions of John Bell Hood, Bushrod Johnson, and Joseph B. Kershaw directly in front of the gap created by the removal of Wood and Sheridan. Within minutes of the Federals' departure, and before Davis could have a chance to march his division into position, the Confederates launched a massive strike directly at the unoccupied space between McCook and Thomas. The Rebel assault caught the Federals completely by surprise. Longstreet's men surged forward, taking McCook's men in flank and pouring in upon Crittenden's reserves like an irresistible wave. Bushrod Johnson thought that "The scene now presented was unspeakably grand, The resolute and impetuous charge, the rush of our heavy columns sweeping out from the shadow and gloom of the forest and into the open fields flooded with sunlight, the glitter of arms, the onward dash of artillery and mounted men, the retreat of the foe, the shouts of the hosts of our army, the dust, the smoke, the noise of firearms — of whistling balls and grapeshot and of bursting shell — made up a battle scene of unsurpassed grandeur."[39]

The Federals found no such grandeur in the situation unfolding before their eyes. The Union line had been severed at its center, and the men of McCook and Crittenden were quickly being overpowered and put into a state of panic. Charles Dana was present at Rosecrans's headquarters when the breakthrough occurred. He had not slept for two nights, and was attempting to catch a couple of winks on the ground when the crash of battle awakened him. Dana said that the "first thing I saw was General Rosecrans crossing himself— he was a very devout Catholic. 'Hello!' I said to myself, 'if the general is crossing himself, we are in a desperate situation.' ... I had no sooner collected my thoughts and looked around toward the front, where all this din came from, than I saw our lines break and melt away like leaves before the wind. Then the headquarters around me disappeared. The gray-backs came through with a rush, and soon the musket balls and cannon shot began to reach the place where we stood. The whole right of the army had apparently been routed."[40]

Indeed, McCook's Corps was being routed from the field, and Crittenden's men were following suit. Longstreet's men were accomplishing what they had not done some two months before on the fields of Gettysburg. They had broken the Union line, albeit with the help of Rosecrans, and stood poised to cripple or destroy the beaten foe. Davis's Division was crushed, Van Cleve's was put in wild disorder, and Sheridan's seemed to evaporate. Rosecrans tried briefly to rally the men and restore order, but the rout was already beyond redemption. As Colonel Gates P. Thruston, of McCook's staff, put it, "No order could be heard above the tempest of battle. With a wild yell the Confederates swept far to their left. They seemed everywhere victorious."[41] The only organized force still intact on the right was Wilder's Brigade, who, with their seven-shot Spencer repeating rifles, were holding their own against the Rebel onslaught. Rosecrans was compelled to surrender his headquarters at the Widow Glenn House and flee for his life amid the tide of refugees running from what had once been his line of battle. Rosecrans tried to join Thomas, but his path was barred by Longstreet's men. Unable to join the left, he opted to take the Dry Valley Road toward Chattanooga, the destination most of the right flank was making their best time to reach.

Wilder had also determined to join Thomas and continue the fight. "At this juncture Wilder conceived the idea of putting through the rebel lines and fighting his way straight down to Thomas. He had five regiments and a battery of artillery." Wilder was confident that his repeating rifles would enable him to cut his way through to Thomas, and was preparing the brigade for the movement when Assistant Secretary Dana arrived and "gave positive orders not to do so, but draw his forces off and down upon the Chattanooga road near the city." A soldier in Wilder's Brigade was much chagrined by the orders and called Dana a "coward," stating that he "had authority at a time when he should have had no authority."[42]

James A. Garfield, Rosecrans's aide, volunteered to try to reach Thomas and inform him of the disaster that had befallen the right. Rosecrans gave Garfield permission to make the attempt, and told him to relay to Thomas that he had permission to withdraw his men, at his own discretion. By 4:00 P.M., Rosecrans had reached Chattanooga, so shaken by the calamity at hand that he had to be helped from his horse.[43] To the south, the sounds of battle could still be discerned from the direction of Thomas's position, and all knew that he was holding firm against the combined weight of the entire Confederate army. Instead of pursuing Rosecrans's fleeing mob, Longstreet faced his men northward, toward Thomas, intent on joining with Polk to sweep this remaining pocket of resistance from the field.

McCook and Crittenden were effectively out of the fight, and it appeared that they were leaving Thomas's reinforced corps to face the entire Confederate army alone. But such was not the case. When Longstreet's men were first charging into the gap in the Federal line, help was already on its way to Thomas. On the night of September 19, Rosecrans had instructed General Gordon Granger to have his Reserve Corps in readiness to support Thomas, if the need arose. In compliance, Granger moved his corps from Rossville to McAfee Church, three miles from Rossville, and a mile and a half from the Lafayette Road. From this location, he was only five miles from Thomas's line, and within easy supporting range. Granger and his division commander, Brigadier General James B. Steedman, had been listening to the sounds of the battle from the time Breckinridge first assailed Thomas at 9:45 that morning. The ever increasing crescendo convinced both officers that the army was being sorely pressed, and they decided to march to the sound of the guns and reinforce Thomas. After the war, many of Steedman's and Granger's men claimed that the march had been made without orders, or even against orders. They asserted that Granger and Steedman were due all the credit for making the decision to go to Thomas's aid, and that no one else had a hand in it. The fact of the matter is that Rosecrans had ordered Granger to put himself in a position to do precisely that the previous night. Furthermore, Thomas had been in almost constant contact with Granger from the inception of the fighting that day. Never one to leave anything to chance, Thomas had informed Granger of his plans on the morning of the 20th, and had inquired as to the exact location of the Reserve Corps and its availability for support. When Granger moved, it was in response to positive orders he had already received from both Rosecrans and Thomas, and not by his own initiative. By 11:00 A.M., Granger had Steedman's men on the road headed toward Thomas. He had his assistant adjutant general send a message to Thomas's chief of staff advising him of the movement:

Col. Flynt:
    General Granger is moving Steedman with two brigades to General Thomas' assistance.
        W.C. Russell,
        Captain and Assistant Adjutant-general.[44]

The head of Granger's Division reached Thomas by 1:00 P.M., and the entire division was on the ground a half hour later. Their arrival could not have been more timely. Thomas's men had been sorely pressed ever since the collapse of the right flank. The first fighting had been initiated shortly after 9:30 A.M., when Breckinridge made contact with Baird's left flank, on Thomas's line. Brigadier General Benjamin Hardin Helm, an in-law of Abraham Lincoln, commanded a brigade in Breckinridge's force, and fell mortally wounded shortly after the fighting began. The Confederates drove Baird's men back, until they were met by troops from the divisions of Negley, Johnson, and Palmer, when the Confederates were checked and repulsed. Cleburne's Division was then sent forward in support of Breckinridge, striking the troops of Palmer and Reynolds, who were fighting from behind strong barricades of logs and rails. Cleburne's assault was short-lived before the galling fire from the Union position forced them to retire as well. Brigadier General Sterling A. Wood, of Cleburne's command, was then sent forward against Reynold's position. The right of Wood's brigade was soon repulsed, but the left made progress, forcing back the right of Reynold's position. Wood then joined with A.P. Stewart in attacking Brannon's Division, but Brannon held firm, and the Confederates were once more compelled to retire. Brigadier General States Rights Gist came to the support of Cleburne and ordered his division forward in the space between that officer and Breckinridge. His men charged the works held by Baird and Johnson, but were themselves repulsed with heavy loss. General Liddell's Division of two brigades joined the fray in support of Gist. Brigadier General Edward C. Walthall's Brigade was sent around the left of Gist's Division to connect with Cleburne's right flank. Colonel Daniel C. Govan's Brigade went to the right of Gist. The time was now about 11:00 A.M., and the continual pressure by the Confederates was beginning to push the Union line to its breaking point. Fortunately for the Union cause,

Brigadier General August Willich of McCook's Corps, and Colonel Ferdinand VanDeveer of Thomas's, both had recently arrived on the scene with their brigades, met Goven's advance, and threw it back half a mile.[45]

As Thomas's line was repulsing these latest assaults, Longstreet's wing was rushing into the gap created by the removal of Thomas Wood's Division, and the Union right was beginning to crumble and melt away. Thomas could hear the sound of fighting extending down the line to his right, and knew that the rest of the Army of the Cumberland was being heavily engaged, but he had no idea of the catastrophe that was then being visited upon the rest of the army. Longstreet's men were fanning out from the breach in the Union line, and were facing northward, in the direction of Thomas' position. Bushrod Johnson's Division of Longstreet's wing, supported by the divisions of Evander Law and Joseph Kershaw, struck Thomas's right flank, under Brannon, and swept the Federal troops from the field. The brigades of Colonel George P. Buell, Brigadier General Samuel Beatty, Colonel John M. Connell, and Colonel John T. Croxton were thrown into the breach, and with the assistance of several pieces of artillery, were successful in blunting the further advance of Johnson and Kershaw. In the process, many of the defenders were surrounded and captured.[46]

Thomas was continuously employed in establishing lines of defense and shifting units to meet the repeated blows of the enemy. He now collected the detachments of broken commands and placed them in line on the crest of Horseshoe Ridge, running west from the Snodgrass house. Part of David Stanley's Brigade was posted on the ridge, south of the Snodgrass house. Colonel Charles G. Harker's Brigade, which had attached itself to Thomas following the rout of McCook's Corps, was assigned to extend the horseshoe-shaped line on the ridge curving to the east of the Snodgrass house. Thomas was occupying a good defensive position, with interior lines, but owing to the disparity of numbers arrayed against him, was still in a precarious situation. VanDeveer's Brigade, after turning Govan's attack back, assumed a position to the right of Stanley's line, connecting to Harker on his left. The Union forces had been so roughly handled that VanDeveer's Brigade was the largest organized unit Thomas had at his disposal at this time.

The Confederates now attacked Thomas's new line. The Confederate right nearly gained the crest before being driven back with heavy losses. Their left, under Bushrod Johnson and Thomas C. Hindman, was making significant progress, however. Meeting only slight resistance, they were gaining ground against the Federal right, and threatening to punch through Thomas's line.[47] It was at this critical juncture that Granger's advance, under Steedman, marched onto the field to save the day. His additional brigades were sorely needed to restore the line and repel the Confederate attackers, but Granger brought with him something that was in as short supply as manpower at that time: ammunition. The reserve ammunition train of Thomas's Corps had been swept away in the retreat of the right flank of the army, leaving Thomas's men with only the cartridges they carried with them with which to fight. Many of the Federals were already out of ammunition and were taking what they could from the dead and wounded in their front in order to continue the fight. Granger had thought to bring his own reserve supply of ammunition with him, and he had 10,000 badly needed cartridges to put into the hands of the beleaguered Union troops when his men joined in the defense of Horseshoe Ridge.

The cloud of dust raised by Granger's advancing men was seen long before Thomas knew whether the force was friend or foe. Thomas sent a captain of the 2nd Indiana Cavalry forward to ascertain the identity of the column, as the soldiers in the ranks looked over their

Picture of the Snodgrass House on Snodgrass Hill, Horseshoe Ridge. Thomas's men defended this area against repeated Confederate attacks, and withdrew only after nightfall had brought a close to the hostilities (United States Army Military History Institute).

shoulders and wondered if they were presently to be surrounded and attacked from the rear. When the Federal trooper approached the column he asked "Whose troops are these?" "Mine, sir," was the simple reply received from an officer riding at their lead. When asked his name, the officer responded, "I am General Steedman, commanding the First Division of the reserve corps." When Steedman rode up to the Union line Thomas greeted him with, "General Steedman, I have always been glad to see you, but never so glad as now. How many muskets have you got?" Steedman responded that there were 7,500 men in his division. "It is a good force," Thomas said, "and needed very badly." Granger was on the scene before all of his men had marched into Thomas's lines, and the immediate peril was somewhat abated.[48]

Thomas was not intimidated by his situation, though he exhibited about as much relief as his reserved personality would allow when he greeted Granger with the words, "I am very glad to see you, General." Steedman inquired as to where his men should be posted, and Thomas pointed to the crest of the ridge to their right, where Hindman and Johnson were threatening to sever the line. "You see," was his only response. As Steedman departed to ready his men for the advance, he overheard Thomas tell one of his aides to instruct Colonel Harker to shift his brigade to the right as well, to add his weight to Steedman's two brigades in blunting the Confederate charge. The aide asked, "Where will I find you, General, when I return?"— evidently thinking that Thomas would withdraw his headquarters in the face of such danger. But the Virginian had determined to be stubborn this day. No thought was given to surrendering his position, and Thomas glared at the officer as if he were shocked at the suggestion that was being implied. "Here," was the short but emphatic reply.[49] Steedman had been trained by Thomas while he was still a colonel at Camp Dick Robinson. He was well acquainted with the qualities of the man, and much amused by the exchange he had just heard between his commander and the aide.

Forming his men for the attack, Steedman personally raised the banner of one of his regiments and led the troops forward toward the crest. Steedman's men pitched into the waiting Confederates with a vengeance, as the struggle for the ridge became a test of endurance and will. Much of the fighting was done at close range with bayonets, clubbed muskets, rocks, and fists. General Palmer observed the action and stated that "In all my experience I have never witnessed such desperate hand-to-hand fighting. The sound of musketry was so incessant and rapid that it was a continuous roar."[50] The Confederates mounted three different counterattacks against the Union right, but with the support of VanDeveer's and Hazen's brigades, each attempt to seize the crest was beaten back. The cost was severe, however. Fully one-half of Steedman's men had fallen in the struggle to hold the crest. But the Confederates had suffered similar losses, and were, at length, compelled to give ground and retire to the southern base of the ridge. A long-range duel of artillery and musketry then ensued between the opposing lines, punctuated by intermittent thrusts by individual Confederate brigades or divisions, which were all repulsed with heavy casualties.[51]

James Garfield was riding toward Thomas's position to inform him of the plight of the rest of the army and give him Rosecrans's message advising him to withdraw his forces at his own discretion. With him were his two orderlies and Captain R.M. Gano, who had delivered a message from Thomas's headquarters to Rosecrans earlier in the day, and was serving as a guide for Garfield. The little band was forced to make a wide loop in the direction of Rossville to avoid contact with Confederate forces that now ranged over the entire countryside. When only a few miles from Thomas's position, the party stumbled upon a force of Confederates and shots rang out. One of Garfield's orderlies was killed, and Gano's leg was broken when his horse fell with a bullet through its lungs. Garfield's horse was shot twice, but was able to continue onward for the ten minutes it took to reach Thomas's lines.

Garfield recorded the time when he arrived at Horseshoe Ridge as being 3:35 P.M. His message from Rosecrans was "the first reliable information" Thomas had received "that the right and center of our army had been driven." Thomas had been fighting for approximately four hours with no knowledge that he was standing alone against the entire Confederate army. He had suspected that events were not going well with the right wing of the army, but was unaware that it had departed the field and was retreating toward Chattanooga. This revelation did not dampen his determination nor alter his plans. When informed that Rosecrans had given permission for him to withdraw, he confidently declined to do so. His optimism was evident in the message General Granger was detailed to deliver in person to Rosecrans at Chattanooga. "Longstreet's Virginians have got their bellies full.... I believe we can now crown the whole battle with victory."[52]

The left of Thomas's line was receiving a respite following the repulses of Polk's Confederates during the morning. For unknown reasons, Bragg was allowing his army to fight piecemeal once again, instead of utilizing the superiority of numbers he enjoyed to its fullest advantage. Bragg had approximately 60,000 men on the field. Thomas had only around 25,000 men in line to oppose him, but given the nature of the Confederates' uncoordinated assaults, he had been able to shift men to counter each new thrust. One Union survivor on the right remembered "They came in great, destructive waves, one after another, charge after charge, assault after assault, in continuous lines all that dreadful afternoon."[53] Had Polk's wing joined in a concerted effort with the assault being waged by Longstreet's men on the Federal right, Thomas would have been denied the opportunity to use his interior lines, and might possibly have been overpowered. Edwin K. Martin, a soldier in the 79th Pennsylvania Infantry, observed Thomas during the fighting that had been taking place and noted the calmness of his demeanor. The general issued orders in a polite and conversational tone, and showed no signs of distress or harassment. "There is no figure in military history more sublime than that of General Thomas in the midst of this line of fire that nearly encircles the Horseshoe Ridge," Martin thought, "wrenching victory from the jaws of defeat ... making amends for the sins of a whole campaign."[54]

During the lull on the left, and prior to the arrival of Steedman's Division, the commanders of the divisions holding the left of Thomas's line discussed their situation and planned for future contingencies. Baird, Johnson, Palmer and Reynolds all felt that a crisis was at hand. They had not received any definitive orders from Thomas for some time, that officer being occupied with affairs on the right. Another assault from General Polk's wing was anticipated at any time. Rumors had it that Rosecrans, Thomas, McCook, and Crittenden had all been killed or captured, and the officers on the left felt that a general needed to be selected to take control of their divisions to lead them off the field to safety should the need arise. Reynolds was the senior officer of the four, but he declined to assume responsibility for conducting any retreat. Palmer emphatically declared that he would have nothing to do with leaving the battlefield. Baird also refused to accept command, preferring to stick it out on the current line of battle. This left only Johnson, and that officer made the consensus of the division commanders unanimous by both refusing to assume command, and by voting to stay the course. It was but a short time after these officers had met that Steedman's men went into the fight and restored the line on the Union right.[55]

The assault that the division commanders on the left anticipated did not materialize until about 4:00 P.M. Granger returned from delivering Thomas's message to Rosecrans shortly thereafter, bringing orders from the army commander for Thomas to assume command of the army on the field and to withdraw it toward Chattanooga by nightfall. Rosecrans had begun to write out detailed orders concerning troop movements and specifics of the withdrawal when he was interrupted by Granger. "Oh, that's all nonsense, general," Granger said. "Send Thomas an order to retire. He knows what he's about as well as you do." Rosecrans acknowledged the truth of Granger's statement and wrote out only a brief order of intent, leaving Thomas to attend to all the details.[56]

Rosecrans had been awaiting news from the front to dictate his course of action. McCook had requested instructions, but was told that Rosecrans was waiting for a report from Garfield that "will enable me to give more definite instructions both to you and General Crittenden." In the meantime, Rosecrans told McCook to "lie down and rest." The commander told him, "I am nearly worn out and I want someone with me to take command, if necessary to assist me."[57]

A Union veteran who had participated in the retreat of the right flank had been listening to the sounds of battle coming from Thomas's front all afternoon from his position near Rossville. Intently he followed "the distant rumble and roar of the guns of the Fourteenth Army Corps, sounding like the last mutterings of a great storm that had spent its strength and was drawing to a close from sheer exhaustion."[58] Both sides were exhausted, to be sure, but the soldier had been incorrect in assuming that the contest was ended for the day. It was about to be renewed with even greater effort, and only the coming of night would cause a cessation to the deadly struggle being waged.

Longstreet committed his remaining division, that of Brigadier General William Preston, to an all-out effort to break the Federal lines. Thomas's strength was now far diminished from that with which he had begun the day. It is estimated that some 25,000 men served under him during the day, but only about one-quarter of those were still in the fight at the time of Granger's arrival on the field. The disparity in numbers had now become acute, as Preston's brigades enveloped the Union line and probed along its length for a weakness. Shadows were beginning to gather as evening drew near, but the promise of darkness only spurred the Confederates to increased effort. By Longstreet's own account, no fewer than 25 different attacks were made by his men against the battered defenders of the ridge.

But the Federals were meeting grim determination with pluck and resolve. Each new assault was thrown back with heavy casualties to both sides. Thomas had placed his artillery for maximum effectiveness, and his experienced eye ensured that the big guns would play an important role in maintaining the line. At one point in the fighting, General Steedman approached a lieutenant named Closskey and ordered him to double-shot his guns in order to increase their deadly power. Closskey replied, "Been doing it for ten rounds." Steedman looked across the lines, where the Confederates were forming for yet another charge, and ordered, "Treble-shot 'em, boys." Closskey stated that he had never heard of a cannon firing three shots at once, but he immediately gave the order to his gunners to do so. When the lanyards were pulled, the cannon roared from the discharges that were so violent as to tear away the rifling from the guns. The effect was equally as powerful to the ranks of the Rebels, however, tearing gaping holes in their advancing lines.[59]

Brigadier General Archibald Gracie Jr. led his newly enlisted brigade in one of the most successful Confederate attacks of the day. Gracie's men went forward into the hail of lead to within a few feet of the Federal breastworks, where they engaged in hand-to-hand combat before being forced to retire. The 1st Alabama Battalion lost 65 percent casualties during this fight, while the flag of the 2nd Alabama Battalion was pierced by 83 different bullet holes. Garfield reported back to Rosecrans that Thomas was "standing like a rock," thus providing him with the nick-name that would engender his everlasting fame. From this time onward, Thomas would be known simply as the Rock of Chickamauga.

As darkness settled over the opposing lines, Thomas made preparations for evacuating his remaining men from their works and removing them to the relative safety of McFarland's Gap. Reynolds's Division, the southernmost in the line, was the first to be pulled from the defenses. But the Confederates had other ideas. As Reynolds was preparing to leave, St. John Liddell's Confederate division launched a fierce attack upon him. Reynolds was in danger of crumbling, so Thomas, who was on the scene, ordered General Turchin to make a counterattack with his brigade. "There they are. Clear them out," were his only instructions to the Russian-born general. Turchin's men went forward with a rush, and the ferocity of their charge stunned the Confederates and sent them tumbling backward. Reynolds was then free to resume his withdrawal, joined by Turchin. One by one, the Federal divisions left the line and took up the march behind Reynolds.

In the end, only three regiments remained on the field to cover the retreat: the 21st and 89th Ohio Infantry and the 22nd Michigan Infantry, of Brannon's Division. Thomas and Granger were still with this rear guard when the Rebels formed for yet another assault. Thomas called out to Granger, "The enemy are forming for another assault; we have not another round of ammunition — what shall we do?" Granger mirrored the steadiness of his commander by answering "Fix bayonets and go for them." It was approximately at this time that Garfield witnessed Thomas taking the hand of a soldier in the ranks and thanking him for his valor and courage. The private stood stunned for a moment, then called out, "George H. Thomas has taken this hand. I'll knock down any mean man that offers to take it hereafter!"[60] An observer watched as "Along the whole line ran the order 'Fix bayonets.' On came the enemy — our men were lying down. 'Forward,' was sounded. In one instant they were on their feet. Forward they went to meet the charge. So impetuous was this counter-charge that one regiment, with empty muskets and empty cartridge-boxes, broke through the enemy's line, which, closing in on their rear, carried them off as undertow." All three regiments were surrounded and overpowered by Preston's men, suffering 322 killed and 563 captured, but their gallant action had served to hold back the Confederates until the remainder of the 14th Corps was safely out of reach.

Darkness now effectively ended the fighting, and brought a close to what would be the bloodiest two-day battle of the war. The Confederates had lost 18,454 in killed, wounded, and missing, while Union casualties were 16,179.[61] Chickamauga had truly lived up to its name. The River of Death had witnessed some of the most savage combat ever to take place on the North American continent, and one of the greatest stands in American military history. By his actions, Thomas had saved the Union army from certain disaster, and had elevated himself to legendary status for posterity.

Several accounts of the battle credit Sheridan with being present during the final thrusts made by the Confederates that day. As such, Sheridan stood in line to receive accolades similar to those accorded to Thomas, Granger, and Steedman. The fact of the matter was that Sheridan was nowhere near Horseshoe Ridge when the fighting for that place was raging. This discrepancy arose due to an incorrect message sent by Garfield to Rosecrans shortly after the former's arrival at Thomas's command. "I arrived here ten minutes ago, via Rossville. General Thomas has Brannon's, Baird's, Reynolds', Wood's, Palmer's and Johnson's divisions still

General Phil Sheridan. Caught up in the stampede created when the corps of McCook and Crittenden were driven from the field, Sheridan claimed to have joined Thomas on Horseshoe Ridge in time to take part in the fighting there. The evidence does not support his claim, however (United States Army Military History Institute).

intact after terrible fighting. Granger is here, closed up with Thomas, and is fighting terribly on the right. Sheridan is with the bulk of his division, but in ragged shape, though plucky and fighting."[62] Garfield does not specifically state that Sheridan is with Thomas, but that is implied by the manner in which the message is worded.

In fact, Sheridan was at McFarland's Gap, along with Negley and Davis, with a total force of some 7,000 men. Thomas had sent word to these officers, by way of Colonel Thruston, chief of staff of McCook's 20th Corps, ordering them to support his right, and the message was delivered at 4:00 P.M. Davis started his command, along with some of Negley's men, in a march for Thomas's lines, but he did not proceed far before giving up the effort. Thomas's messenger reported that Sheridan "insisted on going to Rossville." He went on to state that Negley was also "vacillating," and that he "finally went to Rossville" as well. In his *Life of Thomas*, Don Piatt describes the encounter between Thruston and Sheridan in greater detail. He states that Thruston "omitted from the writing precisely what General Sheridan did say, and this language the gallant young chief of staff omitted from a mistaken sense of propriety. The fact is, the insubordinate subordinate, in a sentence glaring with profanity, swore he would obey no such orders and take his men into a slaughter organized by fools.... A braver man never trod the field of danger. His mind was clear and his nerves calm, and he knew that in that roar that rose behind him as he marched away brave men were being done to death, while heroic officers were looking eagerly to the right and left for aid in this hour of blood-tainted anxiety."[63] Negley was brought before a court of inquiry and was stripped of his command as a result of his failure to follow Thomas's orders, but somehow Sheridan escaped a similar fate.

In his battle report for Chickamauga, Sheridan attempts to clear his actions by asserting that he was endeavoring to reach Thomas via Rossville. He claims that he reached the vicinity of Horseshoe Ridge at about 5:30 P.M., at the approximate time that Reynolds and Turchin were repelling the attack by St. John Liddell on their lines.[64] This claim is unsupported by the reports of Thomas, or of any other officer serving with him. The claim that Thomas ordered Sheridan to hold a position on the right of his line until the center and left could be evacuated, as stated on a historic marker placed on the battlefield some 40 years after the battle, is totally unsubstantiated, and, for that reason, the tablet was removed from its position in the 1930s. Sheridan would share in the fame of Thomas, Granger, and Steedman for years, and his biographers would laud his courage and decisiveness on that blood-stained field, but the historic record denies the laurels thus obtained. Sheridan partisans have continued the controversy for decades, but the truth of the matter is that Little Phil performed no heroic deeds in the afternoon or evening of September 21 on the field of Chickamauga. To Thomas, and the band of subordinate commanders with him, is reserved all the credit, glory, and fame.

Chapter Eleven

Chattanooga and Missionary Ridge

Following the withdrawal of the Federal troops, Longstreet allowed his men to fill their cartridge boxes while he gathered together stragglers and reorganized his command. No further pursuit was contemplated until morning, when all could be prepared and in readiness. Amazingly, General Bragg had retired for the night, and General Polk had to interrupt his slumber to report that the whole Federal army was now in flight and could possibly be destroyed. Bragg refused to accept the information, however, and a Confederate soldier who had been captured and escaped was brought before him to corroborate the story. The soldier told him that he had seen the entire Federal army in retreat before making his way to friendly lines, but Bragg caustically discounted the man's testimony, asking him, "Do you know what a retreat looks like?" The soldier answered the question in a tone sarcastic enough to match that of his commander, "I ought to, General, I've been with you during your whole campaign." Even when the Confederate commander had become satisfied that the battle was fairly won, he could not be induced to press his advantage. To one suggestion of pursuit he testily responded: "How can I? Here is two-fifths of my army left on the field, and my artillery is without horses." He was also short on supplies, and did not have sufficient horses to pull his wagons. Nathan Bedford Forrest argued that the army could get all the supplies it needed in Chattanooga, but Bragg could not be swayed. Forrest, in a rage, would later complain to his officers, "What does he fight battles for?"[1]

On the night of September 21, Thomas's men filed along on the road to Rossville, toward a junction with the rest of Rosecrans's army. The scene they beheld was one of disaster and debris. Wounded soldiers from both sides littered the sides of the road, lying on the ground precisely where their mortal ability to move had denied them further flight. The carnage was not quite as horrid as that which greeted the victorious Southerners in and around the lines at Horseshoe Ridge, but it nonetheless gave witness to the terrible savagery of the day. The cries of the wounded, and the fixed stares of the deceased, were to be heard and seen on all sides. Thomas met with Sheridan during the withdrawal, and they rode together amid the retreating tide. When the pair reached the outskirts of Rossville, they stopped to sit on a fence rail to watch the troops march by. Sheridan later wrote that Thomas was utterly exhausted, and "seemed to forget what he had stopped for and said little or nothing of the incidents of the day."[2] At length, Thomas roused himself and remarked that he had a flask of whiskey in his saddle, and had stopped to offer Sheridan some. The flask was retrieved, and Thomas took a sip, offering the rest to Sheridan, who refreshed himself fully before taking his leave to see to the bivouacking of his men. Thomas later joined Colonel B.F. Scribner, of Baird's Division, for a cup of coffee. Still, he said nothing of the day's work, as he obviously tried to reconcile the bloody events in his weary mind and plan for the operations of his corps on the morrow.[3]

By his efforts, the Army of the Cumberland had blunted the efforts of the Confederates to utterly destroy it, but Thomas was well aware that the Federals were still in a precarious position, and that Bragg could yet achieve the complete victory he desired. Thomas placed detachments to guard the three roads leading out of Rossville, and made dispositions to meet the anticipated threat from the Confederate army, but no Southern thrust was forthcoming. Forrest's cavalry was making a pest of itself along the picket and skirmish lines, but Bragg refused to engage the enemy with any of his infantry. While continuing to prepare for defense at Rossville, Thomas sent a message to Rosecrans on the morning of September 21 advising that the entire army be concentrated at Chattanooga. Rosecrans agreed, and by 7:00 A.M. on the morning of September 22, the entire Union army was safely nestled behind the defenses of the town.

The only problem with Rosecrans's alignment was that he decided not to fortify Lookout Mountain or Missionary Ridge, the two heights that commanded the town and covered two of the Tennessee River ferries vital to supplying the army. He had posted a single brigade on Lookout Mountain, but had withdrawn it on September 23, much to the chagrin of his officer corps.[4] When Bragg became apprised of the situation, he immediately dispatched forces to take the heights, ringed Chattanooga with infantry and artillery, and placed the Federal army under siege. Holed up in their Chattanooga stronghold, the Federal army faced little danger of the Confederates' being able to take the place by a direct assault, but then Bragg would not have to storm the Federal lines to defeat them. If he could hold the enemy in place, they would eventually be starved into submission as a result of their supply lines being severed.

Many of Rosecrans' officers bitterly complained about the lack of foresight in not manning the heights around the town, and all wondered if Thomas's heroic stand at Horseshoe Ridge had not merely postponed an inevitable disaster. The strength of the army was now at 45,000 effectives, and there were but ten days' rations on hand. Major General Joseph Hooker had been ordered to Chattanooga with the 11th and 12th Corps of the Army of the Potomac. Sherman was on his way from Vicksburg with the Army of the Tennessee. Major General Stephen Hurlburt was leading troops from Memphis. Ambrose Burnside was expected to march from Knoxville. Rosecrans's army was not in a position to assume offensive operations until it was strongly reinforced, and those reinforcements were on the way. The only question was whether Chattanooga could be held until they arrived.[5]

There were also other mutterings among the officers of the army. Those who had stood with Thomas held a certain animosity for the officers who had fled the field and not come to the assistance of the left flank. Rosecrans, Cittenden, McCook, and Negley were especially criticized for their actions. It would appear that Thomas took no part in recriminations or fault-finding. He busied himself looking to the defensive placement of the troops and trying to obtain supplies. Though he would later contend that the War Department shared equal blame with Rosecrans because it had ordered a vigorous pursuit of Bragg's army at a time when Thomas felt the Federals should have concentrated at Chattanooga and fully prepared for the next campaign, he kept his opinions to himself while the crisis was at hand.

Among the men in the ranks, Thomas had emerged as the idol of the army. Soldiers strained to get a glimpse of the man already popularly known among them as the Rock of Chickamauga. His mere presence in camp seemed to lift the spirits of the men and infuse them with confidence of final victory for their arms. Charles Dana wrote "I confess I share their feeling. I know of no other man whose composition and character are so much like that

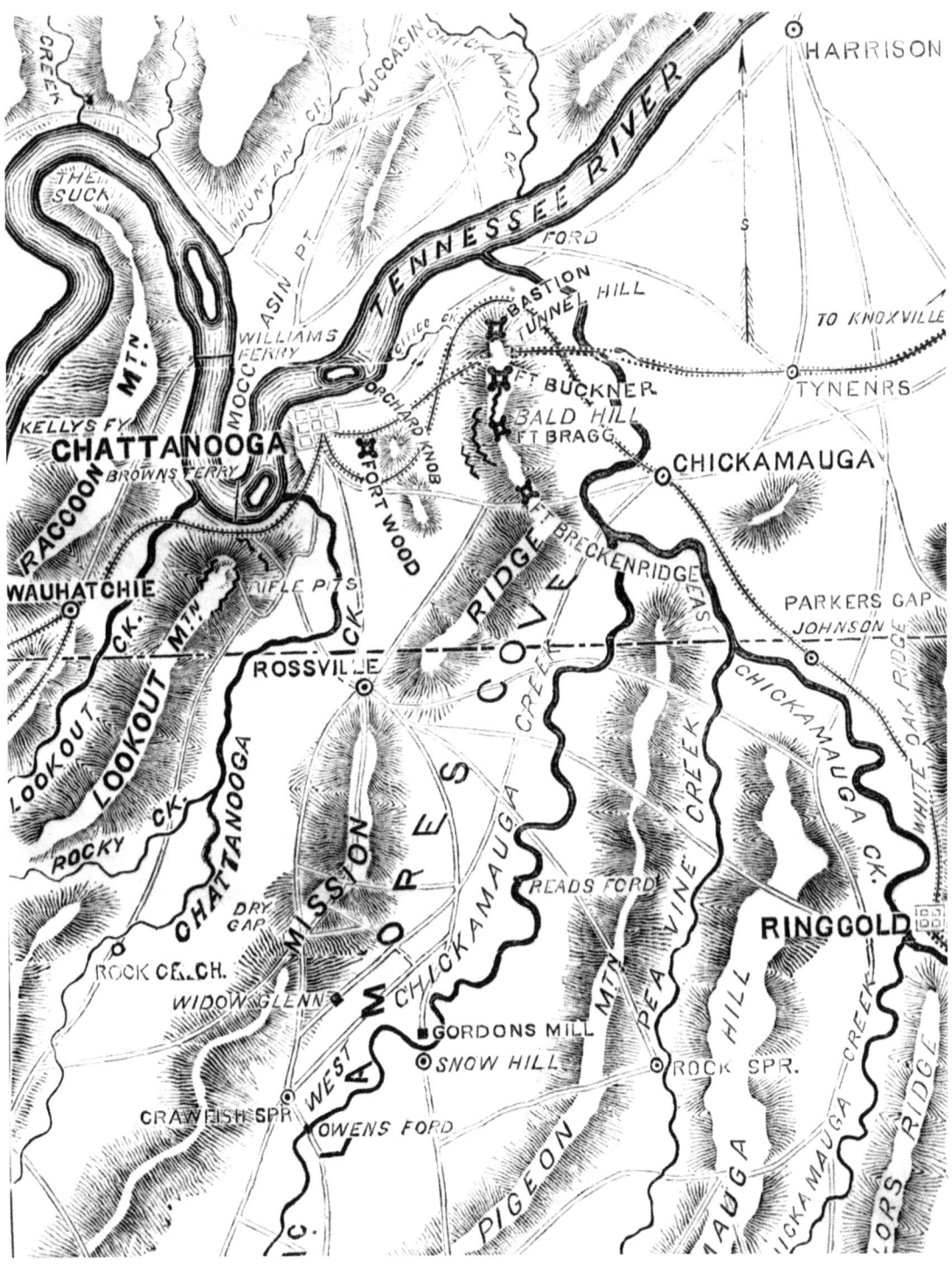

Period map of Chattanooga, Tennessee, showing the natural barriers created by the Tennessee River and the mountainous countryside. From *The History of the Civil War in the United States* by Samuel Schmucker. Published by Jones Brothers & Co., in Philadelphia in 1865.

of Washington; he is at once an elegant gentleman and a heroic soldier."[6] Admiration for Thomas was little less subdued among his Confederate enemies. Moxley Sorrell, a staff officer with General Longstreet, captured the feeling of many in gray when he stated that Thomas "was one of the ablest of their soldiers, perhaps none equaled him, and I heartily wish that he had been anywhere else but at Chickamauga."[7]

Indeed, Assistant Secretary Dana had become quite taken with Thomas, and had voiced his praises in many of the "confidential" communications he had forwarded to the War Department. The administration was duly concerned over the leadership of the army, and a possible replacement for Rosecrans was discussed in a cabinet meeting held ten days following the Battle of Chickamauga. Secretary of the Navy Gideon Welles forwarded the opinion that the Rock of Chickamauga would be the best choice, as no one was "the equal of Thomas, if a change was to be made."[8] Fear of the backlash from Northern politicians that would arise if he promoted a Virginian to command of one of the Union's principal armies led Lincoln to delay the decision for three more weeks, however.

Thomas caught wind of the intentions of the administration, and of Dana's part in bringing the command of the Army of the Cumberland to the forefront, and responded in typical manner. As he had done so many times in the past, Thomas made it known that he stood squarely behind his commander and supported him fully. He sent word to Rosecrans that "spies from Washington now in camp are working for your removal." True to form, he would take no part in anything that smacked of intrigue, and did not even want to have his name attached to it. As such, he told Dana that he was unwilling to replace Rosecrans, if there was any chance that his reputation would be smudged by allegations that he had conspired to do so.[9] Though he very much desired an independent command, and was gaining in popular support for that assignment in the administration, Thomas clung to the code of honor that would not permit him to advance his own career at the cost of a brother officer's reputation, and he would never condone any situation where his own honor or conduct could be called into question. To some, this may seem a character flaw. Thomas was the best man for the job, and everyone connected with the army seemed to know it, including Thomas himself. His code of honor prevented him from fulfilling his own ambitions, but it was precisely this same code of honor that made him the soldier and officer he was, and defined his greatness in command, and was not a personal weakness.

Meantime, the two opposing armies "were lying face to face," wrote General John Beatty. "The Federal and Confederate sentinels walk their beats in sight of each other. The tents of the troops dot the hillsides. We see their signal lights on the summit of Lookout Mountain and on the knobs of Mission Ridge."[10] The Army of the Cumberland was hemmed in, and all efforts were directed toward holding on till help could arrive. A solitary pontoon bridge across the Tennessee River now served as the only lifeline of Rosecrans's army to the outside world. Confederate artillery, placed on Lookout Mountain, had made use of the railroad running into the town impossible. Any supplies destined for Chattanooga could progress by rail only so far as Bridgeport, Alabama, where they had to be loaded on wagons for a torturous 60-mile trek, over harsh mountain roads, that took from eight to twenty days, depending on how much mud the fall rains generated. The road was so steep that 16 mules had to be harnessed to each wagon, and the animals were so overworked that thousands died in making the trips. Mule carcasses lined the road, and one Federal observer thought that if they were "laid lengthwise they would easily cover the entire distance" from Bridgeport to Chattanooga. Fully 10,000 mules and draft animals perished in trying to supply Rosecrans's army.[11] Even with the supreme effort being exerted, the supplies being delivered to the army amounted to a mere trickle, and the men were compelled to subsist on a small fraction of the rations normally issued. The major action between the two armies at this time was in the form of cavalry raids made by the Confederates on the supply trains, which served to further reduce the amount of food being brought into the town. As there was no forage for the mules along the way, it had to be carried in the wagons, decreasing the space available for the much-needed supplies. After a couple of weeks, the food shortage in Chattanooga became so acute that the men scavenged for corn on the ground where the mules had been fed.

General Hooker's 20,000 men from the Army of the Potomac arrived at Bridgeport on October 1, but they did not march to join Rosecrans at Chattanooga. It was felt that Hooker's additional men would only increase the burden on the already starving garrison by increasing the number of mouths to feed. As such, Hooker was instructed to form his men in a defensive perimeter around the railroad and await further developments. Sherman was also advancing, though his four divisions were not making as good time as Hooker's. General Halleck had ordered Sherman to repair the Memphis & Charleston Railroad as they marched, and this assignment seriously impeded their progress.

Back in Chattanooga, the Army of the Cumberland was being reorganized. Rosecrans had relieved McCook, Crittenden, Van Cleve, and Negley from command. Instead of appointing new commanders to the 20th and 21st Corps, he broke up those organizations and assigned their regiments to other brigades in the 14th Corps and Reserve Corps, making them almost as large as divisions. The most important reorganization, however, came from orders issued by President Lincoln.

On October 16, Dana sent a telegram to Secretary Stanton proclaiming Rosecrans to be unfit for command. "The incapacity of the commander is astonishing," he wrote, and avowed that his "imbecility" was "contageous."[12] That same day, Lincoln welcomed General Steedman to the White House. Steedman had traveled to Washington, under orders from the president, for an interview to discuss affairs with the Army of the Cumberland. Shortly after coming into the presence of Lincoln, Steedman was asked his opinion of General Rosecrans. Steedman demurred to respond, but was ordered to do so. When he stated his view that Rosecrans was not the proper person to command a defeated army, Lincoln asked whom Steedman would recommend. "General George H. Thomas," was the response.

Lincoln was now spurred to action. That same day he had orders issued superseding Rosecrans with Thomas. He also had orders cut realigning the command structure of all of the principal armies in the Western Theater. Ulysses S. Grant, then at Cairo, Illinois, received a telegram from Halleck informing him, "You will receive herewith the orders of the President of the United States placing you in command of the Departments of the Ohio, Cumberland and Tennessee." All of the major departments of the west had been combined under Grant's control. He was ordered to have Sherman take over his responsibilities with the Army of the Tennessee, was advised of Thomas's promotion, and was instructed, "It is left optional with you to supersede General G.H. Thomas or not."[13]

Thomas had been hesitant to accept the position, even after receiving orders assigning him to the command. Rosecrans reported that Thomas turned "pale" when he read the telegram, and took a "long breath." Seeing the discomfiture in his brother officer's actions, Rosecrans said, "Thomas, don't say anything; there is no misunderstanding that can come between you and me." Rosecrans then insisted to Thomas that it was his duty as a soldier to accept the command of the army. "Well, I suppose I must do so but I don't like it," said

Thomas, as he resigned himself to replacing a commander he still had confidence in.[14] It must be remembered that Thomas had been a critic of political intervention in military affairs ever since his days with General Taylor in the Mexican War. As far as he was concerned, Rosecrans's failures were not so much of his own making as they were attributable to the interferences and pressures coming from the administration at Washington. Thomas had disagreed with Rosecrans's decision to split the army in a rapid pursuit of the Confederates following their evacuation of Chattanooga, but he put that disagreement aside in loyally supporting the manner in which his superior had conducted his campaign as a whole.

There was also the matter of Rosecrans's political liability to be considered. Prior to the battle of Chickamauga, he had been courted by influential members of both parties with an eye to his becoming their presidential candidate in the 1864 election. Rosecrans had become emboldened enough by his achievements to consider himself worthy of such high office, and his ambitions were fired by the accolades these politicians were sending his way. As such, Rosecrans had become a liability to the administration in several different ways. He had lost the confidence of a portion of his subordinates in the army, as well as of a large number of citizens at home. It was seriously questioned if his leadership was sufficient to save the Army of the Cumberland from ruin. Even if he did so, the credit he thus derived would be used to propel him into candidacy for the presidency, opposing the current administration. By any standard, as far as the Lincoln White House was concerned, Rosecrans had to go, and the logical replacement was Thomas. While that officer detested the prospect of becoming involved in an intrigue against Rosecrans, he was undoubtedly also troubled by the thought that he was now in line to receive the same sort of pressure and interference from above.

While Grant was en route to Chattanooga, he took time to wire Thomas, "Hold Chattanooga at all hazards. I will be there as soon as possible. Please advise me how long your present supplies will last, and the prospect for keeping them up." The Federal soldiers at Chattanooga, impoverished and underfed as they were, took offense at the implications of Grant's message. They were holding firm, and had no intention of abandoning their position before the new commander arrived. Thomas replied to the telegram with a statement that was widely quoted, and only added to the prestige he had already won. After briefly answering Grant's questions concerning the supplies, he boldly stated, "We will hold the town till we starve."[15]

On October 19, General Rosecrans issued a farewell to the army that officially announced Thomas's elevation to command.

> Major General George H. Thomas, in compliance with orders, will assume command of this army and department. The chiefs of all the staff departments will report to him for orders.
> In taking leave of you, his brothers in arms, officers and soldiers, he congratulates you that your new commander comes to you not as he did, a stranger. General Thomas has been identified with this army from its first organization. He has led you often in battle. To his known prudence, dauntless courage, and true patriotism, you may look with confidence that under God he will lead you to victory. The General commanding doubts not you will be as true to yourselves and your country in the future as you have been in the past.... W.S. Rosecrans, Major-General.[16]

Grant made his way to Bridgeport, and from there set out in a rain storm to cover the distance of about thirty miles that separated him from Thomas's army at Chattanooga. Grant was suffering from a leg injury caused when his horse had fallen on top of him. His horse lost its footing on the muddy road and slipped again, adding further injury to the same leg. When Grant arrived in Chattanooga late on the night of October 23, he was in such discomfort that he could not dismount his horse, and had to be lifted from the saddle by members of his staff. Horace Porter, a member of Grant's staff, thought that all things considered, Grant "showed less signs of fatigue than might have been supposed after his hard ride of two days under such trying circumstances."[17]

Grant visited Thomas at his headquarters, and the two men seated themselves at the opposite ends of the fireplace. Thomas gave orders for several generals, and most of the members of his staff, to come to headquarters at once, to meet with the new commander. Welcoming Grant and arranging for a conference of his officers had so engaged Thomas that he failed to notice that the general's clothing was soaked to the point of leaving puddles under the chair on which he was sitting. A staff officer called Thomas's attention to Grant's condition, saying that colds showed no deference for officers. Once made aware of the situation, "All of his old-time Virginia hospitality was aroused, and he at once begged his newly arrived chief to step into a bedroom and change his clothes. His urgings, however, were in vain. The general thanked him politely, but positively declined to make any additions to his personal comfort, except to light a fresh cigar."[18]

The main topic of the officer's conference was how to eliminate the supply problem caused by the Confederate encirclement. Rosecrans and Thomas had previously been working on a plan to open what was being termed a "cracker line," and the following morning Grant, Thomas, and General William F. Smith, chief engineering officer for the Army of the Cumberland, rode out of Chattanooga to examine the feasibility of putting that plan into motion. Adam Badeau, an officer on Grant's staff, recalled the officers and men of Thomas's command as being "downcast, if not desponding," and painted a dire picture of the Federal situation in Chattanooga. He stated that they were "hemmed in on every side by the enemy," and had "no means of supplying themselves." To Badeau, had it not been for the timely arrival of Grant and his staff, the Army of the Cumberland must surely be lost.[19] The fact of the matter is that spirits were high in the Army of the Cumberland. Food was in short supply, but the men had complete confidence in the abilities of their new commander, and Assistant Secretary Dana reported that things were running smoothly and efficiently at headquarters, where "order" prevailed.[20] Grant was merely approving a plan that Thomas and Rosecrans had devised, and Thomas had already put in motion through orders to Hooker before the new commander's arrival. Had Grant not been put in overall command, Thomas would have carried out the attempt to open a new supply line, and the result could not possibly have been other than the way in which it eventually turned out. Thomas was using the men and materials already at hand, and was implementing a mission already planned before Grant arrived. His superior would receive the credit for its success, but he played little more than a spectator's role after providing his only contribution to the operation: his approval that it be carried out.

The date set for the opening of the new supply line was October 27, which happened to be the same day that Thomas's promotion to brigadier general in the regular army went into effect. Grant sent official congratulations regarding the promotion, but there was far from a warm or friendly association between the two men. Though he always observed all of the amenities demanded by the military, and the code of the gentleman, Thomas was usually reserved in his interactions with Grant. While his personal opinions concerning Grant were never recorded, and probably never uttered aloud, Thomas's posturing would lead one to believe that he considered the appointment of Grant as his superior to be a slight. He would serve as an able and efficient lieutenant, and would dutifully perform all assignments given to him, but would always maintain a certain aloofness in his dealings with the overall commander that was not present in his interactions with any other superior.

What could have been the reason for this behavior? Is it possible that Thomas considered himself more suited to the position, and held animosity over serving under an officer he considered as being inferior to himself? That could certainly account for his actions, but it can only answer a portion of the question. Thomas had been serving under officers who were inferior to him since the war began, and had exhibited cordial and friendly relations with all of them, even when he disagreed with their actions. Indeed, in the cases of Patterson, Buell, and Rosecrans, he had fully defended his superiors despite the fact that he had correctly advised courses of action that were rejected, to the failure and embarrassment to Union arms. Nonetheless, Thomas had felt each of these officers to be good men who were trying to do their best, and deserving of his full support and good will. Always an opponent of political intrigue, Thomas possibly resented the maneuvering that had been done on Grant's behalf by Congressman John Sherman, the brother of General Sherman, who just happened to be Grant's best friend.

It can also be conceived that Thomas took offense to the way in which Grant's officers portrayed the Army of the Cumberland as a beaten army in need of rescue. As with the writings of Adam Badeau, many of Grant's staff depicted the Cumberlanders in terms that were insulting to men and officers who had proven their valor on so many hard-fought fields of battle. Many of the men in the ranks held the same sort of disdain at being "rescued" by Grant as members of the 101st Airborne Infantry held for their "rescue" by General George S. Patton's army at Bastogne in World War II. This feeling of aspersions being cast in their direction would play a major part in the Army of the Cumberland's redeeming its honor a few weeks later. Whatever the reasons, Thomas's reserved deportment toward Grant was in contrast with his dealings with any previous commander, and creates a mystery for which there is no clear-cut answer. The members of Thomas's staff were completely devoted to their commander, and imitated his behavior when it came to interaction with Grant or his leading officers.

The point selected for the opening of a new supply line was at Brown's Ferry, on Moccasin Point, just below the city of Chattanooga. Moccasin Point was formed by a bend in the Tennessee River, resulting in a peninsula jutting out toward the mouth of Lookout River and Raccoon Mountain. Thomas's men held Moccasin Point, but the Confederates controlled all the area on the opposite shore of the river, cutting off all contact with the outside world. The terrain on the Confederate side was rugged, and a narrow valley between a range of sharp hills and Raccoon Mountain served as the primary transportation route in the area. The valley was lightly defended by the Confederates, in part because it was so easily defended. Thomas was sure that he could hold the mountainous stronghold against anything that could be sent against him, if it could only be wrested away from the enemy. He proposed a surprise movement by his army, in conjunction with an advance by Hooker's men from Bridgeport. It was for this reason that he had instructed Hooker to concentrate his forces at Bridgeport to await further developments.

At 3:00 A.M. on the morning of October 27, 1,800 men, under the command of General William P. Hazen, embarked in sixty pontoon boats nine miles upriver from Brown's Ferry and made their way to the objective. Brigadier General William F. Smith, chief engineer for the Army of the Cumberland, was assigned overall command of the mission, and another 2,200 men waited out of sight on the north side of the river to add their weight to the mission once a lodgment was made on the Confederate side. It had been decided that approaching the ferry by boat would serve to keep the Rebels off-balance, as they would have no idea where the force intended to land. If the Federals had concentrated Hazen's men opposite the ferry, the Confederates would have been able to discern their intentions and mass an appropriate force to oppose them. Seven of the nine miles the boats would have to navigate were under the fire of Confederate guns, but the darkness and fog prevented their detection. The current was so strong that no oars were needed to propel the boats, and in less than two hours the Federals had landed on the opposite shore. Confederate pickets were quickly overpowered, and by 5:00 A.M., the Union troops were in possession of the hills covering the ferry. Thus far, the operation had been a complete success. Union losses amounted to only a few men wounded, with no one being killed. Materials to finish the pontoon bridge were moved to the north shore of the river, and by the time day dawned the Rebels were surprised to find Federal forces firmly emplaced in the almost inaccessible heights rising from Lookout Valley on the south side of the river. The pontoon bridge was being laid, and would be completed by 10:00 A.M. A second bridge was subsequently laid at Kelly's Ferry. Artillery was then moved across to the south side, and placed to command the roads leading around Lookout Mountain to the Confederate camps. By the time Bragg realized what was taking place, Thomas's men had succeeded in establishing themselves in a position from which only a vastly superior force could dislodge them.[21]

Hooker had been instructed to march his men from Bridgeport to the Lookout Valley to support the operation at Brown's Ferry. General John Palmer had been ordered to facilitate Hooker's movement by taking two brigades and seizing control of the roads over which he must travel. Hooker was thus able to place his army in position for coordinated action with Smith's with no serious impediment coming from the Confederates. Bragg had been warned that the Federals were up to something big on the morning of the 27th, but he discounted the reports as being sensational and exaggerated. It was not until General Longstreet took him to the top of Lookout Mountain, where he could see Hooker's troops with his own eyes, that he began to realize the magnitude of the Federal actions.[22] By the afternoon of October 28, Hooker's advance had reached Brown's Ferry, while his rear was at Wauhatchie, Tennessee. Navigation of the Tennessee River was now open from Bridgeport to Kelly's Ferry. The road from Kelly's Ferry to Chattanooga, by way of Brown's Ferry, was also securely in Federal hands, and a new supply line had been opened for the defenders of the city.

Bragg had been slow in recognizing the Federal threat, and he was even slower in responding to it. On the night of October 28, he finally issued orders for an attack to be made on the forces under Hooker at Wauhatchie, placing General Longstreet in overall command of the mission. Longstreet had been promised two divisions, but at the last moment, Bragg decided to commit only one. The Confederates began their assault at midnight, one of the rare night actions to take place during the war. General John W. Geary's Division absorbed the blow and easily held its ground. Brigadier General Carl Shurz then led a force of 11th Corps men against the attackers, while Major General Oliver O. Howard directed a brigade to make a bayonet charge.

The fight grew hot and lasted for three hours, when one of the unimaginable oddities of war took place. Frightened by the battle, most of the army teamsters had deserted their posts and fled to the rear, leaving their animals unattended. The mules were moved to a state of panic by the rattle of musketry and the roar of the big guns, causing them to break free from their traces and stampede. Luckily for the Federals, they stampeded in the direction of the Confederates "with heads down and tails up, with trace-chains rattling and whiffletrees snapping over the stumps of trees, they rushed pell-mell upon Longstreet's bewildered men. Believing it to be an impetuous charge of cavalry, his line broke and fled." The battle was ended. It was the only attempt Bragg was to make to try to regain control of the disputed area, as he conceded the new supply line to the hands of the Federals. The quartermaster in charge of the mules would later send the following communication: "I request that the mules, for their gallantry in this action, may have conferred upon them the brevet rank of horses."[23]

News of the establishment of the new supply route was cheered by the men in Chattanooga, and Thomas was reported as saying, "We can easily subsist ourselves and will soon be in good condition."[24] A soldier in the ranks commented, "The siege was virtually raised, and it was simply a question of time when we should assume the offensive, tear down the flags now flaunting from Mission Ridge and Lookout, and plant there the stars and stripes."[25] The siege was broken, and Bragg no longer hoped to be able to strangle the Union army into submission. Authorities in Richmond were quick to realize the

General Oliver O. Howard. Howard's 11th Corps, along with Henry W. Slocum's 12th Corps, was sent from the Army of the Potomac to reinforce the Federal army at Chattanooga and assist in lifting the siege (United States Army Military History Institute).

changing fortunes at Chattanooga, and President Davis ordered Bragg to divide his force, sending Longstreet and his 18,000 men to attack Burnside at Knoxville.

When Washington received news of the developments at Chattanooga, the administration despaired for the safety of Knoxville, and ordered Grant to make a demonstration there that would hopefully rescind the order to detach Longstreet. Grant was ordered on November 7 to mount an attack on Missionary Ridge as a diversion in favor of Burnside, and the order was accordingly passed on to Thomas, who was horror-struck. Thomas made a personal reconnaissance of the ridge, and counted the regimental flags and artillery of the enemy. He then reported to Grant that he felt the attack to be ill-advised. In his opinion, the Army of the Cumberland was still too weakened to mount such an attack. Though food supplies had been arriving regularly since the opening of the new supply route at Brown's Ferry, there was a lack of rifles for the men, and horses to pull the artillery were almost non-existent. Thomas warned that an attack at this time would end in failure, uncovering Chattanooga to the Rebels, and suggested that it be postponed until such time as Sherman arrived with his fresh divisions. Grant concurred with Thomas's findings and countermanded the order, though it caused somewhat of a rift between the two men. The assault would have to wait till Sherman was at hand, and Burnside would have to fend for himself against Longstreet.[26] In a very real sense, Thomas helped to save Grant's reputation by talking him out of the attack, which could have resulted in nothing but a serious repulse for the Union army. His refusal to act prematurely saved the Federals from almost certain disaster.

Sherman's advance reached Bridgeport on November 14. Sherman himself had pushed forward, reaching Chattanooga that same day. Grant and Thomas took Sherman on a tour of the area to examine the enemy lines. Almost all of the conversation that took place was between Grant and Sherman, as Thomas was virtually ignored. Grant assigned Sherman the key role in his plan to dislodge the Confederates. The pair had become used to working together, and Sherman was a trusted subordinate to Grant. It is also possible that Grant was still smarting somewhat from Thomas's opposition to making the assault against Missionary Ridge a week earlier. Sherman was ordered to circle the city on the opposite shore, and then to cross the river by night, taking the right of the Confederate army, under Hardee and Cleburne, by surprise. Thomas was to threaten the enemy from his position, while Hooker held fast in Lookout Valley. The date set for commencement of the operation was November 21.

As the generals were returning from their reconnaissance, Thomas pointed out the location of Bragg's headquarters on Missionary Ridge to Sherman. Sherman asked, "Tom, have you seen Bragg or had any communication with him?" The question roused Thomas to anger, and he responded by declaring "Damn him, I'll be even with him yet." Thomas explained that a letter had previously arrived from the north with instructions to send it on by flag of truce. Thomas had forwarded the letter to Confederate lines along with a note to his one-time mess-mate requesting it be sent on to the address inscribed. Instead, Bragg returned the letter with a note stating that it was "Respectfully returned to Genl. Thomas. Genl. Bragg declines to have any intercourse with a man who has betrayed his state." Thomas was deeply wounded by the incident, and carried a lifelong grudge against Bragg because of it. Sherman recalled that Thomas made numerous threats of what he would do when the opportunity presented itself to make amends for the slur against his character.[27]

Sherman returned to Bridgeport to see to the movement of his divisions. Grant's plans were impeded almost from the start. Heavy rains slowed Sherman's advance, and the Confederates compounded the situation by sending rafts down the river to break the pontoon bridges. Grant was forced to postpone the initiation of the operation with each delay encountered. On November 22, Thomas stepped forward to offer a suggestion that would get the advance moving again without further delay. He observed that Sherman's advance could be reinforced by Hooker's 11th Corps, eliminating the need to wait for the Army of the Tennessee division still in the rear to catch up. Hooker's remaining troops, along with the rear elements of Sherman's army, could then make a demonstration against Lookout Mountain, to divert Confederate attention away from Sherman. Grant agreed to allow Hooker's 12th Corps, reinforced by a division from Sherman's army, to attack Lookout Mountain, and instructed Sherman to be in position by the night of November 23. When it became apparent that Sherman would not meet the deadline, Grant decided to follow up on information that had been provided by a Confederate deserter that Bragg's army had withdrawn from its lines, leaving only a strong picket force in front of Chattanooga. He issued Thomas orders to probe the Rebel line on the morning of November 23 in the vicinity of Orchard Knob, a hill directly in front of Missionary Ridge. Oliver O. Howard's 11th Corps had been added to Thomas's five divisions for this reconnaissance in force, which was to begin just after the noon day meal. The divisions were assembled in front of Fort Wood, a strong defensive work that had been constructed to hold artillery with which to shell Missionary Ridge. Thomas utilized his signal corps to introduce a new concept in warfare: remote fire control. The signalmen performed the same service as forward observers in later wars, and helped to make Thomas's barrage a model of deadly efficiency.

The open panorama of the countryside allowed both armies to witness the spectacle as if watching a parade, and the Army of the Cumberland men knew full well that all eyes were upon them. General Thomas Wood's Division deployed in line of battle for the assault on Orchard Knob, and swept forward with a steady, measured gait. Wood's men surged ahead, stunning the defenders who were permitted to view the whole extent of the force arrayed against them, and captured the knob on his left flank with relative ease. His right flank met slightly stiffer resistance from the defenders of Indian Hill, a lower ridge that extended from Orchard Knob, but these were routed after a spirited bayonet charge by the Federals. Thomas signaled Wood, "You have gained too much to withdraw. Hold your position and I will support you." Grant complimented the Cumberlanders by stating, "The troops moved under fire with all the precision of veterans on parade." Sheridan moved his division forward to support Wood, and assumed a position on the right of Wood's line. Howard's 11th Corps men were brought up on the left. By 4:00 P.M., General Granger had established his corps headquarters on Orchard Knob, and the men were throwing up breastworks some three and one-half feet deep, and preparing to defend their gains against any efforts by the Confederates to retake the ground. The reconnaissance had gained far greater results than had been hoped for when Grant had issued the orders. In fact, it had reaped benefits that the Federal commanders were not yet fully aware of. Unaware of the Federal intentions, Bragg had felt compelled to order W.H.T. Walker's divisions away from Lookout Mountain to bolster his left flank on Missionary Ridge. Lookout Mountain was thus left lightly defended by the Confederates.[28]

At 8:00 A.M. on November 24, Thomas's men in front of Missionary Ridge were allowed to be spectators to the next phase of operations against the Southern defenses. As Thomas had suggested, Hooker was being set loose against the Rebel positions at Lookout Mountain. In his attacking force of 10,000 men, he would have a division each from the three armies then at Chattanooga: Brigadier General John Geary's Division of his own 12th Corps, Brigadier General Charles Cruft's Division from the Army of the Cumberland, and Brigadier General Peter J. Osterhaus' Division from the Army of the Tennessee. Hooker split his force to attack the Confederate from two directions. Geary, with his own division and a brigade from Cruft's, was sent south to Wauhatchie, where they were to cross Lookout Creek at a ford. Osterhaus, with Cruft's other brigade, was to cross the creek at a bridge a mile and a half north of Geary's position. Hooker's intention was not to capture Lookout Mountain. Instead, he sought to clear the valley between the mountain and Missionary Ridge of Confederates. If the situation presented itself, he would assail the heights, but the Confederates holding the precipice were not his main concern.

The Federal advance over the rugged terrain was toilsome, but resistance was found to be exceedingly light. The Confederates had 7,000 men posted on Lookout Mountain, more than a sufficient number to be able to hold against Hooker's force if they were concentrated to meet it. The problem was that no such concentration existed. Southern troops were spread all over the mountain side, and the Rebel commander was unfamiliar with both the lay of the ground and the deployment of his men. Major General Carter L. Stevenson had been assigned to assume command of the defenses on the evening of November 23. He had not arrived at the mountain until after dark, and was unable to ascertain the location of all of his forces by the time Hooker launched his attack. The defense of Lookout Mountain therefore devolved upon the shoulders of Brigadier General John K. Jackson, a division commander who had experienced lackluster success thus far in the war.

By 10:00 A.M., Geary's men rounded a shoulder on the mountain and ran into 1,489 men under the command of Brigadier General Edward C. Walthall. A dense fog enveloped the entire mountain, and Walthall's men were surprised by the sudden appearance of Hooker's army in their front. Even so, they fought valiantly against the superior force arrayed against them. Confederate artillerists on the summit attempted to support their hard-pressed comrades, but found that they could not depress their cannon sufficiently to fire upon the Federals. Walthall called for support from Brigadier General John C. Moore, on his right, but Moore's men lost their way in the fog and were late in arriving. Still, Walthall's men, now reinforced by Moore, doggedly held on. After three hours of fighting, the Confederates had only been driven a distance of 400 yards.[29]

By 1:30 P.M., the brigade of Brigadier General Edmund W. Pettus had marched down from the mountain top to reinforce the beleaguered Confederates. They arrived on the scene just as Walthall was about to give way from lack of ammunition. Pettus's men relieved Walthall's troops in the line, while the latter retired to reform and resupply. With fresh ammunition in their cartridge boxes, Walthall's men waded back into the fight, forming to the left of Pettus's line. The Federals in Chattanooga and the Confederates on Missionary Ridge all gazed intently toward the fog-shrouded Lookout Mountain. The forms of men could not be seen, but the flashes from muskets and artillery defined the action and allowed the spectators to follow the fighting. To the Federals' delight, and the Confederates' dismay, the sounds of the battle were drawing closer, a clear indication that the Union troops were gaining ground. The fighting would be dubbed the Battle Above the Clouds, and would be romanticized as a heroic victory for Joe Hooker. In reality, it was little more than a large skirmish, and the Federals were being held back by a force significantly inferior to their own. Moreover, Hooker's men were running dangerously short on ammunition themselves, and it looked as if the assault would have to be called off for the day. General Thomas, learning of the shortage, sent a brigade scrambling up the mountain with as many cartridges as the men could carry in an effort to resupply Hooker. By the time the ammunition arrived, however, darkness had covered the battlefield and the fighting had come to a close.

During the night, the fog drifted away, and the lines of the opposing forces could clearly be identified by their campfires, stretching from the summit to the base of the mountain. The intermittent fire of skirmishers added to the spectacle, but was upstaged by a rare lunar eclipse. Soldiers on both sides felt the eclipse to be an evil omen for the Confederates. Bragg withdrew his forces from Lookout Mountain, fearing that they had little chance of holding their position the following morning. Not willing to lose the services of these troops, he pulled them out of harm's way and shifted them to the north end of Missionary Ridge to bolster Hardee's command. Hooker's men detected the evacuation in the pre-dawn hours of November 25, and Captain John Wilson, along with five comrades from the 8th Kentucky Infantry, climbed to the peak to raise a United States flag just before sunrise. As the sun cast its rays upon the fluttering banner, the Federals in the valley below could clearly see that the mountain was in Union hands, and the sight was greeted with wild cheering and the playing of bands. With Lookout Mountain in their possession, the Federals had eliminated any further threat to their supply line and had forced Bragg from a formidable position of defense. Hooker's

Period drawing of the Battle of Lookout Mountain, known as the Battle Above the Clouds by the soldiers who witnessed it (United States Army Military History Institute).

force had sustained casualties of 480 men, while the defending Confederates suffered 1,251 losses, of which 1,054 were captured or missing.[30]

Grant was now ready to initiate the final phase of his plan to break Bragg's hold on Chattanooga. He desired to turn one of Bragg's flanks in order to facilitate an attack against the center of the Confederate line. Hooker was ordered to march his men to Rossville Gap, in an attempt to find and attack the Confederate left. Sherman was assigned the task of attacking the Confederate right. Thomas, with the Army of the Cumberland, was to hold his position in the vicinity of Orchard Knob. If the Federals could turn one of Bragg's flanks, Thomas would be unleashed against the center. Sherman was issued orders to mount an attack at daylight on Tunnel Hill, on the right of both Missionary Ridge and the Southern line. It was to be the primary effort in Grant's overall plan, and it was assigned to his favorite and most trusted subordinate. Sherman was to attack with six divisions, totaling 26,000 men. The Confederate line at this point was manned by two divisions, or some 10,000 troops, under the command of Patrick Cleburne and Carter Stevenson. Stevenson had just recently gotten his men into position after their withdrawal from Lookout Mountain. On paper, Sherman should have had the better of the situation, enjoying more than a two-to-one superiority, but the Confederate position was formidable and compensated for their lack of numbers.

Sherman's assault began to unravel from the start. He had difficulty getting his men into position, and it was not until mid-morning, about 10:00 A.M., that he was finally ready to order them forward. The blue-clad line received a furious fire of artillery and musketry from the Confederate defenders. Though Sherman's men persisted in mounting charge after charge against the enemy lines, the Confederates proved just as dogged in holding their lines. On several occasions, the Southerners swarmed out of their lines to drive back the attackers with bayonets and clubbed muskets. Sherman suffered some 2,000 casualties in making the attack, but was unable to dislodge Cleburne or Stevenson from their breastworks. In writing about the affair, Sherman tried to shift blame for the failure to turn the line to Thomas. Sherman insisted that Thomas's orders were to support his assault "early in the day." While describing the final episodes of his own failed attack, he sarcastically writes, "I had watched for the attack of General Thomas 'early in the day.'"[31]

This would lead one to believe that Thomas's attack was to be in concert with Sherman's, and that the former was derelict in performing his duty and supporting his comrade. Such is simply not the case. The center of the Confederate line was thought to be the strongest point in their defenses, and Grant was unwilling to mount an assault against it unless one of the Rebel flanks had been turned, increasing the chances of success. Sherman had been given the starring role in the battle, and he had failed to deliver. This is not a condemnation of either Sherman or his men. Cleburne and Stevenson were in a strong position and fought like tigers. It was simply too much for Sherman's veterans to accomplish. The author finds two interesting points here, however. First is Sherman's unsoldierly attempt to shift responsibility for the failed attack to Thomas. Second is the fact that Sherman, with six divisions, failed to accomplish what Grant had ordered Thomas to do eighteen days before, with only four divisions, and without the support of either Hooker or Sherman. Sherman's failure seems to fully justify Thomas's stance against making the attack on November 7, which could have ended in no other way than complete disaster for the Union.

Thomas would have the opportunity to assail the Confederate center, but it would be Hooker, and not Sherman, who turned an enemy flank and made it possible. It may be remembered that Thomas had favored a movement against the Confederate left in his discussions of strategy with Grant. Once more, he was proven correct in his assessment of a battlefield situation. Hooker's men had also begun their drive at 10:00 A.M. By noon, he had his columns at Chickamauga Creek, but the Confederates had destroyed the bridge, and it took the Federals three hours to repair it. By 3:00 P.M., Hooker's men had located the left of the Confederate line, defended by Brigadier General Henry D. Clayton's Alabama brigade. Clayton's two regiments were heavily outnumbered, and could do little against the Union onslaught but fight a delaying action. Hooker's three divisions pushed the defenders back, gained the crest of the ridge, and captured hundreds of enemy prisoners.

Grant was observing the action from a vantage point on Orchard Knob, and upon seeing that the Confederate left flank was indeed folding, he ordered Thomas to send his divisions forward. Darkness would soon be upon the field, and the Federal commander wished to gain as much as he could from the advantage Hooker had given him before night time ended the fighting. Grant did not have a great deal of confidence in the men of the Army of the Cumberland, so the orders he gave Thomas were for only a limited objective. The Army of the Cumberland was to advance and seize only the enemy rifle pits at the base of Missionary Ridge.

General Granger was assigned direct command of the attack, but the heroic commander of the Reserve Corps at Chickamauga was strangely dilatory this day. Granger became obsessed with the artillery, manning one of the cannon himself with the ardor of a school-boy. An hour after he had been given the order to attack, Granger was still "playing" with the artillery, and had not made any preparations to advance. Thomas accosted him abruptly, admonishing him,

Contemporary drawing of the battle of Missionary Ridge, showing Thomas's men in their impetuous assault on the Confederate strongpoint (United States Army Military History Institute).

"Pay more attention to your corps, sir!" Grant publicly reprimanded him by saying, "If you will leave that battery to its captain and take command of your corps it will be better for all of us."[32]

Granger was sufficiently shocked to his senses, and got his four divisions in line in surprisingly short order. Baird's Division was on the left, followed in line by Wood's, Sheridan's and Johnson's. In all, there would be some 20,000 men making the charge. The lines were formed with a precision that had come to define the Army of the Cumberland, and the efficient manner with which the men marched even brought forth a compliment from Grant. Six rapidly fired shots from the artillery was the predetermined signal to advance, and when the final gun sounded the line surged forward. The Cumberlanders were anxious to redeem their reputation and to show Sherman's and Hooker's men the true measure of their valor. Noncombatants, such as cooks and teamsters, took up muskets and found a place in the line. Their enthusiasm was such that the main line quickened its step until it had caught up with the skirmish line. As they neared the first line of rifle pits, they were met by a volley, but the gaps in the line were closed and the attack surged forward.

Bragg had issued orders to the men in the first line of works that they were to fire only one volley if attacked. They were then to withdraw up the hill to the main line. The only problem was that not all of the men in the forward entrenchments received those orders, and as Granger's divisions pushed forward, some of the Confederates fled, while others stayed behind to be gobbled up by the onrushing Yankees. Hundreds of prisoners were taken, as their comrades scurried up the slope to safety. The jubilant Federals had little time to savor their accomplishment. Almost as soon as they gained the works, they came under a destructive fire of artillery and small arms from the main line on the crest. As one soldier in the attack described it: "The order under which the line had charged was now obeyed, but it was evident that something more must be done. With such a storm of iron hail falling thickly around, it was impossible to remain — they must either advance or retreat. To retreat was out of the question, after such a success, and over such a plain, and yet there were no orders to advance."[33]

Grant and Thomas watched as the men decided their course of action. Individually, and in small groups, men were seen climbing the slope to the summit, soon to be joined by the entire Army of the Cumberland. With a cheer, they began to scale the heights — as the Comte de Paris once termed it, they "fled forward" — into the face of galling musketry and artillery fire. Grant could not believe what he was seeing. He turned furiously to Thomas and demanded to know "who ordered those men up the ridge?" Thomas replied that he had not given any such orders. Grant then wheeled around to Granger and snappishly asked if he had issued the orders. "No," Granger said, "they started without orders. When those fellows get started, all hell can't stop them." Grant knew that the Cumberlanders were probably attacking a force equal to, if not stronger than their own, firmly entrenched in a formidable position, and he feared a terrible repulse. As he watched helplessly, he was heard to mutter, "It's all right if it turns out all right. If not, someone will suffer."

General Ulysses S. Grant. Given overall command of the Federal forces collected at Chattanooga, he received credit for the Confederate defeat at that place, even though Grant himself admitted he had nothing to do with it (United States Army Military History Institute).

The Union troops were not to be denied. At times, they were forced to climb up on their hands and knees to ascend the steep incline, but onward they came. The Confederates on the summit watched in amazement. There was even speculation that the troops making this charge must be drunk. As the ascent continued, the Southern defenders were hampered by the fact that their retreating comrades from the first line of rifle pits were between them and the advancing enemy. The defenders were forced to withhold their fire until they reached the safety of the summit, lest they shoot down their own men. Also, the earthworks had been constructed in such a fashion that the defenders were forced to expose themselves in order to fire at the advancing enemy. These two factors combined to place the Confederates at a disadvantage, and the resistless charge of the Cumberlanders created panic among the solid veterans of a score of hard-fought battles. The retreat of the Confederates at the summit started in the same manner as the advance of the Federals had begun at the base. Individually, and in small groups, Confederate soldiers began to throw down their weapons and flee to the rear. Soon, the entire line crumbled and followed suit. Braxton Bragg watched as his line melted away. "A panic, which I had never before witnessed, seemed to have seized upon the officers and men, and each seemed to be struggling for his personal safety, regardless of his duty or his character."[34]

Federal banners could be seen floating from the crest of Missionary Ridge, as the Cumberlanders raised cheer after cheer to celebrate their victory. General Wood, in a gleeful mood, threatened to arrest his men for winning a battle without orders. Grant had intended for Sherman to be the hero of Chattanooga. When he summoned him from Vicksburg he had said, "I hope you will be in time to aid in giving the rebels the worst, or best, thrashing they have had in the war." But Thomas, with the Army of the Cumberland, and not Sherman, with Grant's own Army of the Tennessee, emerged with the glory for the victory at Chattanooga. When General Hooker later congratulated Grant for his great victory, the commander gruffly snapped "Damn the battle! I had nothing to do with it."[35]

Grant seemed to be genuinely perplexed by Thomas's success at Chattanooga. Was this the residue of petty jealousy stemming from Grant's replacement by Thomas during the Corinth campaign, or was something larger afoot? Is it possible that Grant viewed Thomas as his leading competitor for top command in the army? Did he worry that the administration would one day recognize Thomas's ability to win important battles with minimum casualties, instead of the head-on, bloody tactics Grant employed? Grant enjoyed the strong political influence of the Congressional delegations from both Ohio and Illinois, and had the support of a core of high-ranking officers, including Sherman and Sheridan. Thomas, on the other hand, benefited from no political affiliations. Being Southern born, he was always looked upon suspiciously by those in power in the government, and had very little chance of supplanting Grant for the top job in the army. But Grant seems to have always been in awe of Thomas and his ability, and his efforts to limit the opportunities the general would have to distinguish himself show an effort to keep

General Patrick R. Cleburne. His division was the only Confederate unit to hold firm after collapse of the defenses on Missionary Ridge, and the rear-guard action performed by Cleburne and his men saved Bragg's army from being destroyed. Cleburne would later be killed at the Battle of Franklin (United States Army Military History Institute).

a potential rival at bay. These limitations would continue to be invoked by Sherman, when he succeeded Grant in command of the western armies.

Grant should have been thankful for the actions of Thomas and his army. His orders to the Army of the Cumberland were a colossal mistake that, if followed to the letter, could have resulted in nothing more than a blood-bath for the Cumberlanders. If Thomas's men had remained at the first line of rifle pits their ranks would have been decimated by enemy fire. If they had attempted to withdraw, that same fire would have cut them down as they retreated over open ground to the rear. The impetuous assault redeemed a bad situation created by Grant, and for the second time in the Chattanooga campaign his reputation was saved by the actions of Thomas and his men. It may be argued that the victory at Chattanooga was directly attributed to Thomas and his men, but it is a matter of fact that on two occasions they circumvented what must have been a certain defeat for Union arms.

Following the victory at Missionary Ridge, Thomas took the opportunity to join his victorious men on the summit. "I fell among some of my old soldiers, who always took liberties with me — who commenced talking and giving their views of the victory." When Thomas attempted to compliment the men for their actions, "One man very coolly replied: 'General, we know that you have been training us for this race for the last three weeks.'"[36]

Patrick Cleburne was assigned to cover the retreat of the Confederate army, as Bragg relinquished his hold on Chattanooga and marched his army back into Georgia whence it had come. The Union was now in sole possession of the city, and the heartland of the Confederacy was open to invasion. Thomas had increased the national fame he had won as a result of the determined stand at Chickamauga, and newspaper reports of the heroic charge of the Army of the Cumberland at Missionary Ridge thrilled the folks back home in the North. As 1863 drew to a close, it foreshadowed great events to follow with the coming of a new season of campaigning. Thomas would play a key role in the events that were to make 1864 the bloodiest year of the war.

Chapter Twelve

With Sherman Through Georgia

Thomas and Hooker mounted a pursuit of Bragg's retreating forces that was to last until November 27. Hooker pushed in the direction of Ringgold. Upon reaching that place, he was met with resistance so stiff as to cause him to halt and await the arrival of his artillery. He then shelled the Confederate position for a couple of hours before General Grant showed up to call off further pursuit. Thomas advanced through Rossville into the Chickamauga Valley, meeting no serious opposition. All along the line of march could be witnessed the effects of a precipitate and disorderly retreat. Tons of supplies were set ablaze by the fleeing enemy, or were seen scattered along the road. Though Thomas was meeting little resistance, Grant decided to call off his pursuit as well, and the Confederates were left to gather themselves together in Georgia without further molestation from the Union army. The pursuit had proved to be as damaging to Bragg's army as the loss of a battle, as some 6,100 prisoners, 7,000 muskets, 40 cannon, and a large quantity of wagons had been captured.[1]

Grant's reason for calling off the pursuit stemmed from political intervention rather than coming from military propriety. President Lincoln was much distressed for the safety of Knoxville, and Ambrose Burnside's army stationed there, and cautioned Grant that he needed to do what he could to prevent Longstreet from capturing them. Grant sent Sherman and Granger with their commands to lift the siege and rescue the beleaguered garrison. At least that is what they thought. After a torturous march over winter roads, the relief column arrived at Knoxville to find Burnside snugly behind strong works, with a surplus of food and ammunition at his disposal. Longstreet's Confederates were actually the ones in need of support. Sherman was greatly agitated by the march, and when Grant sent a message asking if he could pursue Longstreet into South Carolina, he tersely answered in terms indicating his reluctance to do so and the operation was forgotten. Instead, Sherman and his men were allowed to rest and reorganize in the vicinity of Bridgeport and Huntsville, Alabama. Granger's force was permitted to retire to Nashville for the same purpose.

Thomas and Hooker remained in Chattanooga to keep an eye on Bragg's beaten army, but it was evident that the Confederates would require time to refit, reorganize, and recruit before being able to undertake further operations against the Federals. Both sides were content to go into winter quarters to recuperate and regain their strength, and the prospect of active campaigning before the spring season seemed small, indeed. General Oliver O. Howard suggested to Thomas that the circumstances afforded an excellent opportunity for him to take a short leave from the army to visit his wife. Thomas rejected the proposal, stating, "Something is sure to get out of order if I go away. It was always so, even when I commanded a

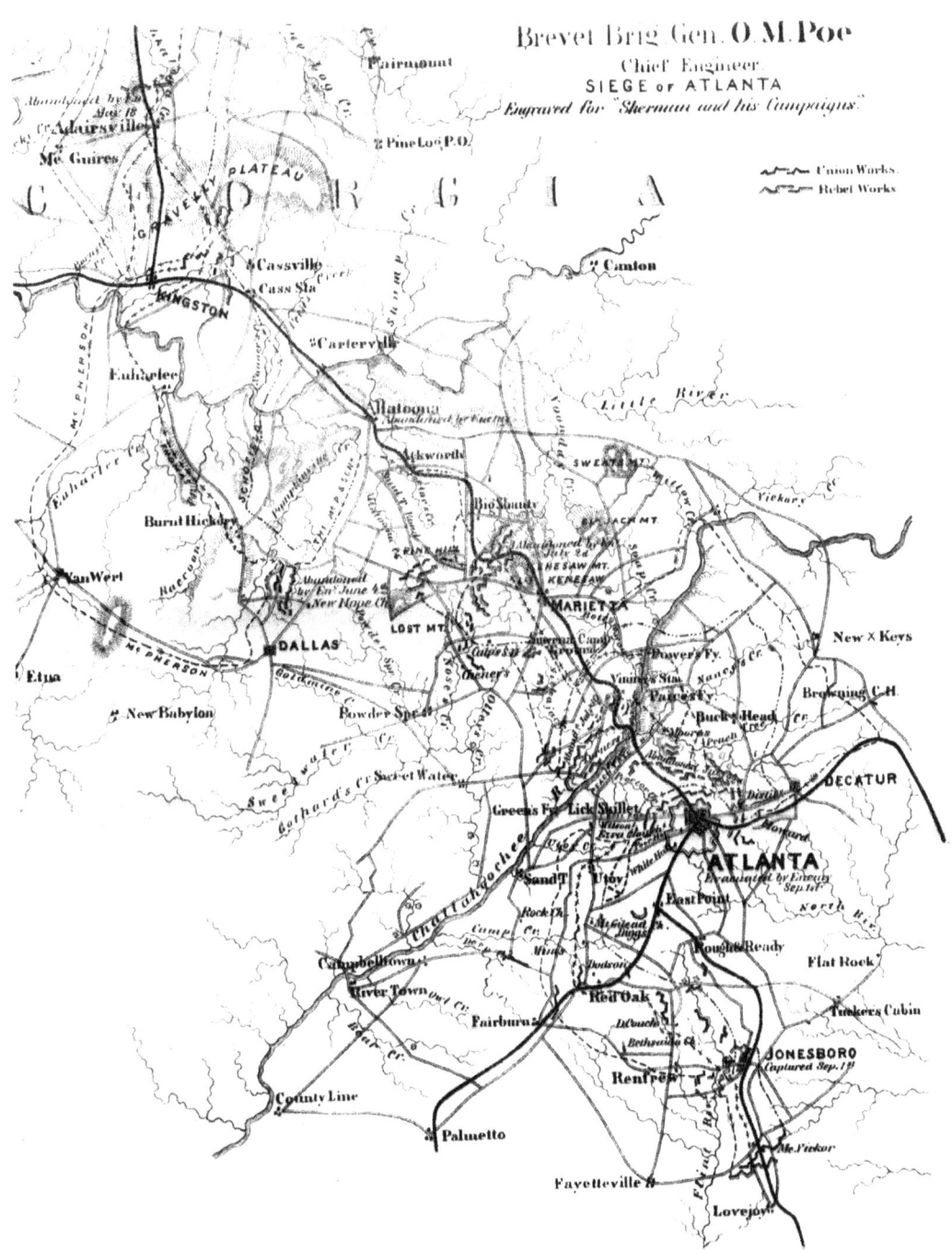

Contemporary map showing the area of northwest Georgia in which the Atlanta campaign was conducted. From *The History of the Civil War in the United States*, by Samuel Schmucker. Published by Jones Brothers & Co., in Philadelphia in 1865.

post."[2] Always a devoted and diligent commander, Thomas felt his proper place to be at the front, caring for the needs of the men in his army.

Back in Washington, talks were being held concerning the status of the Army of the Potomac, the principal Union force in the east, and the army that received the greatest scrutiny from the Northern home front. The administration was less than satisfied with the performance of Major General George G. Meade as commander of that army. Meade had endured a great deal of unfair criticism for allowing Robert E. Lee's army to escape back into Virginia following its defeat at Gettysburg. Other than the abortive Mine Run campaign, the army had been allowed to remain idle for the remainder of the year, and to many it seemed as if Meade was indisposed to fight. James Garfield happened to be in Washington, at the War Department, when the topic of command in the east came up. Stanton confided to Garfield that his leading choice for commander of the Army of the Potomac was George H. Thomas. Garfield praised Stanton's judgment, and gave voice to his hopes that the transition would come to pass.[3] Future events would show that the administration settled upon another plan of action, and Thomas would remain with the Cumberlanders.

In Richmond, Jefferson Davis's administration was also looking to make changes in army command. Braxton Bragg had come under a storm of criticism for his defeat at Chattanooga. Private citizens, and the men under his command, called for his removal, and Davis was forced to bow to these sentiments, even though he remained a loyal and supportive friend to Bragg. General Joseph E. Johnston was given the top spot with the Army of Tennessee, despite the fact that he and Davis had been embroiled in a personal feud that erupted following the Battle of First Manassas. Bragg was ordered back to Richmond, where he assumed the position of chief of staff for the Confederate armies, and served as a personal advisor to Davis.

Joseph E. Johnston was one of the most respected commanders in the Confederate army, even if his relations with his commander in chief were somewhat less than cordial. He had been the first commander of the Army of Northern Virginia, but his wounding at the Battle of Fair Oaks in early 1862 necessitated his replacement in command. Robert E. Lee was thus afforded the opportunity to display his vast talents, and went on to become the leader commonly associated with the exploits of that glorious army. In 1863, Johnston had been sent to Mississippi to assume overall command of the operations in the Vicksburg area, but he really held little authority, as Major General John C. Pemberton, the commander of Vicksburg, constantly received contrary orders from the government in Richmond. Following the capitulation of Vicksburg, Johnston was without a field command, and was the best choice available with which to replace Bragg.[4] Johnston was known for his prowess in defensive

General Joseph E. Johnston. Assigned to replace Braxton Bragg as commander of the Army of Tennessee, Johnston tried to induce Sherman to attack him in one of his fortified positions. Sherman refused to do so, however, conducting a campaign based more on maneuver than muscle (United States Army Military History Institute).

tactics, and the common watchword in both armies was to beware of Lee on the offensive and Johnston on the defensive. Military talent was not the only comparison between Lee and Johnston. Both men enjoyed the complete confidence of the soldiers they led, and Johnston was as much revered by the men in the Army of Tennessee as Lee was in the Army of Northern Virginia. His appointment to command showed immediate positive results in the ranks, where men rejoiced at the prospects of having a competent leader at the helm once more, instead of the much-despised Bragg, whom most of the troops held in contempt. Johnston concentrated his army in the vicinity of Dalton, Georgia, where he increased its ranks, improved its morale, and prepared it for the contest that was sure to come in the spring. The Confederates would return to Tennessee the following year, but the fighting around Chattanooga had placed the South in a position from which it would never recover. The tie that had tethered the Confederacy together had come undone, and Atlanta and the heart of the Southern nation were laid open for invasion and conquest. Many more months of desperate fighting lay in store, but the Union victories around Chattanooga signaled the beginning of the end for the war in the west, and George H. Thomas had been responsible for a lion's share of the credit for his accomplishments.

Thomas spent Christmas of 1863 in camp, surrounded by several of his favorite officers. Captain Sanford Kellog, his nephew and aide, sent out invitations for Christmas dinner to Generals Palmer, Johnson, and Baird, among others. Palmer, the only member of the group not to attend West Point, joked with Thomas that he did not know the meaning of R.S.V.P., to which the general stated that the invitations were of Kellog's doing, and he had no intention for the affair to be so formal. Even so, Palmer wrote that the dinner was a refined event, and remembered that "all was etiquette, all seated and served according to rank and the utmost decorum prevailed."[5] Hearty conversation and a brandy toast served to add a touch of home to the otherwise military banquet, as these comrades thought of family and friends far removed from them.

The celebration of Christmas was surely a welcome respite for Thomas, who was stretched to the limit attempting to accomplish the assignments General Grant had entrusted him with. He had been given the responsibility for virtually all of the staff work to be conducted for the armies of the Cumberland, Ohio, and Tennessee. To Thomas was also assigned the task of distributing rations to all three armies. This proved to be a daunting mission for the officer who had first been assigned to perform commissary duty in the swamps of Florida more than two decades before. The major difficulty came from the dilapidated condition of the railroads. Though Thomas detailed large numbers of his own men to repair the lines, there was simply too much work to be done, and the amount of supplies reaching the armies did not meet the demand. Major General John G. Foster, who was placed in command of the Federal troops in Knoxville when Burnside was relieved, complained bitterly about the lack of supplies he was receiving. Thomas took the complaint to heart, obviously seeing it as a condemnation of his own abilities, and wrote directly to Foster: "From the condition of supplies here I do not know how you can be supplied with anything like half rations. The railroad management is unequal to the emergency, and as that management is not under my control, I cannot say how we shall succeed after the road is open to that point. My animals are dying from starvation. And seeing this inevitable state of affairs, I have decided to starve with them until we can better their condition as well as our own. My only hope is that we can stand things longer than the enemy."[6]

On the surface, it might appear that Thomas was making excuses and attempting to shift the blame for the current situation, which was something totally out of context with his character and conduct. Such was not the case, however. The management of the railroads was truly inept, and the fact that they were not under his control and he could do little about it was driving Thomas to distraction. John B. Anderson had been appointed as the civilian director of railroads for the Army of the Cumberland. He seemed unequal to his assignment, and overawed by the task at hand, making decisions that left Thomas vexed and outraged. In one instance, 1,200 railroad workers had been hired to repair the lines, a number not nearly sufficient to accomplish the job, but Anderson had agreed to accept only 500 of them. Thomas complained of this and many other instances to Grant and Halleck, and at length Anderson was replaced by David McCullum, who had previously been in charge of military railroads in Virginia. McCullum proved to be an efficient administrator, and conditions improved considerably following his assignment. By February 15, 1864, Thomas could report that several of the roads were in good order, and that he expected to have a line completed all the way to Ringgold, Georgia, by March.[7] Thomas was just the man to oversee the railway lines, as he was possibly the most railroad-savvy general in the Union army, behind General Herman Haupt. Thomas had pioneered the use of railway cars to serve as field hospitals so that proper medical assistance could be maintained as close to the front as possible. His innovation did not stop there, however. Thomas hired Mary Walker, the first female doctor contracted to the United States Army, and the only woman to win the Medal of Honor in the Civil War.

The repairs to the supply lines, combined with the fact that the spring season would soon be upon them, prompted Grant to begin to plan offensive operations within his sphere of influence. As early as the end of January, he had put in motion plans to move against Atlanta, Mobile, and Montgomery: "I look upon the next line for me to secure to be that from Chattanooga to Mobile; Montgomery and Atlanta being the important intermediate points. To do this, large supplies must be secured on the Tennessee River, so as to be independent from the railroad from here [Nashville]." Grant determined to make Mobile a second base of operations, stating, "I do not look upon any points, except Mobile in the south, and the Tennessee river, in the north, as presenting practicable starting points from which to operate against Atlanta and Montgomery." Sherman was issued orders for an advance deep into Mississippi for a strike against Meridian, as the opening gambit in the proposed campaign for Mobile. Brigadier General William Sooy Smith was placed in command of some 7,000 cavalrymen and ordered to move out from Memphis on February 1, on a line of march to Meridian. Sherman was to follow with his infantry, from Vicksburg, on February 3. Smith's job was to deal with the enemy cavalry under Nathan Bedford Forrest, and it was felt that this should be an easy task, as the Federal troopers outnumbered the gray-clad horsemen almost two to one. Smith would have a distance of two hundred fifty miles to traverse, while Sherman's infantry would have to trudge one hundred fifty miles to reach the objective.

On February 14, Sherman's infantry marched into Meridian, as the Confederates retreated across the Tombigbee River toward Selma and Mobile. The Federals set to work destroying everything in the town that aided the Confederate war effort. Smith's progress had not been so satisfying. He had delayed his advance from Memphis until February 11, ten full days after it was supposed to have begun. By February 22, he had advanced only to West Point, where he was confronted by Forrest's cavalry. Though the Federal force was double the size of Forrest's, the Confederates were able to defeat Smith's cavalry, and the Union commander retreated back to his place of origin, closely followed by Forrest. Sherman, in the meantime, pushed forward to Hillsborough and Canton, where his army remained until March 3.[8] Sherman had accomplished the deepest penetration into Confederate territory thus far attempted in the war. He had also succeeded in inflicting serious damage to the enemy supply and communications lines in the region.

In early February, Thomas received instructions to concentrate his army for offensive operations against Joseph E. Johnston's Confederates at Dalton, Georgia. Grant feared that Johnston might be able to shift men from his army to face Sherman if he were not held in place, so Thomas was ordered to mount a diversion in favor of the operations taking place in Mississippi. Major General John M. Schofield received similar orders to use his Army of the Ohio to keep Longstreet from reinforcing the Confederates in Mississippi. On February 12, Grant directed Thomas to "make a formidable reconnaissance toward Dalton, and, if successful in driving the enemy out, occupy that place and complete the railroad up to it." Thomas replied that he could accomplish the mission, provided Major General John Logan's Division was returned to him. Logan had been dispatched to east Tennessee to guard against incursions by Longstreet, but Grant agreed to release him from this duty.[9]

Thomas was held up by heavy rains for over a week and was unable to move his army forward. He did, however, keep a close eye on the enemy, and was able to report to Grant that Johnston had only detached a single brigade from his army, presumably for the assistance of the Confederates in Mississippi. The Army of the Cumberland marched forward on February 22 and 23, as Johnston's army withdrew before them without offering battle. Thomas advanced to Dalton, but was forced to retire back to Chattanooga because his nearly starved teams could not bring up enough supplies to subsist the army until the railroad was repaired. Grant, in his memoirs, seems to have discounted the difficulties faced by Thomas, and casts aspersions on him in recounting the affair.[10]

On February 28, Thomas reported to Grant that Major General Daniel Butterfield had informed him that the railroad line between Chattanooga and Nashville could be held by a force of six thousand men. Thomas believed that the line from Nashville to Decatur could be held by a relatively small force, and offered the opinion that both routes could be secured by a force of six thousand infantry and two thousand cavalry. This being the case, he suggested that he could move against the enemy with his own Fourteenth and Fourth Corps, supported by Oliver O. Howard's Corps from the Army of the Potomac. He proposed an aggressive campaign to be conducted along the route of the rail line, all the way to Atlanta. Had Thomas's suggestion been approved, it is possible that the war might have been shortened by a number of months, but Grant and Sherman had other plans for the prosecution of the war against the Confederacy, and there would be a new command structure in place when those plans were pushed forward.[11]

Grant had received the lion's share of the credit for lifting the siege of Chattanooga, even though he had personally admitted that he had little to do with the successful assault that served to drive Bragg's army from the environs of the city. Nonetheless, his perceived success at Chattanooga, combined with his capture of Vicksburg and his earlier captures of Forts Henry and Donelson, propelled him to a stature unequaled by any other officer in the Union army. Grant was seen as the greatest leader in the North, and steps were being taken on his behalf to elevate him to supreme command of all the Union military forces. A bill had been introduced in Congress by the representative from Grant's hometown, Elihu Washburne, to revive the rank of lieutenant general in the United States army. Washburne's intention in so doing was to reward Grant by bestowing the title upon him and making him the ranking general in the North. To be sure, the Confederates had issued the rank to scores of officers, and had even promoted eight generals to the rank of full-general, but tradition had kept the North from following suit. George Washington had been the only officer to hold the rank of lieutenant general in the history of the United States army, and it was commonly held that no other officer was entitled to such lofty position. True, Winfield Scott was named lieutenant general late in his career, but it was only a brevet or honorary appointment. A great deal of controversy and discussion followed Washburne's introduction of the bill, as all knew that Grant would be nominated for the grade if it passed, and would therefore be elevated to a status equaling Washington. At length, the bill received enough votes to pass, and on March 4, 1864, Grant wrote to Sherman: "The bill reviving the grade of lieutenant-general in the army has become a law, and my name has been sent to the Senate.... I now receive orders to report to Washington immediately in person, which indicates either a confirmation or a likelihood of confirmation."[12]

Grant's intuition proved correct, as he received the rank of lieutenant general, as well as overall command of the Union armies in the field. The decision was made that he would make his headquarters with the Army of the Potomac in the east, which left vacant the post he had just held in the west. To fill this, Grant looked no further than his old friend, William T. Sherman. Sherman was appointed command of the armies of the Cumberland, Tennessee, and Ohio, while Major General James B. McPherson was elevated to Sherman's old position as commander of the Army of the Tennessee. A compelling argument could be made that Thomas was the rightful officer to be named to the overall command in the west. In the first place, he outranked Sherman, by virtue of his prior appointment to the rank of major general.[13] That being said, his previous record certainly would have given him claim to the position, but Grant was seeking a replacement that was known to him, an officer he was used to working with, someone with whom he was comfortable. Though Grant and Thomas had experienced no altercations between them, the reserved coolness exhibited by the officers and their staffs at Chattanooga made it evident that Grant and Thomas were not comfortable with each other, even if they did work well together. Sherman's record up to this point was not nearly as impressive as that of Thomas, and Grant could be criticized for allowing friendship and familiarity to impede his judgment in not appointing Thomas to the command. While this is certainly true, it is also true that Grant had the right to pick his own team for the coming spring offensive, and he chose an officer with whom he had previously shared a suitable working relationship over an officer with whom he had experienced limited contact. It is the author's opinion that Grant slighted Thomas in not elevating him to command in the west, but that slight stemmed from a desire to establish cohesion between Grant and his principal commander in that region, and not from an intent to do harm to the reputation or abilities of Thomas. Regrettably, that is exactly what happened, regardless of intent.

For Thomas's part, the slight was noted, but it did not impair his devotion to duty, or his intentions to perform his assignments to his utmost capacity, even though this was the second time he had been passed over in favor of an officer junior to him. When another officer brought the matter up, Thomas stated "I have made my last protest against serving under juniors. I have made up my mind to go on with this work without a word, and do my best to help get through this business as soon as possible."[14] Thomas's rigid sense of honor and decorum must have been sorely tested by this latest ingratitude on the part of the military, but his character was such that it would not allow him to vent his frustrations over the lack of appreciation being shown for his service and accomplishments.

On March 17, Grant and Sherman met in Nashville to plan the campaigns against the two main armies of the Confederacy. Grant would operate with the Army of the Potomac against Robert E. Lee and his Army of Northern Virginia. Sherman, with his three armies now consolidated into the newly created Military Department of the Mississippi, was to engage Johnston's Army of Tennessee in Georgia. The movements were to be conducted simultaneously, so as to prevent the Confederates the ability of shifting men and resources from an idle theater to one that was threatened, as had been done prior to the Battle of Chickamauga. In conjunction with these campaigns, Major General Franz Sigel was to invade the Shenandoah Valley, and Major General Benjamin Butler was to advance up the Virginia Peninsula to threaten both Richmond and Petersburg. Grant intended to make the Confederate armies the objective in this nationwide campaign, knowing that the Rebels could not long endure a war of attrition with the numerically superior forces of the Union. For the first time in the war, the North was about to use all of its muscle at the same time, instead of the independent and uncoordinated efforts that had defined the conflict to date. Grant set the beginning of May as the time for the combined operations to begin.

As all of this was going on, Thomas was spending time overseeing two pet projects. First was the organization of Negro regiments. Thomas kept a daily vigil on the progress of their training, until by April 5 he was able to report that six full regiments of infantry were ready for duty, with another three regiments of infantry and a battery of light artillery in the process of forming. His second pet project was the establishment of a national cemetery on the slopes of Orchard Knob, and he diligently watched over the interment of fallen comrades into this final resting place. When an army chaplain asked Thomas if the solders were to be buried according to the states from which they served, the general quickly responded: "No, no, no. Mix them up. Mix them up. I am tired of states-rights."[15] The spring season brought with it an offense to the senses that had been stifled by the frigid winter temperatures. The thousands of army mules that had perished bringing supplies into Chattanooga were decomposing in the April warmth. As a soldier in the 92nd Illinois Mounted Infantry recalled, "the atmosphere gave off the odors from the remnants of the dead mules that lined the valleys."[16] Thomas was seeing to the burial of the Union soldiers, but the dead army mules were not a priority and would have to wait.

Sherman would have some 98,357 men in his combined army with which to begin his campaign against Johnston. Of this total, 60,733 were members of the Army of the Cumberland, while the Army of the Tennessee and the Army of the Ohio contained 24,065 and 13,559, respectively. As such, Thomas would command almost two-thirds of Sherman's entire force, and the Army of the Cumberland would provide the muscle for the ensuing campaign.[17] Thomas's army was divided into three corps, the Fourth, Fourteenth, and Twentieth, commanded by Generals Howard, Palmer, and Hooker. Each corps consisted of three divisions, commanded by seasoned veterans of numerous hard-fought campaigns. In addition to his infantry, Thomas also had two divisions of cavalry, commanded by Major Generals Edwin M. McCook and Kenner Garrard. A third division of cavalry, under Major General Judson Kilpatrick, also belonged to the Army of the Cumberland, but had been detached to serve under McPherson's command. Both McPherson and Schofield complained to Sherman about the disparity in numbers between their commands and that of Thomas, in an effort to have the troops more evenly distributed among the three armies. Sherman provided a glimpse of his evaluation of Thomas when he responded to these complaints by saying, "I keep you on the flanks in order that if anything happens to either of you I would have 'Old Thom' left; and as you both know, nothing could budge him."[18]

Thomas's army would provide the bulk of the force Sherman would use in his advance on Atlanta, and Thomas himself would do the majority of administrative work for the combined forces. As independent commanders of field armies, McPherson and Schofield were responsible for attending to the details of matters of supply, intelligence, maps, and more. Thomas's abilities in these areas were without equal, causing the other two army commanders to defer the administration of these details to his capable supervision. His expertise caused him to become saddled with the administrative operations of all three armies, and freed McPherson and Schofield from such distasteful duties. Even the clerical duties of all three armies, the military paperwork and record keeping, fell on Thomas's shoulders. In essence, he performed the function of a chief of staff for Sherman's combined forces, while at the same time serving as the commander of an independent field army.

By the end of April 1864, Joseph E. Johnston would report having 52,992 men in his army with which to oppose Sherman. These were divided into two corps, commanded by Lieutenant Generals John Bell Hood and William J. Hardee. By the time the armies first met, that total would be increased to approximately 67,000 with the addition of Leonidas Polk's Corps, and during the course of the campaign, it would continue to swell till it reached approximately 84,000 men of all arms.[19] The reader can quickly see that, at the outset of the campaign, the Army of the Cumberland was a pretty even match for the Confederates by itself, and that Thomas commanded a force almost equal to that of Johnston.

Grant telegraphed Sherman on April 28 that he intended to open his offensive against Lee on May 4, and directed that operations against Johnston commence the following day. The Confederates were dug in around Dalton, and Sherman felt that the position was too strong to risk a frontal assault, so he adopted the strategy of attempting to flank it and maneuver Johnston out of his stronghold. Johnston had established his main defensive position at Rocky Face, an imposing elevation in the Chattanooga Mountains. Buzzard's Roost was the name given to the steep cliffs of the mountain that controlled the gorge created by Mill Creek, along which route the Chattanooga Road wound its way into Dalton. Johnston had created an imposing defensive position all along the sides and summit of Rocky Face, and the mountain literally bristled

General Leonidas Polk. Episcopal bishop and corps commander in the Confederate army, this veteran leader was killed by Union artillery fire on Pine Mountain during the fighting that culminated in the failed assault on Kennesaw Mountain (United States Army Military History Institute).

with entrenched lines of his infantry and artillery. The Confederates had dammed Mill Creek in order to flood the gorge and provide a natural barrier to complement their man-made defenses. As Johnston waited for Sherman to make the first move, he hoped that he could induce him to batter his army against this formidable and imposing obstacle.

On May 1, Sherman telegraphed Grant that he had issued orders to his army commanders. Thomas was to concentrate his army at Ringgold, from which point he would advance directly on Dalton and Rocky Face. McPherson was already on the march to Chattanooga, and was directed to make his way to Villanow, on Thomas's right. Schofield was to march from Charleston to Catoosa Springs, via Cleveland, where he would take up position on Thomas's left. The Army of the Cumberland was to be the anchor upon which the other two armies were to attach themselves. It would also directly oppose the strongest point in the enemy line.

Sherman and Thomas were well-known to one another, and could trace their association all the way back to their days at West Point. Sherman had many times stated his great friendship for Thomas, and the two seemed to have enjoyed an amicable working relation in all of their prior encounters. The beginning of the Atlanta campaign would also witness the beginning of a rift between the two generals that would end with Sherman's playing more the part of a detractor than a friend. In April, Thomas had proposed to make an advance against Johnston's left flank, through Snake Spring Gap, which he knew to be unguarded by the enemy. This would cut Confederate communications between Dalton and Resaca, fifteen miles south, and would force the Confederates to either attack Thomas or withdraw to the east through difficult terrain. "Let me take the Army of the Cumberland, move through Snake Spring Gap and get in the rear of Johnston," he suggested. "He must come out and fight me, and I can whip him with the Army of the Cumberland alone," Thomas stated confidently, adding that "if he should get the better of me, you can come upon him with the Armies of the Tennessee and the Ohio and between us, we can rub him out. His men will take to the mountains, but he must abandon his artillery and trains, and there will be an end to the matter." Sherman rejected Thomas's plan, and the manner in which he did so became a source of contention between these two proud officers. Sherman informed Thomas that "the Army of Tennessee are better marchers than the Army of the Cumberland and I am going to send McPherson." Thomas was so insulted by the statement that he put on his hat and immediately left Sherman's headquarters, "for I saw the game was up."[20]

The logic of Thomas's suggestion was beyond question. The movement that he proposed required strength behind it to force Johnston into doing what the Federals wanted him to. The Army of the Cumberland contained such a force; the Army of the Tennessee did not. Even if Sherman's inappropriate comment about the Tennesseans' being better marchers were true, what good would it do to have them reach their destination if, when the mission was accomplished, the blocking force would number less than half of the available enemy force? As Thomas correctly foresaw it, Johnston would be able to easily parry a thrust like this, even if it compelled him to abandon his hold on the strong defensive line at Rocky Face. If that took place, nothing would be accomplished other than changing the venue on which the armies would be facing one another. Thomas sought to force Johnston's army into a battle it could not hope to win, and to end the campaign for Atlanta in its initial stroke, in the northwestern corner of Georgia. He would later write that his proposed movement would have forced the enemy "either to retreat toward the east, through a difficult country, poorly supplied," or it would have made Johnston "attack me, in which event I felt confident that my army was sufficiently strong to beat him."[21]

At daylight on May 6, the Army of the Cumberland stepped out on the march toward Dalton, amid great excitement in the ranks. John Tomey, a sergeant in the 27th Indiana Infantry, recorded in his diary that the regiment left camp at 7:00 that morning, and bivouacked at 4:00 that afternoon, within six miles of Tunnel Hill, at Rocky Face Mountain. There had been no real contact with the enemy, and Tomey had little more to jot down in his diary but "We have sore feet."[22] When the columns stopped for the night, they faced the prospect of sleeping under the stars. Sherman had ordered the army stripped down for combat to only the barest essentials, and the troops were not carrying tents with them. Grant was engaging Lee's Army of Northern Virginia in the bloody Battle of the Wilderness on this very day, and Sherman was eager to make contact with the enemy in his front and undertake his part of the overall Union strategy.

The Confederates had braced themselves for the coming offensive. The year of 1863 had witnessed the enrollment of thousands of Negro troops, and the South feared that these black soldiers would be unleashed upon the populace during the spring campaign. Southern propaganda sought to enrage the people, and unite them for what was seen as a struggle between the races, as well as between North and South. "Neither life nor virtue is sacred from these northern barbarians; the old and infirm perish by their bloody hands, while lovely women — our wives and daughters — are reserved for a fate even worse than death. Strike, men of the south and exterminate such polluted wretches and living demons!"[23] Unknown to the people of Georgia, Thomas, the Virginian, espoused the use of black troops, but Sherman, the true Northerner, refused to have them in his army. No Negro combat troops would accompany Sherman in his drive on Atlanta.

The Cumberlanders made contact with Johnston's main body at Rocky Face on May 8 when General Howard's 4th Corps moved against the Southern defenses. General Schofield's Army of the Ohio was assigned to assault the Confederate right flank. One Union soldier described Rocky Face as being "the steepest mountain I ever saw. The sides are almost perpendicular." Another thought that "charging such a place seems like folly."[24] In the pre-dawn hours of May 9 the assault against the summit of Rocky Face was begun. Howard succeeded in getting a portion of his men to the top of the ridge, and they advanced for a mile and a half along the crest before reaching Buzzard's Roost. One Union soldier recalled that the Rebels were "fortified and in a position from which I do not believe they could have been driven." Howard's men were separated from Buzzard's Roost by a narrow ravine over which no more than a company could advance at a time. Confederate defenders stood ready to punish any unit foolhardy enough to make the attempt. From their vantage point on the crest, the Union soldiers could plainly see the Confederate defenses around Dalton. Johnston had constructed four or five lines of rifle pits, and every hill around Dalton had been fortified. Even if Howard could be successful in capturing Buzzard's Roost, the capture of Dalton looked to be a daunting task that would cost the lives of thousands of Federal soldiers. Howard spent the day skirmishing with the Confederates along the crest, but was unable to gain any ground or dislodge the defenders from Buzzard's Roost. After dark, he was ordered to withdraw, and further efforts against the crest were abandoned. To the men in the ranks, it seemed as if the day had gone against them. In reality, everything was progressing exactly the way Sherman intended.[25]

McPherson had been sent on a flanking movement through Snake Spring Gap, with orders to seize the railroad line at Resaca, some fifteen miles in Johnston's rear. Thomas's attack on Rocky Face was merely a diversion to occupy the Confederates' attention while McPherson

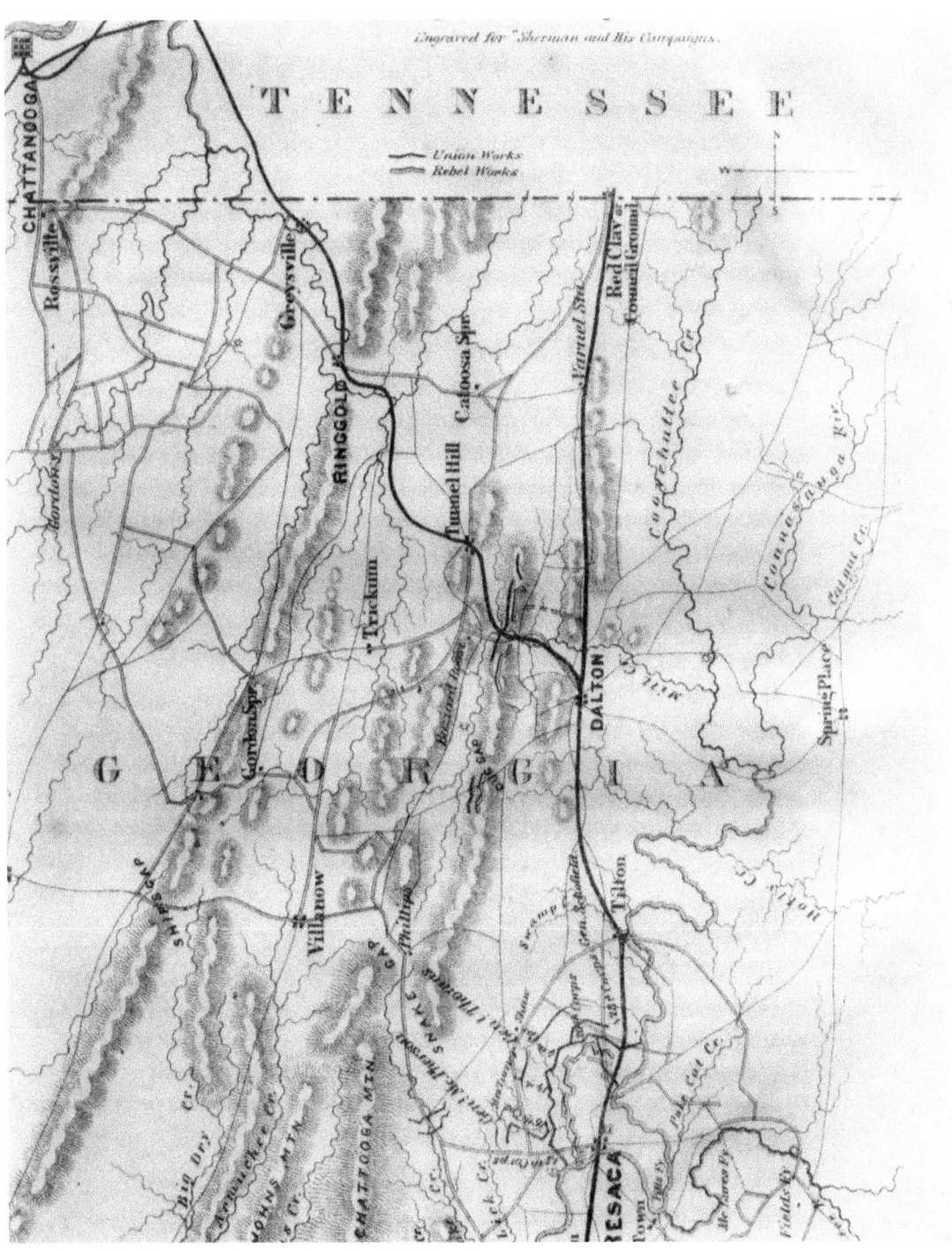

Period map showing the operations of the Union and Confederate forces around Resaca, Georgia. From *The History of the Civil War in the United States*, by Samuel Schmucker. Published by Jones Brothers & Co., in Philadelphia in 1865.

delivered the death blow. Thomas's phase worked to perfection. Johnston's men were preoccupied with Howard's assault and were unaware that McPherson was marching around their flank until the Federals suddenly appeared about five miles from Resaca. Sherman was sure that he had accomplished his goal of trapping Johnston. "I've got Joe Johnston dead!" he bellowed after receiving reports of McPherson's proximity to the railroad. The news that came from the direction of Resaca that night was not nearly so encouraging. McPherson reported that he had encountered strong entrenchments north of Resaca, and had been unable to seize his objective.

In the meantime, Johnston had become aware of Sherman's true intentions and had pulled his army out of Dalton and moved them into previously prepared positions at Resaca. Nothing had been gained, and only the venue was changed. "I regret beyond measure you did not break up the railroad," Sherman wrote to McPherson. The next day, when they met in person, Sherman said, "Well, Mac, you missed the opportunity of your life." In his report to Washington, however, Sherman was careful not to assess any blame to McPherson, and even stated that he had acted under orders.[26] It was only just that Sherman protect his old friend from censure. After all, it was not McPherson's fault that the flanking movement had failed. Thomas had predicted it before the movement was undertaken. Had Sherman accepted Thomas's suggestion, his flanking force would have been sufficient to deal with any situation that arose. McPherson simply did not have enough men in his army to get the job done without the support of the "slow footed" Cumberlanders.

Thomas had suggested that Howard fortify his position in front of Buzzard's Roost to keep Johnston's men pinned down in their defenses while Hooker's Corps was sent to aid McPherson in capturing the railroad. Such a move could still have redeemed Union fortunes and resulted in the outcome that Sherman sought. But the Federal commander once more rejected Thomas's advice, in part because he disliked General Hooker and did not trust him. May 10 was spent deliberating the next Union move. By the end of the day, Sherman had decided to accept Thomas's advice. On May 11, Howard was left at Buzzard's Roost to confront the enemy, while the remainder of the Army of the Cumberland was pushed through Snake Spring Gap. The one day delay afforded Johnston time to react, however, and he had pulled the bulk of his forces out of Dalton on the night of May 10. Sherman had insulted the Army of the Cumberland, and its commander, when he referred to them as being slow. Sherman proved to be the slow one at Dalton, and missed an opportunity to possibly end the campaign in its initial stroke. For the second time, he had rejected Thomas's advice, and thousands of Union casualties in the upcoming battles would attest to the error in doing so. Sherman realized fully the mistake he had made, and would later comment on Dalton, "Such an opportunity does not occur twice in a single life."[27]

On May 13, sharp skirmishing broke out when the Union troops made contact with the Confederate defenses north and west of Resaca. Major General Jacob D. Cox, from Schofield's Army of the Ohio, attacked the left flank of the Southern position, where he captured a portion of works held by troops under Major General Thomas C. Hindman. But Cox was repulsed when he tried to capture even stronger works to his front. On Cox's right, Brigadier General Henry Judah's Division connected Schofield's army with the Army of the Cumberland. Judah's men surged forward, along with the Cumberlanders, but Judah allowed his division to become entangled with Thomas's men, resulting in confusion and disorganization. Judah did not stop to reorganize his lines. Instead, he pushed forward for 400 yards, making contact with the Confederate defenses. When the Southerners unleashed a volley, the confusion in Judah's ranks turned to panic, and the men were quickly demoralized.

Now it was the Confederates' turn to assume the offensive. Cox's Division had been stopped cold, and Judah's had been routed. This left the division of Major General David Stanley exposed and in the open. Johnston ordered Lieutenant General John Bell Hood forward with two divisions of his own, and four additional brigades from the center of the Confederate line. Hood crashed into Stanley, causing his division to stampede from the field, and only the timely arrival of Major General Alpheus Williams's Division prevented a rout from occurring on the Federal left flank. Darkness fell before Hood could reorganize to make another attack.[28] Johnston held the Federals at bay for several days at Resaca, inflicting 4,740 casualties in the process. Of these, 3,500 were sustained by the Army of the Cumberland, which had once more held the center of the Union line.

Thomas was irritated by the frontal assaults Sherman made at Resaca, but took solace in the fact that his army was fighting well and was in good spirits. At Resaca, he had undertaken a personal intervention regarding a captain in Howard's Corps that epitomized his no-nonsense approach to situations. It seems that the captain had been arrested for some minor infraction of the military code, but he refused to go to the rear. Howard's signal corps men had sent several flag messages to Sherman's headquarters concerning the incident, and requesting information about what should be done. Thomas became agitated by all the fuss and bother and interceded, directing Howard, "Restore him to duty, and if he behaves well as a soldier in battle, I will take care of the charges."[29]

Sherman had attempted to envelop Johnston's army at Resaca, but on the night of May 15, Johnston ordered a pontoon bridge to be built across the Oostanaula River, his only remaining escape route. By May 16, he had evacuated his army and was withdrawing south toward Atlanta, looking for a suitable location to make his next stand. On the night of May 17, Johnston found what he was looking for. The road to Cassville forked, with one fork going east, directly to Cassville, while the other went south to Kingston, before turning east to Cassville as well. Johnston sent Hardee's Corps on the road to Kingston, while he led the main body over the more direct route to Cassville. Johnston correctly deduced that Sherman would divide his forces to march over the roads in a like manner. If Hardee could arrive in Cassville before Sherman's main body, Johnston would be able to attack the Federals in detail, while the column on the Kingston road was still on the march. But Sherman's columns did some hard marching of their own and were able to rapidly concentrate north and west of the town before Johnston could spring his trap. On May 19, Union cavalry probed the Confederate line, and established itself on the right flank and rear of the Confederate defenses. Artillery was brought up, and the shelling made it impossible for the Confederates to hold the line. On the night of May 19, Johnston pulled his men out of their positions and once more headed them south toward Atlanta.[30]

By this time, Sherman had covered over half of the distance between Chattanooga and Atlanta, and he had firmly established his method of operating against Johnston. McPherson and Schofield would always operate on the flanks, looking to turn the Rebel line or get into its rear. Thomas, with his large army, would always occupy the center, and serve as the battering ram of the Union army. To McPherson and Schofield would fall all of the dashing and glorious assignments. The Army of the Cumberland would be relegated to perform the grunt work, and slug it out against Johnston's main lines while the armies of the Tennessee and the Ohio grabbed the headlines.

Johnston next stopped at Allatoona Pass, where he established a line in the 1,000 foot mountains that dominated the area. Sherman had served in the area some twenty years before as a young lieutenant, and was well aware of the strength of any defensive position located there. Sherman declined to oblige Johnston and attack him in this newest stronghold, which he felt to be more formidable than the one at Rocky Face. Instead, he opted to once more slip around the Confederate flank and try to place his army between the Confederates and Atlanta. The Federal commander proposed to cross the Etowah River and strike east, toward Marietta. This would necessitate his breaking free from the rail line that was serving as the supply source for his army, and meant that rail supplies could not be resumed until he reached Marietta. Sherman ordered his wagon train to be loaded with twenty days' rations for the men, and started his men toward the little crossroads town of Dallas.[31]

Johnston anticipated Sherman's move and raced his columns southward to block him. When Sherman arrived at Dallas he expected to find the town free for the taking. Instead, he found the Army of Tennessee formed and ready for battle behind freshly constructed earthworks. General John Geary's Division of Thomas's army was in the lead as the Federals approached Dallas. Four miles northeast of the town, at a place called New Hope Church, he made contact with two regiments of enemy infantry at 10:00 A.M. on the morning of May 25. Geary quickly routed the enemy and drove them back, only to discover a strongly entrenched line to their rear. Prisoners informed him that John Bell Hood's entire corps was in his front, and that the corps of Polk and Hardee were within supporting distance. Geary, with his lone division, had stumbled onto the entire Confederate army, in position and ready to fight. He immediately called off his attack and instructed the men to throw up log breastworks for defense.

Thomas was accompanying Geary, and he took charge of the situation. Fearing that the men might become timid if they were fully apprised of the desperate situation, he determined to assume a bold front. He summoned Captain Henry Stone and quietly ordered him "to ride back to Howard as fast as I could and hurry up the 4th Corps." Stone took the order literally, and, jumping on his horse, started out at a gallop to secure the reinforcements. Thomas called him back, however, and admonished him to walk his horse until he was out of sight of the men. There was no sense in causing a panic, and Thomas wanted nothing to seem alarming in Stone's ride to the rear. When Stone reached Howard he relayed Thomas's message, only to be informed that an increased pace would use up the men. Stone then found Alpheus Williams of Howard's Corps, and in him found a more willing accomplice. Williams hurried his division forward. Along the way, the column passed General Sherman, who was becoming enraged by what he thought to be a useless delay. "I don't see what they are waiting for in front now," he snapped. "There haven't been twenty rebels there today."[32]

Confederate fire was increasing substantially by the time Williams' men arrived at New Hope Church. Williams threw them into the fray, losing 800 men in twenty minutes of fighting. Geary had sustained 500 casualties in his own command. The two Federal divisions were being roughly handled by the "twenty rebels" Sherman felt to be in front of Thomas. By this time, it became obvious to all that the entire Southern army was present at New Hope Church. Geary waited for most of the morning and early afternoon as Hooker brought up the other two divisions of his corps and prepared to make an assault. Hooker aligned his divisions for battle by column of brigades, meaning that the brigades of each division were stacked up one behind the other. While this alignment provided strength for the attacking force, it meant that each of the trailing brigades would be under fire from the enemy, but would be unable to respond from fear of hitting the friendly troops in front of them.

Hooker launched his attack at 4:00 P.M., against a portion of the line held by General Alexander P. Stewart's Confederate division, supported by three batteries of artillery. Though

Hooker outnumbered Stewart by more than three to one, the Confederates were able to take advantage of the faulty alignment of the attacking troops. More than 1,500 rounds of shell and canister were fired into the close-packed columns by the Southern artillery, opening huge gaps with each explosion. Though the fighting lasted for three hours, Hooker was unable to gain the Rebel works, and at 7:00 P.M., when the clouds opened up in a torrential downpour, the attack was called off. Hooker had lost 1,665 men in the abortive assault, while Hood's forces had suffered less than half that number.[33] Thomas's vanguard had stumbled into a precarious situation, but by the cool and calculated actions of its commander, a possible disaster was avoided.

During the night of May 25, the remainder of Sherman's army arrived at New Hope Church and went into line opposite the Confederates. Sherman determined to try another flanking movement on the 26th, and sent General Howard with 14,000 men to attack the Rebel right flank. The only problem was that Sherman did not know exactly where the right flank of the enemy was located. The spot against which he sent Howard was not the flank, but merely a bend in the main Confederate line. Howard was in position by 2:30 on the afternoon of May 26, and the line was ordered forward, with the brigade of Brigadier General William B. Hazen in the lead. Hazen ran in to Patrick Cleburne's entire division, two miles north of New Hope Church at Pickett's Mill. Brigadier General John Kelly's brigade of dismounted Confederate cavalry took Hazen's line by the flank, as the Federals advanced through a murderous fire. Hazen's line made it to within twenty paces of Cleburne's line before they were forced to withdraw, after losing 500 casualties.

Howard sent in the other two brigades of Thomas Wood's Division at forty minute intervals, meaning that each was attacking independently and unsupported. Colonel William Gibson's Brigade was the next to test Cleburne's line. Though Gibson's men advanced to within fifteen paces of the enemy, they were thrown back with the same result that had befallen Hazen. Casualties were heavy, as typified by the fifty percent losses suffered by the 49th Ohio Infantry, prompting one survivor to write "This is surely not war, it is butchery." When Howard committed the remaining brigade of Wood's Division, it was not to press another assault on Cleburne's line, but merely to hold his own. The firing gradually died down, but at 10:00 P.M., Brigadier General Hiram Granbury had the men of his Texas brigade fix bayonets and led them in a charge against the Federals in their front. Granbury's men captured 232 prisoners, and brought a close to the fighting for the day. Howard had suffered some 1,600 casualties, while Cleburne had sustained only about one-third that number.[34]

A Confederate officer who walked the ground around New Hope Church following the end of the fighting noted that he beheld much "that I cannot describe; and which I hope never to see again, dead men meet the eye in every direction, and in one place I stopped and counted 50 dead men in a circle of 30 ft. of me. Men laying in all sorts of shapes ... just as they had fallen, and it seems like they have nearly all been shot in the head, and a great number of them have their skulls bursted open and their brains running out, quite a number that way." The officer stated that he had seen many dead men before, "but I never saw anything before that made me sick, like looking at the brains of these men," and he believed that he "would have fainted if I had not passed on and got out of that place as soon as I did."[35]

On May 27, following the fighting at Pickett's Mill, Sherman continued his march toward the railroad at Marietta. McPherson was detailed to hold the ground previously covered by Howard and Hooker, as those troops were pulled out of line and marched around the flank of the Southern position. The military dance that was becoming the Atlanta campaign was about to take its next turn.

June was ushered in with almost constant rains that slowed the advance as the Federals slogged through the Georgia mud. By June 3, Sherman had arrived at Ackworth, twelve miles north of Marietta. Johnston was still in front of him, however. On the night of June 4, the Confederates moved into a new defensive position, eight miles south of Ackworth on a ten-mile line that intersected the Western & Atlantic Railroad. The defining features of the Southern position were four mountains. In a line, from left to right, were Brush Mountain, Pine Mountain, and Lost Mountain. Pine Mountain was slightly in advance of those to the left and right, and curved toward the Federal line. Two miles to the rear stood Kennesaw Mountain, 700 feet high and two miles long. Johnston placed his artillery on the heights and had his infantry throw up earthworks along the slopes. What resulted was a formidable defensive position that seemed to defy the successful possibility of a frontal assault. Sherman went into line with McPherson on the left, Thomas in the center, and Schofield on the right, and began probing for a weakness.

The rains fell incessantly for the next several days as the Federals searched for a likely spot to attack. Thomas had not taken Sherman's orders regarding tents to pertain to him when the campaign began, and he tenaciously clung to his eleven Sibley tents for the comfort of himself and his staff. Sherman reined in his horse in front of Thomas's headquarters and asked whose tents it was that lined the street. "General Thomas's, general," was the reply. "Oh yes, Thomastown — Thomasville, a very pretty place, appears to be growing rapidly," Sherman snapped. Thomas noticed that Sherman had only a single wall-tent for his headquarters, and thought that insufficient, given the recent inclement weather. He thereby ordered a company of sharpshooters to pitch a number of new tents to be used as army headquarters, and Sherman gladly accepted their use for the duration of the campaign.[36]

The Federal campaign had been immensely successful thus far. Though Sherman had not destroyed Johnston's army, he had forced it out of a series of well-prepared defenses with a minimal number of casualties. He had kept his army well in hand, and had marched deep into enemy territory, to within twenty-two miles of his objective. All in all, Sherman was proving to be a brilliant strategist and tactician, and a master of maneuver. The wonder is not that Sherman did as well as he was doing; it was that he did not do better, for the Federal commander was constantly in possession of the Confederate plans. In fact, he received Johnston's orders at the same time the subordinate Confederate commanders did. One of his signal officers had broken the Confederate flag code back in Chattanooga, and had made up code books which were distributed to all of the signal officers in the Federal army. Sherman was daily informed as to enemy troop movements, casualties, and supplies, and was able to base his own decisions upon the full and certain knowledge of the enemy's dispositions and intentions. Shortly before the armies arrived at Kennesaw Mountain, a reporter for the *New York Herald* caught wind of the story and thought it would make excellent reading for the folks back home. When his story was run, Confederate agents in New York immediately notified Johnston that his code had been breached, and it was accordingly changed. Sherman was outraged. He had the reporter arrested, and vowed that he would be hanged as a spy. At length, the reporter was merely banished to a quiet section of Ohio, where he could do no further damage to the Union cause.[37]

At Kennesaw Mountain, however, Sherman would be operating blind for the first time in the campaign. From that point forward, he would be forced to make his own decisions, without the benefit of knowing Johnston's plans or the placement of his forces. While this is not a widely known piece of information, it goes a long way toward explaining the outcome of the fighting at Kennesaw.

Chapter Thirteen

From Kennesaw to the Gate City

The rains that ushered in the month of June lasted for two weeks, and were coupled with cold temperatures that added to the misery of the men in both armies. By June 14, the skies began to clear. Sherman had been growing increasingly impatient because of the delay in front of the Kennesaw defenses, and he planned to resume his offensive as soon as the roads dried up enough to permit the passage of his army.

On that same day, General Hardee asked Johnston to examine his line on Pine Mountain, as he feared it was vulnerable to a flanking attack by the Federals. Johnston and Hardee rode along the crest and stopped to dismount for a better look at Thomas's forces on the plain below. They had been joined by General Polk, and the three officers soon attracted the attention of a small crowd of enlisted men who strained to get a glimpse of their famous leaders. They also caught the attention of General Sherman, who was then inspecting his own lines. Sherman ordered a few rounds of artillery fire to break up the gathering, and Captain Hubert Dilger's Ohio battery responded. The first shell landed dangerously near the Confederate generals, prompting Johnston and Hardee to seek cover. Polk refused to scurry away, and walked slowly and defiantly, possibly intending to set an example for the men. Dilger's second shell struck Polk in the left arm, tore through his body, and exited through his right side, killing him instantly. Sherman had no idea who the officers were when he ordered Dilger to fire, but because of his actions the Confederacy was deprived the services of one of the three corps commanders in the Army of Tennessee.[1]

On June 15, Sherman could wait no longer, and abandoned the flanking maneuvers that had thus far become a fixture of his campaign. Possibly it was because some Northern editors were questioning his willingness to fight, or perhaps it was because he wished to avoid another stalemate. Whatever the reason, Sherman elected to attempt to drive Johnston out of his prepared positions by an attack with his entire army. The assault on the 15th gained little benefit for the Federals, and the attacks were repulsed all along the line. On June 16, Brigadier General Milo Hascall's Division of Schofield's Corps was successful in forcing the Rebel cavalry from Lost Mountain, on the Confederate left. More indecisive fighting took place on June 17. The following day, three divisions of Thomas's Army of the Cumberland attacked a salient in the Southern line held by the division of Major General Samuel G. French, exposing the enemy to a deadly enfilading fire. Johnston had seen enough. On the night of June 18, he abandoned his forward positions and concentrated all of his strength on Kennesaw Mountain.[2]

On June 18, as Johnston was preparing to withdraw his men from the advanced lines on Brushy, Pine, and Lost Mountains, Sherman sent a personal letter to Grant that greatly defamed

Thomas and the men in his command, and planted the seeds of speculation that were to grow in legend and lore for the rest of the war and in the decades beyond. He complained to Grant, "My chief source of trouble is with the Army of the Cumberland which is dreadfully slow. A fresh furrow in a plowed field will stop the entire column and all begin to entrench. I have again and again tried to impress on Thomas that we must assail and not defend ... and yet it seems that the whole Army of the Cumberland is so habituated to be on the defensive that ... I cannot get it out of their heads."[3] Sherman's words seem ridiculous, even to a casual observer, and appear to be the rantings of an officer who had not yet won, or even fought, a battle on his own responsibility. The Cumberlanders were the same men who had done the impossible and broken the Confederate line on Missionary Ridge some six months before. They had gained the crest at Rocky Face, sustained more than 75 percent of the casualties suffered by the Federals at Resaca, and saved the Union army from a possible disaster at New Hope Church. Sherman had rejected advice from Thomas on several occasions, and each time, Thomas's appraisal of the situation had proven to be correct. If Sherman had listened to Thomas at Dalton, the campaign might have been ended shortly after it started. If Thomas had listened to Sherman at New Hope Church, the Federals might have blundered into the trap set by the "twenty" Rebels Sherman credited as being in front of his army.

The fact of the matter is that Sherman was being overshadowed by the accomplishments of Grant in Virginia, as the bloody battles of the Wilderness, Spotsylvania Court House, and Cold Harbor were getting all the press. He even complained that the "whole attention of the country was fixed on the Army of the Potomac and that his army was entirely forgotten."[4] Grant was outperforming him in Virginia, and Thomas was correctly second-guessing his movements in Georgia. Sherman felt the need to justify his limited success to his old friend, and he used Thomas as a scapegoat, deflecting responsibility from himself and placing it squarely on the shoulders of his most capable subordinate. For his part, Grant did an even greater injury to Thomas when he later allowed the letter to be published for the world to read. The commonly held misconception that Thomas was "slow" started with this letter, but would be expanded upon by both Sherman and Grant through to the final days of the war.

On June 25, Sherman issued orders for a general attack on Kennesaw Mountain to take place on the 27th. General McPherson opposed the decision, stating that Johnston could just as easily be flanked out of his position. Sherman's mind was made up, however. He told McPherson that "it was necessary to show that his men could fight as well as Grant's."[5] Thomas had also proposed a flanking movement, similar to the one used at Snake Spring Gap. This time, he suggested that McPherson's Army of the Tennessee be the flanking force, as that army had been increased by the addition of 9,000 men, and was now strong enough to undertake such an endeavor. When Thomas read Sherman's order for the attack, his adjutant general, William Whipple, heard him to remark "This is too bad." When asked why he didn't submit a written protest to the orders, Thomas replied "I will not do it. I have protested so often against such things that if I protest again Sherman will think I don't want to fight."[6]

Kennesaw Mountain was actually two connected crests, in the shape of a foot. Big Kennesaw rose to a height of about 700 feet, and resembled an ankle. Little Kennesaw was 100 to 150 feet lower than its big brother, and served as the instep, extending south for about 1,000 feet, where it ended in small mounds at the intersection of the Burnt Hickory and Marietta roads. Johnston's works were well concealed by woods and protected by numerous obstructions. The position was a very strong one, and Johnston felt he could hold it against any attacks the Federals might make upon it. On June 27, Thomas made a personal reconnaissance of the position, accompanied by Captain Henry Stone. A thorough half-day search revealed foreboding fortunes for the Union army. As Captain Stone recalled, "During the entire search of almost half a day I did not see one place that seemed to me to afford the slightest prospect of success." That being the case, "The place selected was chosen more because the lines were nearer each other than because the enemy's lines seemed vulnerable."[7]

At 8:00 A.M. on the morning of June 27, Thomas sent Major General Jefferson C. Davis's Division of the 14th Corps, and Major General John Newton's Division of the 4th Corps, forward against the Confederate stronghold. Major General David Stanley's Division was in support of Newton, while Major General Absalom Baird's Division supported Davis. Hooker's force was held in reserve. The assault had been ordered after a massive artillery barrage on the Rebel positions, but the big guns had been ordered to fire for only fifteen minutes, and little real damage was done to the defenders on Kennesaw. When the barrage was lifted, Davis's brigades, under Colonel Dan McCook and Colonel J.G. Mitchell, moved forward under a terrible fire from enemy artillery and musketry in an attempt to cover the 600 yards that separated them from the Confederate line. The Federals gallantly advanced to a point just under the enemy guns, but they could go no further. Newton's attack brigades were led by Brigadier Generals Charles Harker and George Wagner. As Thomas described it to Sherman in a message at 10:45 A.M., "General Harker's brigade advanced to within twenty paces of the enemy's breastworks, and was repulsed with canister at that range, General Harker losing an arm. General Wagner's brigade, of Newton's division, supporting Harker, was so severely handled that it is compelled to reorganize. Colonel Mitchell's brigade of Davis's division, captured one line of rebel breastworks, which they still hold. McCook's brigade was also severely handled, nearly every colonel being killed or wounded. Colonel McCook wounded. It is compelled to fall back and reorganize. The troops are all too much exhausted to advance, but we hold all we have gained."[8]

Thomas was being optimistic in his assessment that the attacking units could hold onto the ground they gained. They were being punished unmercifully by the Confederate defenders, and the losses were steadily mounting. It was impossible to advance further, and a retreat would place them out in the open, and could possibly lead to the complete destruction of the attacking brigades. Thomas took steps to back up his bold statement when he sent tools forward so the men could entrench and gain some level of safety in their exposed positions. Exposing themselves to dig the works caused even further casualties, however. The brigades of Newton's Division had been repulsed in their charge, and were not pinned down in the precarious situation that confronted Davis's brigades. Thomas's men had suffered almost 1,600 casualties, while the Confederates sustained only 236, and no positive results had come from all this loss.[9]

While Thomas was assaulting the center of Johnston's line, McPherson and Schofield were busy operating against the Rebel flanks. McPherson demonstrated against the left flank at Little Kennesaw, but the men of the Army of the Tennessee were never ordered to make an attack upon the defenses. Schofield made some progress against the right flank, in the vicinity of Olley's Creek. Sherman was obviously smarting from the repulse of his attacks. At 11:45 A.M., he sent Thomas the following instructions: "McPherson's columns reached near the top of the hill through very tangled brush, but was repulsed. It is found almost impossible to deploy, but they still hold the ground. I wish you to study well the position, and if it be possible to break the line, do it; it is easier now than it will be hereafter. Hold fast all you make."[10]

At 1:30 P.M., Sherman informed Thomas that both Schofield and McPherson were stopped cold, and inquired if he felt he could carry any portion of the enemy line. Thomas responded by saying:

> Davis's two brigades are now within sixty yards of the enemy's entrenchments. Davis reports that he does not think he can carry the works by assault on account of the steepness of the hill, but he can hold his position, put in one or two batteries, tonight, and probably drive them out tomorrow morning. General Howard reports the same. Their works are from six to seven feet high and nine feet thick. In front of Howard they have a very strong abatis. Davis's loss in officers has been very heavy. Nearly all the field officers in McCook's brigade, with McCook, have been killed or wounded. From what the officers tell me, I do not think we can carry the works by assault at this point to-day, but they can be approached by saps and the enemy driven out.[11]

Sherman was determined to try to salvage something out of what had thus far been a disappointing day for his army. At 5:00 P.M., he showed his inclination toward ordering another attack on the center of Johnston's line. Thomas was adamant in his opposition to making another attempt: "The Army of the Cumberland has already made two desperate, bloody, and unsuccessful assaults on this mountain. If a third is ordered, it will, in my opinion, result in demoralizing this army, and will, if made, be against my best judgment, and most earnest protest."[12] Thomas's stand caused Sherman to change his mind and give up further plans for an attack that day. The fighting at Kennesaw was ended. Total casualties around Kennesaw totaled some 3,000 for the Union, while the Confederates had lost only about one-fifth that number. For the first time in the campaign, Sherman had thrown his troops against one of Johnston's fortified positions, and the result was a dismal failure. He had ordered the assaults in an effort to massage his damaged pride, and to show that his army was as deserving of headlines as the one Grant was leading in Virginia.

On June 28, Sherman received a message from Grant telling him that his army was not required to hold Johnston's forces where they were, and allowing him discretionary authority to act independently of the Confederates. Sherman immediately made plans to strike at Johnston's communications. On July 1, he issued orders for McPherson to march his army around the Confederate left to threaten Johnston's rear on the following morning. Thomas was ordered to hold the line in front of Kennesaw. McPherson's movement caused Johnston to abandon his lines on the night of July 2. Thomas followed the Southern army, on the direct road to Atlanta, after halting to reorganize at Marietta. Thomas's views had been correct in every case at Kennesaw. He had favored just the sort of movement that McPherson eventually made, confident that it would pry Johnston out of his entrenchments. When Sherman opted for a frontal attack, Thomas was opposed to the idea, just as confident that the effort would end in a bloody failure. Though Sherman would never admit that the order for the attack had been an error, he was clearly embarrassed by the outcome, and the tension between Thomas and himself would continue to grow as a result.

Johnston was inching ever closer to Atlanta, but his continual withdrawals were exactly according to his plan. The Confederate leader was attempting to compensate for the disparity of numbers between his army and Sherman's by constantly assuming the defensive and forcing the Federals to be the aggressors. By the time he vacated his lines at Kennesaw, Johnston calculated that he had inflicted five times as many casualties on Sherman's army as his own army had sustained, and he planned to assume offensive operations of his own against what should now be more favorable odds. But Johnston's calculations were incorrect. He had indeed inflicted more casualties on the Federals than he had suffered himself, but it was nowhere near as many as he estimated, and the Union army still enjoyed a vast numerical superiority.

Sherman and his officers felt that Johnston would not make another stand until after he crossed the Chattahoochee River, placing that natural barrier between himself and the Union army, but Johnston surprised them by taking up a position at Smyrna, four miles southeast of Marietta. On July 4, the Union army made contact with the Confederate position at Smyrna. Johnston offered battle, but Sherman declined to attack, the taste of his defeat at Kennesaw still fresh on his lips. Instead, he ordered Thomas to skirmish with the enemy, while Schofield and McPherson were moved around their left flank, in an effort to get between the Rebel army and Atlanta. The Federals found the flank lightly guarded by cavalry and state militia troops, which they easily brushed aside. That night, Johnston relinquished yet another strong position and withdrew. He still did not cross the Chattahoochee, however. Unknown to Sherman, the Confederates were falling back to another prepared position. More than 1,000 slaves had been working on fortifications on the west bank of the Chattahoochee for more than two weeks, and Johnston had another series of prepared works waiting for his army to occupy. The Federals pursued, and from their vantage point in front of the Confederate works they got their first glimpse of the prize for which they had been fighting for the past two months. John Tomey of the 27th Indiana recorded in his diary for July 5 that at sundown they were "in sight of Atlanta."[13]

Johnston's line was six miles long and one mile deep. The rifle pits had been strengthened by the addition of numerous redoubts, twelve-foot-thick forts made of logs and earth, with artillery batteries and heavy siege guns at intervals along the line. Sherman described it as being "one of the strongest pieces of field fortification I ever saw," and he had no intention of throwing his army against it. Instead, he once more looked for a way to maneuver the Confederates out of their stronghold. He placed Thomas's and McPherson's armies in front of the works, while a division of cavalry was sent south, to convince the enemy that he was searching for a ford of the river in that direction. In the meantime, General Kenner Garrard took another division of cavalry twenty miles north, toward Rosswell, Georgia, with orders to capture the bridge at that place. When Garrard arrived at Rosswell, he found that the Confederates had already destroyed the bridge, and was unable to find another suitable place for the army to ford.[14]

All of the Federal commanders busied themselves searching for a place to ford the Chattahoochee, and Thomas was no exception. General Wood's Division of the Army of the Cumberland occupied the left flank of Thomas's line, connecting to Schofield's Army of the Ohio. About eight miles upriver from Johnston's defenses, at a place called Pace's Ferry, a ford was located where the Soap River, one of the tributaries of the Chattahoochee, flowed into it. Thomas ordered pontoons from Chattanooga, and by July 9, a full division of Schofield's and Wood's men was on the opposite shore. Johnston received word that he had once more been flanked, and prepared to move his army across the river and fall back even closer to Atlanta. The Federals crossed the river in an almost festive atmosphere. One soldier in the 24th Wisconsin described the scene as this last natural obstacle in their path to Atlanta was breached: "You can see at any time shoals of merry swimmers splashing in the clay colored stream, and sinking in its treacherous quick sands, from morning to night, and 'tattoo' and 'taps' scarcely prevail to bring them out of the waves. In another place men are seen patiently waiting for the small catfish, which alone inhabit the river, to come by their way."[15]

Since the middle of June, Confederate engineers had been strengthening the defenses of Atlanta, particularly in the area of Peach Tree Creek, as that was the direction from which the Federal Army would be approaching. Johnston had secured the promise of seven heavy sea-coast

Contemporary picture of the Confederate defenses around Atlanta. At the time of the campaign, Atlanta was one of the most heavily fortified places in the country, and Johnston hoped that Sherman would batter his army in futile frontal attacks against it (United States Army Military History Institute).

cannon, from Major General Dabney Maury in Mobile, to be placed in embrasure batteries along this front. Johnston pressed forward the work, knowing that the issue of the campaign was soon to be decided, but confident that he could emerge victorious with such strong defenses from which to fight. Sherman must take Atlanta. There could be no more maneuvering once he reached that place, and Johnston was anxious for the chance to finally be able to defend one of his strongest fortifications against the frontal assaults of the Federal army.

But the government in Richmond did not share in Johnston's optimism over the prospects of saving Atlanta from Sherman's horde. Jefferson Davis had watched with increasing anxiety as the Southern army retreated ever closer to the city, and following the evacuation of the Chattahoochee line, he could contain himself no longer. On July 17, the same day that the Federal army had completed its crossing of the river, Johnston received the following telegram:

"Lieutenant-General John B. Hood has been commissioned to the temporary rank of general under the law of Congress. I am directed by the Secretary of War to inform you that, as you have failed to arrest the advance of the enemy to the vicinity of Atlanta, and express no confidence that you can defeat or repel him, you are hereby relieved from the command of the Army and Department of Tennessee, which you will immediately turn over to General Hood. S. Cooper, Adjutant and Inspector General." Johnston issued the appropriate orders at once, and the next morning sent his response to Richmond. "Your dispatch of yesterday received and obeyed — command of the Army and Department of Tennessee has been transferred to General Hood. As to the alleged cause of my removal, I assert that Sherman's army is much stronger, compared with that of Tennessee, than Grant's compared with that of Northern Virginia. Yet the enemy has been compelled to advance more slowly to the vicinity of Atlanta than to that of Richmond and Petersburg, and penetrated much deeper into Virginia than into Georgia. Confident language by a military commander is not usually regarded as evidence of competence."[16]

Johnston was incorrect in his assessment of the situation in Virginia. Lee's army was facing equally long odds in opposing Grant's Army of the Potomac, and the Federals had not gained more ground in the Old Dominion State than they had in Georgia. Nonetheless, he was correct in taking offense at his removal, as his conduct of the campaign thus far had been exemplary. He had successfully parried every thrust Sherman had thrown against him, while keeping his own army well in hand and vigilant for an opportunity to administer a repulse to the invaders. The Federal failure at Kennesaw had caused Sherman to become timid in regard to frontal assaults, and Johnston had every reason to be confident that he could defend Atlanta from behind his formidable fortifications, which could be attacked by Sherman only if he was willing to sustain heavy casualties.

The government in Richmond was also not taking into account the effect the campaigns in Virginia and Georgia were having with the Northern people as a whole. The summer of 1864 had been an absolute horror to the North, with new casualty lists appearing in the newspapers on a daily basis. From May to July, Grant's army alone had lost some 60,000 men in its march from the Wilderness to Petersburg. The Northern populace examined the fearful cost and noted that, even with this expenditure, Richmond and Atlanta were still in Confederate hands. To most Northern citizens, the Union was no closer to winning the war than it had been in the spring, and the ever increasing casualty lists were but a testament to the futility of trying to coerce the South back into the Union by force of arms. With a presidential election looming in the fall, this feeling of futility among the electorate could pay huge dividends to the Confederates, if they could only hold their positions and continue the image of an undefeatable foe that most Northerners already held.

For his part, Hood was reluctant to accept command of the army, even though Johnston's removal came largely because of intrigue he had planted with Davis questioning Johnston's fitness to command. Hood felt it an inopportune time to take the reins of command, and earnestly tried to convince Johnston to ignore the order until after the impending battle was fought. The commanders of the other two corps of the army, Hardee and Stewart, agreed with Hood and tried to persuade Johnston, to no avail. The corps commanders next sent a message to President Davis, in Hood's name, stating "There is now heavy skirmishing and indications of a general advance. I deem it dangerous to change the commanders of this army at this particular time, and to be to the interest of the service that no change should be made until the fate of Atlanta is decided." Davis sent the same response to all three corps commanders, telling them that he had made the move only as a last alternative, "and I cannot suspend it without making the case worse than it was before the order was issued."[17] Like Thomas before Perryville, Hood had realized that the current commander was best suited to fight the army under the circumstances. Unlike Lincoln, however, Davis persisted in following through with the change in command, and the fate of Atlanta, and the Southern nation, hung in the balance. The change in commanders had been made even though Robert E. Lee expressed his personal opposition to it. Lee felt Hood to be too rash in his actions, too much the lion and not enough of the fox.

Sherman was not well acquainted with Hood, and when he learned that he had been elevated to army command, he went in search of intelligence concerning his new foe. Schofield had been a classmate of Hood's at West Point, and Thomas had served as one of his instructors, as well as being his superior in the 2nd United States Cavalry. The general opinion was that Hood "was bold even to rashness and courageous in the extreme."[18] Sherman welcomed the information, as it seemed to forebode a change in the way the campaign would be fought. By all indications, Hood was not the sort of officer to wait to be attacked from behind prepared works. He had earned a reputation as a hard-hitting offensive commander when he led a division in the Army of Northern Virginia, and Sherman felt sure that he would continue his aggressive characteristics as commander of the army. If that turned out to be the case, a pitched battle was imminent, and the Federals would be able to fully take advantage of their superiority in numbers for the first time since leaving Chattanooga.

Sherman left Thomas's Army of the Cumberland to face Atlanta and its defenders. McPherson's and Schofield's armies were sent to the left, in the direction of Decatur, to destroy the railroads leading into the city. Sherman was convinced that Hood would come out of the city to attack Schofield and McPherson, in order to protect his lines of communication. When that happened, Thomas would be free to walk into the city unopposed, and Hood would be left without a base of operations. But Hood did not respond the way Sherman anticipated. He planned to eliminate the immediate threat to Atlanta, in the form of the Army of the Cumberland, before addressing the activities of McPherson and Schofield. Joe Wheeler's cavalry was detailed to keep an eye on McPherson and Schofield, while the rest of the army was concentrated against Thomas. General Hardee was entrusted the responsibility of leading the attack

On July 20, responding to Sherman's order to detach two divisions of Howard's Corps to the left, in an effort to partially plug the gap between the Army of the Cumberland and the forces under McPherson and Schofield, Thomas then advanced toward Peach Tree Creek. Hood wanted to catch Thomas's army in a vulnerable position, as it was astride Peach Tree Creek, but he set the time of the attack at 1:00 P.M., giving the Federals a good portion of the day to effect their crossing. At 12 noon, Thomas reported to Sherman that General Davis's men were skirmishing with the enemy, while Palmer's and Hooker's Corps, with Newton's Division, were advancing one mile beyond the south bank. When Newton's men ran into enemy skirmishers, they halted to erect rail barricades. No one knew what Hood was up to, but Newton did not like the look of things. Hood was not able to coordinate his attack until nearly 4:00 P.M., granting Thomas even more time to consolidate his position on the Confederate side of the creek.

Finally, three divisions of General William Hardee's Corps, and two divisions of General A.P. Stewart's Corps were sent forward, crashing into the Union army. "On the sound of the first shot every man jumped to his feet and into line," reported a soldier with Thomas. "There was no waiting for orders, the men knew what was required to get where they could make a defense.... Meanwhile the musketry firing was coming closer and closer, the yells of the enemy louder and louder, and the bullets began to sing and whistle around us and through the trees over our heads. We realized the critical position we were in and the necessity of immediate deployment into line of battle; should we be struck while still in mass formation it would mean both defeat and slaughter."[18]

The Rebel assault initially threw back the Federal line and threatened to capture a bridge in the rear of Newton's position that would have cut off the Federal line of retreat. Colonel Benjamin Harrison's Brigade was flanked on the right and left, and Harrison was given permission to withdraw, but he resolutely declared "Here we shall stay." Thomas was quick to respond, ordering a battery of artillery to be placed on the left of Newton's line to bolster his position. He assembled all available guns along Newton's line, and personally directed their fire against the Confederates.[19] When the big guns added their fury to the musketry of Newton's infantrymen, the result was to throw back the Confederate attackers, under Major General William B. Bate, with heavy loss.

As the battle raged, Thomas received a message from Sherman prodding him to advance his army into Atlanta, as there were "none of the enemy's troops between Peach Tree Creek and Atlanta."[20] Sherman was so sure that Hood would react to his operations against the Confederate communications that he lost control of that strategic situation by assuming the Schofield and McPherson had the entire Confederate army in their front. Those forces were screened only by Wheeler's cavalry, however. Even after he was made aware that Thomas was heavily engaged, Sherman failed to recognize that his plan to pry Hood out of Atlanta had failed, and continued to grossly overestimate the strength of the forces in his front. In a message to Thomas, he stated, "I have been with Howard and Schofield all of the day and one of my staff is just back from McPherson. All report the enemy in their front so strong that I was in hopes none was left for you."[21] Hardee was throwing some 30,000 men against Thomas's flank, which numbered approximately 20,000 men. Sherman failed to grasp the situation even after Thomas notified him that he was heavily engaged, and seemed so intent that Hood's main force was in his front that he seemed perturbed with the performance of the Army of the Cumberland in not having captured the city. His mindset was such that he never offered assistance to Thomas from the other Union armies. The Cumberlanders would have to fight it out on their own.

General Joseph Wheeler, one of the leading cavalry commanders on either side. Wheeler's Confederate troopers were a constant menace to Union troops on the march (United States Army Military History Institute).

On Newton's right, Confederates under the command of Brigadier General George Maney were trying to exploit a gap between Newton's right flank and the division commanded by Brigadier General William Ward, posted some distance to the rear. Two of Ward's brigades were ordered forward, driving Maney's men before them and securing the gap. General Newton observed Thomas to be "calm and resolute" during the fighting. With the final outcome still in doubt, the general issued orders to his bodyguard to "hold the bridge across Peach Tree Creek and cut down any armed soldier who attempted to cross." All along the line, the Confederates were being repulsed by the stiff resistance of the Cumberlanders, and Thomas was everywhere, issuing orders, placing troops, and instilling confidence in his men. A soldier recorded that when Thomas "saw the rebels running, with us after them, he took off his hat and flung it to the ground and shouted, 'Hurrah! Look at the Third Division. They're driving them!'"²²

By 6:00 P.M., the Confederate assault had stalemated, prompting General Hardee to order his reserve division, under Patrick Cleburne, to add its weight to the attack, in hopes of winning the battle before nightfall ended the fighting. As Cleburne was getting his men into line, a message arrived from Hood informing Hardee that McPherson's Federals had advanced to within artillery range of Atlanta. Wheeler's cavalry would not be sufficient to protect the city from this threat, and he required a division of infantry be sent at once to counter the Union force. Cleburne's men got the assignment, and marched away from Thomas's army. Cleburne's departure, combined with the coming darkness, ended the Battle of Peach Tree Creek.

The attack had been a disaster for the Confederates. Hood's army had suffered 4,796 casualties, while only inflicting 1,710 on the Army of the Cumberland, and it had completely failed in driving the Federals from the environs of Atlanta.²³ Thomas's men had stood tall against the onslaught, and had severely punished their assailants in the process. Peach Tree Creek served as Thomas's first introduction to the mindset of Hood as an army commander. He would utilize this insight to its fullest in the coming months when the two men became engaged in a struggle for the control of Tennessee.

The Battle of Peach Tree Creek was Hood's best opportunity to defeat the Federal army, and served as the decisive engagement in the fighting for the Gate City. Hood had been given the opportunity he was looking for when Sherman divided his army, leaving Thomas's Army of the Cumberland isolated and beyond supporting distance from the forces of McPherson and Schofield. Sherman was unaware as to the exact location of the Confederate army, which had been concentrated in front of the Cumberlanders. If Hood had been able to crush Thomas, the ability of the Union forces to capture Atlanta would have been seriously impaired. But Thomas responded in the same way he had at Stones River and Chickamauga, and Hood discovered what others before him already knew: where Thomas defended the line held firm.

General George Maney. His troops were repulsed with heavy casualties by Thomas's men during the Battle of Peach Tree Creek (United States Army Military History Institute).

Hood spent July 21 reorganizing his command and planning for his next move against the Federals. On July 22, he ordered an attack on McPherson's Army of the Tennessee, advancing on Atlanta from the east. Major General Benjamin Cheatham's Division was assigned to hold McPherson in front, while Hardee's Corps, supported by Wheeler's cavalry, marched around McPherson's left to assault him in flank and rear. The plan began to unravel almost from the start. Hardee was to attack in the early morning of July 22, but Hood had underestimated the distance he would have to march to get in position. No consideration had been given to the oppressive heat that would force him to slow his pace, either. Hardee did not know the ground and had no reliable guides, and a great deal of time was wasted searching for his assigned place. When Hardee finally did arrive on the ground, at approximately 1:00 P.M., he prepared to launch his attack. Unknown to him, however, he was not on the left flank of the Federal army. McPherson's 16th Corps, under Major General Grenville M. Dodge, had been squeezed out of the line of march due to the narrowness of the approach to Atlanta, and had been ordered to take a place on the left of the line. Thus, when Hardee attacked, it was directly into the jaws of the waiting 16th Corps, and not into the flank and rear of McPherson's army.

General James B. McPherson. A favorite of both Grant and Sherman, this commander of the Army of the Tennessee was killed in the severe fighting at the Battle of Atlanta (United States Army Military History Institute).

Even so, the battle opened well for the Confederates. The 16th Iowa Infantry was overwhelmed and forced to surrender, and Major General Giles Smith's Federal division was driven from its fieldworks. Several Union cannon were captured, and General McPherson was killed while trying to rally his men. But the attacks were poorly coordinated. General Cheatham did not launch his assault until nearly 3:30 P.M., by which time Hardee's divisions were running out of steam. The Battle of Atlanta raged for six hours, but each Confederate thrust was eventually thrown back in disorder. In the end, it had been nothing more than another costly failure for Hood. His army was bloodied by 8,499 additional casualties, while the Army of the Tennessee counted 3,641 in killed, wounded, and missing.[24]

As with the Battle of Peach Tree Creek, Sherman allowed one of his armies to face Hood's Confederates alone. Though McPherson's Army of the Tennessee faced the prospect of being overpowered, no reinforcements were ordered to his aid from either Thomas or Schofield. In his *Memoirs*, Sherman cast aspersions upon Thomas by stating that he had implied that he "take advantage of the opportunity to make a lodgment in Atlanta if possible," and the commanding

Artist's depiction of the Battle of Atlanta, where Hood concentrated his forces in an attempt to crush the Army of the Tennessee (United States Army Military History Institute).

general felt that the engagement with McPherson had given him that opportunity. But he had issued no orders whatsoever to Thomas, who was fronted by two entrenched lines and strong artillery positions. In truth, Sherman had not issued orders for Thomas or Schofield to assist McPherson because, as he himself put it, "if any assistance were rendered by either of the other armies the Army of the Tennessee would be jealous."[25] Sherman was deferring to the Army of the Tennessee, his old command, and wished for it obtain the glory of the campaign. He had sent it on the flanking movement toward Decatur in hopes that Hood would attack it, and the Battle of Atlanta had given him the opportunity he desired. Thomas's army was to have the empty victory of marching into a deserted Atlanta, while McPherson was to get credit for defeating Hood's army. Though McPherson's men had stood firm against the assaults thrown against them, Sherman's favoritism could have had tragic results. Sherman was negligent in not utilizing either Thomas or Schofield on July 22. After the fact, he resorted to what was becoming a familiar pattern by trying to shift responsibility to someone else. His failure to take control of the battle was twisted into an implied allegation that Thomas had failed to show initiative and was hesitant to fight.

On July 23, Sherman and Thomas met to discuss a possible replacement for the fallen McPherson as commander of the Army of the Tennessee. General John Logan had assumed command when McPherson had been killed, and was the likely candidate to be named to the position. But Thomas held a less than favorable opinion of Logan as an army commander, and suggested Oliver O. Howard as an alternative. After a lengthy discussion, Howard was accepted. This decision created the need for another replacement in the Union high command. General Hooker protested the fact that Howard had been given the command, since Hooker was his superior, and he requested to be relieved. Thomas accepted Hooker's resignation and

Sherman appointed Major General Henry Warner Slocum to replace him. Slocum had been serving on detached duty ever since Chattanooga, because he had refused to serve under Hooker. Howard's spot as commander of the 4th Corps was filled by Major General David S. Stanley. A few days later, it became necessary to find a new commander for the 14th Corps as well. General Palmer had declined to support a movement of Schofield's in front of Atlanta based on the fact that Schofield was his junior. Though Palmer was a personal favorite of Thomas, no allowance could be made for such pettiness or prideful dereliction of duty, and Thomas advised Sherman to relieve the sulking general. Jefferson C. Davis was then given command of the 14th Corps.

While the command structure of the Union army was being reorganized, General Hood was planning yet another foray to drive the Yankees away from the gates of Atlanta. On July 27, Sherman had ordered Howard's Army of the Tennessee to march to the extreme right of the army to sever the Macon & Western Railroad, the only remaining rail line still in Confederate hands. The defenses of Atlanta were too strong for Sherman to assault by frontal attack, and he hoped that by cutting off all of Hood's lines of supply he could force him to evacuate his position. On July 28, Hood attacked Howard with his own corps, now under Lieutenant General Stephen D. Lee, and A.P. Stewart's Corps, at Ezra Church. Lee engaged the Federals late in the morning, without waiting for Stewart to get into position, and made several charges that were repulsed and thrown back. The Federals had become adept at building fieldworks, and they stoutly defended them against each new thrust launched by the Confederates. At 2:00 P.M., Stewart was finally in position, and added his weight to the assault. Wave after wave of attacks were made for the next three hours, but each met with the same bloody result. Finally, at 5:00 P.M., the attack was called off and the Confederates withdrew back into the city. The fighting at Ezra Church had cost Hood's army another 4,642 casualties, while inflicting only about 700 on the Federals.

Jefferson Davis had desired a more aggressive commander when he replaced Joseph Johnston with Hood, and he got exactly that. But Hood was aggressive to the point of rashness, and his three ill-fated assaults had now cost the Confederate army one-third of their numbers in casualties, while inflicting only minor losses on the enemy. The disparity in numbers between the contending foes was

General John Bell Hood. President Davis selected Hood to replace Johnston as commander of the Army of Tennessee when he tired of Johnston's defensive posture. In Hood, he indeed found a fighter, but the three assaults the new commander threw at the Federals resulted in costly repulses that led to the evacuation of Atlanta (United States Army Military History Institute).

widening to the extent that the Confederates would no longer have a legitimate chance of facing the Federals in a pitched battle.[26]

The campaign for Atlanta now became a siege. Sherman was unwilling to test the strong defenses that lined the city, and Hood no longer had the manpower to mount any offensive actions. His army had only been about half the size of Sherman's when he took over from Johnston, and the three forays he had launched against the Federals had reduced it to the extent that it now numbered but one-third the total of the enemy. Hood was compelled to hunker down behind his works and watch Sherman's movements, hoping that the Federal commander would make a mistake he could capitalize upon. In the meantime, Sherman undertook a daily bombardment of Atlanta with his artillery, with military and civilian targets sharing equally in the destruction. Heavy siege guns had been ordered in by rail, and they would add their immense firepower to the field batteries that were already playing havoc upon the soldiers and residents of Atlanta.

On July 29, 10,000 Union cavalry, under Brigadier General Edward McCook and Major General George Stoneman, were sent to Lovejoy's Station to destroy the Western & Macon Railroad at that junction. Stoneman was to meet McCook at Lovejoy's, but he had received permission to detour by way of Macon and Americus, in an effort to release the Union captives being held at Andersonville Prison. McCook arrived at Lovejoy's Station with 3,500 troopers, who tore up the track and destroyed two locomotives. He then headed his column north to rejoin the main body. At Newman, Georgia, McCook's command was surrounded and attacked by five regiments of cavalry commanded by Joe Wheeler. McCook ordered his men to cut their way out of the encirclement as best they could, but Wheeler's men killed and captured about 600 of the Federals before they were able to escape the trap. Wheeler next turned his attention to Stoneman, attacking his column at Clinton, Georgia. Stoneman was also surrounded by the enemy, and 700 Federal prisoners were taken, including Stoneman himself, before the Union cavalry could cut its way out.[27]

On August 6, Sherman made a final attempt to force his way into Atlanta when he ordered General Schofield to attack the Confederate left, under General William B. Bate. Schofield was repulsed with heavy losses. He then tried to flank Bate's Division, but the Confederates simply withdrew into their main line of fortifications and further offensive movements by Schofield were called off. Sherman would risk no more attacks on the Rebel lines. From this point forward, he would be content to allow his heavy guns to blast the enemy into submission, or to try to maneuver the Confederates into the open.[28]

On August 26, Sherman decided to start shifting his forces away from the front of Atlanta, and sent them south to cut the railroads that McCook's and Stoneman's cavalry had failed to destroy. Howard's Army of the Tennessee moved out first, and swung right to allow Thomas's army to fill in on his left. Schofield's Army of the Ohio would form the left flank in a three-pronged movement on Jonesboro, twenty miles south of Atlanta. Slocum's 20th Corps was moved back to Johnston's old Chattahoochee River defenses, to protect the rail line running from Chattanooga, and to guard against an attack from Hood. On August 28, Thomas and Howard reached the Atlanta & West Point Railroad, and the destruction of Hood's last remaining rail supply line was begun in earnest. Hood had been frozen in Atlanta, trying to guess what Sherman was up to. Realizing the intention of the Federal commander, Hood ordered Hardee to take his corps, along with Stephen D. Lee's Corps, and attack the forces around Jonesboro. Only Stewart's Corps remained in Atlanta. On the morning of August 31, Thomas observed a dust cloud two miles away from his position at Renfrew, Georgia. He knew that it signified a heavy force of enemy infantry on the move, and asked Sherman's permission to attack the Confederates in the flank, while they marched. Sherman refused to grant permission, however. Hardee's two corps were marching directly toward Howard's entrenched army at Jonesboro, and the commander feared for the safety of the Army of the Tennessee. An observer recalled that Sherman "would not allow Thomas to move out of position from which he could quickly go to its support."[29]

Hardee assailed Howard's prepared positions, and the Confederates were severely punished by the determined Federal defenders. Thomas dispatched a division from his army to support Howard, and by late afternoon Hardee called off the attack and withdrew. The attack against Jonesboro had been repulsed, and Hood's army had lost about 2,000 more men in the process. The 14th Corps of Thomas' Army of the Cumberland routed the Confederates and captured Brigadier General Daniel Govan and a majority of his brigade.[30] One is left to contemplate what might have been the results if Sherman had allowed Thomas to attack Hardee's forces in the flank while Howard faced them in front. It is almost certain that the Confederate losses would have been significantly higher than they ended up being, and it is reasonable to imagine that the entire force could have been captured or crushed.

Thomas now sought to move his army to Lovejoy's Station, to cut off the line of retreat of the enemy, but Sherman once more vetoed his suggestion to make the Rebel army the main objective of the campaign. Sherman continued to make the destruction of the railroads his primary focus, and ordered Schofield and Stanley to march from Rough and Ready to Lovejoy's Station, tearing up the Macon and Western Railroad as they came. The resultant delay in destroying the tracks allowed Hardee to get to Lovejoy's Station first, and the opportunity to seal off the Confederates' line of retreat to Macon was lost.

On September 1, at 5:00 P.M., Hood ordered the evacuation of Atlanta, and the following day General Slocum's troops marched into the city to accept its surrender from Mayor James M. Calhoun. The four-month campaign was ended, and the Gate City was finally in Union hands. The South was to be deprived of the great manufacturing center that was Atlanta, and the heart of the Confederacy was laid open to invasion by Sherman's army.

The most significant result of Sherman's campaign was not of a military nature, however. The fall of Atlanta caused the Northern populace to take heart and believe that the end of the war was truly at hand. Public opinion was instantly altered, as the people girded themselves to see the struggle through to its conclusion. The war weariness that had threatened to turn Lincoln out of office subsided. Sherman had almost single-handedly ensured that the Republicans would be reelected in the fall, and that sounded the death-knell of the Confederacy.

Chapter Fourteen

Back to Tennessee

Sherman wired news of the capture of Atlanta to Lincoln, but he failed to mention that Hood's army, though greatly reduced, had not been destroyed. After distributing commissary stores that could not be moved among the citizens of the city, and blowing up all of the ordnance and ammunition that could not be carried with him, Hood consolidated his army at Lovejoy's Station, where Hardee waited. Brigadier General Francis A. Shoup, Hood's chief of staff, recorded in his diary "all quiet along the lines" from their position at Lovejoy's. The Confederates anxiously watched for the assault they were sure would come from the Federal forces, but Sherman declined to advance his army. The Federal commander explained that "after due reflection, I resolved not to attempt at that time a further pursuit of Hood's army, but slowly and deliberately to move back, occupy Atlanta, enjoy a short period of rest, and to think well over the next step required in the progress of things."[1] Hood's army now numbered only about 40,000 men, while Sherman's forces added up to slightly more than twice that total. Even so, the Confederates still presented a real danger to the Federals. Sherman's army was deep in enemy territory, connected to its supply base at Nashville by a tenuous rail line that could be severed by an aggressive enemy. If the Federals were cut off and deprived of supplies, sufficient force could yet be brought against them to turn the campaign into a failure for Union arms. Atlanta held no strategic value for Sherman, and he could derive no benefit from holding the place, so, after due consideration, the general decided to abandon it. Before doing so, however, Sherman determined to destroy its future capacity to serve as a staging point for any Confederate army. He had no intention of siphoning off manpower from his army to garrison the city, or to protect an ever-lengthening supply line. There were already nearly as many Federal soldiers employed in guarding the rail line from Nashville into Georgia as there were at the front with Sherman.

The Confederates realized that the Union supply line was a weakness that could be exploited, and this was the basis for Hood's plan of campaign following the loss of Atlanta. As early as September 6, Hood was communicating his views to President Davis. "The army is much in need of a little rest. After removing the prisoners from Andersonville, I think we should, as soon as practicable, place our army upon the communications of the enemy, drawing our supplies from the West Point and Montgomery Railroad."[2] Hood planned to accomplish through destruction what he could not achieve by force: he would lure Sherman away from Atlanta, and lead him back into Tennessee to protect his vital supply lines. Davis not only approved of Hood's plan, he did all in his power to aid him in accomplishing it. All of the Confederate troops along the Mississippi River were transferred to Hood's command, in the hope that, along with new recruits and returning veterans, a sufficient force could be assembled with which the Rebel leader could recover some of the ground that had been lost.

The effort to concentrate their dwindling forces was a subject that had been advocated for some time by General P.G.T. Beauregard. Beauregard's plan was radical in the extreme, however, and called for the abandonment of all major cities in the South, with the garrison forces being brought together to form an army capable of invading the North. Northern cities would then be subjected to the same destruction that the Confederacy had endured. Beauregard stated that the army could subsist on the vast quantities of supplies that would be captured along its line of march, and felt that the terror and consternation such a move would produce would be sufficient to compel the Union to sue for peace.[3] His plan failed to account for the fact that such a concentration would allow the Federals to also concentrate their forces, which would still greatly outnumber the Confederates, to operate against an enemy army that would be trapped on unfriendly ground, far from assistance or support. Hood's plan was not nearly so outlandish. He would seek to merely recover some of the territory that had been lost during the past year, in an effort to bolster the morale of the Southern people and weaken the resolve of the Northern populace.

The timing of his move seemed fortunate, as Sherman had allowed large numbers of men to be furloughed from his army following the successful conclusion of the Atlanta campaign, leaving him somewhat reduced in numbers. Hood began his campaign in late September, when he marched his army to the southwest, around Sherman's flank, headed for the Tennessee River. Hood was going to operate along Sherman's line of supply in Georgia, while Nathan Bedford Forrest, with his cavalry, would do the same in Tennessee. Sherman had dispatched Major General John Newton's Division of the 4th Corps, along with Brigadier General James D. Morgan's Division of the 14th Corps, to deal with Forrest in Tennessee. Thomas, with two of his corps, was detailed to Chattanooga, where he arrived on September 29. As Hood's army advanced in a northerly direction that roughly traced the line of the campaign it had just concluded, communications between Thomas and Sherman were cut, causing a brief period of uneasiness in Washington. Sherman took up the chase from Atlanta with five corps. Hood crossed the Chattahoochee River and fanned out his army as they marched north, over ground already made famous in the military history of the nation. When Hood captured Dalton, General Grant feared that Chattanooga was his primary target, and issued Thomas orders to withdraw his men from Columbus and Decatur.

Thomas, on the other hand, was convinced that Hood would not risk an attack on the strongly fortified city, and took action to cut off his expected line of march to skirt the stronghold. He sent General Schofield, with Newton's and Morgan's divisions, to block his march from Lafayette. When Hood moved in the direction of Bridgeport, Thomas shifted this force to Caperton's Ferry. Hood was planning to cross his army at Gunter's Landing, preparatory to linking up with Forrest's men for a drive against Nashville. Thomas's dispositions would have placed Schofield's force precisely where it needed to be to blunt Hood's march. Sherman countermanded, however, ordering Schofield to lead his men to Lookout Valley, leaving the way open for Hood to cross. But Hood's plans were altered when he received word from Forrest that he could not join him, causing the Confederate army to continue forward to Decatur.[4]

By October 12, Hood had reached Resaca. To Colonel James B. Weaver, the Federal commander of the garrison stationed there, he sent the following message: "Sir, I demand the immediate and unconditional surrender of the post and garrison under your command, and, should this be acceded to, all white officers and soldiers will be paroled in a few days. If the place is carried by assault, no prisoners will be taken." Weaver responded, in part, by stating "Your communication of this date [October 12] just received. I have to state that I am somewhat surprised at the concluding paragraph, to the effect that, if the place is carried by assault, no prisoners will be taken. In my opinion I can hold this post. If you want it, come and take it."[5] Weaver was daring Hood to assail his fieldworks, even though he was vastly outnumbered by the Confederates. Hood shied away from the challenge, still smarting from the ghastly losses his forays in front of Atlanta had inflicted on his army, and he refused to back up his bluff with any show of force. Resaca was bypassed, and Weaver's men were the final victors in this game of brag and bravado.

Thomas was preparing for a joint operation with Sherman, and was making plans to trap Hood's army between himself and his commander. On October 11, Thomas wired Secretary Stanton that he was "making such disposition of my force as will, I hope, prevent his [Hood's] crossing the Tennessee River ... and while I hold him in front, Sherman will attack him in the rear."[6]

Sherman, for his part, was exerting no great efforts in overtaking Hood and his army and bringing them to battle. In fact, he had already determined to ignore the Confederate army altogether, and was planning a grand offensive in the opposite direction to that which Hood was marching. On September 9, Sherman had wired Grant asking permission to march his army east, away from Hood, with his destination being the port city of Savannah, Georgia. General Thomas would be left in Tennessee to contend with Hood. In his seaward march, Sherman proposed to destroy "roads, houses, and people," and he convinced Grant "I can make the march and make Georgia howl."[7] Grant had concerns, but Sherman quickly overcame them, and the general-in-chief granted his consent and put the matter before the administration. General Halleck was not nearly so quick to accept the plan. Sherman had previously planned to operate on the line of Montgomery and Selma, Alabama, heading south for an eventual link-up with Union forces near Mobile. The wheels were already in motion, sending massive amounts of supplies to Mobile and Pensacola, Florida, to support this

General Nathan Bedford Forrest. Following the capture of Atlanta, Forrest's cavalry operated against Sherman's supply lines in the Federal rear, hoping to lure the Federals back in to Tennessee (United States Army Military History Institute).

movement and the subsequent change of base from Nashville. Halleck felt that the Alabama plan offered the best chance of success. The distance was shorter to Mobile than it was to Savannah, and it was less exposed to an attack by the enemy in Sherman's rear. The Alabama River was more navigable by Union gunboats than was the Savannah River. Tennessee and Kentucky could more easily be screened from Alabama than they could from the Georgia coast. Halleck also believed that Selma, Montgomery, and Mobile had greater military significance than Savannah, Augusta, and Millen. Despite Halleck's less than flattering opinion of Sherman's plan, Grant gave him the go-ahead on October 11, the day before Hood arrived at Resaca.[8]

Sherman returned to Atlanta to organize his army for what would become the famed March to the Sea. The Atlanta he returned to was far different from the one he had left. It was deserted, save for the garrison troops that had been left behind when Sherman marched north in pursuit of Hood's army. On September 11, Sherman had arranged a ten-day truce with Hood for the purpose of removing all of the civilians from the city and transporting them north or south, depending upon their politics. Hood had strongly protested what he felt to be a barbaric action against the non-combatants of Atlanta, but Sherman refused to countermand his orders for the evacuation of the civilians. In one exchange of correspondence, he told Hood, "You might as well appeal against the thunder-storm as against these terrible hardships of war." In all, 446 families were displaced and became refugees as a result of the order, and Atlanta became an armed camp of the Union army.[9]

The army that Sherman proposed to make Georgia howl with consisted of the 14th and 20th Corps from Thomas's Army of the Cumberland, the 15th and 17th Corps from the Army of the Tennessee, and Schofield's Army of the Ohio. Thomas was to return Morgan's and Newton's forces, along with 5,000 fresh volunteers who had recently arrived in Chattanooga, that Sherman planned to use as replacements in his own regiments. This left Thomas with David Stanley's 4th Corps and the remnants of Grenville Dodge's 16th Corps, which had been broken up following Dodge's wounding during the Atlanta campaign. Sherman would have an army of 60,000 to 65,000 men, hand-picked to assure that he commanded the best of the best that had previously been his combined army. Thomas would get what was left over, and would be expected to deal with Hood and Forrest with the material Sherman did not want.[10]

In a message to Thomas dated October 20, Sherman outlined his own plans, as well as his expectations for Thomas's future conduct.

> I propose to demonstrate the vulnerability of the South and make its inhabitants feel that war and individual ruin are synonymous terms. To pursue Hood is folly, for he can twist and turn like a fox and wear out an army in pursuit.... I know I am right in this.... I propose to remain along the Coosa watching Hood till all my preparations are made, viz till I have repaired the railroad, sent back all surplus men and material and stript for the work. Then I will send Stanley with the 4th Corps.... I want you to retain command in Tennessee and ... will give you delegated authority over Kentucky and Mississippi, Alabama, etc. whereby there will be unity of action behind me. I will want you to hold Chattanooga and Decatur [Alabama] in force and on the occasion of my departure ... you shall have ample notice to watch Hood close. I think he will follow me at least with his cavalry in which event I want you to push south.... We must pursue a large amount of secrecy.[11]

Sherman's plan was, oddly enough, the same as one suggested to him by Thomas some time previous. After the fall of Atlanta, Thomas had approached Sherman saying, "Now you have no more use for me, let me take my little command and go eastward to the sea." Sherman told him that he could not authorize such a movement without Grant's permission, but he promised to consult with him on the matter while the railroads were being repaired and the reorganization of the army was taking place. Thomas heard nothing more about his suggestion until Sherman informed him that he was going to make the march, with the main body of the Union forces. What Thomas had proposed was a large scale raid through Georgia, while the primary army in the region, Sherman's, held Hood's forces in check. Sherman intended to make the march with the bulk of his army, leaving the smaller force behind. Thomas had expressed his concerns over the situation when he stated, "There is one thing however I don't wish — to be in command of the defenses of Tennessee, unless you and the authorities at Washington deem it absolutely necessary."[12] He had no desire to be the one left holding the bag if the Confederates invaded the state, and could divine that conditions were shaping up in just such a manner. It would all be fine if he were allowed to retain the services of his own Army of the Cumberland, but that was not to be the case. Two of his three corps had already been designated by Sherman to accompany him to the sea.

Thomas protested against losing the services of the 14th Corps, the nucleus of which he had commanded since his days at Camp Dick Robinson and the Battle of Mill Springs. He had been instrumental in raising and training this corps, and knew well the mettle of the men it contained. Sherman was also aware of the quality of the men in the 14th Corps, and informed Thomas, "It is too compact and reliable a corps for me to leave behind. I can spare you the Fourth Corps and about five thousand men not fit for my purpose, but which will be well enough for garrison duty at Chattanooga, Murfreesboro and Nashville. What you need is a few points fortified and stocked with provisions and a good moveable column of twenty-five thousand men that can strike in any direction."[13] The most glaring problem with Sherman's statement was that the force he planned to leave behind did not even amount to 25,000 men. How was Thomas to garrison more than a dozen towns and cities while gathering together a strike force to deal with Hood when his total command was less than the number Sherman set for the "moveable column"?

When Schofield showed no inclinations to participate in Sherman's march, his 10,000 man Army of the Ohio was redesignated as the 23rd Corps and transferred to Thomas's command. This addition elevated Thomas's force to some 31,000 men, on paper, but that total was somewhat deceiving. Major General Andrew J. Smith and his two divisions of the 16th Corps that were assigned to Thomas had recently been engaged in driving General Sterling Price's Confederates out of western Missouri, and were not readily available. Though these men were listed as being part of Thomas's army, Smith's divisions would not complete their march across Missouri and arrive at St Louis until November 24. For more than a month, they would exist on Thomas's rolls in name only, far from supporting distance of the threatened regions in Tennessee.[14] Quite simply, Thomas was given the assignment of guarding the entire state of Tennessee with a force far inferior to that which Hood and Forrest commanded. He was to defend all vital military positions in the state, while at the same time being responsible for ousting the Confederates from the Volunteer State should they decide to mount an invasion. In short, he was presented with an impossible task, given the resources at hand, and his first independent campaign as an army commander seemed doomed to failure.

Seemingly, the only good thing to come of his assignment in Tennessee was that he had an opportunity to send for Frances to come to Nashville that October. As Thomas never allowed himself to take a leave from his duties, it would be the first time he had seen his wife since August of 1861. The reunion must have been a joyful one, but the dutiful Thomas had far too many responsibilities placed upon his shoulders to allow their time spent together to be care free.

Sherman's apparent lack of concern for the predicament he was placing Thomas in derived from the fact that he had convinced himself that Hood would never invade Tennessee. Sherman did not think the Confederates capable of mounting a large-scale offensive into the state, and felt that Thomas's main responsibility would be in dealing with isolated raids conducted against Federal garrisons and lines of supply. Sherman told Thomas, "Hood is not going to enter Tennessee. Keep enough force to watch the river below and at the shoals, and let the rest march to me or to reinforce the railroad."[15] Thus, he continued to plan his own vain-glorious campaign, showing little concern for the forces being left behind to deal with the South's second most important field army. His own army would march to capture the headlines while Thomas was once more left to perform the grunt work that would enable the March to the Sea to become the huge success it turned out to be. Moving his headquarters to Nashville, Thomas prepared for the imposing task ahead.

Thomas's forces were spread so thin that they effectively invited the sort of raids that Sherman had contemplated. Nathan Bedford Forrest took advantage of the situation to undertake one of his grandest raids of the war when he struck the Union supply depot at Johnsonville, Tennessee, ninety miles west of Nashville. From November 3 to the morning of November 4, Forrest busied himself with the placement of his forces for an attack on the depot. He positioned a two-gun battery of artillery above and below Johnsonville on the Tennessee River to guard against any Federal gunboats that might come to the assistance of the garrison. In addition to these four cannon, he employed the captured gunboat *Undine*, with her eight guns, as a river defense. Opposed to this, the Federals had six gunboats upriver, under Lieutenant Commander Le Roy Fitch, and three below the river, under the command of Lieutenant E.M. King. These Federal vessels mounted a combined total of more than 100 guns, and put Forrest at a significant disadvantage in firepower. The advantage of position enjoyed by the land batteries somewhat compensated for this disparity, however. Forrest positioned the remainder of his artillery to bear upon Johnsonville, and the depot, and on the morning of November 4, he opened his attack against that point. Though the *Undine* was lost, the land batteries were successful in preventing the Union gunboats from reaching Johnsonville.

Confederate shells soon ignited buildings and piles of stores at the depot, and the fires destroyed supplies much needed for Thomas and his army. By the end of the day, when Forrest called off his attack, the Confederates had destroyed or captured three gunboats, eleven steamers, and fifteen barges, and had destroyed one and one-half million dollars' worth of supplies.[16] Schofield arrived in Nashville by rail on November 5, and Thomas immediately dispatched his forces to pursue Forrest, but the effort was in vain. Thomas's ability to deal with Forrest was much impaired by his lack of cavalry. True, Sherman had assigned some 5,000 troopers to Thomas as part of the refitting process for his army at Atlanta, but he had retained all of the horses for himself, leaving these troopers dismounted and of very little use against their Confederate counterparts. Until Thomas could obtain sufficient horses to remount his cavalry, the Rebels would enjoy a distinct advantage in mobility, and Forrest would be able to ride almost wherever he pleased in the state.

While all this was going on, Hood had attacked Allatoona Pass, but the Federal garrison there had managed to successfully defend their position and retain the one million rations stored there. During the end of October, the Confederate army was marching through Gadsden, Guntersville, Decatur, and Tuscumbia, Alabama, in search of a suitable ford of the Tennessee River. Hood had been turned aside at Resaca and Allatoona Pass, but he had captured the garrisons Ackworth, Dalton, Big Shanty, and Tilton. Upon breaking off his chase of Hood and returning to Atlanta, Sherman was heard to remark "If he'll go to the Ohio River I'll give him rations."[17] Sherman was completely disregarding Hood, while Grant still entertained the notion that the enemy army, and not Confederate territory, was the primary objective of his subordinate. Seeing the wisdom of trapping Hood between Sherman and Thomas, and possibly uneasy about Sherman's intention to leave Thomas to face Hood alone, Grant wired his final prompt on November 1: "If you see a chance of destroying Hood's army, attend to that first, and make your other move secondary."[18] But Sherman had no intention of engaging the Confederate army. Indeed, he could already have done so if his pursuit had been conducted with a sense of urgency. Instead, he had trailed Hood at a leisurely pace, quite satisfied to allow the Rebels to roam where they would. His focus was now fixed to the east, and Savannah, and nothing would deter him from it. To Grant, he wired that he was much encumbered by a heavy supply train that made it impossible for him to catch the light-moving Hood. Grant abandoned any further efforts to convince Sherman to engage Hood, and gave permission for him to begin his March to the Sea.

Over the next several days, Sherman and Thomas exchanged a flurry of telegraph messages, as the former saw to all remaining details before leaving Atlanta. On November 12, the telegraph lines were cut to Nashville. The last message that came in from Thomas was, "I am now convinced that the greater part of Beauregard's army is near Florence and Tuscumbia, and that you will have at least a clear road before you for several days, and that your success will fully equal your expectations."[19] Thomas, in referring to Beauregard's army, was noting a change in command in the Confederate army. General P.G.T. Beauregard had been assigned to command of the Department of South Carolina and Florida, which included both Hood's army and that of Lieutenant General Richard Taylor. Beauregard would assume command of either of the armies if he was personally present with them in the field, but the department commander decided to take no such action. He would supervise operations from headquarters, and allow Taylor and Hood to exercise independent command in the field.[20] The army Thomas faced was nominally under the command of Beauregard, but it was Hood that retained immediate command and determined its fate.

Sherman paid little attention to the fact that communications had been cut to

General P.G.T. Beauregard. Placed in overall command of the military district in which Hood was operating, Beauregard chose to allow Hood to conduct his own campaign in Tennessee, and had little or nothing to do with its outcome (United States Army Military History Institute).

Nashville, and did not worry himself that Thomas might be facing impending danger of assault from Hood. On November 16, he marched his army out of Atlanta and headed east on the first leg of a celebrated journey that would win him fame, but would accomplish little toward reducing the striking power of the Confederate military forces in the field. Garrison commands, state militia, and remnants of various other military organizations would be placed in his path, but the Confederacy was never able to gather together a force capable of dealing with Sherman's massive army. The most they could do was to delay and annoy him, as isolated commands were scattered or crushed by his irresistible march. Back in Tennessee, Thomas was facing a similar situation to that of the Confederates in Georgia. His forces were widely dispersed over a substantial area, and the prospect of having them gobbled up individually by Hood's superior army loomed as a very real threat. But this was Thomas, the solid professional, the able strategist and tactician, the brilliant organizer, and the Rock of Chickamauga. He would not allow himself to be forced into a position where his army could be defeated in piecemeal fashion.

Hood had settled in at Tuscumbia, where he rested his men while he established a base of supplies at Corinth. He had drawn Sherman out of the environs of Atlanta for only a brief period of time, but the rest of his plan was working to perfection. With no serious opposition, he had positioned his army within striking distance of Nashville, at a point where it could be more easily reinforced by Taylor's army, on the west bank of the Mississippi River. Sherman was giving up the chase and returning to Atlanta, so the prospects of recovering the city and northwest Georgia seemed unlikely, but that did not mean the campaign was destined to be a failure. He might not be able to liberate Georgia from Federal control, but the prospects of ousting the enemy from Tennessee seemed promising. If Hood could defeat Thomas's scattered forces, tear up the lines of supply and communication to Sherman's rear, and establish a Confederate presence in the state, the North might yet be dealt a setback, and the people of the South would have reason to take heart. It might even come to pass that Sherman would have to cancel his own plans and return to Tennessee to deal with Hood. Indeed, prospects looked good for the audacious Hood during the first week of November, and he was well satisfied with his chances to redeem the loss of Atlanta along with his own tarnished reputation.

Thomas was given a welcome reprieve when Hood spent two weeks at Tuscumbia waiting for his supplies to arrive from Corinth. This time was used to gather together available Union forces to assemble a scratch army to face Hood. Smith was still en route from Missouri with his two divisions. Men were needed to garrison posts at Chattanooga, Murfreesboro, and other strategic points in the state. All those not needed for this duty were banded together into a Provisional Detachment, commanded by General James B. Steedman. This force would eventually contain eight brigades of troops, plus artillery. When added to the garrison force commanded by Brigadier General John F. Miller at Nashville, it would give Thomas the equivalent of an additional small corps.

Approximately half of the men in the Provisional Detachment were black troops: eight full regiments of United States Colored Infantry, along with a battery of Colored artillery.[21] A portion of these were the very same regiments Thomas had supervised in their organization and training back in Chattanooga, following the victory at Missionary Ridge. Sherman had refused to allow any black units to be a part of his army. Thomas showed no such prejudice, though he was still a product of the era in which he lived. Thomas believed that blacks should be enrolled in the military, and felt that they could contribute materially to the war effort, but he questioned their reliability on a battlefield. Thomas felt that blacks were better suited for fatigue duty, or to garrison defensive positions, than to see actual combat on a field of battle.[22] When Thomas inquired of Colonel Thomas J. Morgan, commander of the 14th United States Colored Troops, "if I thought my men would fight, I replied that they would. He said he thought 'they might behind breastworks.' I said they would fight in the open field. He thought not."[23] Time would soon tell which opinion was the correct one, as Thomas was forced by necessity to incorporate the black units into his available army. Morgan would have the opportunity to prove that his men were equal to the task of being soldiers.

Hood spent the two-week respite repairing ten miles of railroad track to Corinth. He was also awaiting the arrival of Nathan Bedford Forrest from west Tennessee to take command of his cavalry, numbering some 6,000 troopers. By November 19, all of Hood's preparations were completed, and he was ready to invade Tennessee and make a run for Nashville. He realized that his delay had given the Federals extra time to get ready, but he believed that he "could still get between Thomas' force and Nashville, and rout them; furthermore, effect such maneuvers as to insure to our troops an easy victory."[24]

Amid terrible storms that pelted the region with rain, sleet, and snow, Hood ordered Forrest's cavalry forward, followed by Stephen D. Lee's Corps. Using pontoon bridges, the advance force was able to cross the Tennessee River and gain the Tennessee side before the bridges were swept away by the rising current. A new set of pontoons were hurried from the rear, and by the following day A.P. Stewart's and Benjamin Cheatham's Corps were also across. Brigadier General Edward Hatch had been assigned by Thomas to watch for a crossing of the Confederates, but he had been lacking in contesting the event. Instead, he hovered cautiously in front of Lee's Corps after it had already crossed the river, and awaited further developments. Hood had now placed his army between Nashville and Pulaski. General Schofield, with his own 23rd Corps and Stanley's 4th Corps, was at the latter place, and in danger of being cut off. This was Hood's intention. He planned to wipe out Schofield's 22,000 men (General Stanley estimated the total to be only 18,000 men) before turning his attention to Nashville.[25]

As soon as Schofield learned that Hood had crossed the river he started his men on a march to Columbia. Hood was also marching for Columbia, by a different road, and it would become a question of who got there first. Hood had the shorter distance to march, but Thomas had ordered General Hatch's cavalry to impede his progress by placing obstructions in his path. The Confederate advance had to contend with felled trees and the constant annoyance of the Federal cavalry. This, combined with the winter storm, and the fact that many of Hood's men were barefoot, made the march to Columbia the worst that many members of the Army of Tennessee could recall. Men wrapped rawhide, hats, and even coat sleeves around their feet to try to protect them from the frozen ground. One Southerner later wrote, "It was a time that tried the strength and spirit of soldiers to the limit."[26] By November 28, however, the weather turned mild, as Indian summer eased the suffering of the Confederates. It now became a foot race for Columbia.

General Stanley stated that Schofield's men "beat Hood to Columbia but only as it were by the hair on our heads." At 9:00 A.M. on the morning of November 29, General Cox's Division of the 23rd Corps reached Columbia just as Union cavalry was being stampeded back toward the town. Cox's men went into line and opened fire on the Confederates, blunting their advance, and giving Schofield's force all day to pass through this crossroads in front of the enemy. Stanley said that Hood "knew our position and forces perfectly well ... and he knew that he had twice as many infantry as we had. By a quick march across from the Lawrenceburg road to our Pulaski road, he could have forced battle, and here a battle might have ruined us and have made him."27

Hood moved his army to strike the Federals four miles above Columbia, on the road to Spring Hill, where he hoped to take Schofield in flank and rear as he marched. Forrest's cavalry was sent ahead to Spring Hill to try to cut off the Federal advance. Thomas had been in constant communication with Schofield, and when he learned of Hood's position above Columbia, he issued appropriate orders to Schofield. "I desire you to fall back from Columbia and to take up your position at Franklin, leaving a sufficient force at Spring Hill to contest the enemy's progress until you are securely posted at Franklin."28 Thomas was well aware of Hood's intentions to try to trap Schofield's force, and his orders were for a speedy withdrawal to Franklin in order to avoid the possibility of the Confederate designs' coming to fruition.

Schofield's withdrawal was not so speedy as Thomas wished, however, and Hood still had the opportunity to cut him off. At 10:00 A.M. on the morning of November 29, when Schofield's vanguard was within two miles of the town, a breathless messenger arrived with news that Forrest's cavalry was within sight of Spring Hill, and was overpowering the pickets of the small garrison. Stanley's Division went forward at the double-quick. Forrest was brushed aside, and a defensive line was begun. The only thing that had saved the Union army from annihilation was one of the quirks that so often happen in war. Hood had issued orders for Cheatham, whose corps was in the path of Schofield's army, to attack while it was still in line of march. For unknown reasons, the order was never delivered, and a golden opportunity was lost.29 By 1:00 P.M., the Federals were prepared to resist any assault by Hood, as Schofield's wagon train rumbled in their rear, on the road to Franklin. At 4:00 P.M., General Cheatham's Corps was thrown against the Union line. In subsequent attacks, Cleburne's, Brown's, and Bate's Divisions were repulsed by Union infantry and artillery until darkness brought an end to the fighting. The Rebels were unable to break through, and Scofield's withdrawal continued that night, his army arriving in Franklin at 9:00 the following morning.30 Hood had been unable to trap Schofield at Spring Hill, and he blamed Cleburne and Cheatham for not pressing their attacks with sufficient vigor. In a surly mood, he determined that this lack of aggressiveness would not be repeated at Franklin. He would crush the Union force once and for all before it could reach Nashville.

By the evening of November 29, Schofield had established a strong defensive hillside position at Franklin and defiantly awaited Hood's arrival. Thomas had wanted Schofield to make a stand at Franklin, pending the arrival of A.J. Smith's divisions, at which time he intended to go on the offensive and drive Hood from Tennessee. But Smith was not yet on the scene, and no word had been received from him since his arrival at Paducah, Kentucky, two days earlier. Though he was expected any time, Schofield would have to face Hood's Confederates with the force he had on hand. His strong works compensated for the disparity in numbers, and Schofield was confident that he could hold at Franklin, should Hood be inclined to attack him. The Confederate commander, still brooding over his failure to crush the Union forces the previous day at Spring Hill, was eager to oblige.

Hood rushed his army in the direction of Franklin, hoping to catch Schofield before he could get his forces across the Big Harpeth River. He felt that a "sudden change in sentiment here took place among the officers and men: the Army became metamorphosed, as it were, in one night. A general feeling of mortification and disappointment pervaded the ranks. The troops appeared to recognize that a great opportunity had been totally disregarded, and manifested, seemingly, a determination to retrieve, if possible, the fearful blunder of the previous afternoon and night."

About 3:00 P.M., General Stewart's Corps made contact with the Federals and filed off to the right of the road and into line of battle. Cheatham's Corps, the next in line, formed to the left of Stewart when it arrived on the field. Forrest's cavalry was divided between the flanks, with orders to descend on the fleeing survivors, should the attack prove successful in shattering the Union line. Lee's Corps was instructed to remain in reserve. Hood had ordered that the attack be made by infantry only, as he was fearful of civilian casualties that might result from his artillery shelling the town. Once his lines were formed, Hood ordered the assault waves forward "to drive the enemy from his position into the river at all hazards."

The gray lines advanced at 4:00 P.M., and quickly drove back the first Union defensive line. The main line then unleashed a volley of musketry that tore huge gaps in the Confederate line, but the attackers continued to press onward. Hood's men were able to penetrate the main line of the Federals, and even turned some captured cannon on the enemy. For a while, it looked as if the Federal defense would be broken, and their army would indeed be pushed into the Harpeth River. At this critical juncture, one of Stanley's brigades mounted a furious counterattack and restored the break in the line, capturing about 1,000 Confederate prisoners in the process. Vicious hand-to-hand fighting erupted, as the opposing lines faced one another separated only by the Union breastworks. Just before nightfall, Brigadier General George Johnston's Division, of Lee's Corps, was ordered forward in support of Cheatham. Johnston's Division struck the Union line in a desperate charge, breaching the position and capturing three stands of colors, but it was, at length, thrown back. Furious fighting continued until 9:00 P.M., and skirmishing did not end till 3:00 A.M. the following morning. Schofield took advantage of the lull in the fighting to pull his men out of their works and start them on the march to Nashville.[31]

The Confederates held the field on the morning of December 1, and they had captured all of the wounded Federal troops Schofield left behind when he evacuated his works. Hood claimed a great victory in his reporting of the battle to Richmond, but he had failed to accomplish any of his goals in regard to Schofield's force. The Federals had been allowed to escape Franklin and continue on their way to Nashville. Hood's army had also experienced the worst of the fighting, taking almost three times the number of casualties the Federals had sustained. Confederate losses at Franklin totaled some 6,252, as opposed to 2,326 suffered by Schofield's army.[32] In addition, Hood's army sustained a frightening number of casualties to its high-ranking officers. Six Confederate generals were killed in the fighting at Franklin, including Patrick Cleburne, States Rights Gist, Hiram Granbury, Otho Strahl, John Adams, and John C. Carter. Generals William A. Quarles, Thomas M. Scott, Francis M. Cockrell, John C. Brown, and Arthur M. Manigault were wounded, and George W. Gordon was captured. In all, Hood lost the services of two major generals commanding divisions, and ten brigadier generals commanding brigades.[33] His command structure would be greatly compromised for the remainder of the campaign as a result of the carnage visited upon his top commanders. On the Union side, General David Stanley had been wounded in the fight, but would soon return to duty with the army.

A Union soldier declared that the sights he saw at Franklin "will haunt me for the rest of my days," and a Confederate recalled that the scene of the Southern dead, lying in piles, "was so appalling that the very thought of it makes me shudder."[34] Hood had won the field at Franklin, but he had paid a terrible price for the victory, a price his army could ill afford. He had also earned the enmity of the soldiers in his command, who were all veterans of the battles around Atlanta. The commander of the Army of Tennessee was fast gaining a reputation for needlessly sacrificing the lives of his men, and they were beginning to lose faith in him as a leader.

Thomas had been anxiously awaiting news from both Schofield and Smith, and elements of the latter's forces began to arrive in the city that day. About 9:00 P.M., he received word from Schofield that Hood's attack had been repulsed, making his face "shine with the fierce light of impending battle." At midnight, the steamers transporting Smith himself and his second division began to arrive at the city's levee, and the long-awaited reinforcements were finally at hand. "We're A.J. Smith's guerrillas," one of his veteran troops announced. "We've been to Vicksburg, Red River, Missouri and about everywhere else ... and now we're going to Hades if old A.J. orders us." The advance of Schofield's army began marching into the city a few hours following Smith's arrival, and the concentration of forces Thomas had been anticipating was finally accomplished.[35] He would now prepare to face the Confederates on his own terms, but before he could do so, he would have to fend off an enemy from within his own ranks.

Thomas was receiving pointed messages from both Secretary Stanton and General Grant, criticizing him for what was being viewed as a lack of initiative on his part. The number and severity of these missives would increase over the following days, as both superiors attempted to prod Thomas into launching an attack on Hood before he was ready to do so. Thomas had sent encouraging word that he was ready to deal with anything Hood might attempt, but this did not seem to satisfy his superiors. "If Hood attacks me here, he will be more seriously damaged than he was yesterday," he had stated. "If he remains until Wilson gets equipped, I can whip him, and will move against him at once."[36]

In response to telegrams received on December 2, prodding for an immediate advance, Thomas replied:

> Your two telegrams of 11 A.M. and 1:30 P.M. to-day are received. At the time that Hood was whipped at Franklin, I had at this place but about 5,000 men of General Smith's command, which added to the force under General Schofield would not have given me more than 25,000 men; besides, General Schofield felt convinced that he could not hold the enemy at Franklin until the 5,000 could reach him. As General Wilson's cavalry force also numbered only about one-fourth that of Forrest's, I thought it best to draw the troops back to Nashville and await the arrival of the remainder of General Smith's force, and also a force of about 5,000 commanded by Major General Steedman, which I had ordered up from Chattanooga. The division of General Smith arrived yesterday morning, and General Steedman's troops arrived last night. I now have infantry enough to assume the offensive, if I had more cavalry, and will take the field anyhow as the remainder of General McCook's division of cavalry reaches here, which I hope it will do in two or three days. We can neither get reinforcements or equipments at this great distance from the North very easily; and it must be remembered that my command was made up of the two weakest corps of General Sherman's army and all of the dismounted cavalry except one brigade, and the task of reorganizing and equipping has met with many delays, which have enabled Hood to take advantage of my crippled condition. I earnestly hope, however, that in a few more days I shall be able to give him a fight.[37]

A large number of Wilson's troopers were still unmounted, and Thomas wished to wait to make his move until proper mounts could be obtained. Every effort was being made to accomplish this goal. When it became evident that there were not enough horses in the region to satisfy the needs of the cavalry, Thomas directed that mules be purchased to make up the difference. He even confiscated the horses of the local streetcar company, as well as those of a traveling circus, and the private stock of Governor Andrew Johnson. Every available mount in Kentucky, Tennessee, and northern Alabama was seized and forwarded to Nashville. Everything that could be done was being done to ensure success in the campaign, but Stanton was not reassured by Thomas's message. After sharing it with Lincoln, Stanton wired Grant, "The President feels solicitous about the disposition of Thomas to lay in fortifications for an indefinite period until Wilson gets replacements. This looks like McClellan and Rosecrans strategy of do nothing and let the enemy raid the country. The President wishes you to consider the matter."[38] Grant sent out two telegrams to Thomas on December 2, prodding him to attack the Confederates before Hood had an opportunity to fortify. He also instructed Thomas to press his quartermaster soldiers, citizens, etc., into service as combat troops and place them in the trenches. Thomas was already doing this when Grant's message arrived. He had taken 5,000 quartermaster employees, along with numerous civilians, and put them to work strengthening the defenses of the city, creating an outer line that shielded an inner line, seven miles long, that ringed the army's hospitals and stores. Abatis and sharpened stakes lined the entire length of the lines, and made the position fearsome to any attacking body.

By December 5, all of the defensive preparations were completed, but Thomas was not yet ready to launch his attack. Hood had previously arrived on the scene, but he was indisposed to commit his army to a repeat of the costly attack at Franklin. Scattered skirmishing and exchanges of artillery fire were the extent of the action. By December 6, Grant and the administration had lost patience with the situation in Nashville, and Grant wired orders to "Attack Hood at once and wait no longer for a remount of your cavalry." Thomas still persisted in getting all things in order before allowing himself to be bullied into a premature strike. On December 8, Grant wired Halleck, "If Thomas has not struck yet, he ought to be ordered to hand over his command to Schofield. There is no better man to repel an attack than Thomas, but I fear he is too cautious to take the initiative." Unknown to Grant, Thomas was finally prepared to kick Hood out of Tennessee, and had issued orders that very afternoon for his troops to be ready to attack in two hours.[39]

But the attack orders had to be canceled. A storm front rolled in, and freezing rain covered the landscape in a thick sheet of ice that made any movement of the army an impossibility. On December 9, sleet and snow continued to fall, freezing both armies in place. Grant was unimpressed by the difficulties facing Thomas, and on December 9 he wired the War Department demanding that he be replaced with Schofield. Stanton drew up the necessary orders, but Halleck protested their issuance, prompting Grant to relent for the moment. He would wait a bit longer to see if Thomas would act, but the stay of execution would be short in duration. That same day, Thomas wired Grant: "General Halleck informs me you are very much dissatisfied with my delay in attacking. I can only say that I have done all in my power to prepare, and if you should deem it necessary to relieve me, I shall submit without a murmur."[40]

Up to this point, Thomas had kept the contents of the various directives from Grant and the War Department a secret. On December 10, he invited all of his corps commanders to his headquarters at the St. Cloud Hotel to lay matters before them. All of the correspondence between himself and his superiors was presented to his generals. Thomas declared that he alone would take responsibility for the delays, but he wanted his officers to know what had been transpiring. Wilson was the first to speak, commending Thomas for his actions and citing the reasons that had made the delays the course of wisdom. Wood (who had replaced the wounded Stanley as commander of the 4th Corps), Smith, and Steedman added their approval to all that Thomas had done, and were quite vocal in their support of his actions. Only Schofield sat silent, refusing to make the opinion unanimous. On December 11, Grant wired a caustic order for Thomas to attack at once. In reply, he received a message from Thomas that read: "I will obey the order as promptly as possible, however much I may regret it, as the attack will have to be made under every disadvantage. The whole country is covered with a perfect sheet of ice and sleet, and it is with great difficulty that the troops are able to move about on level ground."[41]

Thomas did not know it, but he was being undermined by one of his top subordinates. Brigadier General William Whipple, his chief of staff, was the first to suggest that someone was using the telegraph to Washington to give the administration a false sense of the situation at Nashville. Thomas sent for his most trusted subordinate, General Steedman, and discussed the matter with him. Several possible candidates, including Governor Johnson, were ruled out in the discussion, but Steedman agreed to investigate and report his findings. Captain Marshall Davis was assigned to do the detective work, and one trip to the telegraph office resulted in all the evidence needed to support Whipple's assumption. There he found a handwritten message from Schofield to Grant that stated, "Many officers here are of the opinion that General Thomas is certainly too slow in his movements." Steedman took the message to Thomas, who examined it and pronounced his disbelief that Schofield could be capable of such intrigue. Steedman answered that Thomas certainly could recognize the hand-writing of one of his own generals. Putting on his glasses, and holding the message up to the light, Thomas despondently said "Yes, it is Schofield's handwriting.... Why does he send such telegrams?" The honorable Thomas could not understand the means of unrestrained ambition, and Steedman had to explain to him that Schofield, as second in command, stood to replace Thomas if he was relieved. "Oh, I see," said Thomas, as he sadly shook his head.[42]

General Wilson was well-known to Grant, and he used that familiarity to cast his support in favor of Thomas. Writing to the general-in-chief after the battle of Franklin, he commended the manner in which the campaign had been conducted thus far, and expressed the opinion that all concerned were due praise for the way they had coped with difficult circumstances in the face of a superior enemy force.[43]

Grant had apparently seen through Schofield's intrigue before Thomas did, possibly due to Wilson's report, but that did not prevent him from clinging to his stubborn insistence that an immediate attack be made. It is curious to fathom why Grant was so insistent on micromanaging the activities of Thomas when he was so hesitant to do so with his other generals. Sherman, to be sure, was allowed great latitude in his movements, and was shown every consideration by Grant, as were the rest of his subordinate field commanders. It was with Thomas alone that Grant made a point of badgering his command decisions. It is also curious that he was so adamant that Thomas attack Hood, even though he was, at the time, outnumbered by his adversary, given the fact that Grant himself was not taking radical offensive measures against Lee's army in Virginia, even though he outnumbered the Confederates by more than two to one. Grant had been complacent in placing Thomas in command of a ragtag force in Tennessee when he approved Sherman's plans to march to the sea. He was fully aware of the numbers of men Thomas had at hand, the shortages he had to contend with, and the vast area he had to defend. Why, therefore, was he so stubborn in insisting that Thomas fight a battle at a disadvantage, or when weather conditions made the movement of the army almost impossible?

On December 13, Grant ordered General John Logan, who happened to be visiting at City Point, to proceed at once to Nashville for the purpose of assuming command of the army there, if Thomas had not already attacked by the time of his arrival. That very day, the weather around Nashville began to moderate, and the ice started to melt. By December 14, Thomas was issuing assault orders to his commanders and notifying Halleck that he intended to strike Hood the following morning. Logan was on his way to Cincinnati, and Grant was preparing to leave for Nashville himself on the 15th. If Thomas could indeed mount his offensive on December 15, he would be able to negate the orders for his own removal, and would have the opportunity of reaping the rewards for all of his efforts of the past several weeks. The intrigue against him, started by Schofield, could only be undone through a victory on the battlefield.

Thomas was now confident that just such a victory was at hand. Events were about to prove the wisdom of his actions, and his detractors would soon realize their error in labeling him a defensive-minded general.

Chapter Fifteen

The Sledge of Nashville and the End of the War

Hood and his soldiers could have eased Grant's mind concerning the efforts being made by Thomas to bring about the desired battle at Nashville. Since December 2, the Confederate army had been in position in front of the city, so they had a front-row seat to observe Federal movements and preparations for battle. The arrival of reinforcements, the concentration of Wilson's cavalry, and the construction of defensive works all took place in full view of the Southerners, helping to further reduce morale that had been badly shaken at Franklin. They were further demoralized by the storm system that had immobilized Thomas's army and covered the landscape in an icy sheet. One Confederate remembered, "The weather was very severe and the suffering of the men was great. There was no supply of shoes, and the men covered their bare feet with raw hide taken from animals freshly slaughtered." General Forrest's two divisions of cavalry, along with three brigades of infantry, were sent to operate against Murfreesboro and the 3,500-man garrison commanded by Major General Lovell H. Rousseau, and would not be present with the army when Thomas launched his attack.[1] Hood had thus deprived himself of nearly a quarter of his total effective strength, and had but 23,000 men stationed in front of Nashville. By December 15, Thomas's force had grown to approximately 55,000 men, and the balance of power had swung decidedly in favor of the Federals. It must be stated, however, that 12,000, or slightly less than one-quarter of Thomas's men, were raw recruits, and an additional 7,000 were quartermaster's men, having never seen battle. As such, more than one-third of the Federal army gathered at Nashville was green and untested. Thomas estimated the size of the enemy army to be at about 40,000 men, all veterans, and it would have been much closer to that total had not a significant force been sent away to Murfreesboro.

Hood had hoped that recruits from Tennessee would join his ranks and make up for his losses, but fewer than two hundred actually did so. He had also appealed for reinforcements from the Trans-Mississippi Department. Both General Beauregard and President Davis supported the request, but the reinforcements were not forthcoming. General Kirby Smith declined to march his men to Hood's aid, knowing that a large number of them would desert rather than cross the Mississippi.[2] Desertion was a problem in Hood's army as well, as many of the soldiers became disheartened by the campaign. Captain Samuel T. Foster, a member of Cleburne's command, expressed the discord in the Southern army when he wrote in his diary that Hood "had near 10,000 men murdered around Atlanta trying to prove to the world that he was a greater man than Genl Johns[t]on…. And now in order to recover from the merited disgrace of that transaction he brings this Army here to middle Tenn. and by making them false promises and false statements get these men killed."[3]

The Union defensive position at Nashville was some twenty miles long, and circled the southern and western approaches to the city. The outer line started, on the left, at a bend in the Cumberland River, just east of the city, and continued in a southerly direction to the main Federal salient, located on Montgomery's Hill, intersecting the Nolensville Pike, the Franklin Pike, and the Granny White Pike on the way. From there, it continued in a westerly, then northerly loop, crowning a range of hills as it crossed the Hillsboro Pike, the Harding Pike, and the Charlotte Pike. It terminated at another bend in the Cumberland, just west of the city. The inner line began, on the left, at Fort Casino, and stretched in a westerly, then northerly, direction, past Fort Morton, Fort Gillem, and Fort Garesche, terminating just above Hyde's Ferry on the Cumberland. By the time Thomas was ready to take the offensive, Nashville had become the most heavily fortified spot on the North American continent. Brigadier General Zebulon B. Tower had arrived there in October to assume the responsibilities of chief engineer officer, and had completed his assignment in commendable fashion, expanding and strengthening works that were already present:

> The forts were located on hills which studded the 20 miles of breastworks, trenches, and rifle pits. All forts bristled with heavy guns supported by underground magazines and all supplies necessary to withstand a lengthy siege. These great barriers were so skillfully located that they supported each other as well as covering all practical approaches to the city from the south and west. The fieldworks joining the hilltop forts consisted of artillery embrasures at strategic places, earth forts, and trenches and breastworks protected by abatis to impede attacking infantry. The once pastoral scenes through which these ugly scars of war made their abrupt angles had been cleared of all trees and buildings to provide clear paths of fire for the guns of fort and trench.[4] Railroad workers, citizens of Nashville, and impressed slaves had all been used in the construction of the works, which by December 14 were pronounced complete.

The Confederate line was but four miles long, and located just out of range of the Federal big guns. On the right, it was anchored on Rain's Hill, just west of the Nolensville Pike. From there, it coursed southwesterly across the Franklin Pike and Granny White Pike, forming a salient east of the Hillsboro Pike. It then angled almost due south, following the path of the Hillsboro Pike, in an effort to protect the left from any flanking movement of the Federals. Three redoubts were constructed at the angle, with a fourth and fifth marking the terminus of the Rebel line on this part of the field. The inclement weather had delayed construction, and Hood's defensive works were not yet completed by December 15. The opposing lines were two miles apart on the Confederate right, but the distance narrowed to only five hundred yards on the left. General Cheatham's Corps held the right of the Southern line, with Lee's Corps in the center and Stewart's on the left. They were opposed on the Federal side, from left to right, by the corps of Steedman, Schofield, Wood, and Smith.

At 3:00 P.M. on December 14, Thomas called all four of his corps commanders to his headquarters to hold a council of war and discuss the plans of attack. Though they were exactly the same as those he had issued prior to the ice storm that had caused the cancellation of offensive movements, the commanding general wanted to be sure that each man knew his assignment and was prepared to carry it out. Ever the perfectionist, he had taken pains to

Opposite: **Map of Nashville, showing the principal areas of conflict in the campaign. From** ***The History of the Civil War in the United States***, **by Samuel Schmucker. Published by Jones Brothers & Co., in Philadelphia in 1865.**

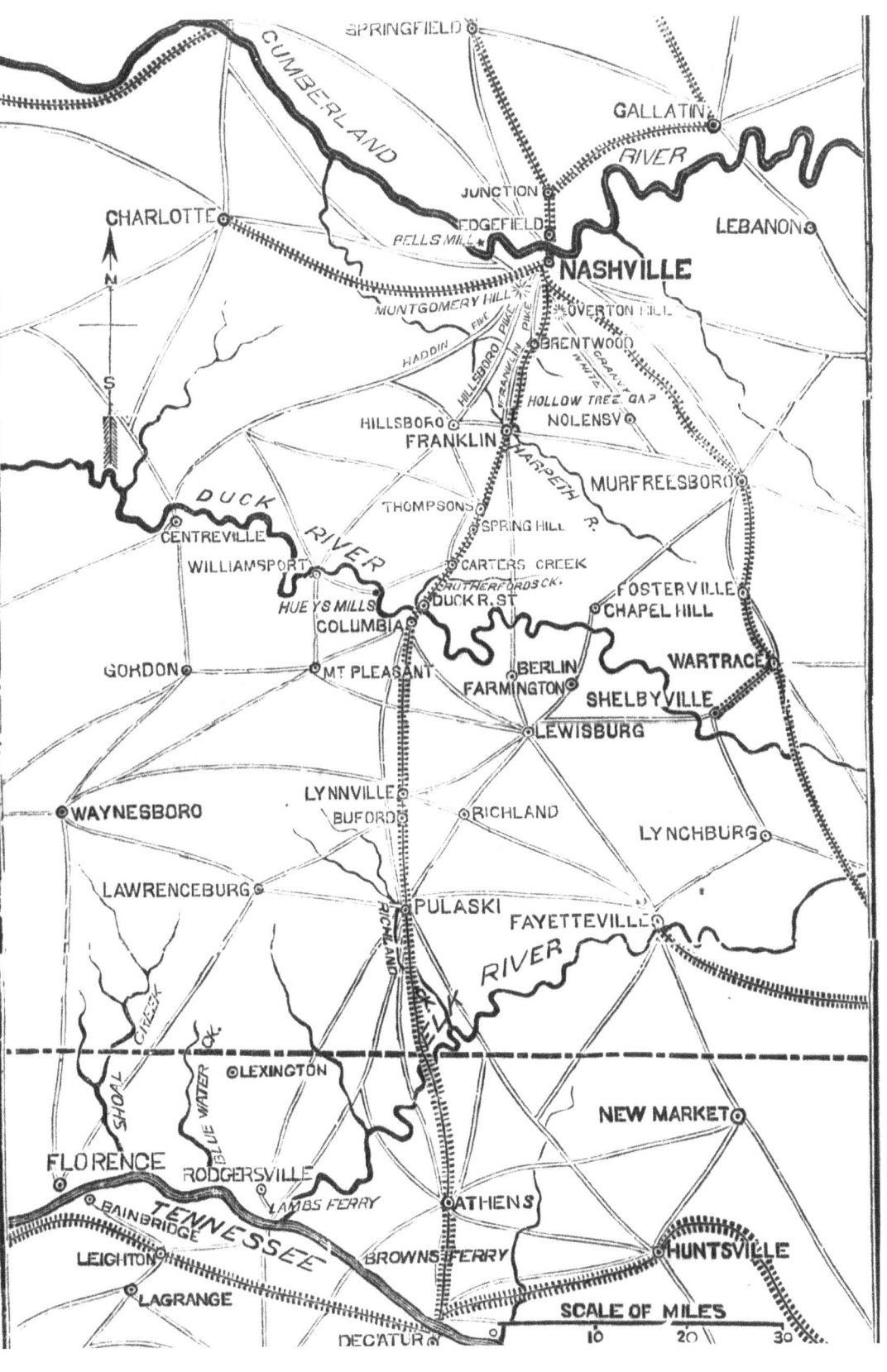

write them out as well, and each officer received a copy of Special Field Orders No. 342, outlining the orders for each. In addition, Thomas had personally met with Commander Fitch, in charge of the naval forces protecting the river approaches to the city, to make sure that all that could be done was being done to ensure that the Confederates could not bypass the city by crossing the Cumberland. All was in readiness, and Thomas was satisfied with the preparations. He went to bed on the 14th completely confident that the following morning would see the beginning of the end for Hood's army.[5]

At 4:00 A.M. on December 15, the waiting Confederates were aroused by the sound of bugles all along the Federal lines. Hood had distributed a circular to his officers several days earlier advising them that he believed a battle would be fought before the end of the year, and admonishing them to keep their men well in hand and stay alert for signs of any threatening Federal movements. The blaring bugles and the shuffling of Union troops behind their works were indeed signs that Hood's warning had been justified, but the Confederates were at a loss as to just what was taking place. A heavy fog blanketed the countryside, and the movements of the Federals could not be discerned in the murky haze. Slightly after 4:00, Schofield's and Wood's Corps marched out of their entrenchments and formed their lines in front of the works. They were replaced in the line by Brigadier General Charles Cruft's Provisional Division and Brigadier General John Miller's garrison troops. These were later joined by Colonel James Donaldson's armed quartermaster's force, and by 6:30 A.M., Steedman's place in the line had been accounted for, and he was forming his troops in front of the works to make his attack.[6]

According to Thomas's plan, Steedman was to make a feint against the Confederate right, hopefully drawing reserves away from other portions of Hood's line. Wood and Schofield were to assault the Rebel center, while Smith, with Wilson's cavalry, was to execute a hammering blow on the Confederate left. Forrest's absence gave Thomas a decided advantage. Wilson's cavalry was now some 12,000 strong, and it would be opposed by only three under-strength brigades of Southern horse, commanded by Brigadier General James Chalmers. Indeed, Hood was so lacking in cavalry that he could not adequately defend his flanks, and his troopers could not hope to stand up against the force Wilson had arrayed against them.

Hood had been concerned over protecting the Franklin Pike and the Granny White Pike in the center of his line, and had massed his forces to cover these

General Benjamin F. Cheatham. This hard-fighting general led a corps in Hood's army during the Nashville campaign (United States Army Military History Institute).

important lines of communication. What resulted was an unbalanced line that found his left held by far too small a force, only two brigades of infantry. When the full operation was put in motion, Smith and Wilson would find themselves facing little more than token resistance.

Thomas arose at an early hour and checked out of his hotel at 5:00 A.M. He made his way to headquarters to monitor the progress of the attack, but news of any forward movement was not forthcoming. Steedman was being delayed by the heavy fog, and it was not until 8:00 A.M. that he was able to begin his assault. Delays were experienced elsewhere along the line as well, with some of the units not moving forward for another hour or two. Steedman's mixed black and white Provisional force moved boldly ahead, brushing aside the enemy pickets in their front and assaulting a battery in the main line. The Federals were not successful in carrying the battery, but the ferocity of their attack caused Hood to shift troops from his center to bolster the threatened right. He was acting exactly as Thomas hoped he would.

On the Union right, Wilson's troopers trotted out in an arc around the Rebel left flank at 10:00 A.M. The fog had only partially contributed to Wilson's delay. Brigadier General Arthur McArthur had inadvertently crossed his men in front of Wilson while getting into position, and the troopers were forced to wait as the infantry trudged past them. With a small portion of his men, Wilson enveloped and pinned down Chalmers's troopers and prevented them from leaving their place in the line. With the rest of his force, Wilson attacked the infantry on the left, fighting his men dismounted when enemy resistance was encountered.[7] When Steedman's men retired to their main line, Hood realized that the attack on his right was probably only a feint, and he began shifting men from Cheatham's Corps to his center and threatened left, where they tried to counter the gains being achieved by Wilson.

Wood's Corps, in the center, was to serve as the pivot point for a left wheel by Smith's and Wilson's men, as the Federal attack employed a vast turning movement to try to smash the Confederate left flank. About half of Thomas's effective force, or some 27,000 men, would be used by Smith and Wilson in the movement. Brigadier General Kenner Garrard's Division of Smith's Corps was formed to the immediate right of Wood's position. On Garrard's right was the division of Arthur McArthur, with Colonel J.B. Moore's Division serving as a

General James Wilson. Thomas placed him in charge of his cavalry at Nashville. By the time of the battle, Wilson had assembled and equipped a mounted arm approximately 12,000 strong, and his troopers played a crucial role in the Union victory (United States Army Military History Institute).

reserve. The wheeling movement of Smith's and Wilson's lines was like a door swinging closed to the left, and the line ended up running north to south and facing east, parallel with the Harding Pike, by the time the motion was completed. The only Confederate unit on that part of the field was a lone brigade, commanded by Brigadier General Matthew Ector. There was little that Ector could do with his limited force against such overwhelming odds. At the first appearance of the Federals, he promptly obeyed previously issued orders to fall back to the main Confederate line, along the Hillsboro Pike, in case of attack.[8]

Wood's Corps had experienced only minor delays from the fog, and was in position in front of their works at an early hour. Skirmishers were pushed forward immediately, and were soon hotly engaged with the enemy. The main body was held back till after noon, however, under orders not to advance until Smith and Wilson had gotten their lines into the assigned position and alignment. Once that was accomplished, Wood ordered his men forward. With Wood's 13,000 veterans added to Smith's and Wilson's forces, Thomas would be throwing 40,000 men into this all-out assault on the Confederate left and center. In his report, Wood stated, "When the grand array of troops began to move forward in unison, the pageant was magnificently grand and imposing. Far as the eye could reach, the lines and masses of blue, over which the nation's emblem flaunted proudly, moved forward in such perfect order that the heart of the patriot might easily draw from it the happy presage of the coming glorious victory."[9]

The battlefield provided a panorama that was witnessed by the largest crowd of spectators that ever watched a battle during the war. One Federal recalled how "citizens of Nashville, nearly all of whom were in sympathy with the Confederacy, came out of the city in droves. All the hills in our rear were black with human beings watching the battle, but silent. No army on the continent ever played on any field to so large and so sullen an audience."[10] The crowd of Northern civilians who had gone to the field at Manassas to watch the first battle of the war had been caught up the stampede of the Union army that followed their defeat. The grand array that Wood described must have looked like an irresistible force, but these Southern civilians were hoping for nothing more than to be caught themselves in another such rout of Union forces.

Wood's men moved forward toward Montgomery Hill, and Colonel Sidney Post's Brigade, of Beatty's Division, was ordered to storm the Rebel works located there. Though the position looked formidable, it was held by only skirmishers, as Hood had moved his main line back from this point five days before. Supported by artillery, Post's men quickly overran the entrenchments and captured the hill. For the most part, Schofield's Corps looked on as spectators. Schofield had been ordered to hold his corps in reserve to support Smith's movements. Major General Darius M. Couch's Division was formed in the rear of Smith's left, with Major General Jacob D. Cox's Division on his left, in front of their works. Schofield's men watched as their comrades overlapped the Confederate line. By early afternoon, the blue-coats were pressing against Hood's main line, and the battle had been joined in earnest. Hood's left had been held by the division of Major General Edward C. Walthall. Designating Walthall's force as a division was indeed a stretch. It contained only two undersized brigades, one of which had numbered only 1,100 men before it lost 432 casualties in the fighting at Franklin. In reality, the division did not even contain enough men to constitute a full-strength brigade. Hood knew how weakly his left was held, and had ordered Major General Edward Johnson's Division, of Lee's Corps, to support it. He later ordered two divisions of Cheatham's Corps, on the right, to shift to Stewart's front and bolster the left.[11]

Datus E. Coon's Brigade, of Brigadier General Edward Hatch's cavalry division, found itself opposite the unfinished and unsupported Redoubt No. 5, on the far left of Hood's line. The Federal troopers dismounted and charged the work with their seven-shot Spencers. The redoubt was defended by a four-gun battery of Napoleon cannon and one hundred infantry, all of which roared into action at the approach of Coon's men. General McArthur sent a brigade from his division to support Coon. When the attackers got close enough, a desperate rush on the defenses ensued. Redoubt No. 5 was speedily overpowered, and almost all of its defenders were captured.

Once inside, the Federals came under artillery fire from Redoubt No. 4, which was already being attacked by the rest of Hatch's and McArthur's divisions. Redoubt No. 4 contained relatively the same number of men and cannon as Redoubt No. 5 had, but resistance here proved to be much stronger. The Confederates here, under the command of Captain Charles Lumsden, were able to hold their position for approximately three hours, despite the fact that they were being assailed by three batteries of rifled cannon, twelve regiments of infantry, and two brigades of dismounted cavalry. After a heroic stand, Lumsden was finally forced to abandon the redoubt only after Federal forces had gained the interior of the work. With the surviving remnants of his command, Lumsden fell back to Walthall's main line.[12]

Smith and Wilson had pushed back the Confederate left, and had captured two of the principal defensive works, but their center was holding firm. Hearing of the success against Hood's left, Thomas sent a message to Wood to prepare to attack the Rebel center. The staff officer Thomas sent could not readily locate Wood, but he communicated Thomas's wishes to his two division commanders. A brigade commander, upon hearing the orders, looked in the direction of Hood's formidable line and questioned "You don't mean we have to go in here and attack the works on that hill?" When an affirmative reply was received, he gazed at the Rebel line, roaring with fire from Hood's artillery, and said, "Why it would be suicide, sir; perfect suicide."[13] Despite the premonitions of the brigade commander, Wood's men were formed and moving forward before the staff officer had a chance to get back to Thomas's headquarters.

In the meantime, McArthur's Division had captured Redoubt No. 3, and had turned its attention to Redoubts No. 1 and 2. Brigadier General Nathan Kimball's Division, of Wood's Corps, joined in the attack on Redoubt No. 1 at about 4:30 P.M., and his men, along with McArthur's, stormed the work and captured the position without serious opposition, the defenders having already been ordered by Stewart to withdraw. Thomas now ordered Wood to move east, toward the Franklin Pike, and form his line facing south. The coming of darkness prevented the completion of this movement, and Wood was forced to halt his advance after crossing the Granny White Pike and wait for morning.[14] Although the Union army had gotten a late start, it had been a successful day. Some 1,200 prisoners and sixteen cannon had been captured, and the entire Confederate line had been shoved back several miles toward Cheatham, on the right. Hood used the lull in the fighting brought on by darkness to withdraw his forces two miles, to another fortified range of hills. Federal losses in the day's fighting amounted to 825 killed, wounded, and missing.[15]

Thomas, in his official report, stated, "The whole command bivouacked in line of battle during the night on the ground occupied at dark, whilst preparations were made to renew the battle at an early hour on the morrow." Indeed, the general was pleased with the events of the day. On his way back to Nashville from the front to wire Grant a report of the proceedings, he remarked, "Unless Hood decamps tonight, tomorrow Steedman will double up his right, Wood will hold his center, Smith and Schofield will again strike his left while the cavalry work away at his rear."[16] His message to Grant informed his superior that he had indeed "attacked the enemy" and had driven their army "about eight miles."[17] This was welcome news to Grant, who by that time had reached Washington, as a first stop on his way to Nashville, where he planned to assume overall command of the situation there. Word of Thomas's offensive caused Grant to retrace his steps back to City Point to coordinate actions against Petersburg and Richmond. It also meant that the orders previously given to General Logan were now void, and that he would not be replacing Thomas as commander of the Army of the Cumberland. Logan was en route to Nashville from Cincinnati, but it would be a wasted journey. Thomas's attack had saved his command. He would now save his reputation, and enhance it far beyond the laurels previously won at Mill Springs, Stones River, and Chickamauga.

Congratulations and accolades began to roll in almost as soon as the fighting concluded on December 15. Secretary Stanton said "I rejoice in tendering you and the gallant officers and soldiers of your command the thanks of this department for the brilliant achievement of this day." Grant telegraphed "Please accept for yourself, officers and men the nation's thanks." Lincoln sent a greeting with an admonition: "You have made a magnificent beginning; a grand consummation is within your easy reach. Do not let it slip."[18]

Thomas was essentially planning to repeat his battle plan of the previous day when the battle was rejoined. The only obvious exception was the fact that Schofield's Corps would play a more active role, as it had been moved from its reserve status to extend Smith's line on the right. Hood spent a busy night moving troops and trying to establish a new defensive position. On his right, he placed Lee's Corps, with Lee's right flank being anchored on Peach Orchard Hill, just east of the Franklin Pike. Stewart's Corps filled in on Lee's left, with his line stretching west across the Granny White Pike. The main portion of Stewart's line was placed behind a rock wall, where a shallow trench had been dug. Cheatham's Corps was shifted from the right of the line to the left, and extended Stewart's left flank to the west, with Cheatham's left flank being anchored on Shy's Hill. The entire line was approximately three

General John A. Logan. Sent by Grant to relieve Thomas of command of the army at Nashville, he had only reached Ohio before news of Thomas's victory was received. Thomas suspected that Grant intended to relieve him, but these suspicions were not confirmed until after the war (United States Army Military History Institute).

and one half miles long, and Hood began moving his army into their assigned positions around midnight on the 15th. The rest of the night was spent in feverish efforts to dig and construct hasty entrenchments.[19]

Dawn on December 16 witnessed renewed fog, but it was not nearly so thick as the previous day. Thomas was up at an early hour, and made his way to the front to supervise the movements of his army. While he and his staff were riding out of the city, they passed a group of wounded Confederate soldiers who were not receiving medical attention. Thomas sent an orderly back to the city to secure an ambulance and surgeon to care for the wounded men, and detailed another orderly to stay with them and make sure they received attention. Before resuming their ride to the front, the party passed around numerous flasks among the suffering men, who welcomed the stimulants against the pain and cold.[20]

The morning of December 16 also differed from the previous day because of the exceptionally heavy bombardment of the Union artillery against the entire Confederate line. The barrage was one of the heaviest and most sustained of the war, and lasted throughout the day. The Confederates were punished by the shelling from three sides, and their efforts to answer the blistering cross-fire were ineffective. The best most Southerners could do was to keep their heads down, behind their defensive works, and await the infantry charge that all knew would follow shortly.[21] Thomas was bringing together all of his talents and acquired knowledge from twenty years of military service. Lessons learned with the old 3rd Artillery and 2nd Cavalry were being brought to bear, as he used these support arms to their utmost capacity in his movements against Hood. All segments of his army were moving together in perfect unity, as could only be accomplished by a commander who fully understood the inner workings of each individual branch. From Sherman's castoffs, Smith's veterans, and various garrison troops, he had created a formidable and well-organized army that he was about to unleash in full fury against the waiting Army of Tennessee.

The end result of the previous day's fighting was that the Union line extended beyond both of Hood's flanks and overlapped his position. There was a real danger that Wilson, with his large cavalry force, might swing around behind the Confederates and block off their routes of retreat, causing Hood's forces to be virtually cut off and surrounded. Steedman initiated the fighting, just as he had the prior day, by attacking the Confederate right in the vicinity of Peach Orchard Hill. Several probing thrusts were made throughout the day, seeking a weak spot, but each foray was repulsed.

About noon, as a cold rain began to fall, Thomas directed General Wood to cooperate with Steedman in an attempt to take the hill. The combined assault went forward at approximately 3:00 P.M., but met with disappointing results. Steedman's black regiments were roughly handled by the Confederates, who took renewed enthusiasm from the sight of Negro troops in their front. One Rebel officer reported that it was with great difficulty that he was able to restrain his men from going over the works to attack the black troops. Another Confederate recalled that they had "the negroes in our trap, and when we commenced firing on them, complete demoralization followed. Many jumped into the [railroad] cut and were either killed or captured." A gray-clad veteran attested, "I have seen most of the battlefields of the west, but never saw dead men thicker than in front of my two right regiments, the great masses and disorder of the enemy enabling the left to take them in flank, while the right, with a coolness unexampled, scarcely threw away a shot at their front. The enemy at last broke and fled in wild disorder."[22]

Union efforts to crack Hood's defensive line on the right were meeting with abject failure, and casualties were piling up. The situation on the left was quite another matter. Wilson's cavalry had gained the rear of the Confederate left flank, and, fighting dismounted, was exerting great pressure against this portion of the line. The defensive line had been turned back, into a fish hook configuration, and was resisting as best it could, but Cheatham's Corps here did not enjoy the same formidable defenses that Lee's Corps occupied on the right. The works on Shy's Hill had been improperly placed by the engineers, who, in the darkness of the previous night, had placed the line too far back from the brow of the hill. This gave the defenders only a limited view of the ground to their front, and made it impossible for them to protect the angle in the line with flanking fire. On top of this, no provisions had been made to place abatis or obstructions in front of the line to impede assaulting infantry. To make matters worse, Cheatham was forced to spread his troops dangerously thin to cover the section of the line entrusted to him, and was further weakened when he had to pull men out of the line to guard against Wilson's attacks in his rear. Wilson recognized the importance of the position he had gained in Hood's rear, and set about turning it to his advantage. He formed a line of battle, one and one half miles long, and, with 4,000 dismounted troopers, ordered it to press forward, toward Nashville, directly in Cheatham's rear. Wilson's force was comparatively equal in size to the number of men Cheatham commanded, and it was heading right for his vulnerable rear. Confronted by the forces of Schofield and Smith in his front and flank, and facing a blistering bombardment by Union artillery, Cheatham was caught in a tight place from which he had little hope of extricating himself.

Wilson described the scene at this critical moment: "My dismounted men, their guidons fluttering in the air, flanked and covered by two batteries of horse artillery, were in plain sight moving against the left and rear of the enemy line." Wilson directed Thomas's attention to his cavalry, and urged an immediate attack by the infantry. "He lifted his glasses and coolly scanned what I clearly showed him. It was a stirring sight, and gazing at it, as I thought, with unnecessary deliberation, he finally satisfied himself. Pausing only to ask me if I was sure that the men entering the left of the enemy works were mine ... he turned to Schofield and as calmly as if on parade directed him to move to the attack with his entire corps."[23] Thomas then rode over to Smith, and pointing to the hills occupied by the Confederates merely said "Order the charge."

At about 4:00 P.M., Wilson's, Smith's and Schofield's men all advanced, and Cheatham's Corps was attacked simultaneously from three sides by a vastly superior force. The Confederates could not hope to withstand such an onslaught, and the angle in their line was quickly overrun. When the breakthrough occurred, Brigadier General Matthew Ector's Brigade was subjected to the full force of the attack. The consolidated fragments of the 2nd, 10th, 15th, 20th, 30th and 37th Georgia regiments attempted to hold their ground, but were quickly gobbled up. Only 65 members of these regiments were able to make good their escape, and the command was virtually wiped out. While large numbers of Cheatham's men sought to escape from the trap, many more stood resolutely to face the impending disaster and be cut down or captured by the Federal horde. Generals Thomas B. Smith and Henry R. Jackson were captured, along with a large number of their commands, while attempting to rally their men.[24]

Cheatham's Corps crumbled so quickly that Stewart did not have time to organize a defense of his now exposed left flank. The Federals pushed east and slammed into Stewart's surprised men. It was only a matter of minutes before Hood's center caved in and joined Cheatham's survivors in a headlong flight toward the Franklin Pike. Lee's Corps, on the right, now became the only organized Confederate force remaining on the field. They had just thrown back the combined assaults of Wood and Steedman, and were jubilant over the victory they had achieved when they were greeted with the realization that the rest of the army was defeated and in retreat. Lee's Corps could not hope to hold its place in the line against the entire Union army, and it was ordered to retire along with the rest of Hood's battered forces. Lee was able to maintain discipline among his men, however, and retired in an orderly fashion, providing a rear guard for the army as he did so. He was ordered to hold the Franklin Pike while the rest of the beaten army marched south over that road in an attempt to make good its escape. Lee's able disposition of his forces, combined with a less than energetic pursuit by General Wood, allowed Hood's crippled army to evade its complete destruction or capture.

Even so, the crushing victory Thomas had orchestrated at Nashville all but eliminated the Army of Tennessee as an effective fighting force for the remainder of the war. Though the Confederates gave no official tally of casualties, estimates place their total losses for the two days of fighting at approximately 15,000 men, with about 4,000 of these being captured. Hood's force in front of Nashville at the commencement of the fighting numbered only about 23,000 men, meaning that he had sustained losses of about two-thirds of his effective force. Even with the addition of Forrest's command, and the two brigades of infantry that had been sent to operate against Murfreesboro, he would probably have fewer than 15,000 effectives remaining from an army that a few short months before had numbered close to 70,000 men. Thomas's total losses were 2,140, leaving him with a force of about 68,000 men, or more than four times that of the enemy.[25] Hood could hope to do little or nothing against such odds, and sullenly marched his remaining forces south, toward the Tennessee River.

The commanding general paused long enough to commend his soldiers for the victory they had won, then, after assigning various duties to his aides, rode off alone down the Granny White Pike. General Wilson, still pursuing the fleeing Confederates, heard a rider approaching from the rear at a gallop. Darkness concealed the identity of the horseman, but Wilson intuitively believed it to be Thomas. He was proven correct when Thomas called out his name. "Dang it to hell, Wilson, didn't I tell you we could lick 'em, didn't I tell you we could lick 'em?" Thomas gushed. Not waiting for a reply, he turned his horse back up the pike, shouted a word of praise for the cavalry, and ordered, "Continue the pursuit as far as you can tonight and resume it as early as you can tomorrow morning." With that, the sound of his galloping hoof beats disappeared into the darkness.[26] The commander was so elated over the events of the day that his enthusiasm even overpowered the fearful back pain that usually confined his equestrian activities to a slow trot. Thomas was galloping!

The Federals took up the pursuit again on the morning of December 17, and for the next ten days a running battle was conducted between the opposing armies. Cold rains turned the roads into mud during the day, but they froze at night into deep ruts that posed a challenge to both man and beast. The elements showed no favoritism to blue or gray, as both sides plodded forward in the miserable winter conditions. But the fleeing Confederates suffered far more than did their pursuers. Ill-equipped, short on rations, and lacking in clothing, particularly hats and shoes, the Southern army marked the route of its retreat by the bloody footprints left on the frozen ground.

General Forrest received news of the disaster at Nashville on the evening of December 16. He also received orders to fall back from Murfreesboro and concentrate his command in the vicinity of Pulaski. Sending detachments to bolster the rear guard, Forrest joined them with his main force on December 18 at Columbia, where he was entrusted with the responsibility of conducting the delaying action. The rear guard consisted of Forrest's cavalry, along with 1,900 infantry, under the command of Major General Edward C. Walthall. Some 400 of Walthall's men were barefoot, and Forrest directed that they be conveyed in wagons to protect them from the bitter cold. When the Union pursuit got too close for comfort, these barefoot soldiers would be formed up in line of battle until the danger was past, and then loaded onto the wagons again for the retreat south.[27]

Forrest carried out his assignment with the rear guard in exemplary fashion. The Union forces were kept sufficiently far away from Hood's main body to prevent them from impeding the retreat or cutting the Confederates off. Forrest made sure that hardly any bridges were left standing in the rear of the retreating army. Each river and stream the Federals came to required a delay in the pursuit while the means to cross them were obtained. Thomas was in dire need of his old 58th Indiana Regiment, who had been trained under his tutelage as pontoniers and bridge-builders, but they were among the regiments from the Army of the Cumberland that Sherman had chosen to accompany his march to the sea.[28]

Thomas had won a great victory at Nashville, but he was now being harassed by both Grant and the War Department as if he had accomplished only a minor task in routing the Confederate army. Telegrams chastised him not to allow the Rebels to escape, and intimated that he was not doing all he could to prevent that circumstance from taking place. The pursuit was being conducted through some of the most heavily foraged areas of the Confederacy. Supplies were almost nonexistent for man or beast, and Wilson's cavalry had already worn out more than 5,000 horses. Thomas was indignant over the apparent lack of confidence in his actions, and the implied tardiness of his pursuit. On December 21, he sent General Halleck a telegram in which he not only defended himself, but fairly stated the reasons for problems his army was encountering. He also took the opportunity to officially complain for the situation he had inherited in Tennessee:

> General Hood's army is being pursued as rapidly and as vigorously as it is possible for one army to pursue another. We cannot control the elements.... I am doing all in my power to crush Hood's army and, if it be possible, will destroy it. But pursuing an enemy through an exhausted country, over mud roads completely drenched with heavy rains, is no child's play.... I hope, in urging me to push the enemy, the department remembers that General Sherman took with him the complete organization of the Military District of the Mississippi, well equipped in every respect, leaving me only two corps partially stripped of transportation.... This army is willing to submit to any sacrifice to crush Hood's army or to strike any other blow which may contribute to the destruction of the rebellion."[29]

Possibly, in an effort to redress the wrongful harassing Thomas had been enduring, and to soothe his ruffled feathers, Stanton sent a telegram to Thomas on December 24 informing him that he had just been nominated to become a major general in the regular army: "With great pleasure I inform you, that for your skill, courage and conduct in the recent brilliant military operation under your command, the President has directed your nomination ... as a major general in the United States Army, to fill the only vacancy in that grade. No official duty has been performed by me with more satisfaction, and no commander has more justly earned promotion by devoted, disinterested and valuable services to his country."[30]

Thomas's delicate sense of pride was aroused by this apparent peace offering. So far as he was concerned, he had long ago earned the recognition now so belatedly being given. He had been passed over following Mill Springs, Stones River, Chickamauga, and Chattanooga, and had been forced to watch as Meade, Sherman, and Sheridan were promoted ahead of him. Sheridan's promotion must have been particularly galling to Thomas, as it had come recently as a reward for his victory at Cedar Creek, Virginia, a battle that had almost been a Union disaster because Sheridan was absent from his army. Now, owing to George B. McClellan's resignation from the army, another commission at the grade of major general was open, and Thomas's services were being tardily recognized. When an officer suggested that the promotion was better late than never, Thomas responded "I suppose it is better late than never but it is too late to be appreciated. I earned this at Chattanooga."[31] Nevertheless, he tried to compose as dignified a response to Stanton as he could muster. "I am profoundly sensible of the kind expressions in your telegram," he wrote, "instructing me that the President had directed my name to be sent to the Senate ... and I beg you to assure the President and yourself that your approbation of my services is of more value to me than the commission itself."[32] Thomas's feelings were compounded when rumors began to be reported to him that Grant had ordered his removal from command of the army prior to the battle. The general viewed the promotion as a sort of apology for an intended slight, making it next to meaningless. One of his officers later said, "He [Thomas] feels very sore at the rumored intentions to relieve him and the major generalcy does not cicatrize the wound."[33] The pursuit of Hood's army was continuing, but focus was shifting to matters of politics and intrigue, and Thomas was not adept in either category.

On Christmas Day, the Confederates crossed the Tennessee River at Bainbridge, Alabama, near Florence, and continued the march toward Tupelo, Mississippi, Hood's final destination. Forrest, still with the rear guard, made a stand at Pulaski that same day, and maneuvered advance elements of the pursuit into attacking him on December 26. The Federals were repulsed and Forrest captured a cannon before crossing the Tennessee himself the following day. On December 29, General Thomas issued orders to call off the pursuit, and the Nashville campaign finally came to an end.[34]

Thomas had been on the verge of dismissal on December 14. Now he was hailed as one of the greatest generals in the Union army. He had accomplished far more than Lincoln or Grant could have hoped for, and had done so at an amazingly small cost to his own army. One of the Confederacy's two great armies had been all but eliminated. The once-proud Army of Tennessee had been reduced to a shadow of its old self, and would never again mount any legitimate threat to Union intentions in the middle or deep South. Thomas's victory limited the Confederacy to one formidable military force east of the Mississippi — the Army of Northern Virginia — and it signaled the irreversible death knell for any remaining hopes of Southern independence. So complete was the victory at Nashville that many military historians rank it second only to Austerlitz as the most decisive victory in military history. George Henry Thomas had organized the army. He had devised the plan of operation. He had refused to be bullied into assuming the offensive before he was ready to do so, and now he had gained one of the most significant victories of the war. From Bunker Hill, Virginia, to Nashville, Tennessee, he had proven himself to be among the most dependable and talented officers on either side, and had the distinction of being the only high ranking commander in the war to never make a serious mistake on the battlefield.

Thomas received congratulations from Sherman dated December 25, after Sherman's army had reached the sea. The message gives insight into what might have been a guilty conscience on the part of Sherman over the precarious situation he had left Thomas in when he marched in the opposite direction from the only legitimate enemy force in the region, and left his subordinate to his own devices to deal with the threat. "I have heard of all your operations up to about the 17th and I do not believe your own wife was more happy at the result than I was. Had any misfortune befallen you I should have reproached myself for taking away so large a portion of the army and leaving you too weak to cope with Hood."[35] Clearly, Sherman was admitting that he had placed Thomas in a dangerous situation, and he was justifiably relieved that events had gone in such a manner to relieve him of any questions of poor judgment on his part. Had Hood been victorious, the entire nation would have demanded to know why Sherman had marched his army away from the enemy and left Tennessee open to invasion. As it was, Thomas's ability as a field commander not only saved Sherman's reputation, it made him look like a genius.

Thomas had thoroughly thrashed Hood's army at Nashville. He had all but eliminated it as a threat to Union forces. He had driven the remnants of the once-mighty host completely out of the state, but that was not enough to earn him the respect or consideration of his superiors. Grant continued to hound him, and to insinuate that he was too slow to be an effective commander. When Sherman suggested that Thomas be ordered to pursue Hood to Selma, Alabama, Grant refused to even consider it. In a message to Sherman, he said, "His pursuit of Hood indicated a sluggishness that satisfies me he would never do to conduct one of your campaigns."[36] One of Sherman's campaigns! Exactly what had Sherman faced in his March to the Sea? His powerful army had marched at will through underdefended or undefended enemy territory, with no threat of engagement. The Confederate forces his army had faced were so inconsequential that they could do little other than annoy his movements and try to keep his bummers and foragers from straying too far from the main body. Some state militia, a few scattered garrison commands, and Joe Wheeler's cavalry were all that remained in Georgia. The principal Confederate army was in Tennessee, facing Thomas. Sherman's men had marched through Georgia virtually unopposed, because the Confederates had no sizeable force in the state to oppose them with. It had been a leisurely hike to Savannah, with no major obstacles to disrupt the journey. Moreover, Sherman's men were granted a full month to rest and recuperate once they reached Savannah, with the blessings of Grant. During this same tine, Thomas's men had fought in three major engagements, and had conducted a pursuit of the enemy in horrendous winter conditions, but their commander was being ridiculed for his "sluggishness."

Thomas desired to give his army a rest following the end of the pursuit. He ordered his forces to go into winter quarters: Smith's Corps at Eastport, Mississippi; Wood's Corps at Hunstville and Athens; Wilson's Cavalry near Hunstville; and Schofield's Corps at Dalton, Georgia. But Thomas's men were to receive no such rest as Sherman's men were being allowed to enjoy. On December 31, General Halleck sent a telegram to Thomas informing him, "Lieutenant-General Grant does not intend that your army should go into winter quarters. It must be ready for active operations in the field."[37] These orders did not indicate that Thomas himself was to lead his army in any further campaigns against the enemy. The orders only meant that Thomas's men would be used. Their commander would shortly find himself almost without a command. Sherman had pressed Grant to provide him with additional men before he resumed his march from Savannah, heading north through the Carolinas. Grant responded by ordering Schofield's Corps to report to Sherman, along the coast. This addition would swell Sherman's available force to approximately 89,000 men. Thomas was next ordered to send reinforcements to Major General Edward S. Canby, who was conducting a campaign against Mobile. General Smith's divisions were sent south, closely followed by a division of

Wilson's cavalry, under Brigadier General James F. Knipe. Another portion of Wilson's cavalry, under the command of Major General George Stoneman, was ordered to conduct a campaign in east Tennessee and the Carolinas, destroying railroads and raiding the countryside in support of Sherman's movements. General Wilson observed that Thomas's forces had been "scattered," and wondered what the high command "counted upon or expected from Thomas," who was once again left with little more than a skeleton command.[38] Wilson himself had received instructions that he was to send a force into the heart of Alabama to occupy Forrest's command, and to destroy the infrastructure of the Confederacy's coal and iron producing capability in that area. Thomas had planned for just the sort of raid that Wilson was ordered to make, and had already given orders for its commencement prior to this time, directing that Wilson consolidate and organize his forces in preparation for the raid. By the first of March, Wilson had collected together some 27,000 men, of whom 20,000 were mounted. Of these, 15,000 were armed with Spencer repeating rifles. Wilson commented that it was "the largest body of cavalry ever collected on the American continent."[39] It was also the best armed and best equipped. Wilson prevailed upon Thomas to be able to make the raid into Alabama with his entire command, promising that he would destroy Forrest and capture Tuscaloosa, Montgomery, and Selma if allowed to do so. Thomas agreed with Wilson's assessment and forwarded the suggestion to Grant, who approved the plan, with one major stipulation. Wilson was directed to make his raid as an independent commander, removed from the supervision of Thomas. The largest remaining force in the Army of the Cumberland was not to be under the control of the commander of that army, and Wilson was to effectively assume Thomas's rightful position at it head. Thomas was confident in Wilson's abilities as a field commander, and offered no opposition to the new command arrangement. In the end, Wilson took 12,500 men in a highly successful rampage through Alabama that accomplished all that he had promised. His troopers captured Selma on April 2, the same day that news arrived of the evacuation of Richmond by Robert E. Lee's Army of Northern Virginia. A detachment of his cavalry was even responsible for capturing President Jefferson Davis after he had fled south from Richmond to reestablish the seat of the Confederate government in Alabama. This detachment was acting upon a tip from Thomas's spy network, one of the most sophisticated in the Union army.

During all this time, Thomas had been allowed to remain idle, with no assignments from his superiors and virtually no command at his disposal. He had ordered one hundred guns to be fired at Capitol Hill in Nashville when word of the capture of Richmond arrived, but he had become little more than a spectator of the great events that were unfolding around the country. When Lee surrendered at Appomattox, Thomas sent orders to his commanders at Chattanooga, Knoxville, Memphis, and Murfreesboro that they were to fire two hundred guns at noon on April 10 in commemoration of the event. When word arrived from Wilson that he had captured Montgomery on April 12, Thomas sent his congratulations, along with a letter proposing formal surrender to Lieutenant General Richard Taylor, commanding the Confederate forces in the Military Division of the West. Thomas offered Taylor the same terms that Grant had given Lee. Wilson was miles away from Taylor, however, who surrendered his army to General Canby near Mobile. With hostilities all but over, Thomas planned a parade to be held in Nashville on April 15 to celebrate the end of the war, but the festivities were canceled when word arrived in Nashville that same day that President Lincoln had been assassinated. The intended celebration became a show of mourning. Thomas ordered every flag in the city to be put to half mast, and directed the artillery at Capitol Hill to fire at intervals of one minute until nightfall. He also wired Andrew Johnson a message conveying his condolences and support: "With profound sorrow for the calamity which has befallen the nation permit me to tender to you as President of the United States assurances of my profound esteem and hearty support."[41]

Wilson continued his raid to Columbus, then headed east toward Macon, Georgia, gathering in large numbers of prisoners along the way. On April 20, at Macon, he accepted the surrender of 3,500 more Confederates. On May 6, the Confederacy officially ceased to exist when Secretary of War Breckinridge ordered all Southern forces still in the field to lay down their arms and surrender. A few small bands, like Stand Waite's cavalry in the Oklahoma Territory, and the Thomas Legion in North Carolina, refused to obey the order, but by June even these small remnants had been taken in tow and the fighting was finally over.

Following the official surrender on May 6, the Union army began a wholesale discharge of many of the volunteer regiments in the service. Thomas's 4th Corps was ordered to Nashville, where it was demobilized and the men mustered out of the army. The veterans passed in review as their old commander watched fifty-four regiments, numbering just over 5,000 men, march by him for the final time. They had served together since the early days of the Shiloh Campaign, and had won shared glory on the bloody fields of Stones River, Chickamauga, Chattanooga, the Atlanta campaign, and Nashville. Now, many of these veterans were looking upon the face of the leader who had so ably guided their movements for the last time. One of their number remembered, "Reverently and affectionately they saluted the old hero as they reached the reviewing stand."[42]

The following morning, Thomas set to paper sentiments that his reserved character would not have allowed him voice aloud:

> The General Commanding the Department takes pride in conveying to the Fourth Army

General George H. Thomas in a picture taken in the latter stages of the war. The effects of several years of hard campaigning can be clearly seen on his care-worn face (United States Army Military History Institute).

corps the expression of his admiration, excited by their brilliant and martial display at the Review yesterday.

As the battalions of your magnificent corps swept successfully before the eye, the coldest heart must have been warmed with interest in contemplation of these men, who had passed through the varied and shifting scenes of this great, modern tragedy, who had stemmed with unyielding breasts the Rebel tide threatening to engulf the landmarks of Freedom; and who, bearing on their bronzed and furrowed brows the ennobling marks of years of hardship, suffering and privation, undergone in defense of freedom and the integrity of the Union, could still preserve the light step and wear the cheerful expression of youth."[43]

When the remaining members of the 4th Corps boarded steamers for New Orleans, Thomas was left with but a small garrison force in Nashville. The war was over, and he was virtually without a command. The recently promoted major general was left to await a new assignment in the postwar days of Reconstruction, and he hoped that it would be befitting his rank and experience.

Chapter Sixteen

The Final Years

Thomas was to first learn of his postwar assignment when General Steedman returned to Nashville from an official visit to Washington. Steedman had with him a map of the United States, on which had been drawn the military divisions that were to be imposed during Reconstruction. The nation had been divided into four sections, with a major general assigned to the command of each. Halleck was given the Pacific coast, Sheridan received the region west of the Mississippi River, Sherman got the Midwest and the South, and Meade was assigned to the Atlantic coast down to Georgia. Thomas, the fifth and final major general in the regular army, found that he had been excluded from receiving a military division. Instead, he was being assigned to command only a department within Sherman's division. This indignity was too much to bear. Thomas refolded the map, placed his fist upon it, and made up his mind that this most recent insult would not be allowed to pass. Thomas asked General John Miller, commander of the garrison of Nashville, to travel to Washington to lay his case before the president. Miller had become quite familiar with Johnson while he was governor of Tennessee. Thomas told him to relay to the president "that during the war I permitted the national authorities to do what they pleased with me. The life of the nation was then at stake, and it was not proper to press questions of rank, but now that the war is over ... I demand a command suited to my rank, or I do not want any."[1]

Upon his arrival in Washington, Miller secured a meeting with Johnson, and fairly stated Thomas's objection to the posting he had received. Miller went so far as to suggest that Thomas be permitted to command a military division made up of the various states he had served in during the war. Johnson agreed with Miller that Thomas should have an assignment befitting both his rank and his substantial service to the nation. "You know my appreciation of General Thomas," he said, as he took a pencil in hand and drew a line around the boundaries of Kentucky, Tennessee, Mississippi, Alabama, and Georgia, and indicated to Miller that this would be the military division Thomas would preside over.[2] The new alignment took away a large portion of the divisions that had previously been assigned to Sherman and Sheridan, and meant that Thomas would control the military aspects of Reconstruction in more Southern states than any other commander. Perhaps Johnson intended this to be the case, and it was more than a random drawing upon a map. Thomas was well-known to Johnson, and had earned the respect of the president through his devotion to the Union and common-sense approach to his duty. He was also, like Johnson, Southern-born, and could be counted on to administer his division in a just and unbiased fashion. One is left to speculate as to why Johnson favored Thomas by giving him the division he did, but it is certain that he did so despite the fact that the other four major generals ranked Thomas and enjoyed much stronger political ties.

While Thomas's military rule over his division would be a fair one, it would also conform to the general's personal beliefs concerning the Confederacy and disunion. He had felt all along that the secession of the Southern states had been illegal and in violation of the Constitution. He viewed the resulting war to be a revolt or rebellion, not a revolution, and held the Southern leaders to be traitors to their country. It was only through the generosity of a magnanimous people, he believed, that the defeated Confederates were not punished as criminals. In his beliefs, Thomas echoed words that would have been welcomed by the most ardent of the Radical Republicans who sought to punish the South, but his actions showed a clemency that removed himself from any alliance with this faction of the ruling party and placed him firmly in the camp of the moderates.

One such example would be the aid and assistance he gave to former officers of the Confederate army, and to their families. Thomas petitioned on behalf of the widow of General Richard S. Ewell, and sought presidential pardons for past generals James P. Longstreet, Paul O. Hebert, Gideon J. Pillow, William T. Wofford, and Josiah Gorgas. He even took up the cause of Alexander H. Stephens, the deposed vice president of the Confederacy, who was languishing in prison.[2] Thomas's disposition toward granting forgiveness to ex–Confederates clearly separated him from the more vengeful radicals, even though he agreed with many of their principles on a philosophical level.

One of the more troubling difficulties Thomas was forced to deal with in his division was the open hostility between Southern whites and the newly emancipated Negroes. These tensions were intensified because a large number of the occupation troops in the states under his control were members of United States Colored regiments. The vast majority of the white regiments had been mustered out of the service, their terms of enlistment having expired. Since most of the black units had been raised later in the war, most of them still had time remaining on their enlistments, and they were retained to garrison and occupy points all over the South. Southern resentment of military occupation was multiplied by the fact that most of the soldiers performing the duty were ex-slaves, and confrontations with blacks, both in and out of the army, began to erupt throughout the South.

In Louisiana, in Sheridan's division, a convention to enfranchise the black citizens of the state and adopt the Fourteenth Amendment was met with violence. One black orator proclaimed "I want you to come in your power. I want no cowards to come.... We have 300,000 black men with white hearts. Also 100,000 good true Union white men who will fight beside the black race against the hell-hound rebels.... We are 400,000 to 300,000 and can not only whip but exterminate the other party.... The streets of New Orleans will run with blood." With such rhetoric being bandied about, the flames were fanned for open confrontation and bloodshed.

When a black man participating in a parade of celebration was jostled by a white man, the marcher struck the white, and the blaze went out of control. A policeman tried to arrest a young black boy for inciting trouble, and a shot from the marchers rang out in front of Mechanics' Institute Hall, where the marchers were supposed to meet. The military guard that had been ordered to guard the premises had been ordered to arrive there at a later time, leaving the situation to be dealt with by local police. The initial shot had caused all of the officers at the headquarters to hurry to the site, and when they arrived, they were pelted with bricks and scattered firing from small arms. The marchers then fled into the hall and its anticipated safety. But the fury of the police, as well as many intoxicated white civilians who had gathered, had been raised, and what followed was one of the worst massacres to take place during peacetime in America. The police and the drunken mob stormed the hall, and by the time the horror was ended, 534 black men and three whites were dead. Another 150, mostly blacks, had been wounded.[3]

Instances of violence against blacks were to be found throughout the South, to a lesser degree. In Thomas's division, a race riot erupted in Memphis, sparked by an altercation between Negro troops and Irish policemen, and lasted for three days. Some forty blacks were killed during the rioting. Thomas exerted firm control over the situation, and arrested a number of individuals responsible for the violence, but he was blocked in his efforts to seek punishment for the offenders by a grand jury that "failed to take any notice whatever of the offenders or of the riot."[4] Clashes between blacks and whites even took place within the ranks of the Union army, where white troops showed a particular resentment for their black comrades. All in all, Thomas supported the black troops, and felt that they were performing their duties in an efficient and soldierly manner. He commented on this in a letter to President Johnson, in which he stated, "As a general rule the negro soldiers are under good discipline. I have required all commanding officers to keep their commands in good discipline and ... I believe they have. I believe in the majority of cases of collision between whites and negro soldiers that the white man has attempted to bully the negro, for it is exceedingly repugnant to Southerners to have negro soldiers in their midst & some are so foolish as to vent their anger upon the negro because he is a soldier."[5]

The feeling of resentment Thomas cited served as the basis for the creation of the Ku Klux Klan, which was organized as a potent force of political intimidation in the Maxwell House Hotel in Nashville, in May of 1867. Nathan Bedford Forrest, Thomas's old nemesis from the war, was elected to the national leadership of the Klan as its Grand Wizzard. In Tennessee, the Klan concentrated on influencing blacks and Unionist whites not to vote through midnight forays in which threats and violence were employed. Thomas believed that the Klan was trying to control Southern elections by means of its violent tactics, and took steps to identify and gather information on all known members, which he forwarded to Washington. Once again, his efforts to control his division were blunted by the civil authority, however. Washington did little to combat the Klan, and the eastern press actually discounted Thomas's findings and reported them to be exaggerations. In Tennessee, a law enacted to authorize local sheriffs to organize efforts to arrest Klansmen met with shameful results because so many local officials were members of the society themselves. In September of 1867, Thomas was called to Nashville to protect the polls for a local election that was threatened by violence. Mayor W. Matt Brown had organized the city police in an effort to obstruct the fall election, and Thomas was compelled to shift additional Union soldiers there in order to avoid a clash between army guards and the local constabulatory.

Despite the problems he was experiencing, Thomas proved to be an able administrator within his military division. He was also a favorite with President Johnson because he rarely took action without first seeking permission to do so from the government. This was in stark contrast to the actions of Sherman and Sheridan, who regularly took action, then advised the government of the results. Thomas performed his duties as a servant of the civil authority, not as a military despot enforcing martial law. Sheridan, on the other hand, was particularly heavy-handed in the administration of his division. He regularly removed duly elected officials from office because he did not approve of them, and ordered numerous political arrests within his division. General Grant stamped his approval on all of Sheridan's actions, setting up a power struggle between himself and President Johnson. When Johnson finally tired of Sheridan's heavy-handed and illegal actions, he sought to have him removed as a division commander. Grant sided with Sheridan and protested the dismissal, stating that he had performed his assigned duties in an adequate manner. Johnson countered by using Thomas as an example of what a proper administrator should be, declaring that he "has not failed, under the most trying circumstances, to enforce the laws, to preserve the peace and order, to encourage the restoration of civil authority, and to promote as far as possible a spirit of reconcilliation."[6] Sheridan was removed, but Thomas declined to accept responsibility for the states that had previously been under his control. He cited as his reasons his belief that reconstruction efforts in Louisiana and Texas would be retarded by his appointment, and begged to be excused because of a recent doctor's discovery of a liver ailment, causing him great pain in his side. He also suggested that Winfield S. Hancock would be would be a suitable replacement for Sheridan. The government publicly announced that Thomas's refusal of the post was based on health problems, and all parties were allowed to save face.[7]

The controversy over the removal of Sheridan placed Thomas in a position he neither sought nor wanted in the arena of national politics. Grant had become the standard bearer of the radical wing of the Republican party, and it was widely felt that he would run for president in the 1868 election. Moderates within the government were looking for a candidate who could possibly wrest the nomination away from Grant, and Thomas seemed a likely contender. Early in 1867, the general began receiving messages from various political leaders advocating him to seek the executive office. Thomas rebuked these advances, stating that he did not have the required experience to consider occupying such a lofty office. This argument was countered with the observation that Grant had no more experience than himself, and he was implored that it was his duty to the country to run. But it was more than just a lack of experience that kept Thomas from throwing his hat into the political ring. He really detested political intrigue, and his military background made him ill-suited to canvassing support for himself or his policies. In a statement avowing his refusal to be forwarded as a candidate for the party, he also took opportunity to speak out against the Radical Republicans' persecution of President Johnson that would eventually lead to impeachment proceedings:

> I have not the necessary control over my temper, nor have I the faculty of yielding to a policy and working to advance it unless convinced within myself that it is right and honest. My habits of life ... are such as to make it repugnant to my self respect to have to induce people to do their duty by persuasive measures. If there is anything that enrages me more than another, it is to see an obstinate and self-willed man oppose what is right morally & under law, simply because, under the law, he cannot be compelled to do what is right.... I have no taste whatever for politics, and besides, restrictions have recently been thrown around the President by Congress which virtually deprive him of his just powers and rights.... I could never consent to be deprived of rights and privileges guaranteed ... by the Constitution as long as the Constitution itself remains unaltered.[8]

Thomas had sought neither Sheridan's removal nor political support for high office, but both incidents served to further the gap between himself and Grant. He had never been among Grant's chosen favorites, and now he posed a potential threat to Grant's political aspirations. Fully aware that Thomas's service during the war had placed him in a position of being almost above reproach, Grant knew no overt attacks against him could even be considered. But covert actions were another matter. Once more, Grant, Sherman, Sheridan, and their minions revived the theme of Thomas's slowness in articles and speeches written during this period. These attacks were conducted in a way that was calculated to create an unflattering image, while taking care not to enrage the masses of old soldiers who held Thomas with almost reverent admiration. Thomas was portrayed by Grant and his supporters as being indecisive and ponderous in his activities, and few mentions of his name were not accompanied by derisive nicknames like "Old Slow Trot" or "Pap Thomas." Using false innuendo, Thomas's detractors publicly extolled his virtues while they planted the seeds criticism and doubt. Thomas was portrayed as a kindly old uncle who did not possess the traits or abilities to perform a job, but was successful in spite of himself. When his accomplishments were praised, it was always in an understated manner that included reference to his supposed slowness and lack of activity. Even his nick-name of "The Rock of Chickamauga" served to promote the immobile and stationary image that his detractors wished to convey.

As Grant, Sherman, and Sheridan were the darlings of the controlling faction of the Republican Party, and because of their status as national heroes, their words, and those of their followers, were circulated far and wide by the newspapers and tabloids of the era. Far less coverage was given to speeches and papers given by officers and soldiers who were most familiar with the general's character and accomplishments. Speeches and papers presented to the Society of the Army of the Cumberland by those who knew Thomas best were largely unreported outside the circle of veterans who adored the commander that had led them victoriously through the war. The sentiments presented by Grant and his followers would become the prevailing image by which history would view Thomas and his accomplishments, and would become one of the main reasons why this general who was victorious in all his military endeavors became relegated to the second team of leadership by most historians of the war.

Hated and resented by many of his Southern countrymen, whom he had abandoned to stand by the Union, and beset by detractors from within the government he had forsaken all to save, Thomas found himself to be a man almost without a country. Only the men who had served under him kept a watchful eye on his reputation. Even his former enemies recognized that the treatment he was receiving was unfair. Once, in Louisville, Kentucky, it came to be known that John Bell Hood and Thomas were staying at the same hotel. Hood expressed his desire to talk with Thomas and a meeting was arranged. Thomas heard the clatter of Hood's crutches coming down the hallway and threw open his door to greet his old enemy from more than a dozen campaigns. Solicitous of painful wounds Hood still bore, he tenderly helped him into his room, where the two men spent an hour talking over old times and reliving the moments that had earned them eternal fame. When Hood returned to his own room, he was overcome with emotion, and was heard to remark: "Thomas is a grand man. He should have remained with us, where he would have been appreciated and loved."[9]

In 1866, Grant became temporary Secretary of War when President Johnson attempted to remove Stanton from that office. This left vacant the recently revived grade of lieutenant general, and Sherman was quickly nominated for the promotion in the latter part of 1867. Johnson submitted Thomas's name to the Senate for confirmation at the rank of brevet lieutenant general and full general. It was Johnson's intention to replace Grant with Thomas as general-in-chief of the army, with a view to making him the permanent Secretary of War. Thomas caught wind of the intrigue, however, and on February 22, 1868, he telegraphed Senator Benjamin Wade, leader of the Radical Republicans, a tactful message to remove his name from consideration. "My services since the war do not merit so high a compliment, and it is too late now for it to be regarded as a compliment if conferred for services during the war." The next day, he sent a similar telegram to President Johnson, and the matter of his promotion was brought to a close.[10] No matter how much he might have desired to secure advancement, or how he possibly felt such a promotion would make amends for the times he had been passed over in favor of officers junior to himself, his integrity and sense of fair play would not allow him to accept a commission that was rooted in political intrigue and power struggles rather than based upon merit and accomplishment.

While he turned down advancement for himself, Thomas personally saw to the advancement of a particular family he felt responsible for back in Virginia. In 1857, while stationed in New Orleans, he had purchased a female slave as a servant for his wife when one of her white servants suddenly left her employment. In 1860, he expressed a desire to set the woman free, but Frances opposed the manumission. With war clouds on the horizon, Thomas was at a loss over what to do with the slave. He felt responsible for her situation, and did not want to sell her to another master, and neither he nor Frances could take her with them, so she was sent to Thomaston. After the conclusion of hostilities, Thomas sent for her. By this time she was married, with a family, and Thomas had them all brought to Nashville, where he secured their employment and started them on the road to a new life.[11]

In 1868, the Ku Klux Klan once more demanded Thomas's attention in Tennessee. Clandestine activities intensified as Klan members tried to influence the outcome of the fall elections, and Thomas notified the War Department that he was ready and able to take action against this latest round of intimidation. He was informed that since Tennessee had been readmitted to the Union two years earlier (the first Southern state to regain its place in the Union), only the state legislature could request assistance from the Federal government. Not even the personal appeals of Governor W.G. Brownlow would suffice. In June, when Congressman Samuel M. Arnall was accosted by a band of masked Klansmen who threatened him with death, Brownlow implored Thomas to garrison six counties of the state with Federal troops. Thomas declined, due to his prior correspondence with Washington, and informed the governor that the state must attend to its own internal affairs. The legislature responded by passing strong laws against the Klan, and by calling for additional men for the state militia. But the local militia proved inept at controlling the violence, which only intensified as the size of the militia increased. At length, Thomas was authorized by Washington to take action, and he sent troops into twenty-one of the state's counties to assure the lawful conduct of the fall elections. The Klansmen were not anxious to tangle with regular army troops, and their outrages diminished substantially while Thomas's men were in place. Once the troops were recalled following the election, the atrocities began anew. But the objective of the Klansmen, to influence the outcome of the election, had been thwarted by Thomas and his men.

The violence in Tennessee had become so acute that public opinion began to be swayed against the Klan, even among former Confederates. Many desperadoes and outlaws masked their crimes by wearing the hooded garb of the Klan and passing themselves off as Klansmen, so that the secret society eventually came to be blamed for all the lawlessness in the state. Nathan Bedford Forrest witnessed the deteriorating situation and decided that nothing good could come from the continued existence of the organization. He therefore called for the Klan to be dissolved, and resigned as it leader. Members in other states were slow to accept Forrest's conclusions, however. When Forrest was later called to testify to Congress about the Klan he said, "I am disposed to do all I can to try and fetch these troubles to an end.... I tried to do my duty as a soldier, and since I have been out of the war I have tried to do my duty as a citizen. I have done more probably than any other man in the South to suppress these difficulties and keep them down.... I want our country quiet once more, and I want to see our people united and working together harmoniously."[12]

The mission against the Klan in the fall elections proved to be Thomas's last important duty in the South. In November of 1868, he was called to Washington to preside over a court of inquiry hearing charges of misconduct leveled at Major General Alexander B. Dyer. Dyer, a fellow Virginian and inventor of the Dyer artillery shell, had served as the army's chief ordnance officer in the final phases of the war, after a term as head of the Springfield National Armory. He had been an efficient and capable officer, and had performed his duties in an exemplary manner, but there were so many charges leveled by dishonest contractors and disgruntled investors that Congress insisted on looking into the matter, and Dyer requested a court of inquiry. The duties of the court would engage Thomas for six months, as a steady parade of "political demagogues, charlatan inventors, and knavish contractors" took the stand to testify. In the end, Dyer was exonerated of all charges, and continued to give good service to the Ordnance Department until 1874.[13]

Thomas's time on the court was pleasantly interrupted in December, when a reunion of the western armies was held in Chicago to commemorate the fourth anniversary of the victory at Nashville. Thomas was appointed chairman of the festivities, which were attended by both Grant and Sherman. Some 2,000 former officers and men attended the celebration, and their boisterous activities drowned out the speakers at a banquet held at the Chamber of Commerce Hall. The notable exception was when Thomas stepped up to the podium. When their old commander was announced, the men roared with cheers and applause. As one witness remembered it, the greeting was "such a storm of applause as hardly once in a century falls upon human ears." When Thomas began to speak, his old soldiers listened in silence, and when he ended his brief speech with a toast, the uproar became almost deafening.[14]

President-elect Grant was on something of a victory tour, having just recently won the election, and it was quite appropriate that he was in attendance with Sherman and Thomas at this celebration. Grant's election left vacant the position of general of the army, and all felt sure that Sherman would be elevated into

General John Schofield. When Thomas protested that Schofield was being given a military division that rightfully should have gone to him, President Grant responded by appointing Schofield to be his Secretary of War (United States Army Military History Institute).

that spot. Sherman's promotion would mean that there was an open grade of lieutenant general, and most thought that either Thomas or Meade would be named to fill it. But Grant had other plans. He chose to bestow the rank upon Sheridan, passing over Halleck, Meade, and Thomas. General William W. Averrill, who had served under Sheridan, made his feelings known as to the question of who was deserving of the rank. He noted that Grant's "meager praise of Thomas which he takes some pains to discount afterwards is rather Curious when contrasted with his Constant and unconditional praise of Sheridan." The injustice being done to Thomas made him wonder whether it was possible to believe in any written history "after seeing a page or two of our own made." Thomas not only accepted the selection of Sheridan to become a lieutenant general, he had anticipated it. Noting that Sheridan's commission as a major general predated his own, he said that he had "always supposed the President would exercise the right to appoint his friend to an office in preference to another whom he did not particularly like."[15]

When the court of inquiry finally adjourned in March of 1869, Thomas found a more troublesome situation than Sheridan's promotion to provoke his ire. General Halleck was being transferred from the west coast, and Schofield was being sent to replace him as commander of the Military Division of the Pacific. Thomas's division had by this time been pared down to only the size of a department, and he protested a junior being assigned to command of a division that he felt rightly belonged to him. True, he would rather have been assigned to the Division of the Atlantic, so that he could be closer to his family, but Meade held that post. The Division of the Missouri was also preferable, but the newly created lieutenant general was stationed there. The vacated Division of the Pacific was the only open posting commensurate with Thomas's rank and service, and he was not about to allow Schofield, of all people, to be appointed to a position that should have been his. Thomas contacted Sherman to protest the appointment, and threatened to make his protest public if a change in the assignment was not made. Sherman cowed at this threat and secured the approval of Grant to name Thomas to the post in Schofield's stead. Grant completed his snubbing of Thomas by making Schofield his superior anyway by naming him to be Secretary of War instead of a divisional commander.[16]

Thomas reported for duty at San Francisco, where his appointment was heralded with praise from an admiring public. He was met in the city by his old friend, Erasmus D. Keyes, who noted that the years of hardship caused by the Civil War had left their mark upon the general. Keyes found the change to be profound, especially in one who was still only fifty-two years of age. "White lines bordered his lips and his eyes had lost their wonted fires.... He made no complaint but applied himself with customary strictness to his duty."[17]

Thomas would occupy most of his time in travel while serving as commander of the Pacific division. In June, he began an inspection tour of the division, visiting forts in Nevada, Arizona, California, Idaho and Washington Territory. He would also visit recently purchased Alaska. His administration was competent and just, and he exercised good judgment in matters like suggesting that regulations be put in place by Congress for the fur trade in Alaska, and advocating that soldiers be posted in the new territory to monitor fortune seekers in the event a major gold discovery was made. In November of 1869, he reported in person to the War Department, at which time he made arrangements for Frances to accompany him back to California. His aides were overjoyed when he returned to San Francisco with his wife, as they had begun to worry over the general's declining health. Tired and worn to the bone from almost thirty years of continual military service, Thomas would log nearly 14,000 miles of travel during his short tenure as commander of the Military Division of the Pacific. Given the rugged travel conditions of the mid–1800s, that alone would have been enough to wear out a man half his age.

The couple had a few months of peaceful contentment in which to renew their relationship, but that was interrupted early in 1870 when the general came under assault from several different sources. First, there was a motion presented in the Tennessee Legislature that the portrait of Thomas that had been commissioned by the state to commemorate his victory at Nashville be sold. Though the motion was defeated by an overwhelming majority, it so infuriated Thomas that he offered to buy the portrait for the $1,000 the state had spent to commission it. He further stated that he would return a gold medal the legislature had presented to him as soon as he could make arrangements to retrieve it from the safe-deposit box where it was being kept in New York.

Hardly had his anger subsided from this episode before he read in the newspapers a statement from Halleck concerning his intended removal as commander of the army at Nashville in 1864. Though Thomas had long believed that Grant had desired such a move, he had never received official confirmation of it. Suspicion is one thing, confirmation is quite another. Knowledge that Grant had issued orders for his removal at Nashville now caused him to seethe, especially since the two principal architects of the intrigue were now his immediate superiors at the War Department and the White House.

An anonymous letter, probably written by Schofield, appeared in the *New York Tribune* on March 12, 1870, that attempted to defend Grant's actions in regard to Thomas. The letter claimed that Thomas had won no great victory at Nashville because the Confederates had been so thoroughly defeated at Franklin, by Schofield, that there was very little fight left in them by the time they arrived at the Tennessee capital. If it was Schofield who had written the letter, he would have been better served to have kept his comments to himself. When the letter was published it unleashed a storm of criticism from former veterans of the Nashville campaign. The letter had played pretty loose with the facts, and these were gladly provided by the officers and men who had been on those Tennessee fields facing Hood's army. Acts of omission were cited, and outright falsehoods were set right, as the men in blue rallied behind Thomas in yet another battle. In the end, what came to light for the public to ponder were the deficiencies Schofield had exhibited in command, and the expression of the veterans that replacing Thomas would have been a fatal error in judgment and a detriment to the Union cause.

Despite the resounding support he was receiving from around the country, Thomas felt obliged to respond to the letter himself. On March 28, 1870, he sat down at the desk in his office to gather his thoughts and compose a reply. His aide, Colonel Alfred L. Hough, left the office as the general was beginning the task. Three hours later, Hough returned to find that the general had almost completed the letter, but was desperately ill. Thomas walked to the outer door of the office, cried out, "I want air!" and fell to the floor. Three doctors were sent for, along with Frances. Stimulants were provided, which had the effect of restoring a measure of vitality to the general. Thomas complained of severe pain in the area of his right temple, but he insisted on rising from the couch upon which he had been placed. This time on his feet was short-lived, however, and he soon consented to resume his place on the couch. The general tried to have a conversation with Frances, but his strength was rapidly ebbing away. Colonel Hough noticed that Thomas was trying to tell him something and bent down to place his ear to his commander's mouth. The general, in a weakened tone, told him that he was feeling a little better and the pain had subsided. Thomas then looked at his wife, who leaned down to hear his last words to her. Colonel Hough stated that after speaking to Frances, the general began to struggle "with a convulsive movement about his chest, and try to rise, which he could not do. I called the physicians from the outer room, and one of them told me ... it was apoplexy.... He remained unconscious and gradually sank until twenty-five minutes past seven o'clock when he died. He did not struggle, only giving a convulsive spasm at the last moment."[18]

Thomas's body was taken to his room at the Lick House Hotel, where it was embalmed. He was placed in a casket with a glass plate over his face, after which he was allowed to lie in state at the Lick House. The outpouring of grief from the citizens of San Francisco was reported as being second only to that shown when Lincoln was assassinated, but Frances refused to permit any public demonstrations to be held in her husband's honor. Following an Episcopalian funeral service, the general's remains were transported to Oakland, where a waiting railroad car had been adorned with crape paper to receive them. The guns from the fort on Alcatraz Island sounded in reverent homage as the hero passed, and a British ship, the *Zealous*, which was anchored in the harbor, fired its own tribute in response, its flag flown at half mast.

The train made its way across the country, the passage marked by the booming of cannons from every military post along the route. When the funeral procession finally arrived at Troy, New York, it was greeted by an assemblage befitting the prestige of a head of state. President Grant and most of his cabinet were joined by Generals Sherman, Sheridan, and Meade, a joint delegation from Congress, the governor of New York, the state legislature, and thousands of soldiers, all waiting to pay a last tribute to the fallen leader. Sherman had ordered the broadcast of a public invitation: "All officers of the Army who can be spared from duty, all civil officers of the General and State Governments, members of the Volunteer armies, civil societies, and citizens generally, are invited to be present to manifest their respect."[19] Twenty-five railroad cars were needed just to bring in the contingent of New York National Guard from Utica. The thousands of mourners who had come to pay their last respects did not include a single member of the general's own family. His sisters told their neighbors, "Our brother died to us in '61," when he turned away from his native South and cast his lot with the Union.[20]

The final rites were administered by Bishop Doane, assisted by four other ministers, at St. Paul's Episcopal Church. The casket was then conveyed to the cemetery in a procession that included four brass bands and more than 140 carriages filled with dignitaries. The streets of Troy were lined deep with the solemn, bare-headed spectators, and above the dirges being played by the bands could be heard the sound of minute guns and tolling church bells. After a brief grave-side ritual, Thomas was laid to rest at Oakwood Cemetery, while rifles barked their saluting volleys. Plans were initiated almost immediately for the construction of the massive granite tomb that now occupies the sight, as well as an equestrian statue to be placed in Washington. It was thought that a little piece of home was needed to complete the general's resting place, and some acorns from the massive oaks at Thomaston were acquired to be planted on his plot. Evidently his sisters were not the only living things still holding a grudge over his decision to support the Union, however, for none of the acorns ever sprouted.

Back at Thomaston, his sister held on to a prized memento: the presentation sword that the people of Southampton County had given him for his services in the Mexican War. It had not been retained as a remembrance, however. Instead, she had kept it as an act of spite.

Thomas had many times written to her requesting the sword be sent to him, but all of his letters were returned unopened, as were the monetary gifts he had forwarded to help his family during their trying times after the war. His sisters had forgotten his name in 1861.

Historians of the war would begin to forget it at the time of his death. No officer did more to advance the cause of the Union, and few did as much, but Thomas was to become relegated to a position of unenviable obscurity as the war's great events were chronicled for posterity. He was not part of the Grant-Sherman-Sheridan circle that dominated the press. His political affiliations had been forever severed when he chose to fight for the Union. His family, neighbors and friends had all favored the Confederacy, and thought of him as a traitor. Only the men who served under him protected his reputation and honored his accomplishments, but then there is no greater tribute a leader can receive than to be honored by those who served under him, even though it was not sufficient to ensure the everlasting glory due this hero of the nation.

Thomas is not mentioned in the middle-school textbook *The American Journey*, published by McGraw Hill, nor in the college textbook *The Enduring Vision*, published by Heath. George Henry Thomas merits far greater consideration from the nation he devotedly served and did as much as anyone to save.

Conclusion

If the preceding pages have given the reader insight to the life of this Virginia gentleman and consummate professional soldier, then the historical aspect of this project has been fulfilled. If this work has kindled a sense of wonderment, or even outrage, that so fine a life could be relegated to a minor role in the history of our nation, then the writer's personal motives in writing this book will have been realized. George Henry Thomas deserves to be mentioned in the same breath with all of the other American folk heroes who emerged from the Civil War, and his name should be as easily recognized, even to those who are not history buffs, as are those of Grant, Sherman, and Sheridan. George Thomas was a man possessing great talent and ability, but he was also a man imbued with high moral character and strong convictions. His sense of honor and duty dictated every decision and action of his life. He made his choices in life based on what he felt to be just and honorable, with no consideration for what was easy or popular. Though he aspired to great heights and desired advancement and recognition, he never once betrayed his own sense of what was right to attain it. For him, promotion and recognition were only worthwhile if they were earned through good deeds and meritorious service. He neither courted nor accepted patronage from political power-brokers. In short, though he never received the measure of fame and glory he earned through his accomplishments, he earned all of the accolades that came his way. That is considerably more than can be said for many of the Civil War heroes who now eclipse the fame posterity has seen fit to bequeath him.

General Thomas is the only corps or army commander on either side never to have committed a serious mistake on the battlefield during the war. He never failed to hold or capture a position assigned to him. General Grant offered a back-handed compliment of his abilities when he wrote his memoirs, stating that "Thomas's dispositions were deliberately made, and always good. He could not be driven from a point he was given to hold." Grant then took away his praise by saying, "I do not believe that he could ever have conducted Sherman's army from Chattanooga to Atlanta against the defenses and the commander guarding that line, in 1864. On the other hand, if it had been given him to hold the line which Johnston tried to hold, neither that General nor Sherman, nor any other officer could have done it better."[1] Grant's assessment conveniently forgets that Thomas's army did most of the heavy lifting in the Atlanta campaign so that McPherson's and Schofield's armies could make the dashing end runs. He also omits the fact that it was Thomas's signal corps that broke the Confederate code, enabling Sherman to conduct his campaign with certain knowledge of Johnston's intentions and movements. Students of the war are fully able to see just how well Sherman conducted the campaign when the Southerners changed their code, just prior to the battle of

Kennesaw Mountain. One can only speculate what might have been the result if Johnston had not been replaced by Hood, and Sherman had been forced to conduct the remainder of the campaign against a formidable foe without the benefit of being able to read his signal messages.

For Thomas, it was not only a matter of doing the right thing on the battlefield, it was knowing what should be done before a battle was even fought. He proved his value as a strategist time and time again, and his advice always proved to be correct. When attached to Patterson's army in 1861, he had correctly suggested that the Union forces advance upon the cloud of dust seen in their front, indicating the march of Joe Johnston's army toward Manassas. Patterson balked at taking the offensive, and the result was the disastrous defeat of the Federal army at Manassas. Following his victory at Mill Springs, he pressed to be allowed to occupy east Tennessee, but was not allowed to do so. During the Perryville Campaign, he correctly divined the intentions of General Bragg and advised a concentration of Buell's army at McMinnville, which would have put it in position to prevent the invasion of Kentucky. In the Tullahoma campaign, he convinced Rosecrans not to make a frontal attack on the strong Confederate defenses at Shelbyville. He later warned Rosecrans that he was inviting disaster by pursuing Bragg's army from Chattanooga with his corps widely separated in mountainous, rugged terrain. Only the failure of Bragg's subordinate officers to launch an attack prior to September 19 prevented the Federal army from being destroyed in detail. At Chattanooga, he had helped to plan, and had already initiated, steps to relieve the siege and open a new line of supply, before Grant and Sherman arrived on the scene. He had pushed for an assault on the Confederate left, instead of the right, as Grant adopted, and which Sherman had failed to carry out. Twice at Chattanooga, he and his army had saved Grant's reputation and the Federal army from disaster, the first time by means of an attack they didn't make, and the second by making an attack they were not supposed to. At Snake Springs Gap, he suggested the exact strategy Sherman employed in prying Johnston out of his defenses at Rocky Face, but Sherman decided to use a force inadequate to accomplish the desired end result of cutting off the Confederates' retreat. After the fall of Atlanta, he once again suggested a plan that Sherman took as his own, a march through the heart of Georgia. Thomas intended the march to be a raid in force, conducted by his own Army of the Cumberland, while Sherman's armies kept a tight hold on Hood. Sherman decided to conduct the march himself, with the bulk of the Union forces in the region, leaving Thomas to defend against Hood as best he could with whatever castoffs Sherman saw fit to leave behind.

It is undeniable that Thomas not only did the right thing on the battlefields on which he fought, he also made all of the right calls in the campaigns in which he was engaged. Had he been in command of the Army of the Cumberland prior to Chattanooga, the history of the war in the west would probably have been far different from the one we now read about. The most heavily reported and famous battles of the war were fought in the east, but the majority of historians agree that the Civil War was won in the West. Had Thomas been in command of the Army of the Cumberland early on, how much sooner could the war have been brought to a close, and how much less would have been its cost in blood? Historian Albert Castel, in his book *Decision in the West: The Atlanta Campaign of 1864*, concluded, "Had Thomas' personal relationship with Grant permitted him to command in Georgia in 1864, almost surely the Union victory would have been easier, quicker, and more complete."[2] Historian Thomas B. Buell believes that if Thomas had been in command, the Atlanta campaign would have been over in a week, instead of the four months it took, and that thousands of lives would have been saved.[3] Biographer Wilbur Thomas called him "the greatest soldier in the Federal Army,"[4] and Earl McElfresh thought that he was "probably the most completely professional soldier of the American Civil War."[5]

Thomas was one of fifteen Union generals accorded the Thanks of the Nation for their services in the war. In his case, this was done for the Battles of Franklin and Nashville. It is curious why this recognition was not tendered for his accomplishments at Chickamauga and Chattanooga. But Thomas was a man of many accomplishments during the war, and he was recognized for painfully few. He helped to introduce the use of map coordinates into battle planning. He introduced the concept of remote fire control with his signal corps at Chattanooga. He was instrumental in the development of folding, portable pontoons. His use of the secret service and spy system was second to none, and was responsible for breaking codes, for disrupting enemy communications, and even for providing information that led to the capture of Jefferson Davis. He introduced the most efficient mess system in the Union army by employing full-time cooks instead of leaving the men to fend for themselves. His use of the telegraph was the most efficient of any army on either side, making possible the concentration of widely scattered forces in minimum time. He established the most effective hospital service in either army, utilizing a mobile system of railroad hospital cars that saved countless lives. Thomas hired the first female doctor ever employed by the United States Army. He established the first National Military Cemetery at a battlefield following his victory at Mill Springs, and established his second at Chattanooga following the defeat of Bragg's army. The tactics he used at Snodgrass Hill, at Chickamauga, are still taught today in the United States Marine Corps assault doctrine. He even provided for the recreation and education of his soldiers by establishing a service to provide them with magazines and books, a forerunner of the USO. Much more than merely a technically correct military strategist and tactician, he was an enlightened visionary who introduced innovations that were ahead of their time. It was many of these same innovations that caused him to be such a favorite with the men he commanded. They could readily see that this was a leader who always looked to their welfare and kept the best interests of his men first and foremost in his actions. When one considers that he achieved his successes with as much economy of losses as any commander in the war, it is easy to understand why his troops adored him and would follow wherever he led.

General Thomas deserves to be remembered not only as one of the greatest commanders to emerge from the Civil War, but as one of the greatest Americans of his age. His life was a shining example of all that is good in American society, and his deportment, devotion to duty, and sacrifice to his country should be sufficient to place him among the ranks of heroes like George Washington and Robert E. Lee. Indeed, he would be listed among the greatest American heroes of all time were it not for the ambition and suspicion of his Northern peers and the resentment of his abandoned Southern brethren. It is hoped that the readers of this work will be able to examine his life free from any of these sentiments and evaluate its worth based solely upon the merits of his accomplishments and character. If that is done, then the writer feels confident that Thomas's wish will finally be realized, and history will do justice to one of the most noble men that America ever produced.

APPENDIX I

General Officers Serving Under Thomas

Baird, Absalom
Beatty, John
Brannon, John M.
Carlin, William P.
Cooper, Joseph A.
Couch, Darius N.
Cox, Jacob D.
Crittenden, Thomas L.
Croxton, John T.
Cruft, Charles
Davis, Jefferson C.
Elliott, Washington L.
Fry, Speed S.
Garrard, Kenner
Geary, John W.
Gilbert, Charles C.
Granger, Gordon
Grose, William
Hammond, John H.
Hascall, Milo S.

Hatch, Edward
Hazen, William B.
Howard, Oliver O.
Jackson, James S.
Johnson, Richard W.
Kimball, Nathan
King, John H.
Kuipe, Joseph F.
McArthur, John
McCook, Alexander McD.
McCook, Daniel
Miller, John F.
Mitchell, Robert B.
Morgan, James D.
Negley, James S.
Palmer, John M.
Reynolds, Joseph J.
Rousseau, Lovell H.
Schofield, John M.
Schoepf, Albin

Schurz, Carl
Sheridan, Philip H.
Smith, Andrew J.
Smith, William F.
Smith, William S.
Spears, James G.
Starkweather, John C.
Steedman, James B.
Stewart, Robert R.
Terrill, William R.
Turchin, John B.
Tyndale, Hector
Van Cleve, Horatio P.
Von Steinwehr, Adolphus
Wagner, George D.
Whitaker, Walter C.
Willich, August
Wilson, James H.
Wood, Thomas J.

Appendix II

Units Serving Under Thomas

Connecticut
5th Infantry
20th Infantry

Illinois
Chicago Board of Trade Battery
1st Light Artillery
2nd Light Artillery
3rd Cavalry
6th Cavalry
7th Cavalry
9th Cavalry
14th Cavalry
15th Cavalry
16th Cavalry
10th Infantry
16th Infantry
19th Infantry
21st Infantry
22nd Infantry
24th Infantry
25th Infantry
27th Infantry
34th Infantry
35th Infantry
36th Infantry
38th Infantry
42nd Infantry
44th Infantry
49th Infantry
51st Infantry
58th Infantry
59th Infantry
60th Infantry
65th Infantry
72nd Infantry
73rd Infantry
74th Infantry
75th Infantry
78th Infantry
79th Infantry
80th Infantry
81st Infantry
82nd Infantry
84th Infantry
85th Infantry
86th Infantry
88th Infantry
89th Infantry
92nd Infantry (Mounted)
95th Infantry
96th Infantry
98th Infantry (Mounted)
100th Infantry
101st Infantry
102nd Infantry
104th Infantry
105th Infantry
107th Infantry
110th Infantry
112th Infantry
114th Infantry
115th Infantry
117th Infantry
119th Infantry
122nd Infantry
123rd Infantry (Mounted)
125th Infantry
129th Infantry

Indiana
2nd Light Artillery
3rd Light Artillery
4th Light Artillery
5th Light Artillery
7th Light Artillery
9th Light Artillery
10th Light Artillery
11th Siege Artillery
12th Light Artillery
14th Light Artillery
18th Light Artillery
19th Light Artillery
20th Light Artillery
21st Light Artillery
22nd Light Artillery
23rd Light Artillery
24th Light Artillery
25th Light Artillery
2nd Cavalry
3rd Cavalry
4th Cavalry
6th Cavalry
8th Cavalry
9th Cavalry
10th Cavalry
11th Cavalry
12th Cavalry
13th Cavalry
17th Cavalry
18th Cavalry
6th Infantry
9th Infantry
10th Infantry
15th Infantry
17th Infantry
22nd Infantry
23rd Infantry
27th Infantry
30th Infantry
31st Infantry
32nd Infantry
33rd Infantry
35th Infantry
36th Infantry
37th Infantry

38th Infantry
40th Infantry
42nd Infantry
44th Infantry
51st Infantry
52nd Infantry
57th Infantry
58th Infantry
63rd Infantry
65th Infantry
68th Infantry
70th Infantry
72nd Infantry (Mounted)
74th Infantry
75th Infantry
79th Infantry
80th Infantry
81st Infantry
82nd Infantry
84th Infantry
85th Infantry
86th Infantry
87th Infantry
88th Infantry
89th Infantry
91st Infantry
93rd Infantry
101st Infantry
120th Infantry
123rd Infantry
124th Infantry
128th Infantry
129th Infantry
130th Infantry
142nd Infantry

Iowa

2nd Light Artillery
2nd Cavalry
5th Cavalry
8th Cavalry
12th Infantry
27th Infantry
32nd Infantry
35th Infantry

Kansas

1st Light Artillery
8th Infantry
10th Infantry

Kentucky

1st Light Artillery
2nd Cavalry
3rd Cavalry
4th Cavalry (Mounted Infantry)
5th Cavalry
1st Infantry
2nd Infantry
3rd Infantry
4th Infantry
5th Infantry
6th Infantry
8th Infantry
9th Infantry
10th Infantry
12th Infantry
15th Infantry
16th Infantry
17th Infantry
18th Infantry
21st Infantry
23rd Infantry
26th Infantry
28th Infantry

Maryland

3rd Infantry

Massachusetts

2nd Infantry
33rd Infantry

Michigan

1st Light Artillery
20th Light Artillery
2nd Cavalry
4th Cavalry
8th Cavalry
1st Engineers
9th Infantry
10th Infantry
11th Infantry
13th Infantry
14th Infantry
19th Infantry
21st Infantry
22nd Infantry
23rd Infantry
25th Infantry
28th Infantry

Minnesota

2nd Infantry
5th Infantry
7th Infantry
9th Infantry
10th Infantry

Missouri

1st Light Artillery
2nd Light Artillery
12th Cavalry
2nd Infantry
11th Infantry
15th Infantry
21st Infantry
23rd Infantry
33rd Infantry
40th Infantry
44th Infantry

New Jersey

13th Infantry
33rd Infantry

New York

1st Light Artillery
13th Light Artillery
8th Infantry
17th Infantry
45th Infantry
58th Infantry
60th Infantry
68th Infantry
78th Infantry
102nd Infantry
107th Infantry
119th Infantry
123rd Infantry
134th Infantry
136th Infantry
137th Infantry
141st Infantry
143rd Infantry
149th Infantry
150th Infantry
154th Infantry
178th Infantry

Ohio

1st Light Artillery
6th Light Artillery
14th Light Artillery

18th Light Artillery
20th Light Artillery
1st Cavalry
3rd Cavalry
4th Cavalry
7th Cavalry
10th Cavalry
1st Infantry
2nd Infantry
3rd Infantry
5th Infantry
6th Infantry
7th Infantry
9th Infantry
10th Infantry
11th Infantry
13th Infantry
14th Infantry
15th Infantry
17th Infantry
18th Infantry
19th Infantry
21st Infantry
24th Infantry
26th Infantry
29th Infantry
31st Infantry
33rd Infantry
35th Infantry
36th Infantry
38th Infantry
40th Infantry
41st Infantry
45th Infantry
49th Infantry
50th Infantry
51st Infantry
52nd Infantry
55th Infantry
59th Infantry
61st Infantry
64th Infantry
65th Infantry
66th Infantry
69th Infantry
71st Infantry
72nd Infantry
73rd Infantry
74th Infantry
79th Infantry
82nd Infantry

89th Infantry
90th Infantry
92nd Infantry
93rd Infantry
94th Infantry
95th Infantry
97th Infantry
98th Infantry
99th Infantry
100th Infantry
101st Infantry
103rd Infantry
104th Infantry
105th Infantry
108th Infantry
111th Infantry
113th Infantry
118th Infantry
121st Infantry
124th Infantry
125th Infantry
173rd Infantry
176th Infantry
179th Infantry
182nd Infantry
183rd Infantry
1st Sharpshooters

Pennsylvania

7th Cavalry
19th Cavalry
27th Infantry
28th Infantry
29th Infantry
46th Infantry
73rd Infantry
75th Infantry
77th Infantry
78th Infantry
79th Infantry
109th Infantry
111th Infantry
147th Infantry

Tennessee

1st Light Artillery
1st Cavalry
2nd Cavalry
3rd Cavalry
4th Cavalry
6th Cavalry

10th Cavalry
12th Cavalry
1st Infantry
2nd Infantry
3rd Infantry
5th Infantry
6th Infantry
8th Infantry
10th Infantry

United States Colored Troops

2nd Light Artillery
12th Infantry
13th Infantry
14th Infantry
16th Infantry
17th Infantry
18th Infantry
44th Infantry
100th Infantry

United States Regulars

4th Light Artillery
5th Light Artillery
4th Cavalry
15th Infantry
16th Infantry
18th Infantry
19th Infantry

Wisconsin

5th Light Artillery
10th Light Artillery
1st Cavalry
1st Infantry
3rd Infantry
8th Infantry
10th Infantry
14th Infantry
15th Infantry
21st Infantry
22nd Infantry
24th Infantry
26th Infantry
31st Infantry
33rd Infantry
44th Infantry
45th Infantry

Appendix III

George H. Thomas Chronology

1816 George H. Thomas is born in Southampton County, Virginia, on July 31, 1816.

1831 Thomas and his family are forced to flee their home at Thomastown during Nat Turner's slave rebellion.

1836 Enters the United States Military Academy at West Point, New York.

1840 Graduates 12th in his class and is assigned to the 3rd U.S. Artillery as a 2nd lieutenant.

1844 Promoted to 1st lieutenant for distinguished service in the Seminole War.

1847 Receives the brevet commissions of captain and major for gallantry in the battles of Monterrey and Buena Vista during the Mexican War.

1851 Receives assignment to act as an instructor of cavalry and artillery at West Point, where he teaches cavalry tactics to Phil Sheridan and J.E.B. Stuart.

1852 Marries Frances Kellogg, of Troy, New York, on November 17, 1852.

1853 Promoted to captain in the regular army in December.

1855 After serving as commander of Fort Yuma, Arizona Territory, Thomas is promoted to major and assigned to the elite 2nd United States Cavalry.

1860 Wounded by a Comanche arrow during a skirmish with the Indians in Texas.

1861 Thomas decides to stay with the Union when Virginia secedes. Promoted to colonel in the regular army and assigned to command of the 2nd U.S. Cavalry when Robert E. Lee resigns. Engaged at Bunker Hill and Falling Waters, Virginia, as a brigade commander, under the command of Robert Patterson. Promoted to brigadier general of volunteers in August and assigned to the Department of the Cumberland, at Camp Dick Robinson, Kentucky, where he trains the recruits gathered there.

1862 Defeats the Confederates at the Battle of Mill Springs, Kentucky, the first Union victory in the west. Promoted to major general of volunteers. Accompanies Buell's army to Shiloh, but does not take part in the battle. Commands a wing of Halleck's army in the campaign to capture Corinth, Mississippi. Serves as second in command to Buell at the Battle of Perryville, Kentucky. First day of the battle of Stones River, Tennessee.

1863 Second day of the Battle of Stones River. Given command of the newly designated 14th Army Corps. Participates in the Tullahoma campaign and capture of Chattanooga, Tennessee. Saves the Union army by his stand on Horseshoe Ridge at the Battle of Chickamauga. Given command of the Army of the Cumberland following the dismissal of

Rosecrans. In November, his Army of the Cumberland charges up Missionary Ridge at Chattanooga, breaking the Confederate lines and relieving the siege of that city. Passed over for top Federal command in the west in favor of General Sherman, even though Thomas is senior to that officer. Promoted to brigadier general in the regular army in December.

1864 Participates in all of the battles during the Atlanta campaign, from Buzzard's Roost to Peach Tree Creek. Is detached, following the surrender of Atlanta, to deal with John Bell Hood's Confederate forces that are invading Tennessee. His forces fight at Spring Hill and Franklin, culminating in the decisive victory at Nashville that completely destroys the Confederate Army of Tennessee. Promoted to the rank of major general in the regular army.

1865 Receives the "thanks of Congress" in March for his Nashville victory. Lee and Johnston surrender the two principal armies of the Confederacy, bringing the Civil War effectively to a close.

1867 President Andrew Johnson attempts to promote Thomas to the rank of lieutenant general and appoint him as Commander-in-Chief of the U.S. Army, supplanting Grant in that capacity. Thomas declines to accept this politically inspired maneuver.

1868 Thomas is nominated for president by the Tennessee State Convention. He declines the honor.

1870 General Thomas dies of a stroke on March 28, while serving in San Francisco, California, as commander of the Military Division of the Pacific. He is buried at Troy, New York.

Chapter Notes

Introduction

1. Society of the Army of the Cumberland, *Yearbook, 1870* (Cincinnati: Robert Clarke, 1871), pgs. 55–56.

Chapter One

1. Henry Coppee, *General Thomas* (New York: D. Appleton, 1893), pg. 3.
2. Wilbur Thomas, *General George H. Thomas—The Indomitable Warrior: A Biography* (New York: Exposition Press, 1964), pg. 48.
3. Thomas, pg. 45.
4. Southampton County Minute Books, 1810–1829, Virginia State Library, Richmond, VA.
5. Frank A. Palumbo, *George Henry Thomas, The Dependable General: Major General U.S.A.: Supreme in Tactics of Strategy and Command* (Dayton, OH: Morningside House, 1983), pg. 3.
6. *Ibid.*
7. William Sidney Drewry, *The Southampton Insurrection* (Washington, D.C.: Neale, 1900), pg. 27; Henry Howe, *Historical Collections of Virginia* (Charleston, SC: Genealogical Publishing, 1945), pg. 472; John Allen Wyeth, *With Saber and Scalpel* (New York: Harper and Brothers, 1914), pg. 261.
8. *Society of the Army of the Cumberland: Reports of the Meetings* (Cincinnati: Robert Clarke, 1875), pg. 56.
9. Coppee, pg. 4.
10. Donn Piatt, *Memories of the Men Who Saved the Union* (New York: Belford, Clarke, 1887), pg. 174; Thomas B. Van Horne, *The Life of Major General George H. Thomas* (New York: Scribner's, 1882), pg. 4.
11. Thomas, pg. 54.
12. Letter from John Mason to Lewis Cass, March 1, 1836, War Department Files, National Archives, Washington, D.C.
13. Letter from Elizabeth Thomas to War Department, Adjutant General's Office, Old Records Division, National Archives, Washington, D.C.
14. Coppee, pg. 5.
15. Coppee, pgs. 322–323.
16. John C. Waugh, *The Class of 1846: From West Point to Appomattox—Stonewall Jackson, George McClellan and Their Brothers* (New York: Warner Books, 1994), pg. 10.
17. Letter from George Horatio Derby to Mary Townsend Derby dated July 2, 1842, George Horatio Derby Papers, United States Military Academy Library, West Point, N.Y.
18. Waugh, pgs. 15–16.
19. Thomas, pgs. 59–60.
20. United States Military Academy, *Library Bulletin Number 1*, "Barracks," pg. 1.
21. Thomas, pgs. 61, 66.
22. *Ibid.*, pg. 67.

Chapter Two

1. Freeman Cleaves, *Rock of Chickamauga: The Life of General George H. Thomas* (Norman, OK: University of Oklahoma Press, 1948), pg. 17.
2. *Ibid.*, pg. 17
3. Coppee, pgs. 7–9.
4. W. Fletcher Johnson, *Life of Wm. Tecumseh Sherman: Late Retired General, U.S.A.* (Edgewood Publishing, 1891), pg. 43.
5. Richard W. Johnson, *A Soldier's Reminiscences* (Philadelphia: J.B. Lippincott, 1886), pgs. 18–20; John T. Sprague, *The Florida War* (New York: D. Appleton, 1848), pgs. 392–393.
6. Johnson, pgs. 20–21.
7. Thomas, pg. 72.
8. Erasmus D. Keyes, *Fifty Years Observation of Men and Events* (New York: Scribner's, 1885), pg. 166.
9. *Ibid.*, pgs. 165–166.
10. Cleaves, pgs. 17–18.
11. Thomas, pgs. 75–76.
12. Keyes, pgs. 166–171.
13. *Ibid.*, pgs. 166–170.

Chapter Three

1. Van Horne, pg. 5; *Encyclopedia Americana* (New York: Stratford Press, 1954), vol. 24, pg. 241.
2. Thomas, pgs. 81–82.
3. Justin H. Smith, *The War With Mexico* (New York: Macmillan, 1919), pg. 182.
4. "Old Shady, with a Moral," *North American Review* 147 (October 1888): pg. 365.
5. Van Horne, pg. 5.
6. Piatt, pgs. 66–67.
7. Piatt, pg. 67; Linus P. Brockett, *Our Great Cap-*

tains: Grant, Sherman, Thomas, Sheridan, and Farragut (New York: Richardson, 1865), pg. 165.

8. Thomas B. Thorpe, *Our Army on the Rio Grande* (Philadelphia: Carey & Hart, 1846), pgs. 231–237.

9. W.S. Henry, *Campaign Sketches of the War With Mexico* (New York: Harper & Brothers, 1847), pg. 104.

10. Smith, pgs. 209–210.

11. Samuel G. French, *Two Wars: An Autobiography of Samuel G. French, an Officer in the Armies of the United States and the Confederate States, a Graduate From the U.S. Military Academy* (Huntington, WV: Blue Acorn Press, 1999), pg. 59.

12. Smith, pg. 238.

13. General Cadmus M. Wilcox, *History of the Mexican War* (Washington, D.C.: Church News Publishing, 1892), pg. 90.

14. *Ibid.*, pgs. 91–92.

15. *Ibid.*, pg. 82.

16. Luther Giddings, *Sketches of the Campaign in Northern Mexico in Eighteen Hundred Forty-six and Seven* (New York: Putnam, 1853), pgs. 168–169.

17. Cleaves, pgs. 32–33.

18. French, pg. 66.

19. William F.G. Shanks, *Personal Recollections of Distinguished Generals* (New York: Harper and Brothers, 1866), pg. 79.

20. Thomas, pg. 101.

21. Cleaves, pg. 35.

22. French, pgs. 69–70.

23. *Ibid.*, pg. 71.

24. Smith, pg. 384.

25. Wilcox, pg. 212.

26. Coppee, pg. 17.

27. Wilcox, pgs. 214–215.

28. *Ibid.*, pg. 220.

29. *Ibid.*, pgs. 223–226.

30. Smith, pg. 116.

31. Holman Hamilton, *Zachary Taylor* (Indianapolis: Bobbs-Merrill, 1941), pg. 240.

Chapter Four

1. Coppee, pgs. 17–18.

2. *Ibid.*, pgs. 18–19; Thomas, pgs. 99–100.

3. Coppee, pgs. 20–21.

4. Thomas, pgs. 100–101.

5. Letter of Braxton Bragg to John Young Mason dated November 17, 1848, Thomas F. Madigan Collection, New York Public Library.

6. Van Horne, pgs. 10–11.

7. Edward R. Snow, *Castle Island: Its 300 Years of History and Romance* (Andover, MA: self-published, 1935), pgs. 25–27.

8. Cleaves, pg. 48.

9. Thomas, pg. 102.

10. Robert E. Lee Jr., *Recollections and Letters of General Robert E. Lee* (New York: Garden City Publishing, 1924), pgs. 17–18.

11. Douglas Southall Freeman, *R.E. Lee: A Biography* (New York: Scribner's, 1962), pgs. 320–321.

12. Cleaves, pgs. 48–49.

13. David Sloan Stanley, *The Memoirs of David Sloan Stanley* (Santa Barbara, CA: Narrative Press, 2003), pg. 59.

14. Richard W. Johnson, *Memoir of Major-General George H. Thomas* (Philadelphia: J.B. Lippincott, 1881), pg. 21.

15. Cleaves, pgs. 50–51; Timothy Hopkins, *The Kelloggs in the Old World and the New* (San Francisco: Sunset Press and Photo Engraving, 1903), pg. 23.

16. Cleaves, pg. 51.

17. Thomas, pgs. 106–107.

18. Letters from George H. Thomas to Major Townsend dated June 1 and July 14, 1854, War Department Files, National Archives, Washington, D.C.

19. Andrew D. Rodgers, *John Torrey: A Story of North American Botany* (Princeton, NJ: Princeton University Press, 1942), pg. 242.

20. California Historical Society, *Quarterly*, June 1942, pg. 97.

21. Thomas, pgs. 107–108.

22. *Ibid.*, pg. 108.

23. Freeman, pg. 360; Emory M. Thomas, *Bold Dragoon: The Life of J.E.B. Stuart* (Norman, OK: University of Oklahoma Press, 1999), pgs. 39–40.

24. Thomas, *Dragoon*, pg. 109.

25. Cleaves, pgs. 55–56.

26. Clifford Dowdey, *Lee* (New York: Bonanza Books, 1965), pg. 107.

27. Thomas, *Dragoon*, pgs. 109–110.

28. Cleaves, pg. 57.

29. *Ibid.*, pgs. 57–58.

30. *Ibid.*, pgs. 58–59.

31. Thomas, *Dragoon*, pgs. 113–114.

32. Johnson, pg. 35.

33. *Ibid.*

Chapter Five

1. Robert P. Broadwater, *Did Lincoln and the Republican Party Create the Civil War? An Argument* (Jefferson, NC: McFarland, 2008), pgs. 44–45.

2. Cleaves, pgs. 62–63.

3. Robert Underwood Johnson and Clarence Clough Buel, *Battles and Leaders of the Civil War*, vol. 1 (New York: Century, 1887–1888), pg. 38, hereinafter referred to as *Battles and Leaders* .

4. Allen Peskin, *Winfield Scott and the Profession of Arms* (Kent, OH: Kent State University Press, 2003), pg. 244.

5. Letter from George H. Thomas to Francis H. Smith dated January 18, 1861, War Department Files, National Archives, Washington, D.C.

6. J. William Jones, *Southern Historical Society Papers*, vol. 10 (Wilmington, NC: Broadfoot Publishing, 1990), pgs. 524–525.

7. Cleaves, pg. 65.

8. Thomas, *Dragoon*, pg. 133.

9. Society of the Army of the Cumberland, *Yearbook, 1870* (Cincinnati: Robert Clarke, 1870), pgs. 65–66.

10. Military Historical Society of Massachusetts, *Critical Sketches of Some of the Federal and Confederate Commanders* (Wilmington, NC: Broadfoot Publishing, 1989), pgs. 172–173; hereinafter *Critical Sketches*.

11. Coppee, pgs. 27–28.

12. Society of the Army of the Cumberland, *Report of the Meetings, 1870* (Cincinnati: Robert Clarke, 1870, pg. 67.

13. *Ibid.*, pg. 68.

14. *Critical Sketches*, pgs.172–173; Alexander K. McClure, *Lincoln and Men of War Times* (Philadelphia: Times Publishing, 1892), pg. 341.
15. Thomas, *Dragoon*, pgs. 74–75.
16. Thomas, *General George H. Thomas*, pgs. 146–147.
17. *Critical Sketches*, pgs. 173–174.
18. Cleaves, pgs. 74–75.
19. Robert Patterson, *A Narrative of the Campaign in the Valley of the Shenandoah in 1861* (Philadelphia: Sherman, Printers, 1865), pgs. 106–107.
20. Thomas, *General George H. Thomas*, pgs. 147–148.
21. Cleaves, pgs. 77–78.
22. Thomas, *General George H. Thomas*, pg. 152.

Chapter Six

1. Thomas, *General George H. Thomas*, pg. 155.
2. *Ibid.*, pg. 156.
3. A. Noel Blakeman, *Personal Recollections of the War of the Rebellion: Addresses Delivered Before the Commandery of the State of New York, Military Order of the Loyal Legion of the United States* (New York: Putnam's, 1907), pg. 330.
4. John Fitch, *Annals of the Army of the Cumberland: 1864 Edition* (Mechanicsburg, PA: Stackpole Books, 2003), pg. 60.
5. Robert N. Scott, *The War of the Rebellion: A Compilation of the Official Records of the Union and Confederate Armies*, series 1, vol. 4 (Washington, D.C.: Government Printing Office, 1881), pgs. 296–297; hereinafter referred to as *O.R.*
6. Ezra J. Warner, *Generals in Blue: Lives of the Union Commanders* (Baton Rouge, LA: Louisiana State University Press, 1964), pgs. 442–443.
7. Thomas Lawrence Connelly, *Army of the Heartland: The Army of Tennessee, 1861–1862* (Baton Rouge, LA: Louisiana State University Press, 1971), pg. 88.
8. Thomas, *General George H. Thomas*, pgs. 162–163.
9. *Ibid.*, pgs. 164–165.
10. *O.R.*, series 1, vol. 4, pg. 339.
11. Cleaves, pgs. 90–92.
12. Warner, *Generals in Blue*, pgs. 51, 443, 501; *Battles and Leaders*, vol. 1, pg. 385.
13. Warner, *Generals in Blue*, pg. 443.
14. *Ibid.*, pg. 51.
15. Thomas, *General George H. Thomas*, pg. 172.
16. *Battles and Leaders*, vol. 1, pg. 385.
17. Van Horne, pg. 51.
18. *Ibid.*
19. *Ibid.*, pg. 52.
20. *O.R.*, series 1, vol. 7, pg. 787.
21. Ezra J. Warner, *Generals in Gray: Lives of the Confederate Commanders* (Baton Rouge, LA: Louisiana State University Press, 1959), pgs, 66, 350.
22. Thomas, *General George H. Thomas*, pg. 175.
23. Letter from George P. Faw to his brother dated January 5, 1862, manuscript collection, East Tennessee State University, Johnson City, TN.
24. George C. Porter, "The Twentieth Tennessee Confederate Regiment," undated newspaper clipping, Confederate Collection, Tennessee State Library and Archives, Knoxville, TN.
25. *Ibid.*
26. Letter from John Simpson to O.P. Morton dated January 28, 1862, 10th Indiana Infantry Collection, Indiana State Archives, Indianapolis, In.
27. Sergeant E. Tarrant, *The Wild Riders of the First Kentucky Cavalry* (Louisville, KY: privately printed, 1894), pg. 63.
28. *Ibid.*
29. Joan W. Albertson, *Letters Home to Minnesota* (Spokane: P.D. Enterprises, 1993), pg. 18.
30. *Louisville Daily Courier*, March 1, 1862.
31. Tarrant, pg. 64.
32. Larry J. Daniel, *Soldiering in the Army of Tennessee* (Chapel Hill, NC: University of North Carolina Press, 1991), pgs. 41–42.
33. Cleaves, pg. 98.
34. *Detroit Advertiser*, January 29, 1862.
35. *Louisville Daily Courier*, March 1, 1862.
36. John Braden and Terry Wantz, *The History of Newaygo County, Michigan Civil War Veterans* (Newaygo County Society of History and Genealogy, 1984), pg. 84.
37. *Jeffersonian Democrat*, February 2, 1862.
38. The Diary or Register of David Anderson Deaderick, Esq., David Anderson Deaderick Papers, Library of Congress, Washington D.C.
39. *Battles and Leaders*, vol. 1, pg. 391.
40. Tarrant, pg. 65.
41. Deaderick Diary.
42. Braden and Wantz, pg. 85.
43. Cleaves, pg. 100.
44. Stephen D. Engle, *Don Carlos Buell: Most Promising of All* (Chapel Hill, NC: University of North Carolina Press, 1999), pg. 145.
45. Thomas Bragg Diary, January 24, 1861 entry, Southern Historical Collection, University of North Carolina, Chapel Hill, NC; Warner, *Generals in Gray*, pg. 66.

Chapter Seven

1. *O.R.*, series 1, vol. 7, pgs. 425–427.
2. Cleaves, pg. 102.
3. William C. Davis, *The Deep Waters of the Proud* (New York: Doubleday, 1982), pg. 118.
4. Fitch, pg. 364.
5. Davis, *The Deep Waters of the Proud*, pgs. 118–119.
6. William C. Davis, *The Orphan Brigade: The Kentucky Confederates Who Couldn't Go Home* (Garden City, NY: Doubleday, 1980), pgs. 78–79.
7. T. Harry Williams, *Beauregard: Napoleon in Gray* (New York: Collier Books, 1962), pgs. 167–168.
8. Jay Wertz and Edwin C. Bearss, *Smithsonian's Great Battles & Battlefields of the Civil War* (New York: William Morrow, 1997), pgs. 557–558.
9. William H. Price, *The Civil War Handbook* (Fairfax, VA: Prince Lithographic, 1961), pg. 67.
10. Wetz and Bearss, pg. 558.
11. Larry J. Daniel, *Shiloh: The Battle That Changed the Civil War* (New York: Touchstone Books, 1997), pgs. 297–300.
12. Judson W. Bishop, *Story of a Regiment* (St. Paul, MN: St. Paul Book and Stationery, 1890), pg. 54.
13. Cleaves, pg. 105; Warner, *Generals in Blue*, pg. 501.

14. Cleaves, pgs. 105–106.
15. Bruce Catton, *Terrible Swift Sword* (Garden City, NY: Doubleday, 1963), pgs. 307–308.
16. *Ibid.*, pg. 310.
17. Cleaves, pg. 107.
18. Letter from George Thomas to Andrew Johnson dated August 16, 1862, George H. Thomas Papers, Henry E. Huntington Library, San Marino, CA.
19. John P. Dyer, *From Shiloh to San Juan: The Life of Fighting Joe Wheeler* (Baton Rouge, LA: Louisiana State University Press, 1961), pg. 39.
20. Dyer, *From Shiloh to San Juan*, pg. 39; Nathaniel S. Shaler, *Campaigns in Kentucky and Tennessee, Including the Battle of Chickamauga 1862–1864. Papers Read to the Military Historical Society of Massachusetts* (Boston: Historical Society of Massachusetts, 1905), pg. 209.
21. Irving A. Buck, *Cleburne and His Command* (Jackson, TN: McCowat-Mercer Press, 1959), pgs. 104–105.
22. *O.R.*, series 1, vol. 16, pt. 1, pg. 150.
23. John Beatty, *The Citizen Soldier: Memoirs of a Civil War Volunteer* (Cincinnati: Wilstach, Baldwin, 1879), pg. 117.
24. Robert M. Frierson, "Gen. E. Kirby Smith's Campaign in Kentucky," *Confederate Veteran Magazine* 1, no. 4, pg. 295.
25. Buck, pg. 108.
26. Dyer, pg. 42.
27. Don C. Seitz, *Braxton Bragg: General of the Confederacy* (Columbia, SC: State, 1924), pgs. 170–171.
28. Price, pg. 67.
29. Stephen Chicoine, *John Basil Turchin and the Fight to Free the Slaves* (Westport, CT: Praeger Books, 2003), pg. 121.
30. *Battles and Leaders*, vol. 3, pg. 44.
31. Van Horne, pg. 425.
32. Warner, *Generals in Blue*, pgs. 173–174; F.B. James, *Perryville and the Kentucky Campaign of 1862: Sketches of War History 1861–1865. Papers Prepared for the Commandery of Ohio, Military Order of the Loyal Legion of the United States*, vol. 5 (Cincinnati, OH: Robert Clarke, 1903), pgs. 162–163.
33. *O.R.*, series 1, vol. 18, pt. 2, pgs, 1050–1051; Shaler, pg. 288; Buck, pg. 112.
34. Stanley F. Horn, *The Army of Tennessee: A Military History* (Indianapolis: Bobbs-Merrill, 1941), pg. 46.
35. L.G. Bennett and William M. Haigh, *History of the Thirty-Sixth Regiment Illinois Volunteers, During the War of the Rebellion* (Aurora, IL: Knickerbocker & Hodder, 1876, pg. 259.
36. *Ibid.*, pgs. 260–261.
37. Bennett, pg. 257; *O.R.*, series 1, vol. 18, pt. 2, pg. 1033.
38. James L. McDonough, *War in Kentucky: From Shiloh to Perryville* (Knoxville, TN: University of Tennessee Press, 1994), pgs. 275–278.
39. *O.R.*, series 1, vol. 18, pt. 2, pg. 1080.
40. Price, pg. 67.

Chapter Eight

1. Lowell H. Harrison, *The Civil War in Kentucky* (Lexington, KY: University of Kentucky Press, 1975), pg. 8.
2. Shaler, pg. 289.
3. Cleaves, pgs. 117–118.
4. Warner, *Generals in Blue*, pgs. 410–411.
5. *O.R.*, series 1, vol. 16, pt. 2, pg. 642.
6. *Ibid.*, pg. 652.
7. *Ibid.*, pgs. 641–642.
8. Warner, *Generals in Blue*, pg. 52.
9. *O.R.*, series 1, vol. 16, pt. 2. pg. 657.
10. *Ibid.*, pg. 663.
11. Piatt, pg. 199.
12. *O.R.*, series 1, vol. 16. pt. 2, pg. 663.
13. *O.R.*, series 1, vol. 17, pt. 2, pgs. 117–118.
14. *Ibid.*, pg. 118.
15. Piatt, pg. 202 and Van Horne, pg. 89.
16. Earl J. Hess, *Banners To The Breeze: The Kentucky Campaign, Corinth, and Stones River* (Lincoln, NE: University of Nebraska Press, 2000), pg. 178.
17. Society of the Army of the Cumberland, *Reports of the Meetings*, 1870, pgs. 80–81.
18. Cleaves, pgs. 123–124.
19. *War Papers: Being Papers Read Before the Commandery of the District of Columbia, Military Order of the Loyal Legion of the United States* (Wilmington, NC: Broadfoot Publishing, 1993), pgs. 12–13.
20. William J.K. Beaudot, *The 24th Wisconsin Infantry in the Civil War: The Biography of a Regiment* (Mechanicsburg, PA: Stackpole Books, 2003), pg. 137.
21. James Street Jr., *The Struggle For Tennessee: Tupelo to Stones River* (Alexandria, VA: Time-Life Books, 1985), pgs. 91–92.
22. Bennett, pgs. 317–319.
23. Wertz, pg. 563.
24. Beaudot, pg. 152.
25. Cleaves, pgs. 126–127.
26. *Battles and Leaders*, vol. 3, pg. 627.
27. Thomas, pgs. 293–294.
28. Cleaves, pg. 127..
29. Wertz, Jay, pgs. 563–565.
30. William C. Davis, *Stand in the Day of Battle* (Garden City, NY: Doubleday, 1983), pg. 8.
31. Street, pg. 149.
32. *Ibid.*, Pg. 150.
33. *Ibid.*, pgs. 152–154.
34. *Ibid.*, pgs. 154–155.
35. Beaudot, pg. 171.
36. W.D. Bickham, *Rosecrans' Campaign With the Fourteenth Army Corps* (Cincinnati: Moore, Wilstach, Keys, 1863), pg. 202.
37. Van Horne, pgs. 96–97; Piatt, pgs. 211–212.
38. *War Papers Read Before the Indiana Commandery, Military Order of the Loyal Legion of the United States* (Indianapolis: Published by the Commandery, 1898), pg. 174–175.
39. Thomas, pg. 300.
40. Alexander F. Stevenson, *The Battle of Stone's River* (Boston: J.R. Osgood, 1884), pg. 132.
41. *O.R.*, series 1, vol. 20, pt. 1, pgs. 785–786.
42. Thomas, pg. 302.
43. Cleaves, pg. 136.

Chapter Nine

1. John Morley, *Life of Gladstone* (New York: Macmillan, 1911), speech made at Newcastle, England, October 7, 1862.
2. Cleaves, pg. 138.

3. *O.R.*, series 1, vol. 20. pt. 2, pg. 306.
4. *O.R.*, series 1, vol. 23, pt. 2, pgs. 255–256.
5. Cleaves, pgs. 138, 141.
6. *O.R.*, series 1, vol. 23, pt. 2, pg. 395.
7. *Ibid.*, pg. 423.
8. *Ibid.*, pg. 415.
9. *Battles and Leaders*, vol. 3, pg. 635.
10. Stanley, pg. 162.
11. *Battles and Leaders*, pg. 635.
12. Claire E. Swedberg, *Three Years With The 92nd Illinois: The Civil War Diary of John M. King* (Mechanicsburg, PA: Stackpole Books, 1999), pgs. 89, 91.
13. *Battles and Leaders*, vol. 3, pg. 636.
14. Stanley, pg. 164.
15. Jerry Korn, *The Fight For Chattanooga: Chickamauga to Missionary Ridge* (Alexandria, VA: Time-Life Books, 1985), pg. 26.
16. *Battles and Leaders*, vol. 3, pgs. 636–637.
17. Stanley, pg. 167.
18. *War Papers: Being Papers Read Before the Commandery of the District of Columbia*, pgs. 6, 19.
19. *O.R.*, series 1, vol. 23, pt. 2, pgs. 402–403, 518
20. Cleaves, pg. 147.
21. Charles A. Dana, *Recollections of the Civil War* (Lincoln, NE: University of Nebraska Press, 1996), pgs. 104–105.
22. Thomas, pgs. 333–334.
23. Swedberg, pg. 108.
24. Fitch, pgs. 457–461.
25. *O.R.*, series 1, vol. 30, pt. 3, pg. 481.
26. Cleaves, pg. 150.
27. Korn, pg. 35.

Chapter Ten

1. *Battles and Leaders*, vol. 3, pg. 638; Warner, *Generals in Gray*, pg. 137.
2. Glenn Tucker, *Chickamauga: Bloody Battle in the West* (Dayton, OH: Morningside Bookshop, 1976), pgs. 86–92.
3. Jeffrey D. Wert, *General James Longstreet: The Confederacy's Most Controversial Soldier* (New York: Touchstone Books, 1993), pg. 304.
4. *Battles and Leaders*, vol. 3, pgs. 673, 676.
5. Van Horne, pg. 106.
6. Chicoine, pg. 145.
7. Tucker, pgs. 29–30.
8. *Ibid.*, pgs. 61–65.
9. *O.R.*, series 1, vol. 30, pt. 3, pg. 264.
10. Tucker, pg. 67.
11. *O.R.*, series 1, vol. 30, pt. 3, pg. 485.
12. *Ibid.*, pgs. 564–565.
13. Tucker, pgs. 66, 69–70.
14. *Ibid.*, pg. 70.
15. Dana, pg. 109.
16. Tucker, pg. 71.
17. *Southern Historical Society Papers*, vol. 2, pg. 241.
18. Wert, pgs. 305–306.
19. *O.R.*, series 1, vol. 30, pt. 2, pgs. 30–31.
20. *O.R.*, series 1, vol. 30, pt. 1, pg. 111.
21. Cleaves, pgs. 155–156.
22. James H. Wilson, *Under the Old Flag*, vol. 2 (New York: D. Appleton, 1912), pgs. 111–112
23. Korn, pg. 45.
24. Cleaves, pg. 159.
25. Thomas Berry, *Four Years With Morgan and Forrest* (Oklahoma City: Harlow-Ratliff, 1914), pg. 243.
26. Korn, pg. 47.
27. Dana, pg. 112.
28. William A. Fletcher, *Rebel Private: Front and Rear — Memoirs of a Confederate Soldier* (New York: Meridian Books, 1995), pg. 98.
29. *United Service Journal*, September 1896, pg. 223.
30. Korn, pg. 52.
31. *Ibid.*, pg. 48.
32. Cleaves, pgs. 162–163.
33. Fitch, pg. 467.
34. Korn, pg. 54.
35. *Ibid.*, pgs. 54–55.
36. Clint Johnson, *Bull's-Eyes and Misfires: 50 People Whose Obscure Efforts Shaped the American Civil War* (Nashville: Rutledge Hill Press, 2002), pg. 127.
37. John C. Ridpath, *The Life and Work of James A. Garfield* (Cincinnati: Jones Brothers, 1882), pg. 153; Johnson, pgs. 127–128.
38. Michael A. Cavanaugh, *Military Essays and Recollections of the Pennsylvania Commandery Military Order of the Loyal Legion of the United States* (Wilmington, NC: Broadfoot Publishing, 1995), pg. 442.
39. Korn, pg. 58.
40. Dana, pg. 115.
41. *Battles and Leaders*, vol. 3, pg. 664.
42. Swedeberg, pg. 123.
43. Jacob D. Cox, *Military Reminiscences*, vol. 2. (New York: Scribner's, 1900), pg 10.
44. Isaac H.C. Royse, *History of the 115th Illinois Volunteers* (Terre Haute, IN: published by the author, 1900), pgs. 120–131.
45. Joseph C. McElroy, *Chickamauga: Record of the Ohio Chickamauga and Chattanooga National Park Commission* (Cincinnati: Earhart & Richardson, Printers and Engravers, 1896), pgs. 14–15.
46. *Ibid.*, pg. 16.
47. *Ibid.*, pg. 18.
48. Thomas, pg. 389.
49. Cleaves, pg. 172.
50. John M. Palmer, *Recollections of John M. Palmer: The Story of an Earnest Life* (Cincinnati: R. Clarke, 1901), pg. 84.
51. McElroy, pg. 18.
52. Cleaves, pgs. 173–174.
53. *War Papers: Being Papers Read Before the Commandery of the District of Columbia Military Order of the Loyal Legion of the United States*, vol. 4 (Wilmington, NC: Broadfoot Publishing, 1993), 429.
54. Tucker, pgs. 348–349.
55. Cleaves, pg 174.
56. Shanks, pg. 273.
57. William M. Lamers, *The Edge of Glory: A Biography of General William S. Rosecrans, U.S.A.* (New York: Harcourt, Brace & World, 1961), pgs. 356–357.
58. *Sketches of War History 1861–1865: Papers Read Before the Ohio Commandery of the Military Order of the Loyal Legion of the United States*, vol. 1 (Cincinnati: Robert Clarke, 1888), pgs. 441–442.
59. Korn, pgs. 66–67; Tucker, pg. 350.
60. Van Horne, pg 427.
61. *Ibid.*, pgs. 68–69, 73.
62. *O.R.*, series 1, vol. 50, pg. 141.
63. Piatt, pgs. 430–431.
64. *O.R.*, series 1, vol. 50, pg. 580.

Chapter Eleven

1. Korn, pg. 72–73.
2. Philip H. Sheridan, *Personal Memoirs of P.H. Sheridan* (New York: Charles L. Webster, 1888), pg. 285.
3. Cleaves, pg. 176.
4. Korn, pg. 78.
5. Dana, pg. 121
6. Cleaves, pg. 178.
7. G. Moxley Sorrel, *Recollections of a Confederate Staff Officer* (New York: Neale Publishing, 1905), pg. 186.
8. Gideon Welles, *The Diary of Gideon Welles*, vol. 1 (Boston: Houghton Mifflin, 1911), pg. 447.
9. Dana, pg. 125.
10. Korn, pg. 78.
11. *Ibid.*, pgs. 78–79, 81, Benjamin P. Thomas and Harold M. Hyman, *Stanton: The Life and Times of Lincoln's Secretary of War* (New York: Alfred A. Knopf, 1962), pgs. 289–290.
12. Cleaves, pg. 181.
13. Carl Sandberg, *Abraham Lincoln: The War Years 1861–1864*, vol. 2 (New York: Dell Books, 1962), pg. 392.
14. Society of the Army of the Cumberland, *Reports of the Meetings* (Cincinnati: Robert Clarke, 1869), pg. 78.
15. Van Horne, pg. 156.
16. *O.R.*, series 1, vol. 30, pt. 4, pg. 478.
17. Horace Porter, *Campaigning With Grant* (New York: Century, 1897), pg. 3.
18. *Ibid.*, pg. 4.
19. Adam Badeau, *Military History of Ulysses S. Grant From April 1861 to April 1865*, vol. 1 (New York: D. Appleton, 1868), pgs. 442–443.
20. Dana, pg. 133.
21. Badeau, pgs. 446–447.
22. Horn, *The Army of the Tennessee*, pg. 293.
23. Porter, pgs. 9–10.
24. *Ibid.*, pg. 10.
25. Bennett and Haigh, pg. 510.
26. *Battles and Leaders*, vol. 3, pg. 715.
27. Cleaves, pg. 192.
28. Bennett and Haigh, pgs. 519–520; Van Horne, pg. 174.
29. Korn, pgs. 130–133.
30. *Ibid.*, pgs. 133–136.
31. Henry Davenport Northrup, *Life and Deeds of General Sherman: Including the Story of His Great March to the Sea* (Harrisburg, PA: Pennsylvania Publishing, 1891), pg. 375.
32. Korn, pgs. 142–143
33. Bennett and Haigh, pg. 526.
34. *Battles and Leaders*, vol. 3, pg. 726.
35. Korn, pgs. 145–147; Cleaves, pg. 199; Clarence Edward Macartney, *Grant and His Generals* (New York: McBride, 1953), pgs. 14–15.
36. Van Horne, pg. 426.

Chapter Twelve

1. Jenkin Lloyd Jones, *An Artilleryman's Diary* (Madison, WI: Wisconsin History Commission, 1914), pg. 144.
2. Oliver Otis Howard, *Autobiography of Oliver Otis Howard, Major General, United States Army*, vol. 1 (New York: Baker & Taylor, 1908), pgs. 495–496.
3. Cleaves, pgs. 202–203.
4. Warner, *Generals in Gray*, pgs. 161–162.
5. Cleaves, pg. 203.
6. *O.R.*, series 1, vol. 32, pt. 2, pg. 82
7. *Ibid.*, pgs. 43, 63, 88, 89, 111, 131, 143, 248, 395.
8. Badeau, pgs. 556–559.
9. *O.R.*, series 1, vol. 32, pt. 2, pgs. 373, 429.
10. Ulysses S. Grant, *Personal Memoirs of U.S. Grant* (New York: Charles L. Webster, 1885), pg. 357.
11. Thomas, pg. 455.
12. William T. Sherman, *The Memoirs of General William T. Sherman: By Himself*, vol. 1 (Bloomington, IL: Indiana University Press, 1957), pgs. 398–399.
13. Thomas, pgs. 455–456.
14. Piatt, pgs. 519–520.
15. Van Horne, pg 213.
16. Swedberg, pg. 187.
17. Thomas, pg. 457.
18. *Ibid.*, pg. 458.
19. *Battles and Leaders*, vol. 4, pg. 281.
20. Cleaves, pgs. 209–210.
21. Howard, pg. 503.
22. Robert P. Broadwater, *On to Atlanta: With the 27th Indiana Infantry Through Georgia* (Baltimore: Publish America, 2008), pg. 47.
23. Lloyd Lewis, *Sherman: Fighting Prophet* (New York: Harcourt, Brace, 1932), pg. 355.
24. Beaudot, pg. 293.
25. *Ibid.*
26. Lewis, pg. 357.
27. *Papers Read to the Military Historical Society of Massachusetts*, vol. 10 (Boston: Military Historical Society of Massachusetts, 1905), pgs. 188–189.
28. Ronald H. Bailey, *Battles For Atlanta* (Alexandria, VA: Time-Life Books, 1985), pgs. 42–43.
29. Cleaves, pg. 214.
30. John P. Dyer, *The Gallant Hood* (Indianapolis: Bobbs-Merrill, 1950), pg. 235; *Battles and Leaders*, vol. 4, pgs. 265–266; Bailey, pgs. 49–50.
31. Bailey, pg. 50.
32. *Battles and Leaders*, vol. 4, pgs. 269–270; Bailey, pgs. 51–52; *Papers Read to the Military Historical Society of Massachusetts*, vol. 8, pg. 408.
33. *Battles and Leaders*, vol. 4, pgs. 269–270; Bailey, pgs. 51–52; William F. Fox, *Regimental Losses in the American Civil War 1861–1865* (Albany, NY: Albany Publishing, 1869), pg. 346.
34. *Battles and Leaders*, vol. 4. pg. 269; Bailey, pgs. 52–56.
35. Milton Meltzer, *Voices From the Civil War* (New York: Thomas Y. Crowell, 1989), pgs 168–169.
36. Van Horne, pg. 230.
37. G. Allen Foster, *The Eyes and Ears of the Civil War* (New York: Criterion Books, 1963), pgs. 11–12.

Chapter Thirteen

1. Bailey, pgs. 61–62,
2. Wertz and Bearss, pg. 169.
3. Piatt, pg. 534.
4. Lewis, pg. 375.
5. *Ibid.*

6. Society of the Army of the Cumberland, *Reports of the Meetings* (Cincinnati: Robert Clarke, 1893), pg. 118.
7. *Papers Read to the Military Historical Society of Massachusetts,* vol. 8, pg. 480.
8. Thomas, pgs. 477–478.
9. Van Horne, pgs. 94–95.
10. *O.R.*, series 1, vol. 39, pt. 4, pg. 609.
11. *Ibid.*, pgs. 609–610,
12. Piatt, pg. 547.
13. Broadwater, *On To Atlanta*, pg. 75.
14. Bailey, pgs. 76–77.
15. Beaudot, pg. 320.
16. *Battles and Leaders*, vol. 4, pgs. 274–275.
17. Dyer, pgs. 247–248.
18. K. Jack Bauer, *Soldiering: The Civil War Diary of Rice C. Bull* (Novato, CA: Presidio Press, 1986), pgs. 146–147.
19. Society of the Army of the Cumberland, *Reports of the Meetings, 1893*, pg. 130.
20. Van Horne, pg. 245
21. *O.R.*, series 1, vol. 38, pt. 4, pg. 196.
22. Cleaves, pg. 231.
23. Price, pg. 68.
24. Wertz and Bearss, pgs. 500–501; Price, pg. 68.
25. Sherman, pgs. 77, 82.
26. Bailey, pgs. 132–136; Price, pg. 68.
27. Bailey, pgs. 136–138.
28. William Key, *The Battle of Atlanta and the Georgia Campaign* (Atlanta, GA: Peachtree Publishers Limited, 1981), pg. 72.
29. Society of the Army of the Cumberland, *Reports of the Meetings, 1893,* pg. 139.
30. *Critical Sketches*, pg. 189.

Chapter Fourteen

1. Dyer, pg. 271.
2. James Longstreet, *From Manassas to Appomattox* (Philadelphia: Lippincott Publishing, 1896), pg. 317.
3. Thomas, pg. 510.
4. John B. Hood, *Advance and Retreat: Personal Experiences in the United States and Confederate Armies* (New Orleans: Hood Orphan Memorial Fund, 1880), pgs. 266–267.
5. Sherman, vol. 2, pgs. 154–155.
6. *O.R.*, series 1, vol. 39, pt. 3, pg. 175.
7. Lewis, pg. 429.
8. Anne J. Bailey, *The Chessboard of War: Sherman and Hood in the Autumn Campaign of 1864* (Lincoln, NE: University of Nebraska Press, 2000), pg. 29.
9. Bowman, John S., *The Civil War Almanac* (New York: World Almanac Publications, 1985), pg. 223.
10. Cleaves, pg. 245.
11. Letter from William T. Sherman to George H. Thomas dated October 20, 1864, Frederick H. Dearborn Collection, New York Public Library, New York, N.Y.
12. Van Horne, pgs. 255–256.
13. *Ibid.*, pg. 261.
14. Cleaves, pg. 246.
15. Van Horne, pg. 256.
16. Robert Selph Henry, *First With The Most: Forrest* (Wilmington, NC: Broadfoot Publishing, 1987), pgs. 371–379.
17. Lewis, pg. 430.
18. Van Horne, pg. 269.
19. *Ibid.*, pg. 259.
20. Dyer, pgs. 276–277.
21. *Battles and Leaders*, vol. 4, pg. 473.
22. Noah Andre Trudeau, *Like Men of War: Black Troops in the Civil War 1862–1865* (New York: Castle Books, 2002), pg. 334.
23. The Rhode Island Soldiers and Sailors Historical Society, *Personal Narratives of Events in the War of the Rebellion: Being Papers Read Before the Rhode Island Soldiers and Sailors Historical Society* (Providence, RI: published by the Society, 1885–1887), pg. 88.
24. *Battles and Leaders*, vol. 4, pg. 428.
25. Cleaves, pgs. 249–250.
26. *Ibid.*, pg. 250.
27. Stanley, pgs. 196–197.
28. *Military Essays and Recollections: Papers Read Before the Commandery of the State of Illinois, Military Order of the Loyal Legion of the United States*, vol. 3 (Chicago: Dial Press, 1899), pg. 273.
29. Cleaves, pg. 251.
30. Stanley, pgs. 196–198.
31. Hood, pgs. 293–295.
32. Price, pg. 69.
33. *Battles and Leaders*, vol. 4, pg. 453; Dyer, pg. 293.
34. James Lee McDonough, *Nashville: The Western Confederacy's Final Gamble* (Knoxville, TN: University of Tennessee Press, 2004), pg. 111.
35. Cleaves, pg. 254.
36. Van Horne, pg. 300.
37. *O.R.*, series 1, vol. 45, pt. 2, pgs. 17–18.
38. Van Horne, pg. 301.
39. *Ibid.*, pg. 303.
40. Piatt, pgs. 570–571.
41. Van Horne, Pg. 306.
42. Cleaves, pgs. 259–260.
43. Thomas, pg. 547.

Chapter Fifteen

1. Gen. Clement A. Evans, *Confederate Military History: Tennessee*, vol. 8 (New York: Blue & Grey Press), pgs. 162–163.
2. Bailey, pgs. 137–138.
3. Samuel T. Foster, *One of Cleburne's Command: The Civil War Reminiscences and Diary of Capt. Samuel T. Foster* (Austin: University of Texas Press, 1980), pg. 151.
4. Paul H. Beasley and C. Buford Gotto, "Fortress Nashville," *Civil War Times Illustrated* 3, no. 8 (December 1964): pg. 26.
5. Stanley F. Horn, "Nashville: The Most Decisive Battle of the War," *Civil War Times Illustrated* 3, no. 8 (December 1964): pg. 6.
6. *Ibid.*, pgs. 8–9.
7. Horn, "Nashville: The Most Decisive Battle of the War," pg. 9; Cleaves, pg. 262.
8. Horn, "Nashville: The Most Decisive Battle of the War," pg. 10.
9. *Ibid.*, pg. 11.

10. *Ibid.*
11. *Ibid.*, pgs. 30–31.
12. *Ibid.*, pgs. 31–32.
13. *Battles and Leaders*, vol. 4, pgs. 459–460.
14. Horn, "Nashville: The Most Decisive Battle of the War," pg. 32.
15. Evans, pg. 165.
16. James F. Rusling, *Men and Things I Saw in Civil War Days* (New York: Eaton & Mans, 1899), pg. 96.
17. Johnson, *Memoir of Major General George H. Thomas*, pgs. 196–197.
18. *Ibid.*, pgs. 197–198.
19. Horn, "Nashville: The Most Decisive Battle of the War," pg. 33.
20. John Watts De Peyster, *General George H. Thomas* (New York: 1875), pg. 13.
21. Horn, "Nashville: The Most Decisive Battle of the War," pg. 33.
22. Horn, "Nashville: The Most Decisive Battle of the War," pg. 33; Trudeau, pg. 343.
23. Wilson, vol. 2, pg. 116.
24. Horn, "Nashville: The Most Decisive Battle of the War," pg. 34.
25. Price, pg. 69.
26. Wilson, vol. 2. pg. 125.
27. Thomas A. Wigginton, "Cavalry Operations," *Civil War Times Illustrated* 3, no. 8 (December 1964): pg. 43.
28. Cleaves, pg. 272.
29. Johnson, pgs. 201–202.
30. Van Horne, pg. 371.
31. Rustling, pg. 104.
32. Piatt, pg. 377.
33. *O.R.*, series 1, vol. 45, pt. 2, pg. 461.
34. Horn, "Nashville: The Most Decisive Battle of the War," pg. 36.
35. Cleaves, pg. 269.
36. Van Horne, pg. 361.
37. *Ibid.*, pg. 376.
38. Wilson, pg. 180.
39. *Ibid.*, pg 180.
40. Cleaves, pg. 281.
41. Letter from George Thomas to Andrew Johnson dated April 10, 1865, Andrew Johnson Papers, Library of Congress, Washington, D.C.
42. Cleaves, pg. 283.
43. *Army and Navy Journal*, June 3, 1865.

Chapter Sixteen

1. Van Horne, pg. 424.
2. Cleaves, pgs. 287–288.
3. Claude G. Bowers, *The Tragic Era: The Revolution After Lincoln* (Cambridge, MA: Literary Guild of America, 1929), pg. 128–129; Robert Selph Henry, *The Story of Reconstruction* (Indianapolis: Bobbs-Merrill, 1938), pgs. 188–189.
4. Letter from George Thomas to Ulysses S. Grant dated August 15, 1866, War Department Papers, National Archives, Washington, D.C.
5. Cleaves, pg. 289.
6. George Fort Milton, *The Age of Hate* (New York: Coward-McCann, 1930), pgs. 458–459.
7. Cleaves, pgs. 295–296.
8. Van Horne, pgs. 421–422.
9. *Ibid.*, pg. 206.
10. Cleaves, pg. 299.
11. Francis McKinney, *An Education in Violence: The Life of George H. Thomas and History of the Army of the Cumberland* (Detroit: Wayne State University, 1961), pg. 83.
12. Selph, *Forrest*, pg. 447.
13. Warner, *Generals in Blue*, pg. 136.
14. Cleaves, pg. 301.
15. *Ibid.*, pg. 302.
16. Van Horne, pg. 434.
17. Keyes, pg. 167.
18. *San Francisco Alta*, March 29, 1870
19. Van Horne, pg. 447.
20. W.H.T. Squires, *The Days of Yester-Year* (Portsmouth, VA: Printcraft Press, 1928), pg. 195.

Conclusion

1. Henry Stone, "Major-General George Henry Thomas," in *Critical Sketches*, pgs, 206–207.
2. Albert Castel, *Decision in the West: The Atlanta Campaign of 1864* (Lawrence, KS: University Press of Kansas, 1992), pg. 565.
3. Thomas B. Buell, *The Warrior Generals: Combat Leadership in the Civil War* (New York: Crown, 1997), pg. 361.
4. Thomas, pg 267.
5. Earl B. McElfresh, *Maps and Mapmakers of the Civil War* (Boston: Henry N. Abrams, 1999), pg. 161.

Bibliography

Primary Sources — Manuscript Collections

East Tennessee State University
Faw Collection

Henry E. Huntington Library
George H. Thomas Papers

Indiana State Archives
10th Indiana Infantry Collection

Library of Congress
Andrew Johnson Papers
David Anderson Deaderick Papers

Mississippi State Archives
Francis Marion Aldridge Papers

National Archives
War Department Files

New York City Public Library
Frederick H. Dearborn Collection
Thomas F. Madigan Collection

Tennessee State Library and Archives
Confederate Collection

United States Military Academy Library
George Horatio Derby Papers

University of North Carolina, Chapel Hill
Thomas Bragg Diary

Virginia State Library
Southampton County Minute Books and Tax Lists

Primary Sources — Books

Albertson, Joan W. *Letters Home to Minnesota*. Spokane: P.D. Enterprises, 1993.
Angle, Paul M. *Three Years in the Army of the Cumberland: The Letters and Diary of Major James A. Connelly*. Bloomington: Indiana University Press, 1969.
Badeau, Adam. *Military History of Ulysses S. Grant From April 1861 to April 1865*. New York: D. Appleton, 1868.
Bailey, George W. *A Private Chapter of the War*. St. Louis: G.I. Jones, 1880.
Balch, William Ralston. *The Life of James Abram Garfield: Late President of the United States*. Philadelphia: J.C. McCurdy, 1881.
Beatty, John. *The Citizen Soldier: Memoirs of a Civil War Volunteer*. Cincinnati: Wilstach, Baldwin, 1879.
Bennett, J.G., and William M. Haigh. *History of the Thirty-Sixth Regiment Illinois Volunteers, During the War of the Rebellion*. Aurora, OH: Knickerbocker and Hodder, Publishers and Binders, 1876.
Berry, Thomas. *Four Years With Morgan and Forrest*. Oklahoma City: Harlow-Ratliff, 1914.
Bickham, W.D. *Rosecrans' Campaign with the Fourteenth Corps*. Cincinnati: Moore, Wilstach, Keys, 1863.
Bircher, William. *A Drummer-Boy's Diary: Comprising Four Years of Service With the Second Regiment Minnesota Veteran Volunteers, 1861 to 1865*. St. Paul, MN: St. Paul Book and Stationery, 1889.
Bishop, Judson W. *The Story of a Regiment*. St. Paul, MN: St. Paul Book and Stationery, 1890.
Blakeman, A. Noel. *Personal Recollections of the War of the Rebellion: Addresses Delivered Before The Commandery of the State of New York, Military Order of the Loyal Legion of the United States*. New York: Putnam's, 1907.
Braden, John, and Terry Wantz. *The History of Newaygo, Michigan, Civil War Veterans*. Newaygo County Society of History and Genealogy, 1984.
Brown, Thaddeus C.S., Samuel J. Murphy, and William G. Putney. *Behind the Guns: The History of Battery I, 2nd Regiment, Illinois Light Artillery*. Carbondale: Southern Illinois University Press, 1965.

Cannon, J.P. *Inside of Rebeldom: The Daily Life of a Private in the Confederate Army.* Washington, D.C.: National Tribune, 1900.
Caren, Eric C. *Civil War Extra: A Newspaper History of the Civil War.* 2 vols. New York: Castle Books, 1999.
Cavanaugh, Michael A. *Military Essays and Recollections of the Pennsylvania Commandery Military Order of the Loyal Legion of the United States.* Wilmington, N.C.: Broadfoot Publishing, 1995.
Cox, Jacob. *Military Reminiscences.* 2 vols. New York: Scribner's, 1900.
Dana, Charles A. *Recollections of the Civil War.* New York: D. Appleton, 1902.
Davies, General Henry E. *General Sheridan.* New York: D. Appleton, 1895.
De Peyster, John Watts. *General George H. Thomas.* New York: 1875.
Drewry, William Sidney. *The Southampton Insurrection.* Washington, D.C.: Neale, 1900.
Evans, Gen. Clement A. *Confederate Military History: Tennessee.* Vol. 8. New York: Blue & Grey Press.
Fitch, John. *Annals of the Army of the Cumberland.* Philadelphia: J.B. Lippincott, 1864.
Fletcher, William A. *Rebel Private: Front and Rear—Memoirs of a Confederate Soldier.* New York: Meridian Books, 1997.
Fordyce, Samuel W., IV. *An American General: The Memoirs of David Sloan Stanley.* Santa Barbara, CA: Narrative Press, 2003.
Foster, Samuel T. *One of Cleburne's Command: The Civil War Reminiscences and Diary of Capt. Samuel T. Foster.* Austin: University of Texas Press, 1980.
Fox, William F. *Regimental Losses in the American Civil War 1861–1865.* Albany, NY: Albany Publishing, 1869.
French, Samuel G. *Two Wars: An Autobiography of Samuel G. French, an Officer in the Armies of the United States and the Confederate States, a Graduate from the U.S. Military Academy.* Huntington, WV: Blue Acorn Press, 1999.
Giddings, Luther. *Sketches of the Campaign in Northern Mexico in Eighteen Hundred Forty-six and Seven.* New York: Putnam, 1853.
Goff, Tim. *Under Both Flags: Personal Stories of Sacrifice and Struggle During the Civil War.* Guilford, CT: Lyons Press, 2003.
Grant, Ulysses S. *Personal Memoirs of U.S. Grant.* New York: Charles L. Webster, 1885.
Guernsey, Alfred H., and Henry M. Alden. *Harpers Pictorial History of the Civil War.* New York: Harper & Brothers, 1866.
Hood, J.B. *Advance and Retreat: Personal Experiences in the United States and Confederate Armies.* New Orleans: Hood Orphan Memorial Fund, 1880.
Howard, Oliver Otis. *Autobiography of Oliver Otis Howard, Major General, United States Army.* 2 vols. New York: Baker & Taylor, 1908.
Howe, Henry. *Historical Collections of Virginia.* Charleston, SC: Genealogical Publishing, 1945.
James, F.B. *Perryville and the Kentucky Campaign of 1862: Sketches of War History 1861–1865. Papers Prepared for the Commandery of Ohio, Military Order of the Loyal Legion of the United States.* Vol. 5. Cincinnati: Robert Clarke, 1903.
Johnson, Richard W. *Memoir of Major-General George H. Thomas.* Philadelphia: J.B. Lippincott, 1881.
_____. *A Soldier's Reminiscences.* Philadelphia: J.B. Lippincott, 1886.
Johnson, Robert Underwood, and Clarence Clough Buel. *Battles and Leaders in the Civil War.* 4 vols. New York: Century, 1880–1881.
Jones, J. William. *Southern Historical Society Papers.* Wilmington, NC: Broadfoot Publishing, 1990.
Jones, Jenkin Lloyd. *An Artilleryman's Diary.* Madison: Wisconsin History Commission, 1914.
Keyes, Erasmus D. *Fifty Years Observations of Men and Events.* New York: Scribner's, 1885.
Keylin, Arleen, and Douglas John Bowen. *The New York Times Book of the Civil War.* New York: Arno Press, 1980.
Lee, Robert E., Jr. *Recollections and Letters of General Robert E. Lee.* Garden City, NY: Garden City Publishing, 1924.
Lewin, J.G., and P.J. Huff. *Witness to the Civil War: First-Hand Accounts from Frank Leslie's Illustrated Newspaper.* New York: Collins Books, 2006.
Longstreet, James P. *From Manassas to Appomattox.* Philadelphia: J.P. Lippincott, 1896.
McClure, Alexander K. *Lincoln and Men of War Times.* Philadelphia: Times Publishing, 1892.
McElroy, Joseph C. *Chickamauga: Record of The Ohio Chickamauga and Chattanooga National Park Commission.* Cincinnati: Earhart & Richardson Printers and Engravers, 1896.
Memorials of Deceased Companions of the Commandery of the State of Illinois, Military Order of the Loyal Legion of the United States. Wilmington, NC: Broadfoot Publishing, 1993.
Military Essays and Recollections: Papers Read Before the Commandery of the State of Illinois, Military Order of the Loyal Legion of the United States. Chicago: Dial Press, 1899.

Military Historical Society of Massachusetts, *Critical Sketches of Some of the Federal and Confederate Commanders*. Wilmington, NC: Broadfoot Publishing, 1989.
Mosgrove, George Dallas. *Kentucky Cavaliers in Dixie: Reminiscences of a Confederate Cavalryman*. Lincoln: University of Nebraska Press, 1999.
Northrup, Henry Davenport. *Life and Deeds of General Sherman, Including the Story of the Great March to the Sea*. Harrisburg: Pennsylvania Publishing, 1891.
Palmer, John M. *Recollections of John M. Palmer: The Story of an Earnest Life*. Cincinnati: R. Clarke, 1901.
Papers Read to the Military Historical Society of Massachusetts. Boston: Military Historical Society of Massachusetts, 1905.
Patterson, Robert. *A Narrative of the Campaign in the Valley of the Shenandoah in 1861*. Philadelphia: Sherman, Printers, 1865.
Piatt, Donn. *Memories of the Men Who Saved the Union*. New York: Belford, Clarke, 1887.
Porter, Horace. *Campaigning With Grant*. New York: Century, 1897.
The Rhode Island Soldiers and Sailors Historical Society. *Personal Narratives of Events in the War of the Rebellion: Being Papers Read Before the Rhode Island Soldiers and Sailors Historical Society*. Providence: published by the Society, 1885–1887.
Royse, Isaac H.C. *History of the 115th Illinois Volunteers*. Terre Haute, IN: published by the author, 1900.
Rusling, James F. *Men and Things I Saw in Civil War Days*. New York: Eaton & Mans, 1899.
Schofield, John M. *Forty-Six Years in the Army*. Norman: University of Oklahoma Press, 1998.
Scott, Robert N. *The War of the Rebellion: A Compilation of the Official Records of the Union and Confederate Armies*. 129 vols. Washington, D.C.: Government Printing Office, 1880–1901.
Shaler, Nathaniel S. *Campaigns in Kentucky and Tennessee, Including the Battle of Chickamauga 1862–1864. Papers Read in the Military Historical Society of Massachusetts*. Boston: Military Historical Society of Massachusetts, 1905.
Shanks, William F.G. *Personal Recollections of Distinguished Generals*. New York: Harper and Brothers, Publishers, 1866.
Sheridan, Philip H. *Personal Memoirs of P.H. Sheridan*. New York: Charles L. Webster, 1888.
Sherman, William T. *The Memoirs of General William T. Sherman: By Himself*. Bloomington: Indiana University Press, 1957.
Sketches of War History 1861–1865: Papers Prepared for the Commandery of Ohio, Military Order of the Loyal Legion of the United States. Cincinnati: Robert Clarke, 1903.
Sketches of War History 1861–1865: Papers Read Before The Ohio Commandery of the Military Order of the Loyal Legion of the United States. Cincinnati: Robert Clarke, 1888.
Society of the Army of the Cumberland. *Reports of the Meetings*. Cincinnati: Robert Clarke, 1869.
_____. *Reports of the Meetings*. Cincinnati: Robert Clarke, 1870.
_____. *Reports of the Meetings*. Cincinnati: Robert Clarke, 1875.
_____. *Reports of the Meetings*. Cincinnati: Robert Clarke, 1893.
_____. *Yearbook, 1870*. Cincinnati: Robert Clarke, 1870.
Sorrel, G. Moxley. *Recollections of a Confederate Staff Officer*. New York: Neale Publishing, 1905.
Sprague, John T. *The Florida War*. New York: D. Appleton, 1848.
Squires, W.H.T. *The Days of Yester-Year*. Porstmouth, VA: Printcraft Press, 1928.
Stevenson, Alexander F. *The Battle of Stone's River*. Boston: J.R. Osgood, 1884.
Stout, Dr. L.H. *Reminiscences of General Braxton Bragg*. Hattiesburg, MS: Book Farm, 1942.
Supplemental Report of the Joint Committee on the Conduct of the War. Washington, D.C.: Government Printing Office, 1866.
Swedberg, Claire E. *Three Years With The 92d Illinois: The Civil War Diary of John M. King*. Mechanicsburg, PA: Stackpole Books, 1999.
Tarrant, Sergeant E. *The Wild Riders of the First Kentucky Cavalry*. Louisville, KY: privately printed, 1894.
Thorpe, Thomas B. *Our Army on the Rio Grande*. Philadelphia: Carey & Hart, 1846.
Van Horne, Thomas B. *The Life of Major General George H. Thomas*. New York: Scribner's, 1882.
War Papers: Being Papers Read Before the Commandery of the District of Columbia, Military Order of the Loyal Legion of the United States. Wilmington, NC: Broadfoot Publishing, 1993.
War Papers: Being Papers Read Before the Commandery of the State of Michigan, Military Order of the Loyal Legion of the United States. Wilmington, NC: Broadfoot Publishing, 1993.
War Papers Read Before the Indiana Commandery, Military Order of the Loyal Legion of the United States. Indianapolis: Published by the Commandery, 1898.
War Papers Read Before the Commandery of the State of Maine, Military Order of the Loyal Legion of the United States. Portland, ME: Lefavor-Tower, 1908.

War Talks in Kansas: A Series of Papers Read Before the Kansas Commandery of the Military Order of the Loyal Legion of the United States. Kansas City, MO: Press of the Franklin Hudson Publishing, 1906.
Welles, Gideon. *The Diary of Gideon Welles.* 3 vols. Boston: Houghton Mifflin, 1911.
Wilcox, Cadmus M. *History of the Mexican War.* Washington, D.C.: Church News Publishing, 1892.
Wilson, James H. *Under the Old Flag.* 2 vols. New York: D. Appleton, 1912.
Wyeth, John Allen. *With Saber and Scalpel.* New York: Harper and Brothers, 1914.

Primary Sources — Newspapers, Magazines, Periodicals

Army and Navy Journal, June 3, 1865
Confederate Veteran Magazine
Detroit Advertiser, January 29, 1862
Detroit Daily Tribune, February 1, 1862
Geauga County Jeffersonian Democrat, February 2, 1862
Knoxville Register, January 26, 1862
Lebanon Weekly Patriot, October 26, 1899
Louisville Daily Courier, March 1, 1862
Marshall, Michigan Statesman, January 29, 1862
Memphis Daily Avalanche, January 28, 1862; January 30, 1862
Nashville Banner, January 31, 1862
North American Review, October 1888
Perry County Weekly, January 29, 1862
San Francisco Alta, March 29, 1870
Southern Bivouac: "Kennesaw Mountain," March 1883; "Hood's Tennessee Campaign," March 1885; "Hood's Tennessee Campaign," August 1885; "The Fifteenth Kentucky," September 1886
United Service Journal, February 1896

Secondary Sources — Books

Bailey, Anne J. *The Chessboard of War: Sherman and Hood in the Autumn Campaign of 1864.* Lincoln: University of Nebraska Press, 2000.
Bailey, Ronald H. *Battles for Atlanta: Sherman Moves East.* Alexandria, VA: Time Life Books, 1985.
Battlefields of the Civil War. New York: Arno Books, 1979.
Bauer, K. Jack. *Soldiering: The Civil War Diary of Rice C. Bull.* Novato, CA: Presidio Books, 1986.
Beaudot, William J.K. *The 24th Wisconsin Infantry in the Civil War: The Biography of a Regiment.* Harrisburg, PA: Stackpole Books, 2003.
Bowers, Claude G. *The Tragic Era: The Revolution After Lincoln.* Cambridge, MA: Literary Guild of America, 1929.
Bowman, John S. *The Civil War Almanac.* New York: World Almanac Publications, 1985.
Boyd, James P. *The Life of General William T. Sherman.* Publishers' Union, 1891.
Boynton, H.V. *Dedication of the Chickamauga and Chattanooga National Military Park, September 18–20, 1895.* Washington, D.C.: Government Printing Office, 1896.
Bridges, Hal. *Lee's Maverick General: Daniel Harvey Hill.* Lincoln: University of Nebraska Press, 1991.
Broadwater, Robert P. *Did Lincoln and the Republican Party Create the Civil War? An Argument.* Jefferson, NC: McFarland, 2008.
_____. *On to Atlanta: With the 27th Indiana Infantry Through Georgia.* Baltimore: Publish America, 2008.
Brockett, Linus P. *Our Great Captains: Grant, Sherman, Thomas, Sheridan, and Farragut.* New York: Richardson, 1865.
Buck, Irving A. *Cleburne and His Command.* Jackson, TN: McCowat-Mercer Press, 1959.
Buell, Thomas B. *The Warrior Generals, Combat Leadership in the Civil War.* New York: Crown, 1997.
Carter, Samuel, III. *The Siege of Atlanta, 1864.* New York: Ballantine Books, 1973.
Castel, Albert. *Decision in the West: The Atlanta Campaign of 1864.* Lawrence: University Press of Kansas, 1992.
Catton, Bruce. *Terrible Swift Sword.* Garden City, NY: Doubleday, 1963.
Chicoine, Stephen. *John Basil Turchin and the Fight to Free the Slaves.* Westport, CT: Praeger Books, 2003.
Cleaves, Freeman. *Rock of Chickamauga: The Life of General George H. Thomas.* Norman: University of Oklahoma Press, 1948.

Connelly, Donald B. *John Schofield & the Politics of Generalship.* Chapel Hill: University of North Carolina Press, 2006.
Connelly, Thomas Lawrence. *Army of the Heartland: The Army of Tennessee, 1861–1862.* Baton Rouge: Louisiana State University Press, 1971.
_____. *Autumn of Glory: The Army of Tennessee, 1862–1865.* Baton Rouge: Louisiana State University Press, 1971.
Coppee, Henry. *General Thomas.* New York: D. Appleton, 1893.
Daniel, Larry J. *Days of Glory: The Army of the Cumberland 1861–1865.* Baton Rouge: Louisiana State University Press, 2004.
_____. *Shiloh: The Battle That Changed the Civil War.* New York: Touchstone Books, 1997.
_____. *Soldiering in the Army of Tennessee: A Portrait of Life in a Confederate Army.* Chapel Hill: University of North Carolina Press, 1991.
Davis, William C. *The Deep Waters of the Proud.* Garden City, NY: Doubleday, 1982.
_____. *The Orphan Brigade: The Kentucky Confederates Who Couldn't Go Home.* Garden City, NY: Doubleday, 1980.
_____. *Stand in the Day of Battle.* Garden City, NY: Doubleday, 1983.
Denney, Robert E. *Civil War Medicine: Care & Comfort of the Wounded.* New York: Sterling Publishing, 1994.
Dowdey, Clifford. *Lee.* New York: Bonanza Books, 1965.
Dyer, John P. *From Shiloh to San Juan: The Life of "Fightin' Joe" Wheeler.* Baton Rouge: Louisiana State University Press, 1961.
_____. *The Gallant Hood.* Indianapolis: Bobbs-Merrill, 1950.
Encyclopedia Americana. New York: Stratford Press, 1954.
Engle, Stephen D. *Don Carlos Buell: Most Promising of All.* Chapel Hill: University of North Carolina Press, 1999.
Flood, Charles Bracelen. *Grant and Sherman: The Friendship That Won the Civil War.* New York: Farrar, Straus and Giroux, 2005.
Foster, G. Allen. *The Eyes and Ears of the Civil War.* New York: Criterion Books, 1963.
Freeman. Douglas Southall. *R.E. Lee: A Biography.* New York: Scribner's, 1962.
Haas, Garland A. *To the Mountain of Fire and Beyond: The Fifty-Third Indiana Regiment From Corinth to Glory.* Carmel: Guild Press of Indiana, 1997.
Hamilton, Holman. *Zachary Taylor.* Indianapolis: Bobbs-Merrill, 1941.
Harrison, Lowell H. *The Civil War in Kentucky.* Lexington: University of Kentucky Press, 1975.
Hattaway, Herman. *General Stephen D. Lee.* Jackson: University Press of Mississippi, 1976.
Henry, Robert Selph. *First with the Most: Forrest.* Wilmington, NC: Broadfoot Publishing, 1987.
_____. *The Story of Reconstruction.* Indianapolis: Bobbs-Merrill, 1938.
Henry, W.S. *Campaign Sketches of the War with Mexico.* New York: Harper & Brothers, 1847.
Hess, Earl J. *Banners to the Breeze: The Kentucky Campaign, Corinth, and Stones River.* Lincoln: University of Nebraska Press, 2000.
Hopkins, Timothy. *The Kelloggs in the Old World and the New.* San Francisco: Sunset Press and Photo Engraving, 1903.
Horn, Stanley F. *The Army of Tennessee: A Military History.* Indianapolis: Bobbs-Merrill, 1941.
Hutton, Paul Andrew. *Phil Sheridan and His Army.* Lincoln: University of Nebraska Press, 1985.
Johnson, Clint. *Bull's-Eyes and Misfires: 50 People Whose Obscure Efforts Shaped the American Civil War.* Nashville: Rutledge Hill Press, 2002.
Johnson, W. Fletcher. *Life of Wm. Tecumseh Sherman, Late Retired General, U.S.A.* Edgewood Publishing, 1891.
Kennett, Lee. *Marching Through Georgia: The Story of Soldiers & Civilians During Sherman's Campaign.* New York: HarperPerennial Books, 1995.
Key, William. *The Battle of Atlanta and the Georgia Campaign.* Atlanta: Peachtree Publishers Limited, 1981.
Korn, Jerry. *The Fight for Chattanooga: Chickamauga to Missionary Ridge.* Alexandria, VA: Time Life Books, 1985.
Lamers, William M. *The Edge of Glory: A Biography of General William S. Rosecrans, U.S.A.* New York: Harcourt, Brace & World, 1961.
Lewis, Lloyd. *Captain Sam Grant.* Boston: Little, Brown, 1950.
_____. *Sherman: Fighting Prophet.* New York: Harcourt, Brace, 1932.
Longacre, Edward G. *A Soldier to the Last: Maj. Gen. Joseph Wheeler in Blue and Gray.* Washington, D.C.: Potomac Books, 2007.
Lowry, Don. *Dark and Cruel War: The Decisive Months of the Civil War, September–December 1864.* New York: Hippocrene Books, 1993.

Macartney, Clarence Edward. *Grant and His Generals.* New York: McBride, 1953.
McDonough, James Lee. *Nashville: The Western Confederacy's Final Gamble.* Knoxville: University of Tennessee Press, 2004.
_____. *War in Kentucky: From Shiloh to Perryville.* Knoxville: University of Tennessee Press, 1994.
McElfresh, Earl B. *Maps and Mapmakers of the Civil War.* Boston: Henry N. Abrams, 1999.
McFeely, William S. *Grant: A Biography.* New York: W.W. Norton, 1981.
McKinney, Francis. *Education in Violence: The Life of George H. Thomas and the History of the Army of the Cumberland.* Detroit: Wayne State University Press, 1961.
McMurray, Richard M. *Atlanta 1864: Last Chance for the Confederacy.* Lincoln: University of Nebraska Press, 2000.
Meltzer, Milton. *Voices From the Civil War.* New York: Thomas Y. Crowell, 1989.
Meyer, Howard N. *Let Us Have Peace: The Story of Ulysses S. Grant.* New York: Collier Books, 1966.
Miller, Francis Trevelyan. *The Photographic History of the Civil War.* New York: Castle Books, 1957.
Milton, George Fort. *The Age of Hate.* New York: Coward-McCann, 1930.
Mitchell, Joseph B. *Military Leaders in the Civil War.* New York: Putnam's, 1972.
Morley, John. *Life of Gladstone.* New York: Macmillan, 1911.
Nevin, David. *The Road to Shiloh: Early Battles in the West.* Alexandria, VA: Time-Life Books, 1983.
Nevins, Allan. *The War For The Union: War Becomes Revolution, 1862–1863.* New York: Scribner's, 1960.
Overmyer, Jack K. *A Stupendous Effort: The 87th Indiana In The War of the Rebellion.* Bloomington, IN: Indiana University Press, 1997.
Palumbo, Frank A. *George Henry Thomas, Major General, U.S.A.: The Dependable General, Supreme in Tactics of Strategy and Command.* Dayton, OH: Morningside House, 1983.
Peskin, Allen. *Winfield Scott and the Profession of Arms.* Kent, OH: Kent State University Press, 2003.
Piatt, Donn. *General George H. Thomas: A Critical Biography.* Cincinnati: Robert Clarke, 1893.
Price, William H. *The Civil War Handbook.* Fairfax, VA: Prince Lithographic, 1961.
Randall, J.G. *Midstream: Lincoln the President.* New York: Dodd, Mead, 1953.
_____, and David Donald. *The Civil War and Reconstruction.* Boston: D.C. Heath, 1961.
Ridpath, J.C. *The Life and Work of James A. Garfield.* Cincinnati: Jones Brothers, 1882.
Rodgers, Andrew G. *John Torrey: A Story of North American Botany.* Princeton, NJ: Princeton University Press, 1942.
Roland, Charles P. *Albert Sidney Johnston: Soldier of Three Republics.* Austin, TX: University of Texas Press, 1964.
Roster, Charles. *The Destructive War: William Tecumseh Sherman, Stonewall Jackson, and the Americans.* New York: 1991.
Sandberg, Carl. *Abraham Lincoln: The War Years 1861–1864,* vol. 2. New York: Dell Books, 1962.
Seitz, Don C. *Braxton Bragg: General of the Confederacy.* Columbia, SC: State, 1924.
Smith, Justin H. *The War With Mexico.* New York: Macmillan, 1919.
Snow, Edward R. *Castle Island: Its 300 Years of History and Romance.* Andover, MA: self-published, 1935.
Stanley, David Sloan. *The Memoirs of David Sloan Stanley.* Santa Barbara, CA: Narrative Press, 2003.
Street, James, Jr. *The Struggle For Tennessee: Tupelo to Stones River.* Alexandria, VA: Time-Life Books, 1985.
Sword, Wiley. *Embrace an Angry Wind-The Confederacy's Last Hurrah: Spring Hill, Franklin, and Nashville.* New York: HarperCollins, 1992.
Symonds, Craig L. *Joseph E. Johnston: A Civil War Biography.* New York: W.W. Norton, 1992.
Thomas, Benjamin P., and Harold M. Hyman. *Stanton: The Life and Times of Lincoln's Secretary of War.* New York: Alfred A. Knopf, 1962.
Thomas, Emory M. *Bold Dragoon: The Life of J.E.B. Stuart.* Norman: University of Oklahoma Press, 1999.
Thomas, Wilbur. *General George H. Thomas—The Indomitable Warrior: A Biography.* New York: Exposition Press, 1964.
Trudeau, Noah. *Like Men of War: Black Troops in the Civil War 1862–1865.* New York: Castle Books, 2002.
Tucker, Glenn. *Chickamauga: Bloody Battle in the West.* Dayton, OH: Morningside Bookshop, 1976.
Warner, Ezra J. *Generals in Blue: Lives of the Confederate Commanders.* Baton Rouge: Louisiana State University Press, 1964.
_____. *Generals in Gray: Lives of the Union Commanders.* Baton Rouge: Louisiana State University Press, 1959.
Waugh, John G. *The Class of 1846: From West Point to Appomattox, Stonewall Jackson, George McClellan and Their Brothers.* New York: Warner Books, 1994.
Wert, Jeffry D. *General James Longstreet: The Confederacy's Most Controversial Soldier.* New York: Simon and Schuster, 1994.
Wertz, Jay, and Edwin C. Bearss. *Smithsonian's Great Battles and Battlefields of the Civil War.* New York: William Morrow, 1997.

Williams, T. Harry. *Beauregard: Napoleon in Gray*. New York: Collier Books, 1962.
_____. *Lincoln and His Generals*. New York: Gramercy Books, 2000.
Wittenberg, Eric J. *Little Phil: A Reassessment of the Civil War Leadership of Gen. Philip H. Sheridan*. Washington, D.C.: Potomac Books, 2002.
Woodward, W.E. *Meet General Grant*. New York: Horace Liveright, 1928.
Woodworth, Steven E. *Chickamauga: A Battlefield Guide With a Section on Chattanooga*. Lincoln: University of Nebraska Press, 1999.
_____. *Leadership and Command in the American Civil War*. Campbell, CA: Savas Wood Publishers, 1996.
_____. *Nothing But Victory: The Army of the Tennessee 1861–1865*. New York: Alfred A. Knopf, 2005.

Secondary Sources — Newspapers, Magazines, Periodicals

California Historical Society, Quarterly
"Catching Up With 'Old Slow Trot,'" *Smithsonian Magazine* 37, no. 12 (March 2007).
Civil War Times Illustrated
Columbiad Journal

Index

Abercrombie, John J. 52
Ackworth, Georgia 174, 195
Adams, John 200
Agua Neuva, Mexico 28
Allatoona Pass, Georgia 171, 195
Alpine, Georgia 116, 117
Altamont, Tennessee 78, 79
Americus, Georgia 188
Ampudia, Pedro 24, 26, 29
Anderson, John B. 162
Anderson, Thomas M. 57
Andersonville Prison 188, 190
Army of Northern Virginia 3, 103, 115, 125, 160, 161, 165, 168, 182, 217, 219
Army of Tennessee 3, 93, 94, 115, 117, 127, 160, 165, 179, 188, 193, 194
Army of the Cumberland 4, 88, 90, 92, 97, 100, 102, 103, 105, 107, 110, 111, 112, 114, 116, 117, 121, 122, 132, 140, 142, 143, 145, 146, 150, 152, 154, 156, 157, 165, 166, 167, 168, 170, 175, 176, 178, 179, 182, 183, 184, 189, 193, 194, 212, 216, 219, 234
Army of the Kentucky 104
Army of the Mississippi 77, 88
Army of the Ohio 64, 72, 73, 87, 88, 111, 163, 165, 168, 170, 179, 180, 187, 198, 201, 213, 215, 217
Army of the Potomac 56, 88, 103, 104, 106, 115, 140, 143, 159, 163, 164, 165, 176, 181
Army of the Tennessee 71, 72, 73, 77, 89, 140, 143, 149, 150, 156, 164, 165, 185, 186, 188, 189, 193
Arnall, Samuel M. 227
Atlanta, Georgia 1, 4, 111, 117, 121, 161, 162, 163, 166, 168, 171, 172, 178, 179, 180, 182, 183, 184, 185, 187, 188, 189, 190, 192, 193, 196, 197, 201, 233, 234
Augusta, Georgia 193
Austerlitz, battle of 217
Averrill, William W. 229

Badeau, Adam 145
Bainbridge, Alabama 217
Baird, Absalom 120, 121, 124, 125, 131, 135, 137, 154, 161, 177
Baker, James 70

Baltimore, Maryland 17
Banks, Nathaniel P. 57
Bastogne, Belgium 146
Bate, William B. 183, 188, 199
Battle of Atlanta 185, 186
Beach Grove, Kentucky 65, 69
Beatty, John 128, 142
Beatty, Samuel 98, 99, 101, 102, 132, 210
Beauregard, P.G.T. 52, 55, 71, 72, 73, 74, 75, 76, 191, 196, 205
Bell, John 46, 51
Bentonville, North Carolina 3
Berry, Thomas 124
Bishop's Palace 24, 25
Bladon Springs, Alabama 76
Blakeley, Archibald 121
Bowling Green, Kentucky 60, 63, 71, 88
Bragg, Braxton 10, 11, 12, 19, 20, 21, 23, 25, 26, 28, 30, 31, 32, 34, 40, 48, 72, 73, 76, 77, 80, 83, 86, 87, 88, 93, 97, 98, 99, 101, 102, 103, 105, 106, 113, 115, 117, 121, 123, 124, 126, 127, 134, 139, 140, 147, 148, 149, 150, 151, 152, 154, 156, 157, 158, 160, 161, 234, 235
Bramlette, Thomas E. 59
Brannon, John M. 120, 123, 124, 129, 131, 132, 137
Brazos de Santiago, Texas 34
Breckinridge, John C. 46, 72, 73, 94, 97, 98, 99, 101, 105, 115, 118, 128, 131, 220
Breckinridge, Joseph 67
Brentwood, Tennessee 105
Bridgeport, Alabama 113, 142, 143, 144, 146, 147, 149, 158, 191
Brown, Jacob 20, 21, 23
Brown, John C. 200
Brown, W. Matt 224
Brownlow, W.G. 227
Brown's Ferry, Tennessee 146, 147, 148
Brownsville, Texas 42
Brush Mountain, Georgia 174
Buckner, Simon B. 57, 58, 59, 122, 123, 127
Buell, Don C. 10, 11, 57, 64, 65, 70, 71, 72, 73, 74, 75, 77, 78, 79, 80, 81, 82, 83, 84, 86, 87, 88, 89, 90, 91, 93, 234

Buell, George P. 132
Buena Vista, Mexico 28, 31, 32, 33
Bunker Hill, Virginia 4, 55, 56, 217
Burnside. Ambrose E. 111, 116, 122, 140, 148, 149, 158
Butler, Benjamin 165
Butterfield, Daniel 163
Buzzard's Roost, Georgia 166, 168, 170

Cairo, Illinois 143
Calhoun, James M. 189
Calhoun, John C. 19
Cameron, Simon 61, 63
Camp Cooper, Texas 42, 43, 44, 45
Camp Dick Robinson, Kentucky 57, 58, 60, 61, 62, 134, 194
Camp Wildcat, Kentucky 60, 61, 63
Canales, Antonio 23
Canby, Edward R.S. 218, 219
Carlisle, Pennsylvania 50, 51
Carter, John C. 200
Carter, Samuel P. 64, 71, 77
Carthage, Tennessee 80
Cass, Lewis 7, 8
Cassville, Georgia 171
Catoosa Springs, Georgia 167
Cedar Creek, Virginia 4, 217
Centreville, Virginia 52
Chalmers, James 208, 209
Chalmette Battlefield 17
Chambersburg, Pennsylvania 51
Charleston, South Carolina 17, 19
Charleston, West Virginia 55, 56
Chase, Salmon P. 87
Chattahoochie River 179, 188, 191
Chattanooga, Tennessee 2, 3, 47, 77, 91, 109, 110, 111, 113, 116, 127, 130, 134, 139, 140, 142, 143, 144, 146, 148, 149, 150, 151, 152, 156, 157, 158, 161, 163, 165, 171, 179, 182, 187, 188, 191, 193, 194, 197, 201, 216, 217, 219, 220, 233, 234, 235
Cheatham, Benjamin F. 84, 123, 124, 185, 198, 199, 200, 206, 209, 210, 211, 212, 214
Chicago, Illinois 228
Chickamauga, Georgia 1, 4, 17, 125, 126, 184, 212, 216, 220, 235
Chickamauga Creek 118, 121, 123, 153

Chickasaw Bayou, Mississippi 3
Cincinnati, Ohio 63, 88, 204, 212
Clayton, Henry D. 153
Cleburne, Patrick R. 109, 118, 121, 125, 126, 128, 131, 149, 152, 153, 157, 173, 184, 199, 200
Clinton, Georgia 188
Cockrell, Francis M. 200
Colburn, John 105
Cold Harbor, Virginia 3, 176
Colorado River 44
Columbia, Tennessee 71, 72, 198, 199
Comanche Indians 42, 43
Connell, John M. 132
Coon, Darus E. 211
Cooper, Samuel 180
Corinth, Mississippi 72, 73, 74, 75, 76, 77, 78, 88, 91, 103, 197, 198
Corpus Christi, Texas 18, 19
Couch, Darius M. 210
Cox, Jacob D. 170, 171, 198, 210
Crab Orchard, Kentucky 63
Crawfish Springs, Georgia 118, 120, 125, 127
Crittenden, George B. 65, 66, 70, 72
Crittenden, Thomas L. 64, 65, 72, 82, 83, 84, 86, 92, 93, 94, 97, 98, 100, 101, 104, 106, 109, 112, 113, 116, 117, 121, 122, 123, 124, 127, 130, 135, 140, 143
Crook, George 37
Croxton, John T. 124, 132
Cruft, Charles 79, 98, 150, 205
Cumberland Gap 58, 61, 64, 70, 71, 77, 79
Cumberland River 65, 66, 69, 71, 80, 205, 206, 208
Curley, Joseph 5

Dallas, Georgia 172
Dalton, Georgia 123, 161, 163, 166, 167, 168, 176, 191, 195, 218
Dana, Charles A. 112, 121, 125, 129, 130, 140, 142, 143, 145
Danville, Kentucky 58
Davis, Jefferson 40, 70, 71, 76, 77, 103, 115, 116, 148, 160, 180, 187, 190, 205, 219, 235
Davis, Jefferson C. 80, 94, 98, 129, 130, 138, 177, 178, 182, 187
Davis, Marshall 203
Deadrick, Robert 69
Decatur, Alabama 193, 195
Decatur, Georgia 182, 186
Decatur, Tennessee 163
Dechard, Kentucky 77
Deshler, James 37
Dilger, Hubert 175
Dodge, Grenville M. 185, 193
Donaldson, James 208
Doubleday, Abner 51, 52
Douglas, Stephen 46
Duck River 73, 109
Dug Gap, Georgia 117, 118, 123, 124
Dumont, Ebenezer 92
Durfee, Joseph 68
Dyer, Alexander B. 228

Eagleville, Tennessee 107
East Tennessee and Virginia Railroad 61, 62, 63
Eastport, Mississippi 218
Ector, Matthew 210, 214
8th Kentucky Infantry 151
89th Illinois Infantry 125
11th Army Corps 140, 147, 149, 150
Etowah River 172
Everglades, the 12, 13, 14, 16, 17
Ewell, Richard 223
Ezra Church, Georgia 187

Fairfax Court House, Virginia 55
Falling Waters, Virginia 4, 52, 53
Faw, George P. 66
15th Army Corps 193
15th Georgia Infantry 214
15th Mississippi Infantry 66, 68
15th Pennsylvania Infantry 52
5th United States Cavalry 56, 57
58th Indiana Infantry 216
1st Alabama Battalion 136
1st City Cavalry of Philadelphia 53
1st Illinois Infantry 28
1st Kentucky Cavalry 66, 67
1st Ohio Infantry 25
1st Ohio Light Artillery 67, 70
1st Tennessee Cavalry 109
1st Tennessee Infantry 68
1st Tennessee Infantry, C.S.A. 85
1st United States Artillery 20
1st United States Cavalry 40
1st United States Dragoons 28
1st United States Infantry 23
Fishing Creek, Kentucky *see* Mill Springs
Fitch, Le Roy 195, 208
Fletcher, William A. 125
Floyd, John B. 43
USS *Forester* 12
Forrest, Nathan Bedford 74, 77, 92, 101, 105, 124, 139, 162, 191, 193, 195, 198, 199, 200, 205, 208, 215, 216, 219, 224, 227
Fort Adams, Rhode Island 34, 36
Fort Belknap, Texas 41
Fort Brooke, Florida 16
Fort Brown, Texas 20, 21, 23, 33
Fort Casino, Tennessee 206
Fort Columbus, N.Y. 10, 11
Fort Dallas, Florida 13
Fort Donelson, Tennessee 71, 72, 163
Fort Garesche, Tennessee 206
Fort Gillem, Tennessee 206
Fort Henry, Tennessee 71, 72, 163
Fort Independence, Massachusetts 35, 36
Fort Lauderdale, Florida 12, 13, 14, 15, 16
Fort Mason, Texas 42
Fort McHenry, Maryland 17
Fort Morton, Tennessee 206
Fort Moultrie, South Carolina 17
Fort Pierce, Florida 12, 13, 14
Fort Pillow, Tennessee 76
Fort Sumter, South Carolina 50, 56, 88
Fort Taylor, Texas 20, 21, 23
Fort Texas, Texas 20

Fort Washita, Texas 42
Fort Wood, Tennessee 150
Fort Yuma, Arizona 38, 39, 40
Foster, John G. 161
Foster, Samuel T. 205
14th Army Corps 104, 105, 116, 118, 121, 124, 135, 137, 143, 165, 177, 187, 189, 191, 193, 194
14th Ohio Infantry 65, 70, 163
14th United States Colored Troops 198
4th Army Corps 104, 163, 165, 168, 172, 177, 187, 191, 193, 194, 198, 203, 220, 221
4th Kentucky Infantry 67
4th Tennessee Cavalry 69
4th United States Artillery 28
4th United States Infantry 18
49th Ohio Infantry 173
Frankfort, Kentucky 80
Frankfort Arsenal 59
Franklin, Tennessee 105, 199, 200, 201, 202, 205, 230, 235
Franklin Pike 206, 208, 211, 212, 214, 215
French, Samuel G. 9, 23, 25, 26, 27, 29, 30, 32, 175
Fry, Speed S. 67, 68, 69, 92, 93

Gadsden, Alabama 195
Gallatin, Tennessee 68, 93
Gano, R.M. 134
Garfield, James A. 4, 49, 50, 107, 130, 134, 135, 136, 137, 138, 160
Garnett, Robert S. 37
Garrard, Kenner 37, 165, 179, 209
Geary, John W. 147, 150, 151, 172
Gibson, Randall 98
Gibson, William 173
Gila Trail 39
Gilbert, Charles C. 82, 83, 84, 86, 92, 94
Gist, States Rights 131, 200
Gladstone, William E. 103
Glasgow, Kentucky 80
Goodling, Michael 84, 85, 86
Gordon, George W. 200
Gorgas, Josiah 223
Govan, Daniel C. 121, 132, 189
Gracie, Archibald, Jr. 136
Granbury, Hiram 173, 200
Granger, Gordon 104, 127, 130, 131, 132, 133, 134, 135, 136, 137, 138, 150, 153, 154, 155, 158
Granny White Pike 206, 208, 211, 212, 215
Grant, Ulysses S. 2, 3, 10, 11, 32, 58, 71, 72, 73, 74, 75, 77, 78, 89, 106, 110, 122, 143, 144, 145, 146, 148, 149, 150, 152, 153, 154, 155, 156, 157, 158, 162, 163, 164, 165, 166, 167, 168, 176, 178, 192, 193, 196, 201, 202, 203, 204, 205, 211, 212, 216, 217, 218, 219, 224, 225, 226, 228, 229, 230, 231, 232, 233, 234
Gruesel, Nicholas 84

Haggard, J.N. 68
Halleck, Henry 64, 72, 75, 77, 81,

89, 90, 91, 104, 107, 111, 112, 114, 117, 122, 143, 162, 192, 193, 204, 216, 218, 222, 229, 230
Hancock, Winfield S. 225
Hanson, Charles 21
Hanson, Roger W. 98
Hardee, William J. 10, 11, 40, 72, 73, 93, 94, 105, 107, 109, 115, 149, 151, 166, 172, 175, 181, 182, 183, 184, 185, 188, 189
Harker, Charles G. 132, 133, 177
Harrison, Benjamin 182
Harrodsburg, Kentucky 86
Hascall, Milo S. 98, 175
Hatch, Edward 198, 211
Haupt, Herman 162
Hawkins, E.S. 20, 21, 23
Hazen, William P. 98, 134, 146, 147, 173
Helm, Benjamin H. 131
Herbert, Paul O. 223
Hescock, Henry 84
Hickman, Kentucky 58
Hill, Daniel H. 10, 115, 118, 123, 127, 128
Hillsboro Pike 206
Hindman, Thomas C. 118, 132, 133, 170
Holly Springs, Tennessee 78
Honnell, William H. 67, 68
Hood, John B. 3, 37, 40, 48, 115, 123, 125, 129, 166, 171, 172, 180, 181, 182, 184, 185, 187, 188, 190, 191, 192, 193, 194, 195, 196, 197, 198, 199, 200, 201, 202, 204, 205, 208, 209, 210, 211, 212, 213, 215, 218, 226, 234
Hooker, Joseph 140, 143, 145, 146, 147, 149, 150, 151, 152, 156, 158, 165, 170, 172, 173, 177, 182, 186, 187
Horseshoe Ridge 17, 132, 134, 135, 137, 138
Hough, Alfred L. 230, 231
Howard, Oliver O. 37, 59, 147, 149, 158, 163, 165, 168, 170, 171, 172, 173, 178, 182, 183, 186, 187, 188, 189
Huntsville, Alabama 158, 218
Hurlburt, Stephen A. 73, 122, 140
Hyattsville, Maryland 57

Imperial Valley, California 39
Indian Hill 15
Indianapolis, Indiana 89
Iuka, Mississippi 88

Jackson, Andrew 7, 8, 12, 17
Jackson, Henry R. 214
Jackson, James S. 83
Jackson, John K. 151
Jackson, Thomas J. 1, 32, 52
Jackson, Mississippi 71, 72
Jefferson Barracks, Missouri 40
Jerusalem, Virginia 6, 7, 32
Johnson, Andrew 57, 61, 62, 77, 78, 79, 80, 87, 202, 203, 220, 222, 224, 225, 226
Johnson, Bushrod 109, 125, 129, 132, 133

Johnson, Edward 210
Johnson, Richard W. 44, 94, 124, 125, 131, 135, 154, 161
Johnsonville, Tennessee 195
Johnston, Albert S. 40, 48, 50, 60, 63, 65, 71, 72, 72
Johnston, George 200
Johnston, Joseph E. 3, 40, 48, 52, 55, 105, 160, 161, 163, 165, 166, 167, 170, 171, 172, 174, 175, 178, 179, 180, 181, 187, 233, 234
Jones, Sam 13
Jonesboro, Georgia 188, 189
Judah, Henry 170, 171

Kellogg, Abigail 38
Kellogg, Frances see Thomas, Frances
Kellogg, Lyman M. 38
Kellogg, Sanford 128, 129, 161
Kelly, John 173
Kennesaw Mountain, Georgia 3, 174, 175, 176, 177, 178, 179, 231
Kershaw, Joseph B. 129, 132
Key Biscayne, Florida 12
Keyes, Erasmus D. 8, 15, 16, 17, 19, 36, 38, 50, 229
Kilpatrick, Judson 165
Kimball, Nathan 211
King, E.H. 195
King, John M. 107, 112
Kingsbury, Charles P. 12, 13
Kingston, Georgia 171
Kingston, Kentucky 79
Knipe, James F. 219
Knoxville, Tennessee 71, 89, 111, 116, 122, 140, 148, 158, 161, 219
Ku Klux Klan 224, 227, 228

La Angostore, Mexico 28
Lafayette, Georgia 117, 118, 121, 191
Lake Worth 15
Lane, Joseph 29
Law, Evander 132
Lebanon, Kentucky 64, 65
Lee, Fitzhugh 36, 44, 49, 50
Lee, George W.C. 36, 37
Lee, Robert E. 1, 3, 5, 10, 32, 36, 40, 42, 43, 44, 48, 50, 51, 88, 103, 104, 116, 160, 161, 181, 219, 235
Lee, Robert E., Jr. 36
Lee, Stephen D. 187, 188, 198, 200, 206, 210, 212, 214, 215
Lee and Gordon's Mills, Georgia 122, 123
Lenoir, T.M. 78
Lexington, Kentucky 58, 59, 63, 79
Liddell, St. John R. 85, 86, 125, 131, 136, 138
Lincoln, Abraham 2, 45, 46, 47, 50, 57, 58, 64, 71, 77, 82, 87, 90, 101, 102, 104, 131, 142, 143, 158, 181, 189, 190, 202, 212, 219
Logan, John 163, 186, 204, 212
Logan's Cross Roads, Kentucky see Mill Springs
Lombardini, Manuel 29
London, Kentucky 63, 64

Longstreet, James P. 10, 11, 17, 115, 122, 126, 127, 129, 130, 134, 135, 136, 139, 142, 147, 149, 158, 163, 223
Lookout Creek 146, 150
Lookout Mountain 113, 117, 120, 121, 140, 142, 147, 148, 150, 151
Lost Mountain 174, 175
Louisa Court House, Virginia 116
Louisville, Kentucky 56, 57, 59, 63, 80, 82, 84, 88, 89, 226
Lovejoy's Station, Georgia 188, 189, 190
Lowd, Allen 21
Lumsden, Charles 211
Lynchburg, Virginia 47

Macon, Georgia 188, 189, 220
Manassas, Virginia 1, 55, 56, 160, 210, 234
Manchester, Tennessee 109
Maney, George 183
Manigault, Arthur M. 200
Mansfield, Joseph K. 22, 23, 24
Manson, Mahlan D. 67, 79
Marietta, Georgia 172, 173, 178, 179
Martin, Edwin K. 135
Martinsburg, West Virginia 53, 56
Mason, John Y. 7, 8, 10, 34, 35
Massie, Robert F. 35, 36
Matamoras, Mexico 20
Maury, Dabney 48, 49, 180
Maynard, Horace 57, 63, 70
Maxwell House Hotel 224
McArthur, Arthur 74, 209, 211
McClellan, George B. 32, 56, 64, 71, 77, 88, 202, 217
McClernand, John 73, 74, 75
McClure, Alexander K. 51
McCook, Alexander M. 37, 64, 72, 82, 83, 84, 86, 92, 93, 94, 97, 104, 106, 109, 113, 116, 117, 121, 122, 124, 127, 129, 135, 140, 143
McCook, Dan 67, 68, 177, 178
McCook, Edwin M. 165, 188
McCown, John 93
McCullum, David 162
McDowell, Irvin 52, 55, 56
McLaws, Lafayette 115
McLemore's Cove, Georgia 117, 118, 120, 127
McMinnville, Tennessee 78, 79, 93, 234
McPherson, James B. 37, 164, 165, 166, 167, 168, 170, 171, 173, 174, 176, 177, 178, 179, 182, 183, 184, 185
Meade, George G. 32, 115, 160, 217, 222, 229, 231
Memphis, Tennessee 47, 76, 122, 140, 162, 219, 224
Mendenhall, John 98, 99, 101
Mexico City, Mexico 26
Mill Springs, Kentucky 1, 4, 65, 70, 71, 72, 103, 194, 212, 216, 234, 235
Millen, Georgia 193
Miller, John F. 99, 102, 197, 208, 222

Missionary Ridge, Tennessee 4, 122, 126, 140, 142, 148, 149, 150, 151, 156, 157, 176, 197
Mississippi Rifles 28, 30, 31
Mississippi River 47, 76, 197
Mitchell, J.G. 177
Mitchell, Ormsby M. 57, 61, 62, 71, 72
Mitchell, Robert B. 92, 93
Mobile, Alabama 34, 71, 1621, 180, 192, 193, 218, 219
Moccasin Point, Tennessee 146
Mohave Indians 39, 40
Monterrey, Mexico 23, 24, 25, 26, 33, 35, 38
Montgomery, Alabama 162, 192, 193, 219
Moore, J.B. 209
Moore, John C. 151
Morgan, James D. 191, 193
Morgan, John H. 77
Morgan, Thomas J. 198
Morton, Levi 80
Mumfordville, Kentucky 80
Murfreesboro, Tennessee 72, 79, 93, 94, 102, 103, 104, 194, 197, 205, 215, 219
Murphy, William 44

Nashville, Tennessee 1, 3, 4, 60, 71, 72, 77, 79, 80, 88, 91, 92, 93, 94, 105, 113, 158, 163, 164, 190, 191, 194, 195, 196, 197, 198, 200, 201, 203, 204, 205, 210, 212, 215, 216, 220, 222, 224, 227, 228, 230, 235
Negley, James S. 80, 92, 94, 96, 97, 99, 102, 117, 118, 120, 121, 128, 131, 138, 140, 143
Nelson, William 58, 64, 72, 73, 79, 80
New Haven, Connecticut 57
New Hope Church, Georgia 172, 173, 176
New Orleans, Louisiana 16, 17, 18, 35, 47, 221, 223, 227
New York, New York 38, 42, 47, 48, 50, 230
Newman, Georgia 188
Newsom's Depot, Virginia 5
Newton, John 177, 182, 183, 191, 193
19th Alabama Infantry 78
92nd Illinois Infantry 107, 112, 165
9th Ohio Infantry 67, 68
9th Ohio Light Artillery 68
Nolansville, Tennessee 94
Norfolk, Virginia 47
Nueces River 18

Oakland, California 231
Oatman, Mary Ann 39
Oatman, Olive 39, 40
Oatman, Royce 39
Okechobee River 13
101st Airborne Division 146
Oostanaula River 171
Orange Court House, Virginia 116
Orchard Knob, Tennessee 149, 150, 152, 153, 165

Ord, Edward O.C. 1, 4, 77
Osterhaus, Peter J. 150

Pace's Ferry, Georgia 179
Pacheco, F. 29
Paducah, Kentucky 58, 199
Palmer, John M. 97, 99, 124, 125, 131, 134, 135, 137, 147, 161, 165, 182, 187
Palo Alto, Mexico 20, 22
Patterson, Robert 26, 27, 51, 52, 55, 57, 82, 234
Patton, George S., Jr. 146
Peach Orchard Hill, Tennessee 212
Peach Tree Creek, Georgia 179, 182, 183, 184, 185
Pemberton, John C. 110, 160
Pensacola, Florida 192
Perez, F. 29
Perryville, Kentucky 83, 86, 92, 93, 181
Pettus, Edmund W. 151
Peyton, Baille 68
Pickett's Mill, Georgia 173
Piedmont, West Virginia 55
Pigeon Mountain, Georgia 117, 121, 123
Pillow, Gideon J. 98, 223
Pine Mountain, Georgia 174, 175
Pittsburgh Landing, Tennessee 72, 73, 75, 90
Poe, Edgar Allan 36
Polk, James K. 18, 19, 26, 34, 60
Polk, Leonidus 58, 71, 72, 73, 85, 93, 94, 101, 105, 109, 122, 123, 127, 129, 130, 135, 166, 172
Pope, John 75, 76, 77, 88
Port Isabel, Texas 20, 23
Porter, Fitz John 37, 51, 55
Porter, George P. 66, 67
Porter, Horace 145
Post, Sidney 210
Prentiss, Benjamin 73
Preston, William 98, 101, 123, 136
Prewitt's Knob, Kentucky 80
Price, Sterling 76, 194
Pulaski, Tennessee 198, 215

Quarles, William A. 200
Quitman, John A. 25, 26, 27

Raccoon Mountain, Tennessee 146
Randall, Samuel J. 53
Readyville, Tennessee 93
Renfrew, Georgia 188
Resaca, Georgia 167, 168, 1701, 171, 176, 191, 195
Resaca de la Palma, Mexico 20, 23
Reynolds, John 20, 27, 30
Reynolds, Joseph J. 120, 123, 125, 129, 131, 135, 126, 137
Reynosa, Mexico 23
Richmond, Kentucky 79
Richmond, Virginia 56, 116, 148, 160, 165, 180, 181, 200, 212, 219
Ringgold, Georgia 122, 123, 127, 158, 162, 167
Rio Grande River 18, 20
Robertson, F.H. 78
Rochelle, James 7

Rocky Face, Georgia 166, 167, 168, 172, 176, 234
Rome, Georgia 111, 117, 121
Rosecrans, Sylvester H. 87
Rosecrans, William S. 10, 11, 36, 87, 89, 90, 92, 93, 94, 96, 98, 100, 103, 104, 106, 107, 109, 110, 111, 113, 114, 115, 118, 121, 123, 124, 125, 126, 127, 128, 129, 130, 134, 135, 136, 140, 142, 143, 144, 202, 234
Rosswell, Georgia 179
Rough and Ready, Georgia 189
Rousseau, Lovell H. 83, 84, 92, 96, 97, 205
Russell, W.C. 131

St. Augustine, Florida 12, 13
St. Louis, Missouri 64, 194
Saltillo, Mexico 24, 26, 28, 29, 30
San Antonio, Texas 42, 47
San Diego, California 39
San Domingo, Mexico 24
San Francisco, California 39, 50, 64, 229, 231
Santa Anna, Antonio Lopez de 18, 28, 29, 30, 31
Savannah, Georgia 12, 192, 193, 218
Savannah, Tennessee 73
Schoepf, Albin F. 60, 63, 64, 65, 66
Schofield, John M. 37, 163, 165, 166, 167, 168, 171, 174, 175, 177, 179, 181, 182, 183, 184, 185, 187, 188, 189, 191, 194, 195, 198, 199, 200, 201, 203, 204, 206, 208, 210, 212, 214, 218, 229, 230, 233
Scott, Thomas A. 53
Scott, Thomas M. 200
Scott, Winfield 2, 26, 27, 28, 47, 48, 55, 164
Scribner, B.F. 139
2nd Alabama Battalion 136
2nd Georgia Infantry 214
2nd Kentucky Infantry 28, 29, 30
2nd Illinois Infantry 28, 29, 30
2nd Indiana Cavalry 132
2nd Indiana Infantry 28, 29, 30, 31
2nd Minnesota Infantry 67, 68
2nd United States Cavalry 40, 41, 43, 49, 50, 51, 56, 57, 182, 213
2nd United States Dragoons 28
Seddon, James 115
Selma, Alabama 162, 192, 193, 219
Seminole War 12, 15, 17
17th Army Corps 193
7th United States Infantry 20, 21, 22, 23
78th Pennsylvania Infantry 118, 121
79th Pennsylvania Infantry 135
77th Pennsylvania Infantry 125
Shelbyville, Tennessee 105, 107, 110, 111, 234
Shepherd, O.L. 97
Sheridan, Philip 1, 3, 4, 10, 37, 78, 94, 96, 100, 129, 130, 137, 138, 139, 150, 154, 217, 222, 223, 224, 225, 226, 229, 231, 232, 233
Sherman, John 2, 146
Sherman, Thomas W. 13, 14, 20

Index

Sherman, William T. 1, 2, 7, 8, 9, 10, 11, 12, 57, 60, 62, 63, 64, 72, 73, 74, 75, 140, 143, 146, 148, 149, 152, 153, 156, 157, 158, 162, 163, 164, 165, 166, 167, 168, 170, 171, 172, 175, 176, 177, 178, 179, 180, 182, 183, 185, 186, 187, 188, 189, 191, 192, 193, 194, 195, 196, 201, 216, 217, 218, 222, 224, 225, 226, 228, 229, 231, 232, 233, 234
Shiloh Church, Tennessee 73, 75, 103
Shoup, Francis A. 190
Shrover, William H. 35, 36
Shurz, Carl 147
Siddle, Casper 44
Sierra Madre Mountains 23, 28
Sigel, Franz 165
16th Alabama Infantry 67
16th Army Corps 185, 193, 194
16th Iowa Infantry 185
6th Kentucky Infantry 97
Slocum, Henry W. 187, 188, 189
Smith, Andrew J. 194, 197, 199, 201, 203, 206, 208, 209, 210, 211, 212, 213, 214, 218
Smith, Charles F. 72
Smith, E. Kirby 40, 77, 78, 79, 80, 83, 205
Smith, Francis H. 48, 49
Smith, Giles 185
Smith, Thomas B. 214
Smith, William F. 145, 146
Smith, William Sooy 162
Smyrna, Georgia 179
Snake Spring Gap, Georgia 167, 168, 170, 176, 234
Snodgrass House 132
Soap River 179
Somerset, Kentucky 63, 64, 65
Sorrell, Moxley 142
Southampton Academy 7
Southampton County, Virginia 5, 6, 7, 10, 32, 33, 34, 38, 231
Southwick, Daniel 38
Sparta, Tennessee 79, 80, 93
Spotsylvania, Virginia 3, 176
Spring Hill, Tennessee 199
Stanley, David S. 37, 921, 93, 99, 107, 109, 110, 132, 171, 187, 189, 193, 198, 199, 200
Stanton, Edwin 81, 87, 89, 90, 104, 110, 111, 112, 114, 117, 143, 160, 192, 201, 202, 212, 216, 226
Starkweather, John C. 84, 86
Steedman, James B. 65, 86, 131, 132, 133, 134, 135, 136, 137, 143, 197, 201, 203, 206, 208, 209, 213, 215, 222
Stephens, Alexander 223
Stevenson, Alabama 113
Stevenson, Carter L. 150, 152, 153
Stewart, Alexander P. 109, 115, 123, 125, 131, 172, 173, 181, 182, 187, 188, 198, 200, 206, 210, 211, 212, 214
Stone, Henry 172, 177
Stoneman, George 188, 219
Stones River, Tennessee 94, 101, 102, 103, 104, 184, 212, 216, 220

Strahl, Otho 200
Streight, Abel 105
Stuart, James E.B. 37, 40, 42, 52, 93
Sumner, Edwin V. 40
Swift, Eban 100

Tampico, Mexico 26, 27
Taylor, Richard 196, 197, 219
Taylor, Zachary 18, 19, 20, 21, 23, 24, 25, 26, 27, 29, 30, 31, 32, 82, 144
Tennessee River 72, 73, 110, 112, 113, 140, 146, 147, 162, 191, 192, 195, 198, 215, 217
10th Georgia Infantry 214
10th Indiana Infantry 67
Terrill, William R. 83
Texas Rangers 23, 47
3rd Indiana Infantry 28, 29, 30
3rd Kentucky Infantry 59
3rd United States Artillery 8, 10, 12, 14, 15, 18, 20, 28, 34, 35, 38, 213
3rd United States Infantry 18, 64
30th Georgia Infantry 214
37th Georgia Infantry 214
36th Illinois Infantry 84, 93, 94
Thomas, Benjamin 5
Thomas, Elizabeth 5, 6, 8, 42
Thomas, Frances 38, 42, 45, 47, 50, 194, 227, 229, 230, 231
Thomas, George H. 1, 2, 3, 4, 5, 7, 8, 9, 10, 11, 12, 13, 14, 15, 16, 17, 20, 21, 23, 25, 26, 27, 28, 29, 30, 31, 32, 33, 34, 35, 36, 37, 38, 39, 40, 41, 43, 44, 45, 46, 47, 48, 49, 50, 51, 52, 53, 55, 56, 57, 58, 59, 61, 62, 63, 64, 65, 66, 67, 68, 69, 70, 71, 72, 74, 75, 77, 78, 79, 80, 81, 82, 83, 86, 87, 88, 89, 90, 91, 92, 93, 94, 96, 100, 102, 104, 106, 109, 110, 111, 113, 114, 117, 118, 120, 121, 122, 123, 124, 125, 126, 127, 128, 131, 132, 133, 134, 135, 136, 137, 138, 139, 140, 142, 143, 144, 145, 146, 148, 149, 151, 152, 153, 155, 156, 157, 158, 159, 160, 161, 163, 165, 166, 168, 170, 171, 172, 174, 176, 177, 178, 179, 182, 183, 184, 185, 186, 187, 188, 191, 192, 196, 194, 195, 196, 197, 198, 199, 201, 202, 203, 204, 205, 206, 208, 209, 210, 211, 213, 214, 215, 216, 217, 218, 219, 220, 221, 222, 223, 224, 225, 226, 227, 228, 229, 230, 231, 232, 233
Thomas, John C. 5
Thomas, John W. 5
Thomas, Lorenzo 63
Thomas Legion 220
Thomaston, Virginia 5, 6, 46, 47
Thruston, Gates P. 130, 138
Tile, John 44
Tomey, John 168, 179
Tower, Zebulon B 206
Tracy, E.D. 78
Travis, Joseph 6
Trimble, Carey 57

Triune, Tennessee 93
Troy, New York 38, 231
Tullahoma, Tennessee 105, 109, 110, 111
Tunnel Hill, Tennessee 152, 168
Tupelo, Mississippi 76, 217
Turchin, John B. 116, 136, 138
Turner, Nat 6, 7
Tuscaloosa, Alabama 77, 195, 196
12th Army Corps 140, 150
20th Army Corps 104, 138, 143, 165, 188, 193
20th Georgia Infantry 214
20th Tennessee Infantry 66, 68
21st Army Corps 104, 143
21st Ohio Infantry 136
24th Wisconsin Infantry 94, 179
29th Tennessee Infantry 66
22nd Indiana Infantry 85
22nd Michigan Infantry 136
27th Indiana Infantry 168, 179
23rd Army Corps 194, 198
Twiggs, David E. 24, 26, 27, 35, 38, 43, 47, 48, 50

C.S.S. *Undine* 195
Unionville, Tennessee 107
Utica, New York 231

Van Cleve, Horatio 98, 130, 143
Van Deveer, Ferdinand 124, 132, 134
Van Dorn, Earl 40, 43, 75, 78, 105
Van Vliet, Stewart 8, 11, 12, 13, 14
Vicksburg, Mississippi 76, 106, 110, 115, 122, 140, 156, 160, 163, 201
Victoria, Mexico 27
Villa Gran, Mexico 27
Villanow, Georgia 167
Virginia Military Institute 48, 49, 50

Wade, Benjamin 226
Wade, Richard A. 14, 15, 16
Wagner, George 177
Waite, Stand 220
Walker, Mary 162
Walker, Samuel H. 21
Walker, W.H.T. 122, 123, 127
Wallace, Lew 74
Wallace, W.H.L. 73
Walnut Springs, Mexico 24
Walthall, Edward C. 131, 151, 210, 216
Ward, William 183
Wartrace, Tennessee 105, 109
Washburne, Elihu 163, 164
Washington, George 5, 10, 164, 235
Washington, John M. 28, 29
Washington, D.C. 47, 58, 63, 77, 111, 112, 125, 143, 144, 148, 159, 160, 164, 170, 194, 203, 212, 222, 224, 227, 228, 231
Watkins, Sam 85
Wauhatchie, Tennessee 147, 150
Weaver, James B. 191, 192
Welles, Gideon 142
West Point, New York 7, 8, 9, 34, 36, 37, 38, 42, 48, 57, 87, 161, 182

Wheeler, Joseph 78, 92, 93, 101, 123, 182, 184, 185, 188, 218
Whipple, William 176, 203
White Oaks Pond, Tennessee 74
Widow Glenn House 125, 130
Wier, Robert W. 37
Wilder, John T. 80, 109, 130
Wilderness, Virginia 3, 168, 176
Williams, Alpheus 171, 172
Williams, Seth 37
Williamsport, Maryland 52
Willich, August 94, 132
Wilson, James H. 201, 202, 203, 205, 208, 209, 210, 211, 213, 214, 215, 216, 219, 220
Wilson, John 151
Winchester, Virginia 4, 52, 55, 56
Wofford, William T. 223
Wood, Edwin B. 67
Wood, Sterling A.M. 85, 121, 131
Wood, Thomas J. 64, 72, 128, 129, 132, 150, 154, 156, 179, 203, 206, 209, 210, 211, 212, 213, 215, 218
Woodbury, Tennessee 109
Wool, John E. 28, 29, 30, 31
Worth, William J. 13, 15, 22, 24, 26
Wright, Horatio G. 82

Yaryan, John L. 100
Yavapai Indians 39
Young, J.K. 125

HMS *Zealous* 231
USS *Zenobia* 12
Zollicoffer, Felix K. 58, 30, 61, 63, 64, 65, 66, 67, 68, 70

www.ingramcontent.com/pod-product-compliance
Ingram Content Group UK Ltd.
Pitfield, Milton Keynes, MK11 3LW, UK
UKHW050538150426
5217IPUK00026B/1985

9 780786 438562